How to Hit Out, Get Ball Control and Play Percentage

TENNIS

An Illustrated Guide to Greater Efficiency and Better Performance

Anthony Stockman

How to Hit Out, Get Ball Control and Play Percentage Tennis

An Illustrated Guide to Greater Efficiency
and Better Performance

Copyright © 2016 Anthony J. Stockman
All rights reserved.
No part of this publication may be reproduced or transmitted in any form
or by any means, electronic or mechanical, including photocopy, recording,
or any information storage and retrieval system, without permission in
writing from the publisher/author.

Cover and Interior Design by Robert Lanphear
www.LanphearDesign.com

Library of Congress Cataloging-in-Publication Data
Stockman, Anthony.
How to Hit Out, Get Ball Control and Play
Percentage Tennis/Anthony Stockman.
Library of Congress Control Number: 2016919587
CreateSpace Independent Publishing Platform,
North Charleston, SC

ISBN: 1519296827
ISBN 13: 978-1519296825

Contents

Foreword v
Introduction: Ball Control and the "Joy of Hitting Out" 1
Chapter 1: Targets and Aiming 7
Chapter 2: Playing the Arcs 41
Chapter 3: Arc Projection—Combining Two Concepts 79
Chapter 4: Strength and Position—The Foundations of Percentage Play 89
Chapter 5: How to Make High-Percentage Shot Selections 105
Chapter 6: How to Play a Point 143
Chapter 7: How to Control Your Brain During Competition 161
Conclusion 173
Glossary 175
Appendix 1: Volley Targets 177
Appendix 2: Service Targets 191
Appendix 3: How to Transistion from a Flat,
            Novice-Type Serve to a Topspin Serve 199
Appendix 4: How to Crush Your Service Return 203
Appendix 5: Grips 215

This book is dedicated to my son Zack,
who made its completion possible.

Foreword

This book is for any tennis player who wants to get good. It is designed for the player who is beyond the beginning stage, but a beginner can also use these tools and techniques. It is about playing singles, but all the techniques described can also be applied to controlling the ball in a doubles match.

The first half of the book will be useful for players of all levels. This includes chapters 1 ("Targets and Aiming"), 2 ("Playing the Arcs"), and 3 ("Arc Projection"). Understanding these concepts will help you improve very quickly and will make the game a lot more fun to play. The second half of the book is directed at players who have some competitive experience; it details shot selection and point tactics. This includes chapters 4 ("Strength and Position"), 5 ("How to Make High Percentage Shot Selections") 6 ("How to Play a Point"), and 7 ("How to Control Your Brain during Competition").

Inexperienced players should understand and master the concepts in the first three chapters before moving on to the second half. For players with a few matches under their belts, the second half of the book will provide them with an excellent logic for playing and winning points—which means playing and winning matches. The appendixes fill in any gaps that were not covered in the "Targets and Aiming" chapter, that have to do with targeting your serve, volley, and service return.

My hope is that this book will demystify the game. Tennis can be very frustrating if you use archaic stroke techniques to control the ball. Interest in tennis has declined in the United States in recent years. I believe this is because the current approach to learning and teaching the game is antiquated and in need of serious updating. My goal is to help you learn how to control the ball, become skilled at the game quickly, and understand the way tennis is played at a highly competitive level. By using the tools described within, you should be able to improve your game exponentially.

This book is for male and female tennis players. I have alternated between the male and female pronoun in the text to make the book "gender neutral" and emphasis its application to players of both sexes.

INTRODUCTION

Ball Control and the Joy of "Hitting Out"

"Hitting out" is a tennis expression that means fearless striking of the ball with no concern about missing. Hitting out all the time—wouldn't that be nice? The true pleasure of the game of tennis is to be able to rip the ball—to really go for your shots without fear of failure. The worst part of the game is being nervous and afraid to hit your shots for fear of missing. This is commonly called "choking." Choking comes from the fear of making a mistake. But the nervous mistakes and the "cement elbow" really can be driven from your game. The techniques needed to do that are here for you to learn.

Tennis should be an out-of-body experience. Your freest, most uninhibited shot-making happens when you are not consciously controlling your body—when you are focusing outside of yourself, shooting for targets, and in the "zone." The game happens out in front of you in the space above the court. This book is about that space. It is about using visual markers out above the court to control the ball without directly manipulating your body.

Ponderous and nervous shot-making occurs when you are thinking about your body. This happens when you are consciously trying to control your stroke: when you are trying to make a specific movement happen with your backswing, follow-through, or footwork. Strokes are important. You need to develop a certain muscle memory and consistent movement of your backswing and forward swing. But you can't control the ball by controlling your stroke. Stroke control is archaic. It's restrictive and internal to the body, and is prone to generating cement elbows and nervous errors. It is inimical to hitting out. You control the ball by shooting for targets and manipulating visual cues around those targets. This book contains a system of visual tools and techniques to develop that control. With those tools you will construct an "aiming architecture." This is a targeting structure you will build to manipulate the flight path of the ball. It is the "ball-control" technique. It is a visual, out-of-body approach. It is freeing and unrestrictive. It embraces going for your shots. This approach enables you to hit out all the time.

Ball Control versus the Traditional Stroke-Control Approach

Alchemy was an ancient form of science whose objective was to transform base metals into gold. A lot of tennis instruction is like medieval alchemy. Those techniques try to control the ball by controlling the body. If you make your stroke just so, the ball will magically go into the court. If you miss, you should try harder to perfect your stroke, or hold your grip more correctly. Bringing together all those physical moves produces the "gold" of a good shot. This is the stroke-control approach to tennis.

Perhaps the stroke-control approach to tennis came about because of the close association between tennis and golf. The same class of people played both games at country clubs, so instructional models for both games developed along similar lines. Stroke tips and conscious control of the body work okay in golf. This is because golf is a static game: when you strike a golf ball, it is lying motionless on the ground. So it is reasonable to try to produce a perfect, identical stroke every time you hit a golf shot. But tennis is very different.

In tennis, the ball is a moving, dynamic object. The only time the ball is *not* moving is when it is stationary for a split second at the top of the toss on your serve. At all other times, the ball is a moving, spinning, and changing force that must be reckoned with. Having the same stroke every time just will not work. Even if you could make the same stroke every time, your shot would change every time as the ball moves differently. Every ball your opponent hits to you has a slightly different arc to its flight path, so your stroke must adapt for each incoming ball. In tennis, the ball, its arc, and its shape, must be "played." This doesn't mean you have to learn an infinite number of strokes. It means you must learn a holistic concept of playing the ball. This approach must be flexible and adapt to the dynamic force of the oncoming shot. The concept is called "playing the arcs." When you learn this method you will be able to handle any shot your opponent hits to you and harness the shot's energy and force.

Playing the arcs is one half of this holistic approach. The other half is the ball-control concept. It focuses on where the player wants the ball to go. To achieve ball control, the player must leave his or her strokes behind and go to a visual, direct-command approach to controlling the ball. This is the opposite of making the *body* do something right in order to get the ball to go into the court. It is making the *ball* go into the court using visual cues. As a result of commanding the ball to go to a certain spot, the body does the right thing. This book is all about changing your approach from stroke control to ball control.

To get your game to a place where you can hit out all the time, you must end your fear of missing. If you use stroke-control techniques, tennis is a mysterious game—those techniques assume that if you miss, then your stroke must be wrong. So you keep trying to make that perfect stroke. When you make the perfect stroke and you still miss, the mystery deepens. Yelling and "tennis psychosis" seep in. You become afraid of missing because errors seem to happen randomly, without reason, even when you make the perfect stroke.

Ball-control techniques are different. Using ball control, you will embrace mistakes. You will learn to use mistakes as a guide to making adjustments and correcting for errors. To achieve ball control, we will take a direct-command approach. That approach uses visual cues to aim the ball at certain target*s*.

After aiming and shooting, you will adjust your aim point to correct for any error and fire your shot again. *Choosing targets, aiming, and continuously adjusting your aim point is the heart of ball control.* Knowing what to do after you make an error will eliminate your fear of missing. That knowledge enables you to go for it. Knowing how to correct for errors will enable you to hit out. This process will, over time, make you extremely accurate with your shots. You will be able to place the ball where you want it to go. Aiming techniques will also free up your body. Instead of rigidly trying to control the movement of your stroke, you will freely and loosely rip the ball, sending it to your target. Hitting out all the time—that is where you want your game to be.

Percentage Tennis

Playing tennis is a bit like gambling, in that both tennis players and gamblers make choices based on the probability of success. Card-counting blackjack players increase their bets when they know the deck is in their favor. Good craps players do not take low-percentage or "sucker" bets, such as a hard eight or playing the field; they know such bets can pay off big, but they also know that in the long run they will lose. Good gamblers play the high-percentage-of-success bets; they play the percentages.

When you play tennis, you also make choices. A good tennis player also makes choices based on the probability of success, but instead of choosing what bet to make, the tennis player chooses what shot to hit. When you play percentage tennis, you choose shots with a high chance of going in the court. You play the percentages by making smart shot selections.

Most tennis players do not have a clue about how to choose a shot, or even what shots there are to choose from. The average player is thinking about controlling her body and making her stroke; she is trying to produce a perfect backswing, stay down to the ball, or make a "good" follow-through.

Taking a shot is like firing a gun: you aim a projectile. It can be a bullet from a pistol, a rocket from a launcher, or the ball coming off your racket. A shot in tennis is the act of aiming and shooting the tennis ball to a specific target. The highest form of shot selection is controlling and creating the complete arcing shape of your shot. Shot selection is choosing *where* to hit the ball, not *how* to hit the ball.

Percentage tennis is simply a matter of choosing the right shot for a given situation on the court. Ball-control techniques enable you to shoot the ball where you want it to go. Ball control enables you to make a shot selection. Getting ball control makes it possible for you to become a percentage-tennis player.

The Six Tools

You will learn six concepts on your way to getting ball control and becoming a percentage-tennis player. They are:
- Targets and aiming
- Playing the arcs
- Arc projection
- Strength and position
- The vector of the oncoming shot
- Vision

Targets and aiming will enable you to leave your strokes behind and start "crushing" the ball freely. You'll learn to shoot the ball where you want, and when you do make a mistake you'll know how to correct for it.

Playing the arcs will enable you to take into account the dynamic flight path of the ball. By playing the arcs, you will learn to hit ripping topspin and backspin shots and create differently shaped arcs when you make your shots.

Arc projection is the highest level of ball control. It is the fusion of aiming and playing the arcs. Using this technique, you will project and create the entire flight path of your shot. You will learn to bend reality to your will and "conjure" the arcing shape of your shot.

Strength and position are tools you will use to know where high-percentage targets are. You will learn how the position of your body affects where you can shoot your shot.

The vector of the oncoming shot also defines those high-percentage targets. When you combine the concepts of strength and position with the vector of the oncoming shot, you will become a complete percentage-tennis player. You'll be able to make high-percentage shot selections in any situation on the court.

Vision introduces a new way of seeing the ball that will help you implement all of these concepts.

Aiming and Targeting Architecture

Once you understand these tools, you'll own them. They'll be yours. You won't need a coach to continuously guide you. You will create an aiming-and-targeting architecture that is unique to your game. This architecture will become more complete every time you play. After you learn these secrets of the game, you will be on your way to becoming as good as you possibly can be.

I have seen a one-hour conversation about these concepts turn an average club hacker into an outstanding competitive tennis player. A single lesson on these tools turned a below-average high-school player into a tennis guru who now makes a living teaching tennis. You can take these concepts, make them your own, and be on your way to exponential improvement of your game.

Order of Learning

It is important to note that aiming and playing the arcs are two connected concepts that must be learned separately.

Aiming and playing the arcs work together like hand and glove. Aiming for targets is how you control the vector of your shot—up, down, left, and right. It's about making shot selections and choosing where to shoot the ball. Playing the arcs is about taking into account the energy of the oncoming shot. It's a flexible technique for playing the ball and it will be your guide to ripping topspin and backspin shots. These two concepts work together holistically, forging a synergy that can unleash your shot-making potential and explode your game. Unfortunately, these two concepts can't be taught at the same time. You will have to learn one and then the other. After you understand both concepts, it will be simple to put them together and use them as a cohesive whole. But for now we must talk about them individually. In chapter 1 you will learn how to aim and choose targets. In chapter 2 you will learn how to play the arcs. Keep in mind that these concepts will be connected together and used as one—once you understand them both.

CHAPTER 1

Targets and Aiming

Most old-school tennis concepts emphasize controlling the stroke, proclaiming that by controlling the stroke, your shot will go in the court. This school of thought suggests that if you miss, you must have made a bad stroke. So to correct for the miss you need to make your stroke more correct. Using this technique, your errors seem random. You miss sometimes even when you've made a perfect stroke. As you keep trying to make that correct stroke, and you keep missing shots, your frustration grows as your logic fails. You don't have a clue about why you keep missing. Einstein's apocryphal definition of insanity is "doing the same thing over and over again and expecting different results." The stroke-control technique produces this kind of tennis madness.

You need to control the ball, not your body. Using ball-control concepts, you will directly manipulate the flight path of your shots by using visual cues. You create targets, aim your shots at those targets, and then make corrections when you miss. Your strokes will change automatically as you move your aim points. By controlling the ball and making it go where you want it to go, you will make your body do the right thing.

Aiming and Shooting

When you aim something (a firearm, ball, arrow, rocket, etc.), you are directing it so that when you release the projectile, it will hit a target or travel along a certain path.

In tennis, you aim the shot. When you hit a shot in tennis, it is like you are firing a gun. This is where the term shot comes from. This "shooting a gun" concept is essential to achieving a freed-up, go-for-it approach to the game. This approach is crucial in enabling you to hit out. Your forehand should feel like a rifle, your backhand a missile, and your service a cannon. You need to let it go. You need to rip your shots. You need to hit out and go for it. The key to achieving this freed-up approach is not worrying about making mistakes.

Using aiming techniques, you will learn that almost every time you hit a shot, you make an error. That is, you almost never hit your target exactly. So, it is okay to make a mistake. As a matter of fact, you must make a bunch of mistakes to improve your control. Errors and adjustments are the building blocks of ball control.

Aiming techniques teach you how to correct for errors. Once you realize that errors are an inevitable, and even good, thing, your frustration level will go down. You will never have to wonder what mysterious thing is wrong with your stroke. By missing and making aiming adjustments, you will continuously improve

Aiming Has a Bad Rap

In many sports the idea of "aiming" has the connotation of nervously, ponderously "pushing" a ball toward a certain spot. Baseball pitchers who are aiming are hindering their pitch by over controlling their bodies as they attempt to get their pitches to go to certain locations. Our concept of aiming is more akin to aiming a gun. When you aim a rifle or pistol or even a howitzer, you are choosing a specific target. Then you pull the trigger and boom! The shot goes downrange. You will learn to aim at a specific target and then let your shot go. Your shots—forehand, backhand, serve, and volley—will explode like gunpowder in a bullet. Connecting each stroke to a target—a specific aim point—and then exploding your shot is the heart of hitting out. With a specific aim point and target you can detach hitting your shot from the fear of missing. This is because, if you miss your target, you have a logical and workable process for making a correction. You will also learn that you rarely hit your target and aim point exactly anyway. In other words, you almost always miss. Sometimes you miss by a lot, sometimes by a little. Once you realize this, you know that missing is both okay and normal. It won't matter if you miss, because you can make a correction on the next shot. And when you choose high-percentage targets, your errors will become great shots—when you miss, your shot will land well inside the court or hit the line for a winner!

your ball control. So instead of freezing up and attempting to not miss, you will be able to adjust and let the next shot rip. The aim-point adjustment technique will also keep you from making the same mistake twice. Making the same mistake twice is the red-letter indicator of someone who does not have ball control.

The Aiming Technique

I first observed aiming techniques by watching a couple of good tennis players in a funny situation. The three of us were sitting on a bench next to a planter. The planter was filled with small pebbles and had a sprinkler head in the corner. My friends started playing a game. They put one small rock on top of the sprinkler head. Then they picked up a handful of pebbles and started taking turns tossing the little rocks at the pebble on the sprinkler head. I realized they were competing to see who could hit the small rock first. I joined in. My friends' shots at the little rock got closer and closer, while my shots did not improve at all. They were able to hit the little rock after three or four tries. I never hit it. I got frustrated, picked up a larger stone, and hurled it at the little pebble, but with no success. I only made a buffoon of myself. My friends smiled knowingly at each other and chuckled at me. They knew a secret: they knew how to control the flight path of the pebble. That method works to control the flight path of any projectile—including a tennis ball.

You might be asking yourself, "What does tossing a pebble have to do with hitting a tennis shot?" A tennis shot is much more complex. You are swinging at a moving object, attempting to get it to go over the net and into the court. There is a backswing, a follow-through, and so on. But whether you toss a pebble or shoot a tennis shot, you are attempting to do the same thing. You are using a technique of some kind to try to control where the pebble or ball will go. You are attempting to control its flight-path vector. What you will learn here is how to use visual cues to control that flight path. You will learn to gain this control using visual cues rather than consciously changing how your body moves. The aiming technique works when you shoot any projectile at any target: a rock at a tree, one pebble at another, or a forehand tennis shot at the tennis court.

Let's go back to the pebble example. Here is what my friends were doing: once they chose their target (the center of the pebble), they aimed at it very specifically. After they tossed their pebble at the target, they measured their error. Then, they changed their aim point for the next toss. After that toss, they measured their error again and changed their aim point again. Using this method, they were able to hit their target, a tiny pebble, with another tiny pebble after just a few tries. Choosing the target, setting the aim point, and then adjusting the aim point based on your error is the aiming technique.

Now let's go over it step by step.

To introduce the target-and-aiming technique, we will start with a simple example that you can do anywhere. We'll shoot a crumpled-up piece of paper at another crumpled-up piece of paper. (You don't have to use paper balls. You can use any target and any projectile for this game—tennis balls, pebbles, or small rocks—anything will do.) Once you learn how to choose your target and manipulate your aim points in this example, you will learn how to choose targets and manipulate your aim points on the tennis court.

Take four pieces of paper and crumple them up into little balls. Now place one paper ball on the floor a few feet away from you. That ball will be your target. The other three balls of paper will be your projectiles.

Step 1. Choose Your Target

The first step is to choose your target very specifically. In the paper-ball game, it is the center of the paper ball. If you are shooting at a different object, it is the exact center of that object.

Step 2. Draw the Aiming Cross

Now, in your mind's eye, draw a cross over your target. Figure 1 is exactly what you should perceive. The center of the aiming cross will be directly over the target. The aiming cross is essential for making aim-point adjustments.

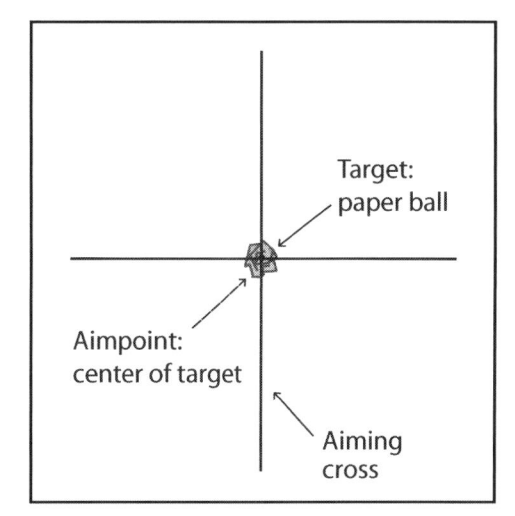

Fig.1 Paper ball with aiming cross

Step 3. Select Your Aim Point

Your first aim point will be the center of the aiming cross. You will focus your eyes, very specifically, on that aim point.

Step 4. Take the Shot

Now focus your eyes on the aim point and shoot. Don't think about how you make your toss. A little overhand toss will do. You can do it side arm or underhand, too; it really does not matter. Don't try to control what your hand is doing. This is very important. When students first try this exercise, they usually start by changing the way their hand moves to change the flight path of the projectile. This is the "no clue" stroke-control approach. You must not do this. Just aim for the target and let it go. Remember, this is all about where you are aiming, not how you are tossing.

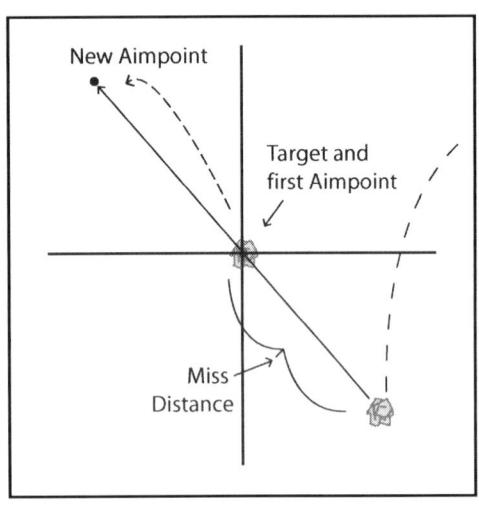

Fig. 2 Miss low and right with correction.

Step 5. Measure Your Error

After your first toss, notice where your shot went. In this example (see Figure 2), the miss was low and to the right. Measure the distance you missed in your mind's eye. This is a visual calculation of the miss distance.

Step 6. Adjust Your Aim Point

This is the aiming rule: You always adjust your aim point in the opposite direction of your mistake. You always adjust your aim point the same distance you missed. Figure 2 shows where you move your aim point after missing low and to the right. Notice how the new aim point has moved in the opposite direction of the error and moved the same distance as the miss. This is the most important part of the aiming technique. To make this correction, draw an imaginary line from your miss through the center of the aiming cross. Continue the line through the cross to the other side, the same distance you missed. This spot will be your new aim point.

Step 7. Take Your Second Shot

Now focus your eyes on the new aim point and take your second toss. I cannot emphasize eye focus enough. This is the beginning of learning vision techniques. The focus of your eyes is truly the sight mechanism of your body. Careful manipulation of your eyes is essential to rapid improvement of your eye-hand coordination. Although there are no guarantees you will hit the target on the second try, I can almost guarantee this: You will not make the same mistake twice. You might miss, but you will miss in another spot. By doing this, you have demonstrated the rudiments of ball control. (Granted, this game actually demonstrates paper-ball control, but the principal and technique are the same.)

The fact that you influenced the projectile's flight path by changing aim points is the essence of ball control. On the tennis court you will choose targets and apply exactly the same aim-point adjustment technique.

Step 8. Make Your Second Correction

The aiming technique is continuous. So after your second toss, measure your error again. (Any number of errors are possible, but for now, imagine your mistakes are as follows; we will go through other possibilities shortly.) If your second shot misses above the target, drop your aim point down. In this example, you move the aim point down because your second error was high, but you keep your aim point over to the left of the target because this lateral correction worked. The distance you move the aim point down will be the distance you missed above the target. This is shown in Figure 3. Notice that the third aim point is lower than the second aim point.

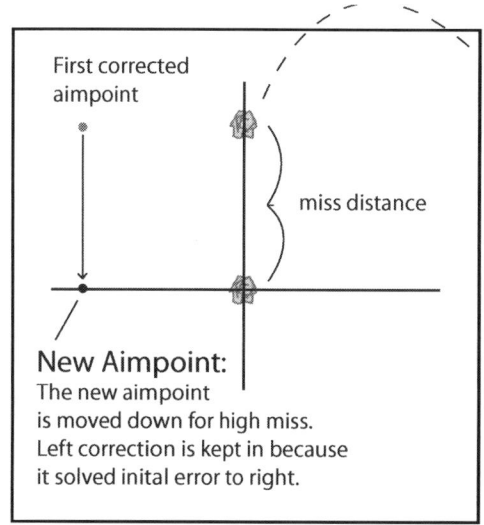

Fig. 3 Second shot miss high.

Step 9. Take Your Third Shot

Focus your eyes on the new aim point and shoot. If you still miss the third shot above the target, you need to move your aim point even lower. Measure the distance you missed high, and move your aim point down the same distance. Figure 4 illustrates how to make this third correction. Now focus your eyes on your new aim point and toss. This shot should come closer to the target.

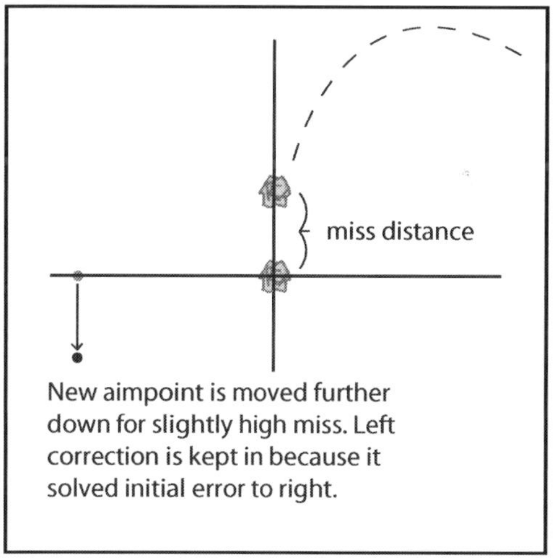

The Aiming Technique Restated

Fig. 4 Third shot: miss slightly above target

The aiming technique is as follows. First, pick out a target. In your mind's eye, draw an aiming cross over the target. Then, set a very specific aim point over the target (the first aim point is always the center of the cross). Take your shot. Measure the error. Move your aim point in the opposite direction of your miss. Make your correction the same distance as your error. Take your next shot.

You could be throwing a ball, shooting a gun, or hitting your serve; the basic aiming technique remains the same. You will use this same technique to aim your shots on the tennis court.

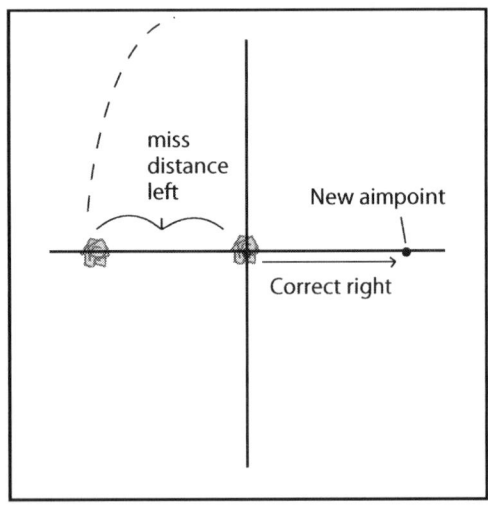

Fig 5a Miss left

Possible Errors and Corrections

Now we will look at examples of errors and how to correct for them. These examples should give you a good feel for aiming, measuring your error, and adjusting your aim point in just about any situation. I will describe various miss possibilities and how to make the first aim-point adjustment. You may skip some of the examples if you grasp the concept, but if you are at all unclear about the technique, follow each example until you feel comfortable.

For these aiming examples, we will use the paper balls. We could use any target and any projectile. Try tossing one tennis ball at another, or toss your paper balls at a light switch.

Miss to the Left or Right

In Figure 5a you can see that the error is to the left of the target. For this mistake, move your aim point to the right the same distance you missed to the left. Now focus on the new aim point and toss.

In Figure 5b the miss is to the right. For this mistake, move your aim point to the left the same distance you missed.

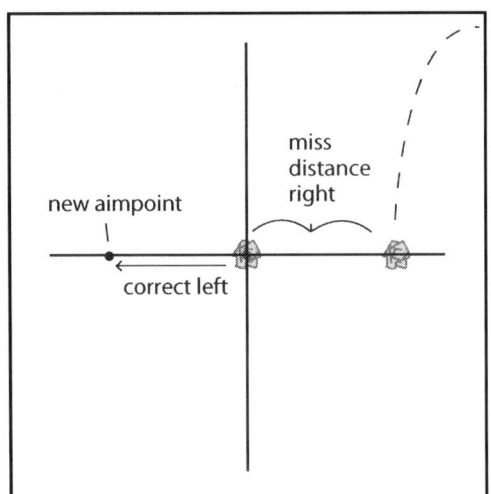

Fig. 5b Miss right

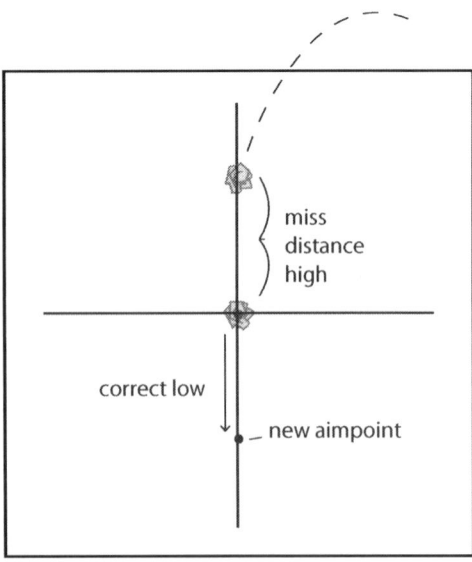

Fig. 6a Miss high

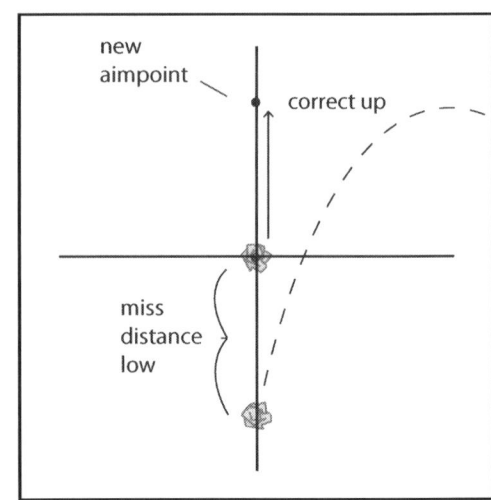

Fig. 6b Miss low

Miss High or Low

In Figure 6a the error is high: above the target. To correct for this error, move your aim point below the target the same distance you missed. Now focus on the new aim point and toss. In Figure 6b the error is low: below the target. When you miss low, move your aim point above the target the same distance you missed.

Miss Low and Right

This error gets a little trickier, but it's actually not very difficult to address (see Figure 7). The mistake here is low and to the right. To correct for this error move your aim point diagonally across the target, high and left. Draw an imaginary line through the center of the aiming cross. Move the aim point the same distance you missed to the other side of the target. Focus on the new aim point and shoot.

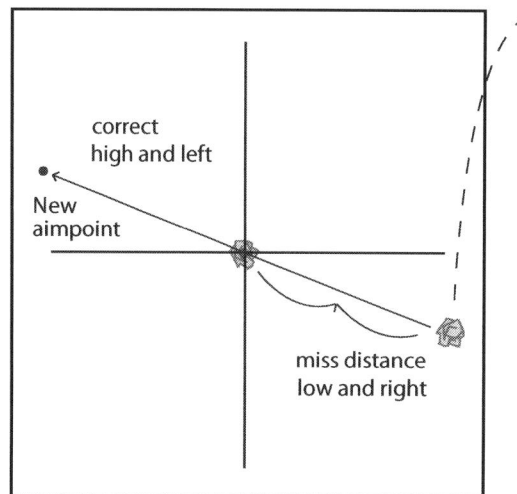

Fig. 7 Miss low and right

Miss Low and Left

Here the mistake is low and to the left (see Figure 8). In this case, to correct for your error, you would move your aim point across the target high and to the right. Once again, you move it the same distance you erred to the other side of the target. Now focus on the corrected aim point and toss again.

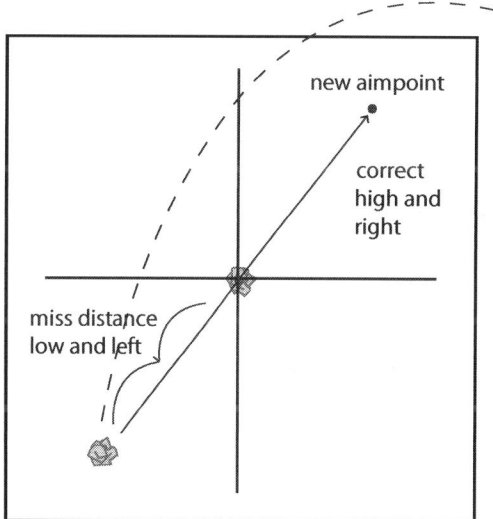

Fig. 8 Miss low and left

Miss High and Right

If the aiming technique is starting to make sense to you, I bet you know how to correct for this mistake. In this case you move your aim point across the target to the opposite side, low and to the left (see Figure 9). Move it the same distance as your mistake. Focus your eyes on the new aim point and shoot.

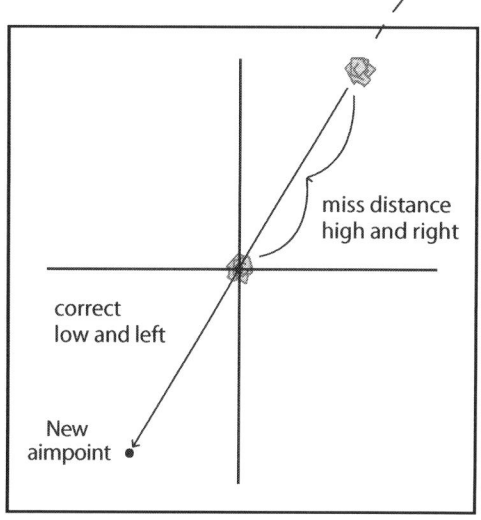

Fig. 9 Miss high and right

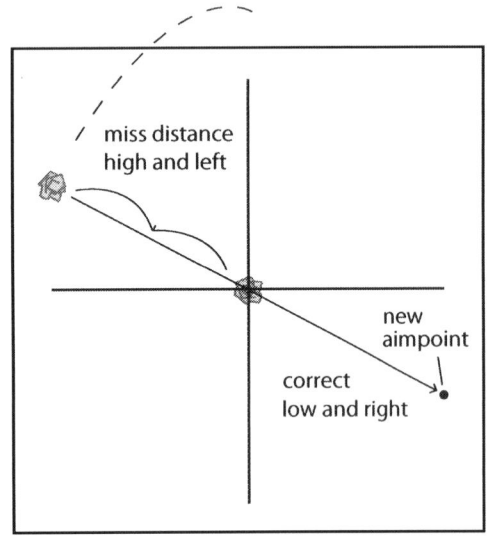

Fig. 10 Miss high and left

Miss High and Left

With this error, move your aim point low and to the right the same distance you missed to the other side of the target (see Figure 10). Take aim with the focus of your eyes and shoot.

A Complete Aiming Sequence

Every error and correction you make will be some variation of those we've just gone through. To make sure you really understand the aiming technique, we will go through a complete sequence of shots you might make with the first, second, third, and fourth aiming adjustments. Remember, this is just an example, and your errors might be completely different than this, but understanding how to make the second and subsequent aim-point adjustments is key. Here we go.

First Shot

Here the shooter misses high and to the left (see Figure 11). You can see that the second aim point is adjusted the same distance missed: low and to the right of the target.

Second Shot

The shooter misses to the right side of the target on his next attempt (see Figure 12). To correct for this mistake, the aim point must be dragged over to the left.

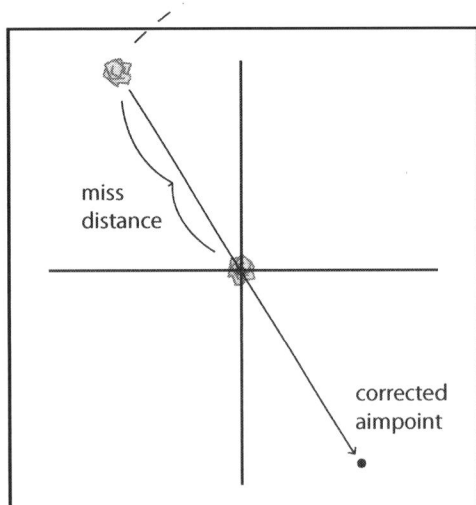

Fig 11 Complete aiming sequence. First shot miss high and left

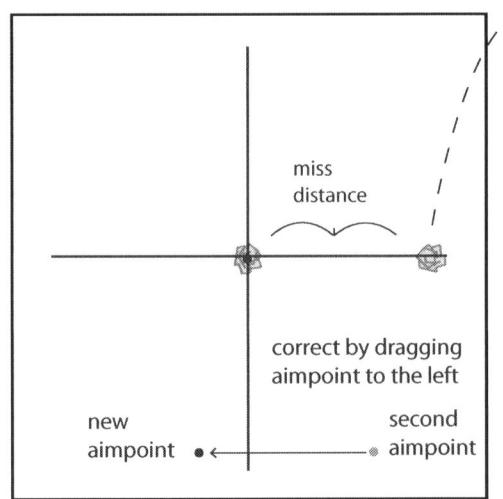

Fig 12 Second shot. Elevation error is corrected, but this shot misses to the right of target, so the aimpoint is corrected to the left the same distance as the miss.

The aim point is moved left the same distance as the miss to the right of the target. The new aim point is now almost directly below the target. In this case the vertical error was solved, but the shooter needs to correct for the miss to the right.

Third Shot

This shot misses directly below the target, near the corrected aim point (see Figure 13). The correction now is to drag the aim point up toward the target. The distance you move the aim point is the same distance you missed below the target. Notice that the shots are getting closer to the adjusted aim point. This is typical. The shooter is getting more accurate. The shots are getting more precise. By manipulating the aim points, our shooter is improving control, and the shots are getting closer to the aim point.

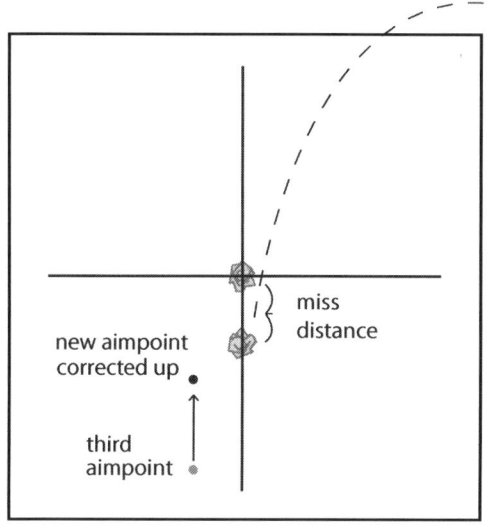

Fig 13 Third shot. The third shot misses low, directly below the target. The aimpoint is moved up to correct

Fourth Shot

This shot misses the target but is dead on the adjusted aim point (see Figure 14). When this happens, bring the aim point directly over the target and fire. Our shooter has improved his control and is hitting where he is aiming.

DRILL

You need to practice this. Try this aiming exercise with any projectile and any target. Play around with choosing a target and manipulating the aim points. Do this until you hit the target or at least get a feel for changing the flight of your projectile using the visual aiming cues. The process of changing the projectile's flight path, with visual cues, is the essence of ball control.

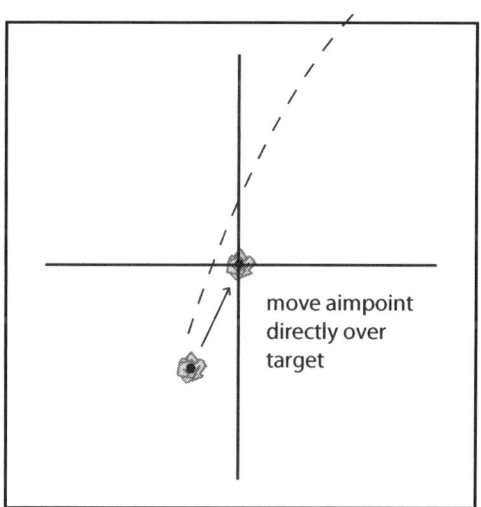

Fig 14 The fourth shot misses the target but hits directly on the corrected aimpoint. The correction here is to bring the aimpoint right back over the target. Your accuracy has improved and you are striking right where you are aiming. This is a common occurance as your ball control improves.

Common Problems with the Aiming Technique

Most people experience one or both of two common problems when learning aiming techniques, as follows.

Problem 1: You make a correction, but you keep missing in the same spot. The most common cause of missing in the same spot over and over is that you really did not try to shoot for your corrected aim point. It is a difficult concept to try to miss a target in order to hit it, and that is what you are doing when you move your aim point away from and off your target. But if you miss your target when you are aiming right at it, and you keep missing your target when you are aiming right at it (like hitting a tennis ball into the net three times in a row), it makes sense that you can hit your target when you aim away from it. If you missed in the same spot, try your corrected aim point again. This time, really focus your eyes on the new corrected aim point and really try to shoot for it. You should see results.

Problem 2: Your aiming correction doesn't change the flight path of your shot, even when you are really shooting for the corrected aim point. In this case, you need to "break out of your error." What I mean here is that you have to make a drastic aim-point adjustment to force your body to change what it is doing. If you try the first solution above but you keep missing in the same spot, correct your aim point twice as far away from the target—double the distance of your initial correction. Now take another shot. This will definitely change the flight path of the projectile. You will find this kind of thing happening to you every once in a while when you are playing tennis. Even though you are using the aiming techniques, you still hit three forehands into the net, or you still double fault, missing at the same spot. If this happens, you need to break out of the error by really exaggerating your aim-point correction.

Things to Notice about the Aiming Technique

When you make a sequence of shots, you are constantly moving your aim point based on the distance and direction that you miss your intended target. You always correct your aim point in the opposite direction of your miss. If you miss high, you aim low. If you miss low, you aim high. If you miss left, you aim right. If you miss right, you aim left. Your shots will usually get closer and closer to your aim point as you use this technique. This is the process of gaining ball control. The more you do it, the more accurate you get. If your shot hits right on your adjusted aim point, then move your aim point directly over your target.

Even after taking many shots, you might not hit your intended target. Don't worry about that. As long as you continue to adjust your aim points, and you don't miss at the same spot twice, you are getting the job done. In tennis and in any other game, you very rarely are able to hit the exact spot you are aiming for. There is always some error. Think about it: when you do hit your target, especially when your aim point is off the intended target, you have made an error anyway! But the "error" in this case is a good shot.

Manipulating Eye-Hand Coordination

When you use the aiming technique, you are directly manipulating your eye-hand coordination. The process of aiming, shooting, and adjusting your aim points builds a database for the vision and motor skills portions of your brain. Using what you see to directly alter what your body does fine-tunes your coordination. This direct manipulation will exponentially develop your eye-hand skills. If applied to your tennis game, your ball control will get better every time you play. You should be able to advance ahead of your practice partners. You will be able to play better with less practice. You will easily beat players who you used to struggle against. You will start beating players who you have never beaten.

The Chair and the Net

You have tossed your paper balls at your target. You have learned the basics of aiming and correcting your aim points up, down, left, and right. Now it's time to try an aiming game that is much closer to the way you will aim on the tennis court.

Fig 15 Choose your target above the chair and draw the aiming cross in your minds eye.

Take a trash can and a chair. The chair should have a back that you can see through. Place the trash can a few feet behind the chair. Sit in front of the chair. Make sure you are sitting low enough so that you do not have a direct shot at the trash can.

How does the aiming technique apply here? You can't aim directly at the trash can; if you did, you would hit the chair. So you have to choose a target that will get the paper ball to go over the chair and in the trash can. To do this we pick a spot above the chair that the projectile must pass through on its way into the trash can.

Fig 16 By shooting the paper ball through the target above the chair you get it into the trashcan.

Pick a spot about eighteen inches above the chair and use that as your target (see Figure 15).

Targeting and aiming require the use of a visual reference point. In this drill, since we can't shoot directly at the trash can, we use the chair as the visual reference point. From this visual reference, you create your target in the space above the chair. You use the physical object you can see to create the phantom target above the chair.

This is an essential skill. You have to be able to hold in your mind's eye an imaginary target above the chair. It isn't easy, but it is a skill you must learn. In your mind's eye, draw an aiming cross over that imaginary point. Now take your shot. By making your projectile pass through the correct spot above the chair, you will get it to go into the trash can (see Figure 16).

For left and right misses of the trash can, the aiming adjustments are the same as in the previous examples. If you miss left, correct right. If you miss right,

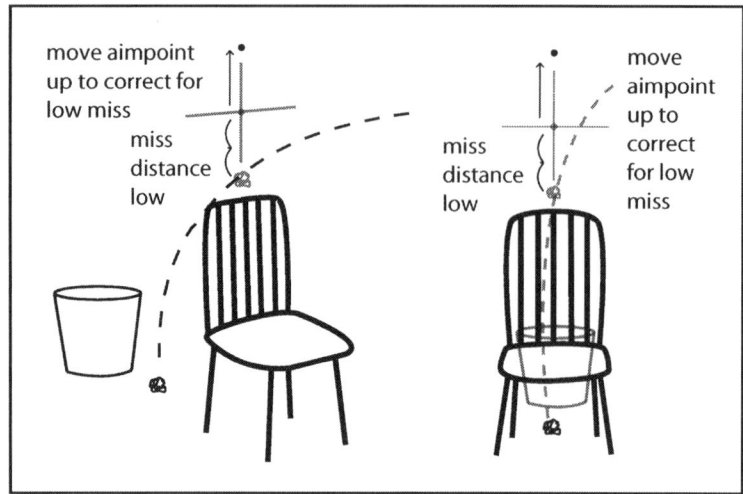

Fig 17 Miss short of trashcan. This is a low miss. Correct by moving your aimpoint up.

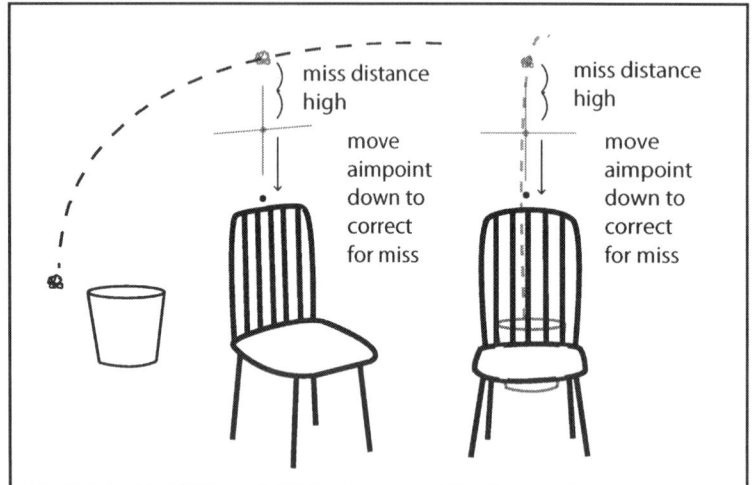

Fig 18 Miss beyond trash can. This is a high miss. Correct by moving your aimpoint down.

correct left. But how do you correct for near and far misses of the trash can? How do you control how far you toss the paper ball?

You control how far your paper ball travels with the up-and-down correction.

If you miss the trash can on the near side, you adjust your aim point up. The corrected aim point will produce a higher trajectory. That higher trajectory will make the projectile travel farther. Notice that you measure your error based on where the projectile passed by your aiming cross. The aiming cross creates a plane that is broken by the projectile as it travels out to the trash can. It is where the projectile breaks this imaginary plane that the error is measured (see Figure 17).

If you miss far—beyond the trash can—then lower your aim point. With a lower trajectory the projectile will travel a shorter distance. Again, the error is measured where the projectile passes by the aiming cross. Calculate and adjust your aim point based on this (see Figure 18). If you miss long, aim lower. If you miss short, aim higher.

Play around with these up-and-down corrections to get your shot into the trash can. You will find a point in space above the chair that will get the paper ball into the trash can every time. When you find this spot, it becomes your target. Move your aiming cross over this spot and make adjustments from there.

This is the same targeting problem you face on the tennis court. You cannot aim directly at different spots on the court. If you do, you will shoot the ball into the net. You have to make your shot pass through a spot above the net to get it to go in the court. The net will become your visual reference point. You will use the net to build your aiming architecture on the tennis court.

You will learn where the targets are—above the net—to get your shots to go where you want them to go into the court. You will keep the ball inside the sidelines with the left-and-right correction and you will control the depth of your shot with the up-and-down correction.

Why It Is Easier to Play Doubles Than Singles

Most tennis players are more comfortable playing doubles than singles. This is due to the visual nature of aiming and targeting. Even though a player may have no clue about aiming or targets, that player is still affected by the visual environment on the court. When you play doubles, you have four big three-dimensional (3D) objects out there for your visual reference: your partner, the net, and your two opponents. These four big objects create a visual corridor to guide you as you hit your shots. Those visual reference points form a ready-made aiming architecture that all players use when they play doubles. Even if a player is not using aiming techniques, the objects on the court provide a reference for shot making; this makes doubles an easier game.

When you play singles you have a big open space in front of you. Nobody is standing on the court, creating an alley to shoot through. Even more challenging is that in singles, unlike doubles, you have to shoot your shots from locations all over the court. As you move from the middle of the court to the left or right side of the court, your targets change. The targets slide around as your shooting position changes. If you don't know where those targets are, your performance will be poor. This is why many players become a bit lost when it comes to making shots on the singles court.

To be competent in singles, you have to create an aiming architecture that is viable from any location on the court. In singles you only have two 3D objects for visual reference: your opponent and the net. Your opponent doesn't help, because she is moving all around the court and can't really be used as a reference point for targeting. The only fixed 3D reference you have for constructing targets is the net.

The rest of this chapter will teach you how to use the net as a targeting reference from any position on the court. Your aiming architecture will be constructed with reference to and around the net.

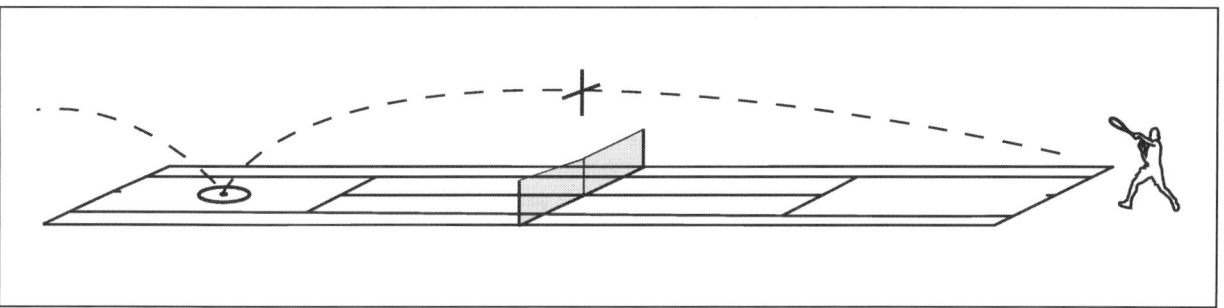

Fig 19 Target above the net to achieve shot goal in center of court between the service line and the baseline.

Direct Fire Versus Indirect Fire

Targets On the Court Versus Targets Over the Net

When a target is exposed you can shoot right at it. This is called direct fire. When an obstacle obscures a target, you cannot shoot right at it. If you do you will hit the obstacle. So you have to shoot at a target that will clear the obstacle and make your shot hit the intended target. This kind of shooting is called indirect fire. These are military terms but they apply perfectly to aiming and shooting in tennis. The net obscures targets on the tennis court. So when you shoot for targets in tennis you have to use indirect fire. That is why we use targets over the net to hit locations on the court.

If you use targets on the court there is no real way to create a visual target for a deeper or shallower shot. If you use targets on the courts surface to control depth you are wishing the ball to go the distance you want it to go. You are not directly changing the vector of your shot. The vector of your shot is the initial direction of its flight path, and that is what you do when you use aiming techniques: you control the vector of your shot.

Aiming techniques directly control the flight path of the ball—up, down, left, and right. That will be the approach here. We'll do this by firing away at aim points higher or lower, left and right above the net.

Targets and Aiming on the Tennis Court

Remember, you must solve only two problems when controlling the tennis ball:
1. You have to keep the ball inside the sidelines. You do this by controlling the left-and-right vector of the shot.
2. You have to ensure that the ball gets over the net and lands inside the baseline. You do this by controlling the up-and-down vector of the shot.

That is all there is to it. It is really a very simple game. You adjust your aim points up, down, left, and right. This is just like the chair-and-trash-can exercise.

Let's start with a very basic example. You are shooting your ground-stroke shot from the middle of the court. Backhand or forehand—it doesn't matter. Your targeting goal is to hit your shot so that the ball lands in the middle of the court between the baseline and the service line (see Figure 19).

To make this shot, we will choose a target that is about three feet above the net, right over the center of the net; (see Figure 19). If your shot passes through this target, it should land pretty close to the center of the court, between the service line and the baseline. After shooting a few shots, you may find that you need to move this target up or down to ensure that your shot has the correct depth. Finding the right height for your targets is one of the first steps in building an effective aiming architecture; this will be covered in the depth drill shortly.

After you take a shot at this target, you will analyze your error and make a correction. The error is marked when the ball passes by the aiming cross. The aiming cross creates an imaginary plane above the net. Where the ball breaks this imaginary plane is the point you measure your error from. All of the aim-point corrections you just learned apply both to this target and to every target you use on the tennis court. But let's go through a few simple examples to show you what it looks like on the court.

High Miss

If you miss your target high, your shot will go too far and land outside the court. For this miss, adjust your aim point down the same distance that you missed high. The error is measured where the ball passes by the imaginary plane created by the aiming cross. Correcting low will give your shot a lower trajectory; the lower trajectory will bring the shot down into the court nearer the target goal between the baseline and the service line. Notice that in this example the corrected aim point is on the net. You are actually aiming *into* the net to correct for the high error. Get used to this. As you use the aiming techniques you will frequently have to aim "to miss." In this example, the correction has you aiming your shot into the net (see Figure 20).

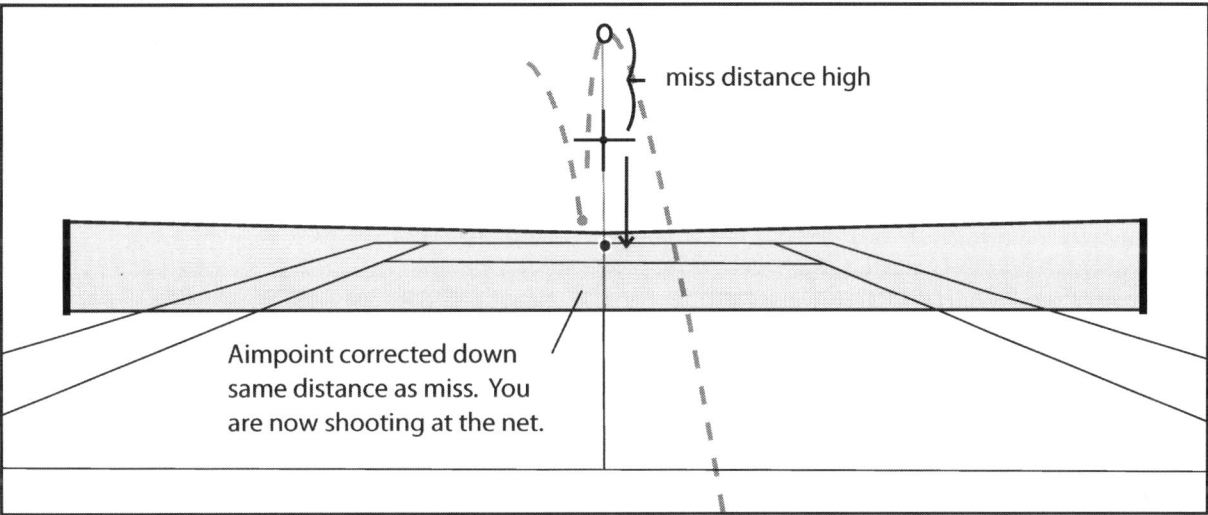

Fig 20 High Miss. You miss your target high and the shot goes long, outside the court. Aim point must be corrected down for the high error.

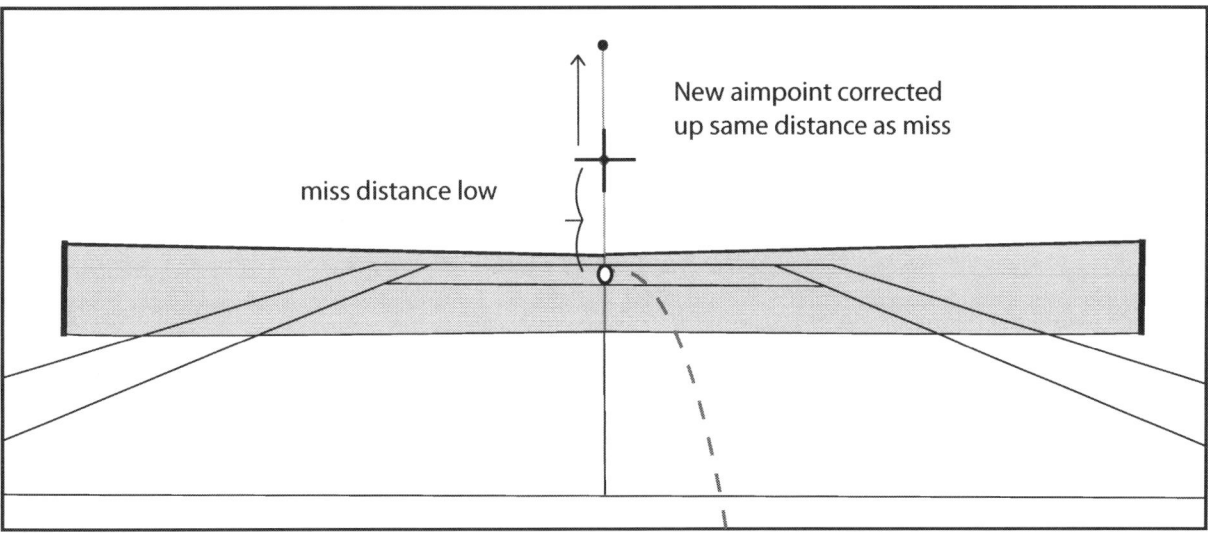

Fig 21 Low Miss. You shot misses low striking the net. Your next aim point is corrected up to give your next shot a higher trajectory.

TARGETS AND AIMING | 21

Low Miss

If you miss your target low, your shot will hit the net or land short in the court. For this miss, adjust your aim point up the same distance that you missed low. Notice that you measure your error based on where the ball passes by the aiming cross (or, in this case, hits the net). This correction will give your shot a higher trajectory. With a higher trajectory, the shot will land deeper in the court (see Figure 21).

Left and Right Miss

These errors are corrected in the same way you learned before. For a miss to the right, move your aim point over to the left. For a miss to the left, move your aim

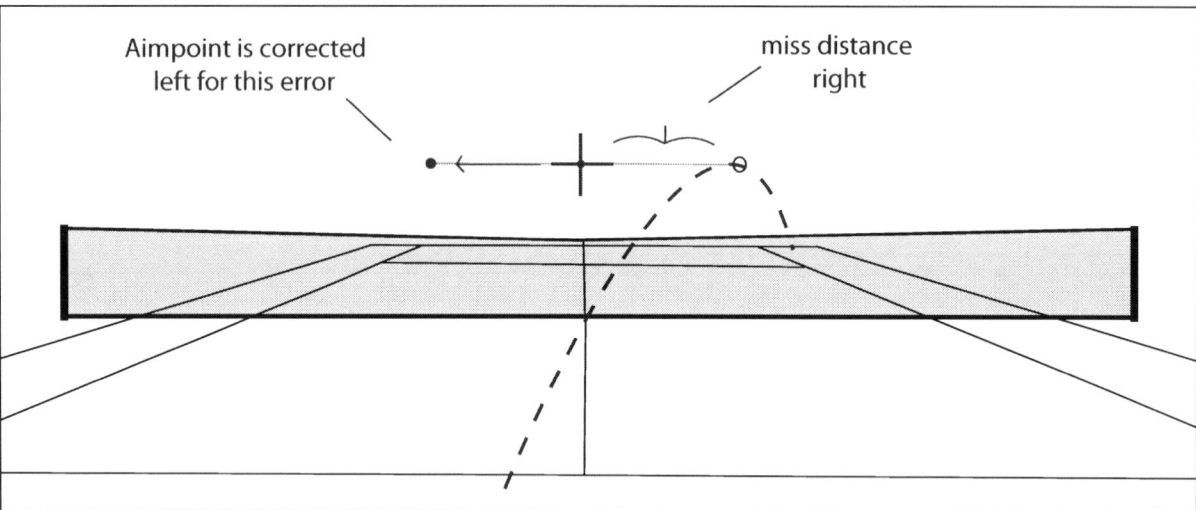

Fig 21a Right Miss. You miss your target to the right. Drag your aim point left to correct for this error.

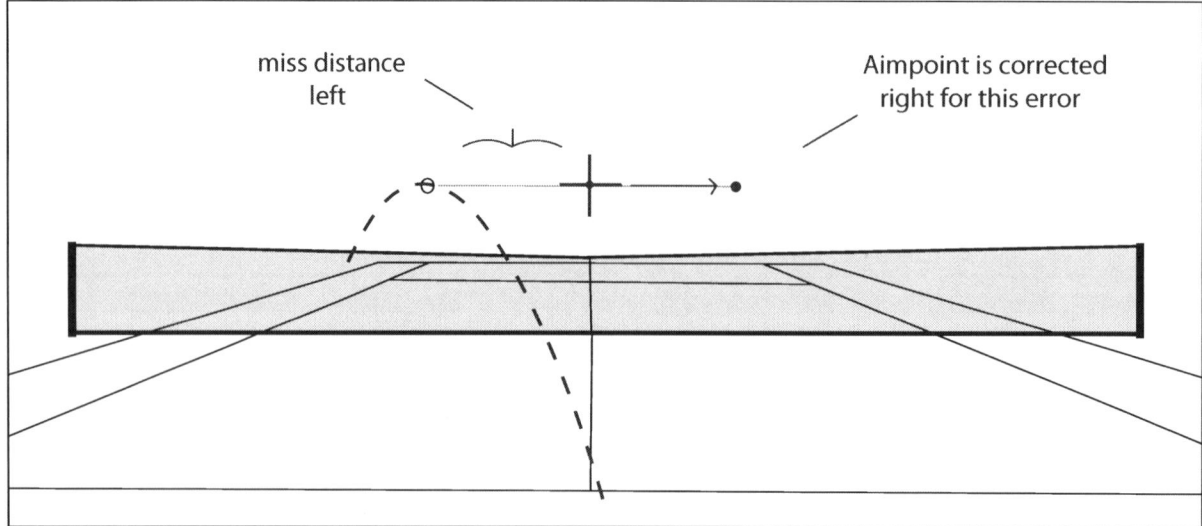

Fig 21b Left Miss. You miss your target to the left. Drag your aim point to the right correct for this error.

point over to the right. Mark your error where the ball passes over the net by the aiming cross. Move your aim point the same distance you missed.

Combination Errors

For errors that miss in both elevation (high or low) and in "azimuth" (left or right), make your aim-point correction as you learned in the tossing examples. Draw an imaginary line through the aiming cross and move your aim point the same distance that you missed to the other side. Figures 22 and 23 show two of these errors and the appropriate corrections.

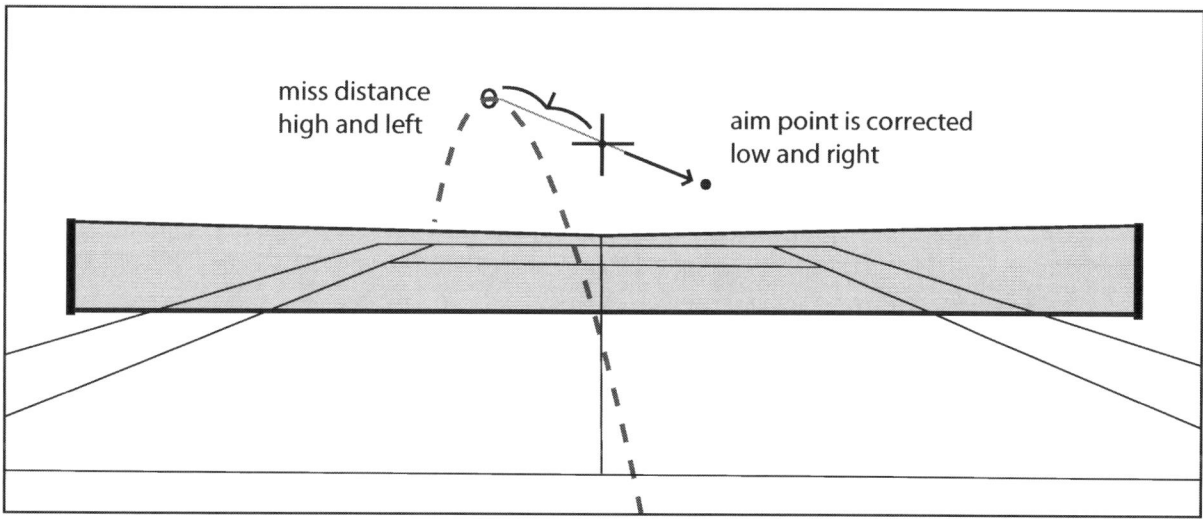

Fig 22 High and Left Miss. For this error your correct your aim point low and right.

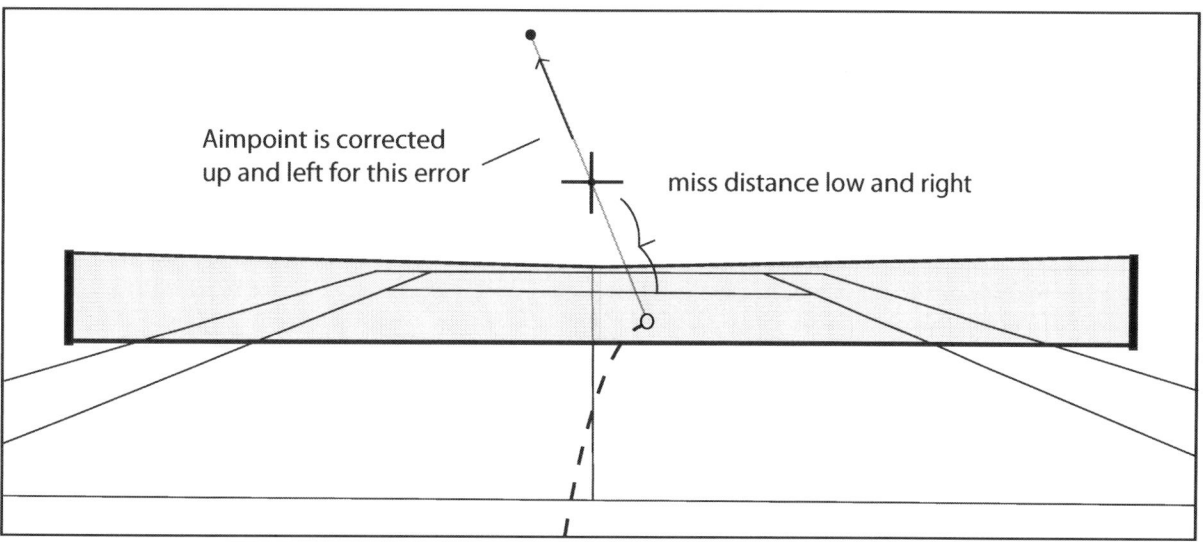

Fig 23 Low and Right Miss. You miss your target low and right, into the net. Drag your aim point up and left to correct for this error.

TARGETS AND AIMING | 23

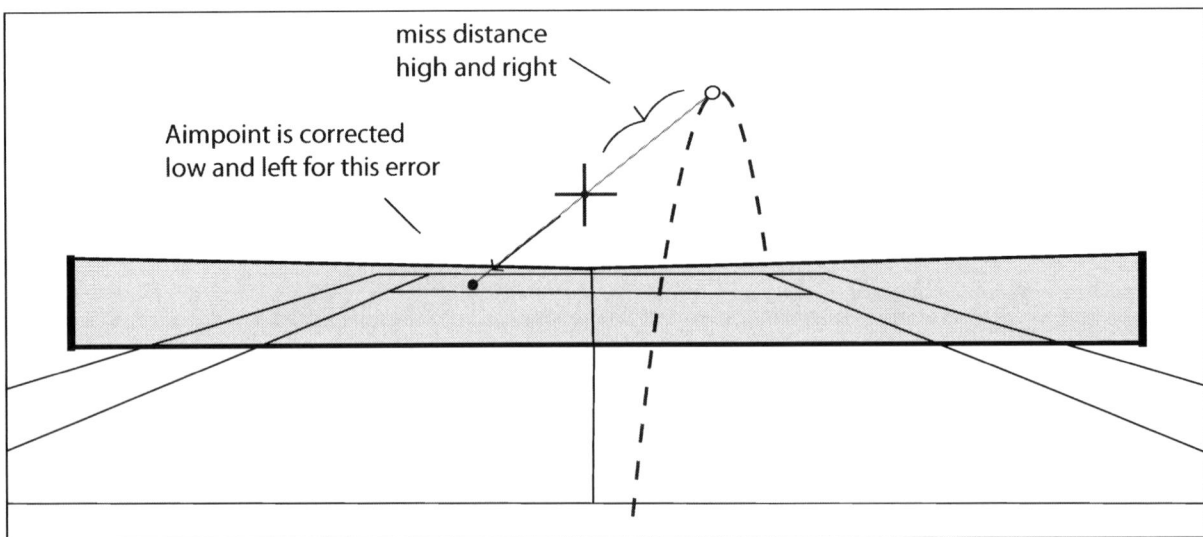

Fig 23a High and Right Miss. You miss your target high and right. Drag your aim point low and left to correct for this error.

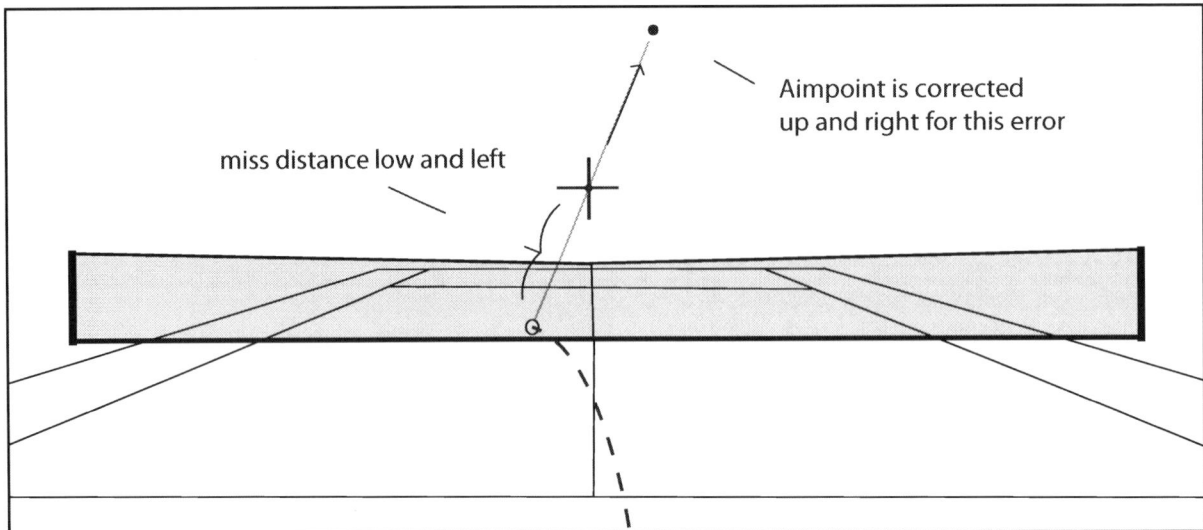

Fig 23b Low and Left Miss. You miss your target low and left, into the net. Drag your aim point up and right to correct for this error.

Get Out on the Court and Try It

Go out on the court with a partner. For some of these drills, it is best if your partner has a basket of balls and can feed you shots, like a tennis instructor. But if this is not possible, you can do it during a rally.

As you start these drills and learn the targets, it is essential that you separate controlling the ball from controlling your strokes. You have to develop a shooting mind-set. When you take a shot on the court, you are firing a ball at a target: whether ground strokes or volleys or serves, you're taking a shot. You must not focus on the details of the movement of your stroke. Focus only on where you want the ball to go. Your strokes will change as you change your aim points. When you control where the ball goes with the aiming process, your body and strokes will comply and do the right thing.

DEPTH DRILL

This drill is designed to give you the feel for using the up and down aim-point correction to control depth. It is similar to the trash-can-and-chair drill. It will also help you define how high above the net to set your target when you play. You will also be doing a process called bracketing. You bracket a target by shooting shots on either side of it. Once this is done, the target is measured and can be hit at will. In this drill, you will first try to hit all your shots long—over the baseline. Then you will hit all your shots short in the court, on the service line or in the service box. After that, you will choose a target between the long and the short targets. This target will put all your shots to the "sweet spot" of the court, between the baseline and the service line. This is the initial construction of your aiming architecture. The bracketing process builds your eye-hand coordination database. You will begin the process of "finding the court" and will significantly improve your ball control.

Keeping It Simple: A Holistic Concept

If anything is important on the tennis court, it's concentration. The ability to focus your mind under pressure and to control your thoughts in a positive way is essential to success in match play. Aiming in two dimensions simplifies your thought process. By taking the aiming concept to its simplest form—left and right and up and down—you are giving your mind a very simple thing to think about. This will be your key to success in competition.

As you know, tennis is a very mental game. You can miss almost any shot at any time. This is commonly known as choking. The usual reason for choking is thinking too much and thinking the wrong thoughts. Think about the last time you double faulted or missed an easy shot in a crucial situation. Analyze your thoughts. I bet the thought or image of missing crept into your mind. For example: "What if I double fault?" or "Don't double fault!" The great thing about using aiming techniques is that they give you a simple and positive action thought. All you have to do is focus on driving the ball to a certain location above the net. If you are thinking positively of hitting the ball where you want it to go, you cannot be thinking about missing. Thinking about missing is the reason for choking. Thinking about aiming for a target and ripping your shot is the exact opposite of those negative thoughts.

Procedure for the Depth Drill

To keep things simple, place your target directly over the middle of the net. This is the "center tape" target. You will use it a lot in the future. We will work on shooting the ball to the left and right side of the court later.

For now, your first goal will be to find the target that drives every ball beyond the baseline. This target will be pretty high above the net: it will probably be eight to ten feet, or more, above the net. Your goal will be to hit all your shots so that they land between the baseline and the fence. You really need someone to feed you a bunch of balls here, since it is hard to rally with someone who is hitting every ball long and out of the court. If you are rallying with someone, your first goal will be to find the target that puts every ball right on the baseline. (This is far less effective, so it is best to try to get someone to feed you balls for this drill.)

When you first start aiming at a target high over the net to get your shots to go long and out of the court, you will probably feel very uncomfortable. Don't "push" the ball. Hit the ball hard. Hit your shots at about 75 percent of your hardest pace. Remember, you are learning to hit out. You have to get used to going for it. Don't be afraid to miss. You might hit a few shots into the fence, or even over the fence. That's okay. You have to make all of these mistakes. Those errors become a database for building ball control. Once you locate the over-the-baseline target and you adjust your aim points accordingly, you will be able to get most of your shots to land between the baseline and the fence (see Figure 24). Once you locate this over-the-baseline target, move on to the next step.

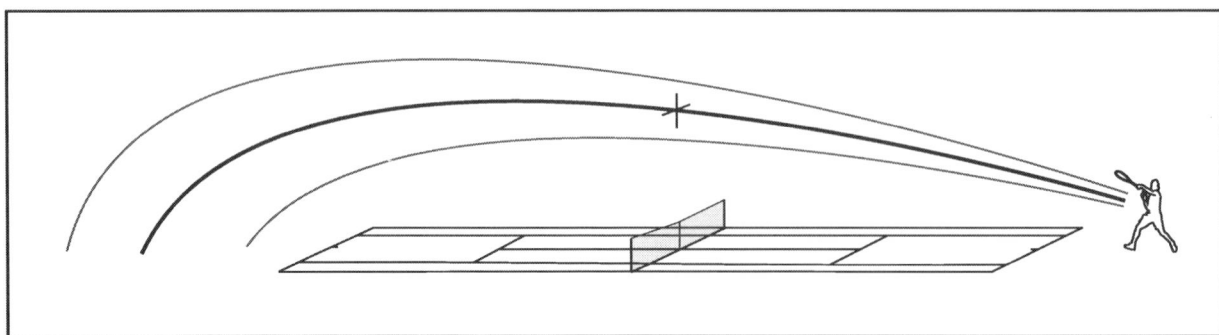

Fig 24 Bracketing: Beyond the baseline target

The next step in this drill is to shoot for the service line. You need to select a lower target this time. Try one about two feet over the net. Once again, it is best to have someone feed you balls, as opposed to rallying. Adjust your aim points around this target until the majority of your shots are landing near the service line or in the service court. We are still shooting for the center of the court, right over the middle of the net. Notice that you will make a lot of errors into the net with this lower target. That's okay. This drill is designed to let you make the mistakes that you need to make in developing ball control. Go ahead and hit out. Don't try to "not miss." Go for your shots. Accept making errors as a part of getting ball control. Hit the ball at about 75 percent power. Use the aim points to continuously adjust up and down around the lower target. Keep shooting for this target until a majority of your shots land near or inside the service line (see Figure 25).

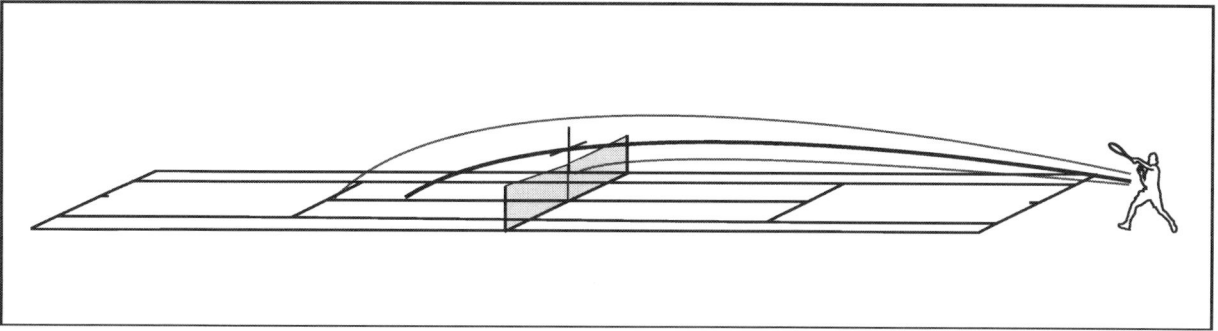

Fig 25 Bracketing: Service line target

What you have done in this drill is bracket the sweet-spot target on the tennis court. By doing this, you've gathered a bunch of data points for building your aiming architecture. You have defined, in your coordination center, the depth of the court. You have also defined visually where the optimum up-and-down target is. The optimum target is between the target that sent all the balls over the baseline and the target that put all your shots on the service line. Remember, you are shooting at targets above the net to get results on the court. By controlling the ball's initial vector and getting your shot to go through the target over the net, you will hit the desired location on the court.

Now it's time to shoot for the target zone you will use in match play. Your goal here is to get all of your shots to land between the service line and the baseline. You have measured your optimal vertical target in the first part of the drill: that target is between the over-the-baseline target and the service-line target. Hold that target in your mind's eye. Have your partner feed you twenty or thirty more balls. Use the aim-point adjustment technique as you make errors around that target. Once again, go for it. You need to hit out. Be ready to make a few errors. Don't cringe when you miss. Enjoy yourself. Do not consider errors to be failures. Get the feel for going for your shots and using your mistakes as tools to improve your ball control (see Figure 26).

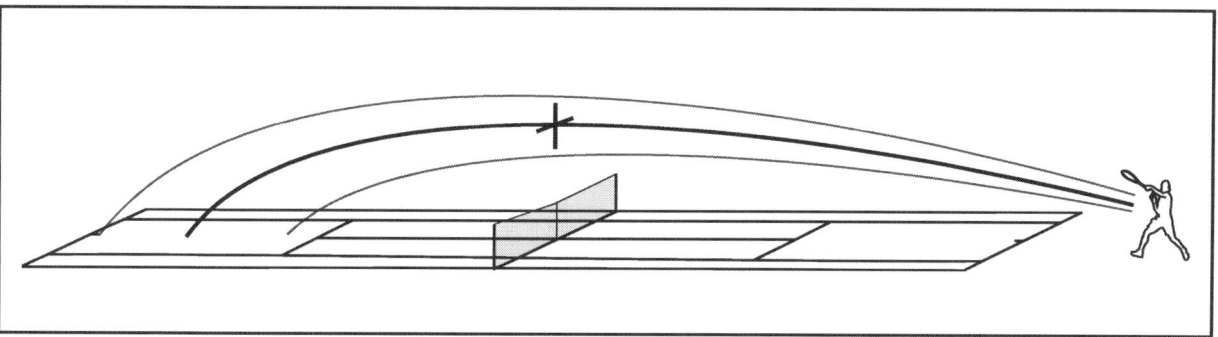

Fig 26 Bracketing: Sweetspot target. Here you want all your shots to land between the baseline and the service line.

At the end of this drill, you should find yourself able to hit a high percentage of your shots between the baseline and the service line. That zone is your goal for almost every shot you will hit.

Controlling Depth with Speed

As far as speed goes, I know what some of you might be thinking: "A hard-hit ball will travel farther than a slowly hit ball." This is true; the distance the ball travels is also a function of its speed. A ball hit at the same height slowly will not travel as far as a ball hit at a faster speed. We will ignore the speed variable for now. You need to learn to control the vector of the ball first. Once you have mastered these aiming techniques, you can start considering the speed of the ball. As a general rule, harder-hit, faster balls must be aimed lower to keep them in the court. Also, slowly hit balls must be hit higher to keep them out of the net and landing deep in the court. A large portion of the speed variable will be taken care of when you learn to play the arcs. So for now, focus on controlling the vector of your shot up, down, left, and right.

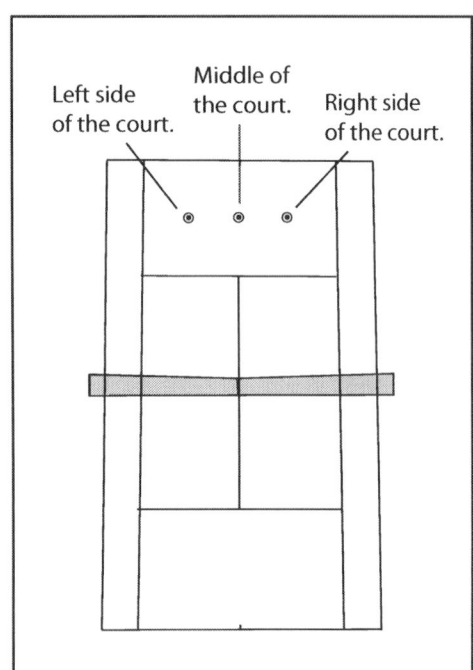

Fig 27 The three shot selections.

Shot Selection and the Three Targets

In the introduction, you learned that shot selection is the key to tennis. Knowing how to choose shots—and knowing where the high-percentage shots are—is how you become a good percentage-tennis player. Well, here are the shots to choose from. There are only three choices. Yes, just three. We will shoot at targets above the net to get the ball to go to the following locations on the court. Here are the shots you can choose from:

Shot 1: Middle of the Court
This is a spot between the baseline and the service line, in the middle of the court.

Shot 2: Left Side of the Court
This is a spot between the baseline and the service line, in the middle of the left side of the court.

Shot 3: Right Side of the Court
This is a spot between the baseline and the service line, in the middle of the right side of the court (see Figure 27).

These shot selections—the middle of the court and the left and right sides of the court—will be your "shot selection" choices. Once again, we will use targets above the net to get your shot to go to these three locations. Why are these goals so modest? You might be asking, "Shouldn't I be trying to make better shots closer to the lines?" The answer is no. The reason is your circle of error.

Circle of error is the average distribution of your mistakes. That sounds really dry, but it is actually not that painful to understand. Take ten shots at a target and make a mental note of where all your shots land. Use the aiming techniques. Adjust your aim points for each error you make. You might hit the target a couple of times, but you will probably make six or seven near misses. If you plotted each miss with a piece of chalk, you would have a picture like the one shown in Figure 28. Now draw an imaginary circle around your target that contains all the shots. That circle is your circle of error.

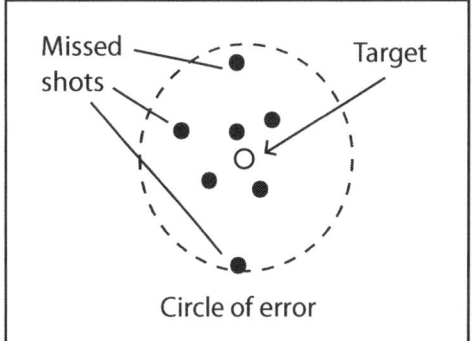

Fig 28 The Circle of Error

Let's say your circle of error on the tennis court is about eight feet in diameter. Draw that circle of error around the three targets on the court. You will see that some of your shots will come very close to the baseline; others will land short in the court. When you aim for the left or right side of the court, some of your shots will land right in the middle of the court and some will land very close to the sidelines.

Using these three targeting goals will get almost all of your shots to land in the court. Your mistakes will be the shots that land in the middle of the court or hit the line for a winner. Using these three shot selections will bring you very close to being a good percentage-tennis player. (You will complete the transition to becoming a percentage-tennis player with the tools of strength and position and the vector of the oncoming shot, but that will come later.)

The Three Targets

To make these three shot-selection choices, we will use three different targets above the net. The targets change depending on where you are standing on the court. As you move from the middle of the court to the left and right sides of the court, the targets will slide left and right. Let's start with the targets when you are standing in the middle of the court.

The center-of-the-court target is directly over the tape at the center of the net, about three feet above the net (see Figure 29).

The target for the left side of the court is about three feet to the left of the tape, about three feet above the net (see Figure 29).

The target for the right side of the court is about three feet to the right of the tape, and about three feet above the net (see Figure 29).

Notice how close all these targets are to the center of the net. Using aiming techniques, you will very rarely choose targets far to the left or right of these spots. The next time you watch a professional tennis match, notice how many balls cross the net very near these three targets. Many cross almost directly over the center of the net. Even on crosscourt passing shots, the ball will pass over the net very close to the center tape. Only on shots down the line does the ball cross over the net near the sideline.

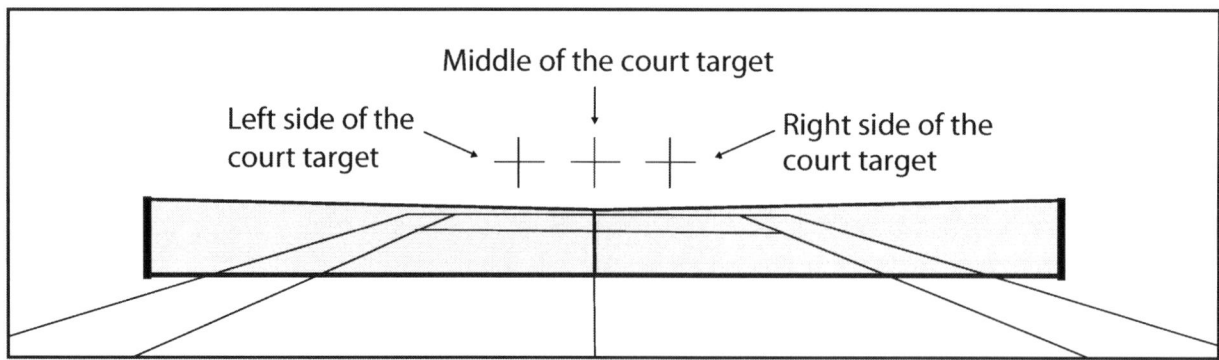

Fig 29 The three targets from the center of the court

Look at the bird's-eye view of these three targets. The dead-center target produces the shot right down the middle of the court. When you draw an eight-foot circle of error around the outcome of your shot, you can see that a lot of balls will go to the left and right of the middle of the court (see Figure 30).

Now let's look at the top view of the left and right targets (see Figure 31 and 32). You can see that the small angle we aim for produces a shot that lands in the middle of the left or right side of the court. When we draw an eight-foot circle of error around the outcome of these targets, you can see that about half of the shots will come very close to the sideline. These errors will be your great shots. These mistakes will be your near winners and outright winners. You want to make winning mistakes instead of losing errors out of the court.

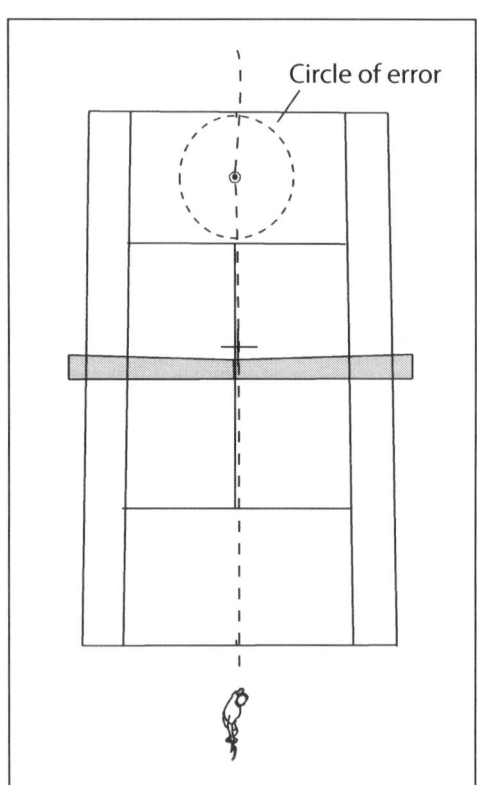

Fig 30 Center of the court target from the middle of the court.

Targets from the Side of the Court

Our shot selections remain the same: we want to shoot the ball to the middle of the court and to the left and right sides of the court. But when we are standing or playing the ball from the side of the court, the targets slide over. The targets to make these three shot selections move as your shooting position moves from the middle of the court to the side of the court. This target shift is the main reason that playing singles is harder than playing doubles.

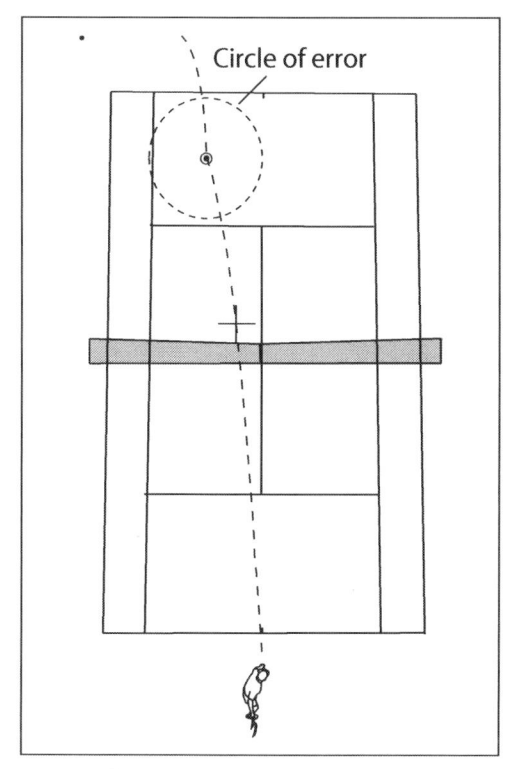

Fig 31 Left side of the court target from the middle of the court.

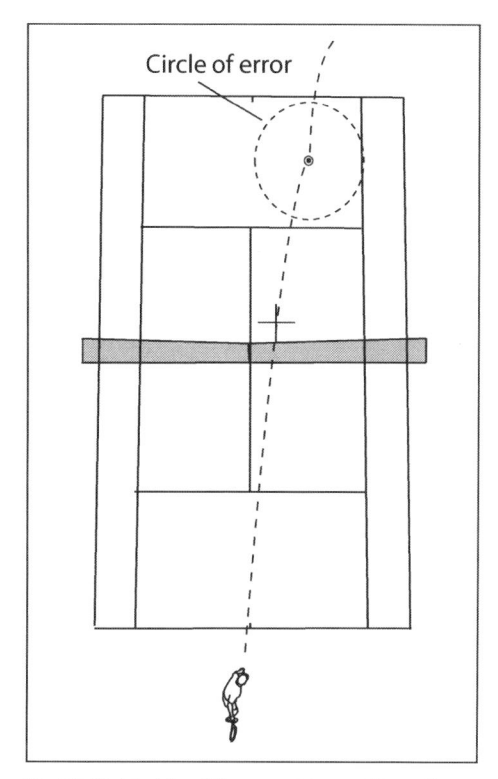

Fig 32 Right side of the court target from the middle of the court

Targets from the Right Side of the Court

Let's start with targets when shooting from the right side of the court. Figure 33 shows the three targets. Because you are shooting from the right side of the court, the targets have moved to the right.

The target that is dead center over the middle of the net is now the target for hitting the left side of the court, cross-court. This center-tape, cross-court target, when shooting from the side of the court, is a "very-high-percentage shot". Here the net is lowest and the court is longest. You can really crush the ball when you are going for

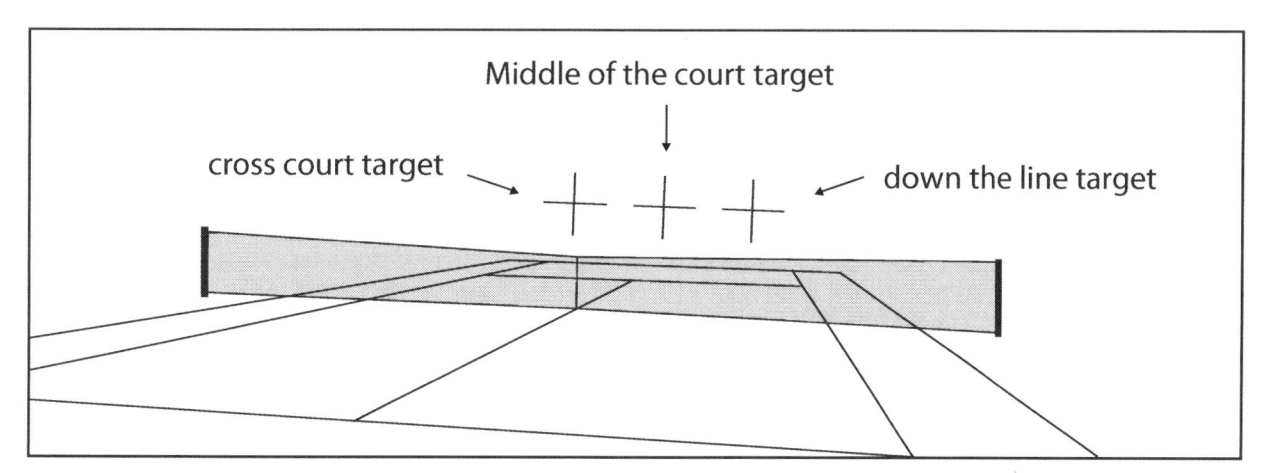

Fig 33 The three targets from the right side of the court

TARGETS AND AIMING | 31

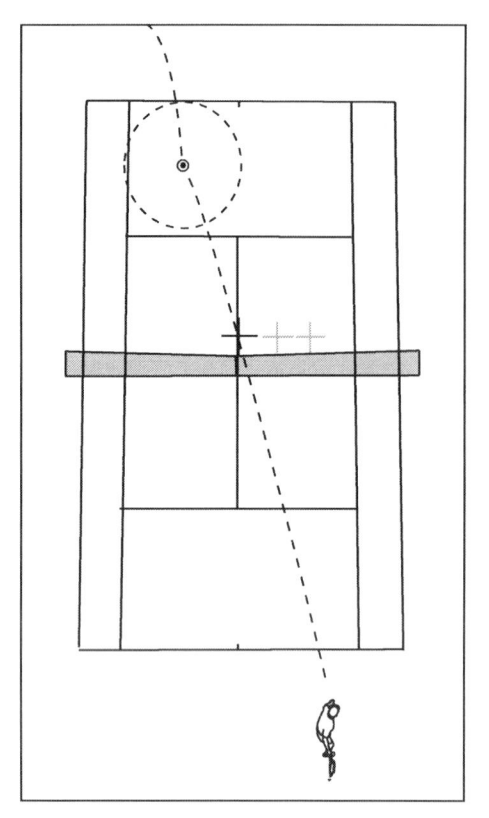

Fig 34 Left side of the court target, shooting from right side. Also know as cross court.

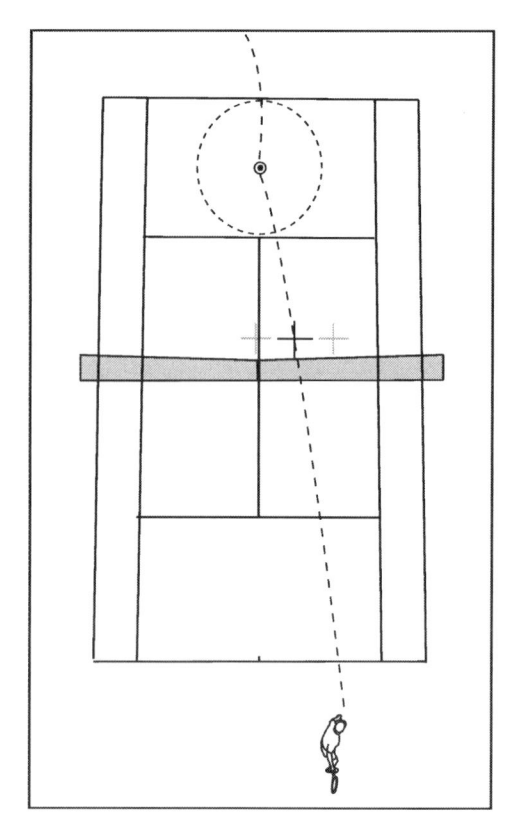

Fig 35 Target for middle of court, shooting from right side.

this target. The next figure shows the bird's-eye view of this target and its outcome when shooting from the right side of the court (see Figure 34). We will call this the "center-tape target" because it is right over the net tape.

The target for hitting the middle of the court has moved to the right: it is a couple of feet to the right of the center of the net. Figure 35 shows the bird's-eye view of a shot at this target.

The third target is the down-the-line target. This target is between the center tape and the sideline. This target is very conservative. It is biased to the middle of the court. This target purposely does not shoot the ball near the sideline. This is because the down-the-line target, when you're shooting from the side of the court, is usually the lowest-percentage shot you can make. There are many reasons for this. First, the net is at its highest; second, the length of the court is shorter, so you do not have as much room to err long in the court. These are the traditional explanations for the down-the-line shot being a low-percentage play. But there are other more important reasons that make it a low-percentage shot. We will go over those reasons in the chapter on strength and position (chapter 4). Suffice it to say that when you shoot the ball down the line, you will have a greater tendency to miss wide of the court. The circle of error for this target is actually more elliptical: it extends toward the sideline of the court. Figure 36 shows the bird's-eye view of a shot at this target and its circle of error.

Targets from the Left Side of the Court

When you play a ball from the left side of the court, the targets slide over to the left (see Figure 37).

Just as from the right side, the center-tape target shoots the ball to the opposite corner, crosscourt. For the same reasons, it is the highest-percentage play you can make. Figure 38 shows the bird's-eye view of this target.

The middle-of-the-court target has moved to the left. Figure 39 shows the outcome of a shot at this target.

The down-the-line target from the left side of the court is between the sideline and the center of the net. This is a conservative target because of the tendency to miss wide of the court. To compensate for this natural error, we use this very conservative target when shooting the ball down the line. We purposely bias this target away from the sideline. If you use this conservative target, you will make a lot of winning mistakes near the sideline (see Figure 40).

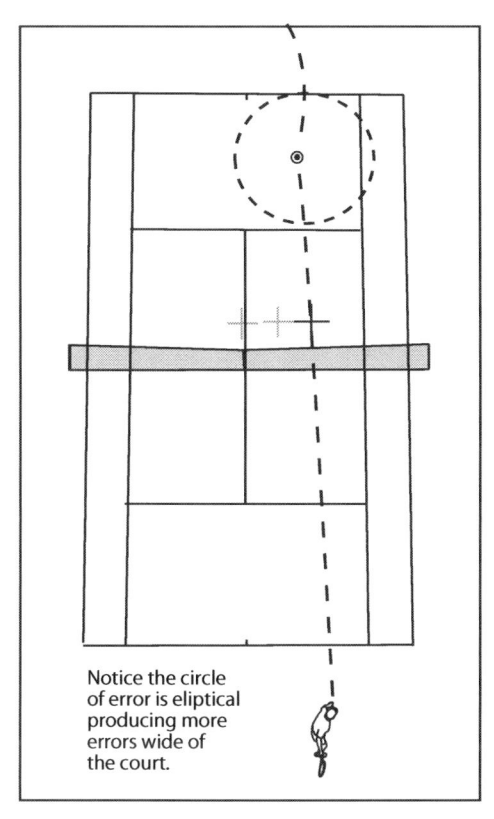

Notice the circle of error is eliptical producing more errors wide of the court.

Fig 36 Target for right side of court, shooting from right side. Also known as "down the line".

BASIC AIMING DRILLS

Now it is time to try a few specific drills to get you started with targets, aiming, and ball control. Go out on the court with a partner. It will be best if your partner has a basket of balls and can feed them to you, but if this is not possible, you can do it during a rally. These drills are ground-stroke drills.

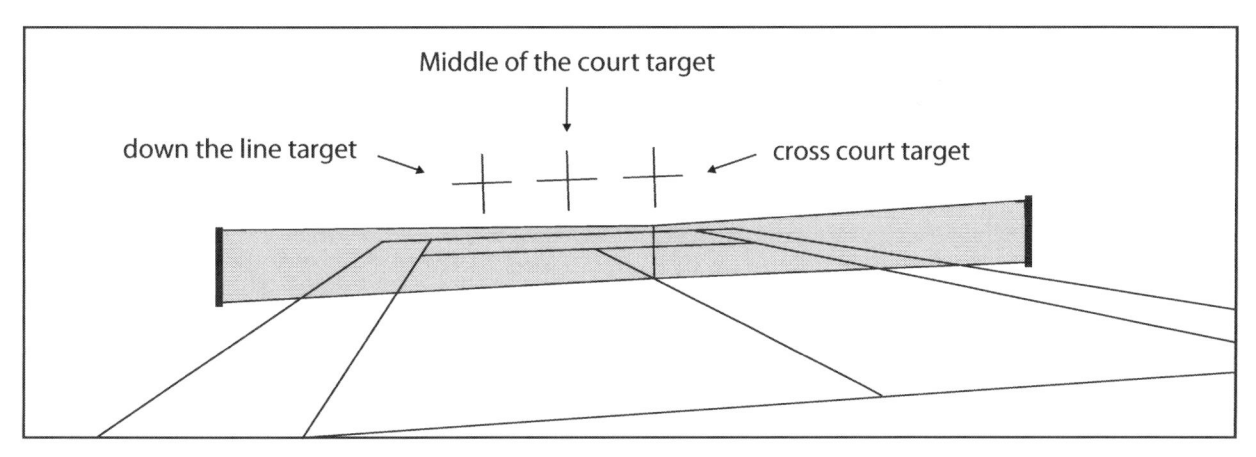

Fig 37 The three targets from the center of the court

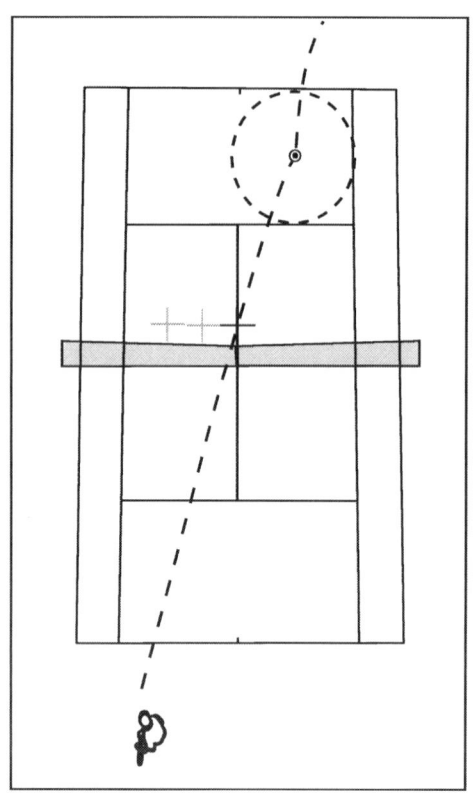

Fig 38 Right side of the court target, shooting from left side. Also know as cross court.

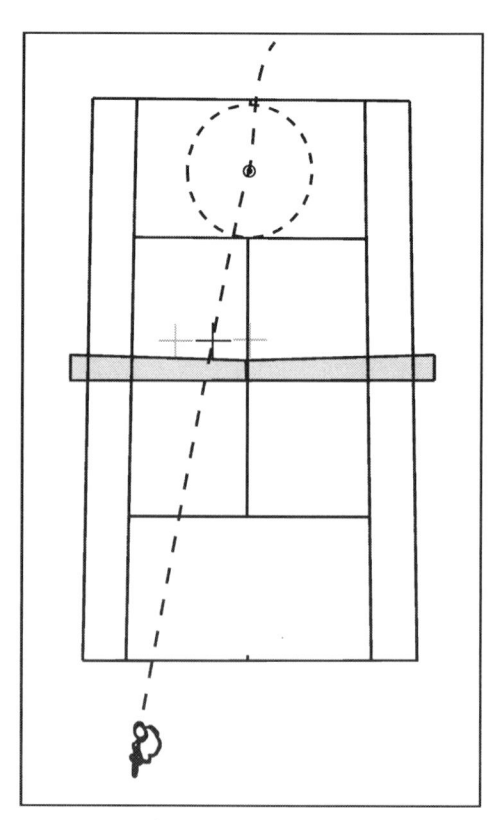

Fig 39 Target for middle of court, shooting from left side.

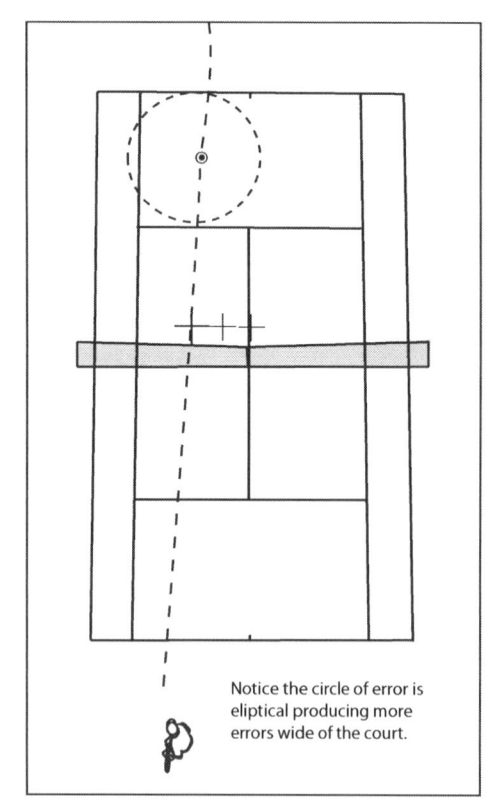

Fig 40 Target for left side of court, shooting from left side. Also known as "down the line".

Notice the circle of error is eliptical producing more errors wide of the court.

DEPTH DRILL

This is the introductory drill that you have already tried. It is the first drill to do to get the feel for aiming in two dimensions—up, down, left and right—to get results in all three dimensions. The third dimension being the depth of your shot—near and far. Refer to page 29 for depth drill instructions.

CENTER-TAPE TARGET DRILL

In this drill, you will try to make every ball you hit go directly over the center of the net, no matter where you are standing in the court. Your target here will be directly over the center tape. Put your target at the optimum height that you found in the depth drill.

It is best to do this drill while rallying with a partner. Your goal in this drill is twofold. First, you are practicing the aim-point technique around this target. Use all the corrections you have learned: use the up-and-down correction and the left-and-right correction. Never accept missing in the same spot twice. The second goal of this drill is to notice how effective this center-tape target is. When you stand in the middle of the court and you hit your shot through the center-tape target, the ball will land in the middle of the court. But when you are hitting your shots from the right side or the left side of the court, and you shoot your shot through the center-tape target, your ball will go into the opposite corner of the court. Keep hammering this center-tape target and observe the outcome (see Figure 29).

Now try playing practice points. Use only the center-tape target, no matter what. You will find that you will miss very few shots. Keep shooting for the target over the center of the net. Keep adjusting your aim points around the center-tape target as you make errors. When you are shooting from the side of the court, your shot will be a vicious crosscourt; when you are hitting from the middle of the court, your shot will be a ball to the dead center of the court. You will find that you can win a lot of points by using this very conservative and very simple shot selection. Don't worry that you are hitting the ball right back to your opponent. When you obey the rules of percentage tennis, you will learn that it is often okay to hit the ball right back to your opponent. Remember, tennis is a game of errors. You don't want to miss. You want to give your opponent a chance to miss.

Once again, you have to go for it. Do not let yourself stiffen up and push the ball. Go for your shots. Make your aim-point adjustments. Embrace making errors as a good thing. Know that you learn from mistakes and that you can immediately correct for them. Hit the ball hard. Use 80 percent power.

Pull Drill

In this drill, you will be getting close to upper-level-percentage play. This drill will introduce you to the strength concept. Strength and position will be explained in detail in chapter 4, but for now you will get a feel for what strength is, and how powerful a concept and technique it is for percentage play.

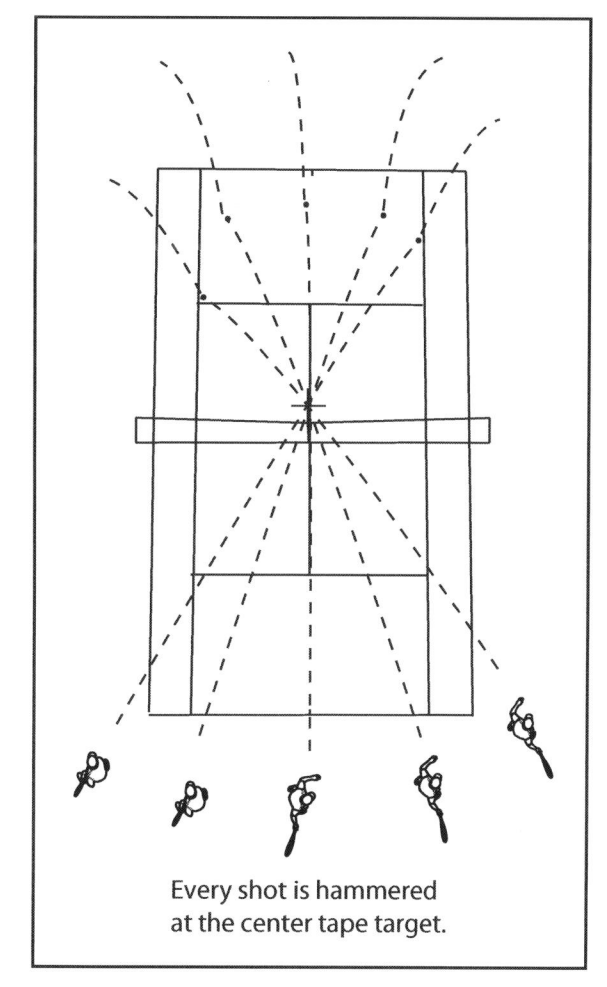

Every shot is hammered at the center tape target.

Fig 41 Center Tape target drill

For this drill, you will "pull" the ball into your strength every time you select a shot. (These directions assume a right-handed player.)

- When you are receiving a ball in the center of the court on your forehand side, use the target to the left of the center of the net. This target is on the strong side of your forehand. You will be pulling the ball to the corner.
- If you are standing on the right side of the court, hitting a forehand, use the center-tape target. This target will shoot the ball crosscourt (see Figure 41).
- When you are receiving the ball in the center of the court on your backhand side, use the target to the right of the center of the net. This target is on the strong side of your backhand. You will be pulling the ball to the corner. (see Figure 41).
- When you are standing in the left side of the court, hitting a backhand, use the center-tape target. This target directs the ball crosscourt.

These targets are on the strong side of your forehand and backhand. In both cases you will be pulling the ball to the corner "in strength" (see Figure 42). (Strength will be fully explained in chapter 4)

You can do this drill with a partner in a rally or practice point, although it's best to make it a practice point, because your opponent will be doing a lot of running. Notice that you will make very few errors, hit a lot of shots into the corners, and often dominate the point.

Now play a couple of games using this plan. Do not vary your shot selection. Choose the targets as they are above. Always choose these "pull" targets.

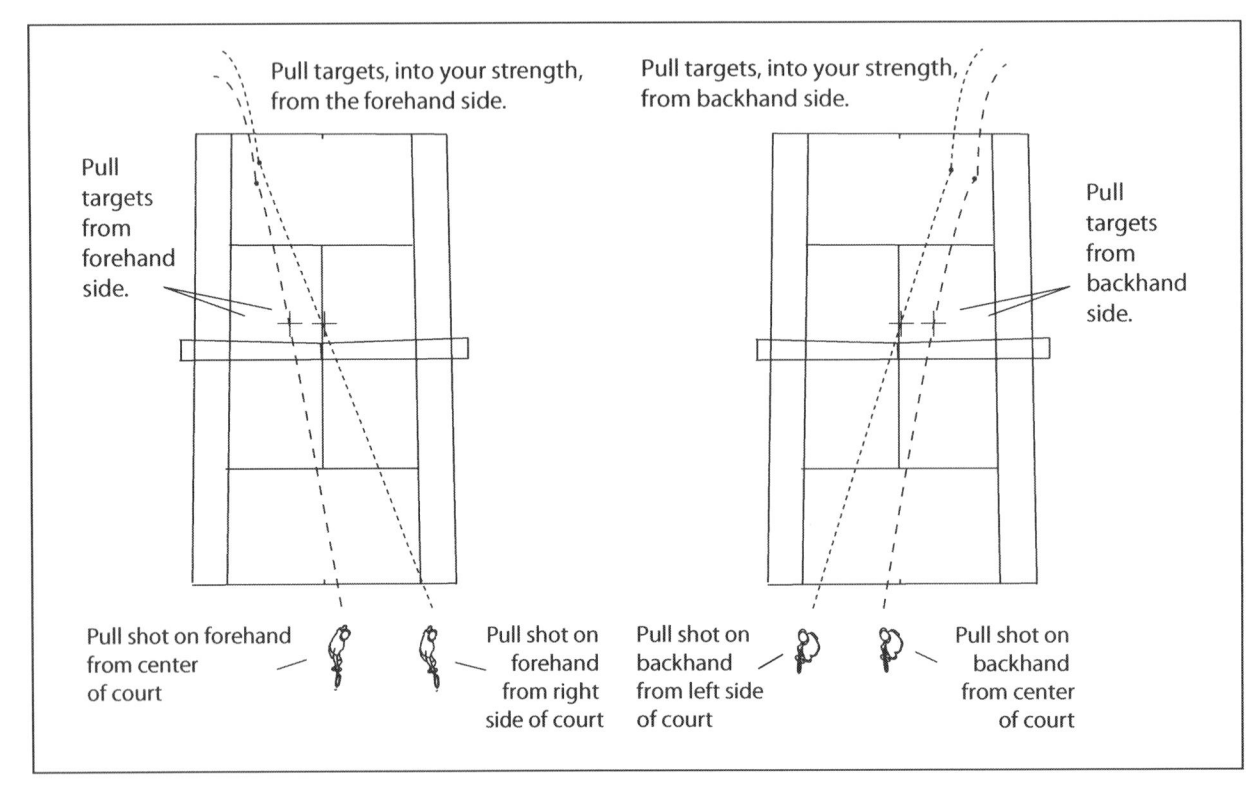

Fig 42 Pull drill

You might remind yourself of Monica Seles in her prime here. By using these shot selections, you are playing a very conservative but high-level game of percentage tennis.

In these practice games you need to go for it. Do *not* push the ball. It is okay to lose every game. You are in the nascent stage of developing ball control. As long as you are correcting for your errors using the aim-point adjustment techniques, you are being successful. What you will find is that you will make a lot of mistakes early on, but as the games progress, you will get more and more accurate. You will hit the ball hard, and you will begin to hit a lot of those hard shots in the court. The "hit out" mind-set is essential to getting ball control and taking your game to the next level. Play a few games or a whole set using the pull targets.

DOWN-THE-LINE DRILL

In this drill you will make shot selections that are usually the opposite of good percentage play. The drill is designed to show you that targeting the ball down the line, or away from your body, will produce a whole lot of errors. The reason for this is that you push the ball away from your body when you select the shot down the line. This is the opposite of pulling the ball to your strength. It is not always a bad shot selection, but it is usually a low-percentage play. The strength concept will be fully explained in chapter 4.

These directions assume you are right-handed. (If you play left-handed, simply reverse the directions.) Here they are:

- If you are receiving the ball in the center of the court on your forehand, aim for the target to the right of the tape. Your goal should be to hit the ball into the right side of the court, down the line.
- If you are playing a forehand from the right side of the court, aim for the target to the right side of the net. This will shoot the ball to the right side of the court. Your goal, again, is to shoot the ball down the line.
- If you are in the middle of the court and are playing a backhand, aim for the target to the left side of the court. Your goal off the backhand is to hit the ball into the left side of the court, down the line.
- If you are standing in the left corner of the court playing a backhand, aim for the target that shoots the ball to the left side of the court. Your goal off the backhand, again, is to shoot the ball down the line.

To simplify: Off the forehand, aim to the right side of the court, and off the backhand, aim to the left side of the court (see Figure 43).

You will find that you will make a lot of errors in this drill. You will miss the ball wide of the court a lot, and you will make a lot of errors long and into the net.

After you try this drill in a rally, play a few practice games. Do not play a whole set using this target plan. It will not be a good experience. You will lose a lot of points. You just need to play a few games to get a feel for what *not* to do. Keep on practicing your aiming techniques during this drill. In chapter 4 you will learn when the down-the-line target is a high-percentage play.

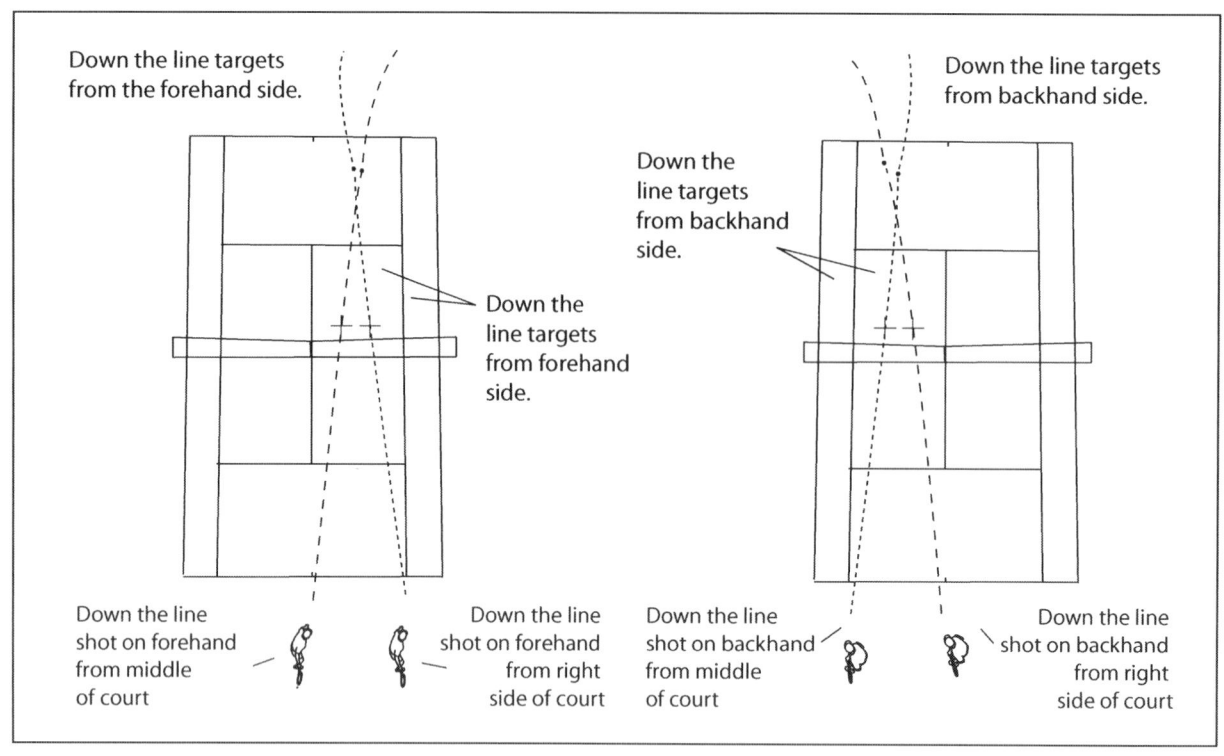

Fig 43 Down the line drill

Aiming Architecture

We have just defined the aiming architecture for ground-stroke targets. Start with these targets. Use the targets every time you go out and play. Demand that you correct for your errors every time you shoot a shot.

Ball control is a matter of knowing *where*—not how—to shoot your shots. Targets and aiming are your tools for finding out where that is. You are building visual cues—visual markers on the court—to guide your ball control. Where you have to aim a shot to get it to go where you want it to go is the quintessential core of tennis. That is the aiming architecture. Your construction of this architecture will grow and become more complete as you work with the targets and manipulate the aim points.

Building your aiming architecture is like filling in the pixels on a digital photograph. Each error you make, and every good shot you hit, places another dot onto the image. Over time the entire picture becomes clearer and more complete. Because you have a logic that uses errors constructively, you will complete this image rapidly. You will build your aiming architecture more quickly than the clueless, who have no ball-control logic. They build the picture haphazardly, almost accidentally, as they play the game.

The targets I have shown you here work, but you will have to manipulate them and tailor them to your game. Your game is unique. You hit your shots with a certain amount of spin at a certain pace, and the targets will be unique to you for those reasons. As you learn to play the arcs in the next chapter, your game will change. You will learn how to impart more spin on your shots. This will change the shape of your shots. As you do this your targets will need to be adjusted. This adjustment is usually in height. Big topspin shots, for instance, need to be aimed higher. Ripped backspin shots need lower targets. Keep this in mind as your game develops. Keep experimenting and learning with every mistake you make.

Sliding Targets

As we've discussed, playing singles is much harder than playing doubles. The reason for this is that you have to shoot your shots from all over the court. The targets change as you move from the middle of the court to the left and right sides of the court; they slide left and right as you move around. Understanding how the targets change is an extremely important part of the aiming architecture. How much the targets slide left and right depends on how far to the side of the court you are shooting from. The farther you are to the side of the court, the more the targets slide with you. The targets for shooting from the side of the court that you saw in all of the illustrations are generic, but they work well. Use them as your initial reference for building your targeting architecture. As you improve and gain experience, you can refine how much the targets slide as you shoot from wider positions on the court.

Volley targets are slightly different from ground-stroke targets. They are explained in appendix 1.

Simple Goals – Shooting for the Three Targets

Its important to simplify and we have. With this new targeting architecture the game is distilled to three shot selections, the left side, the right side, and the middle of the court. The targets are conservative. They are centered between the service line and the baseline. They give you a large "margin of error." You can crush your shots to these locations, using the over the net targets, because you know the majority of your errors are going to go in the court. Some will land right in the middle of the court. Some of them will winning shots on the lines.

Using these three simple targets during a point will reduce uncertainty in your decision-making. You will have a clue. You will know what you are going for. You are taking shots. You must develop this "shooting" mindset. Pull the trigger and let it go. All you have to do is pick out a target and shoot. Go for it. You can hit out and let the chips fall where they may. You are going to miss. But, when you use these three very conservative targets a huge number of your misses are going to go in the court.

In chapters 4 you will learn how to determine which of the three targets are high or low percentage in different situations on the court. Once you understand this you will know how to make high percentage shot selections. Your consistency will skyrocket and your errors will fad away. In chapter 5 you will learn how to use this knowledge to play and win points. A tennis match is played one point at a time. Learning how to win points means learning how to win matches.

Summary

Targets and the aiming technique are the main tools for getting ball control. Have fun experimenting with these tools. Try to get over making mistakes. Mistakes are your friends. You use them to get better. You use them to develop ball control.

The next chapter will teach you how to play the arcs. This is where the fun begins. You will learn how elite players hit the ball really hard, with a lot of spin. You will learn this technique and start to enjoy the game more than you ever have before. You will learn how to play the arc of the incoming ball and control the arc and spin of your shot as it flies out into the court.

CHAPTER 2

Playing the Arcs

Note: Aiming and playing the arcs work together like hand and glove. When combined, they create a synergy that will unleash your shot-making potential and explode your game. Unfortunately, they can't be taught at the same time. You have to learn one and then the other. After you understand both concepts, it will be simple to put them together and use them as a whole. For now we must talk about them individually. You just learned about targets and aiming; now it is time to learn how to play the arcs. Keep in mind: once you understand them, both concepts will be joined together and used as a holistic technique.

The Arc

An arc is something that is curved or arched. Every ball you play on the tennis court travels on an arcing flight path. Understanding the arcs will be your key to unlocking the game of tennis. Playing the arcs will give you a complete and flexible approach to striking the ball in all situations.

A great revelation I heard from a student when I first taught him to play the arcs was, "Wow, this is just like surfing." (The kid was a surfer as well as a tennis player.) His previous tennis instruction had taught him to move his racket like a robot. He had to make his stroke a certain way every time, without change, without relating to any visual cue. When he learned to see the arcs and play them, tennis completely changed for him. This only took one lesson—about thirty minutes. He suddenly saw that tennis was like surfing. The game was based on visual cues of a changing, curving thing. In surfing, the curving thing is the wave; in tennis, it is the arcing flight path of the ball. He saw that the game was not a stiff, rigid thing but a free-flowing, visually oriented activity with a lot of possibilities. You, too, will learn to use the arc as a visual platform for creating your shots. You will learn to carve the arcs like a surfer shreds the waves.

Here are a few facts about the arc: every tennis ball that your opponent hits to you has an arcing flight path as it travels across the net, and every ball you hit back will describe an arc as it travels over the net and into the court.

The arc of the ball is a visual measuring tool. It illustrates every characteristic of the oncoming shot. The arc, or curved path, that the ball travels is a result of several factors. One factor is speed. The faster the ball travels, the flatter the arc will be. Because the ball is traveling fast, it will travel farther and flatter before gravity pulls it back to earth. So, fast shots have flatter arcs. If the ball is hit slowly, it will have a rounder arc. Because the ball travels slowly, it goes a shorter distance before gravity pulls it back to earth. So, more slowly hit balls have rounder arcs.

Spin is the other big factor. A ball hit with topspin will curve down into the court. The more topspin on the ball, the more dramatically the arc will curve down. If a shot is hit with backspin, its arc will be flat; it may even appear to rise initially. Then the ball will fall down into the court as the speed of the shot slows and gravity pulls it back down into the court.

Direction is also important. If the ball is hit high above the net, it will have more of a curved arc as gravity pulls it down into the court. So balls hit high into the air will curve a greater distance into the court. If the ball is hit low across the net, it will take less time and distance to fall into the court and its arc will not be as round.

The arc of the shot your opponent hits to you is a result of its speed, spin, and direction. The shot's arc tells you everything about the ball's energy. It is a visual signature and fingerprint of the oncoming shot. The arc is the analog representation of the shot's digital characteristics: speed, spin, and direction.

Playing the Arcs

To master playing the arcs, you will learn the following:

1. *How to see the arcs.* Here you will change your perception techniques to be able to see and capture the shape of the arc in your mind's eye.
2. *What part of the arc guides your racket.* You use the whole arc of the ball to see and gauge the shot that your opponent hits to you, but you will only use part of the arc to guide your racket. That part is the second half, from the top of the arc to its contact with the court—that is the portion of the arc that is played.
3. *Start with top topspin.* To simplify the discussion and to limit confusion, we will first learn how to play the arcs with topspin. After topspin techniques are clear, playing the arcs with backspin will be explained.
4. *Stroke essentials.* While this isn't a book about tennis strokes, there are a few essential things you must have in the motion of your racket to be able to play the arcs. They are (for topspin shots) a closed racket face and a basic figure-eight motion to your stroke.
5. *How to flip your racket around the arc.* This is the heart of the technique and where you will learn to hit big topspin shots. In fact, it will enable you to put as much or as little spin on the ball as you desire.

Seeing the Arc

Different spins = different arcs. There are three basic kinds of arcs and three basic kinds of spins. Different spins create different arc shapes. It is helpful if you know about an arc's shape as a result of the spin on the ball. So first, we will sort out the arcs by their spin.

Topspin shots have arcs that start flat and then curve rapidly down into the court. The topspin puts pressure on top of the ball, pushing it down and creating

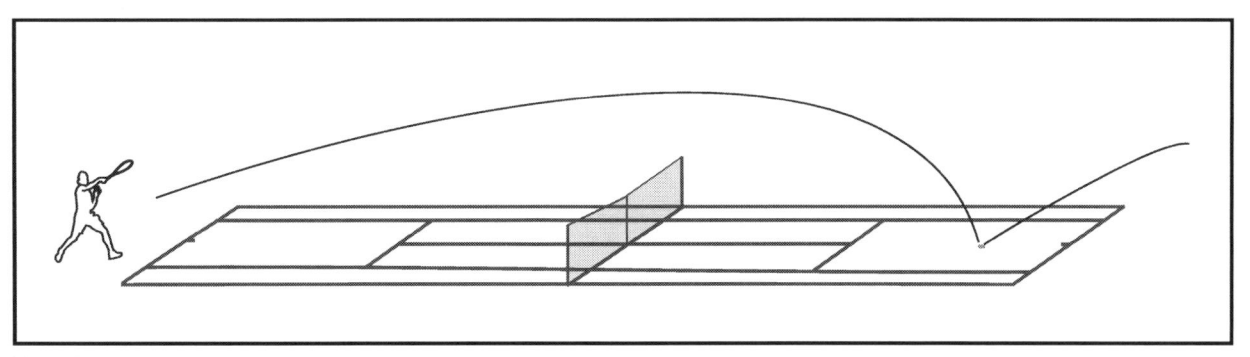

Fig 1 Basic topspin arc

its rounded shape. The general contour of a topspin arc is shown in Figure 1.

Backspin shots have arcs that are initially flat, with a rounded finish. The backspin puts pressure on the bottom of the ball. That pressure holds the ball up, creating the flat portion of the arc. The rounded finish to the backspin arc occurs as the speed of the ball wears off and gravity pulls the ball down into the court. Good players can hit backspin shots hard and down into the court. These arcs look very flat as they hit the court before they slow down. The general shape of a backspin arc is shown in Figure 2 below.

The arcs of flat shots—shots hit without significant spin—curve more constantly as they slow down and gravity pulls them into the court. This is because there is

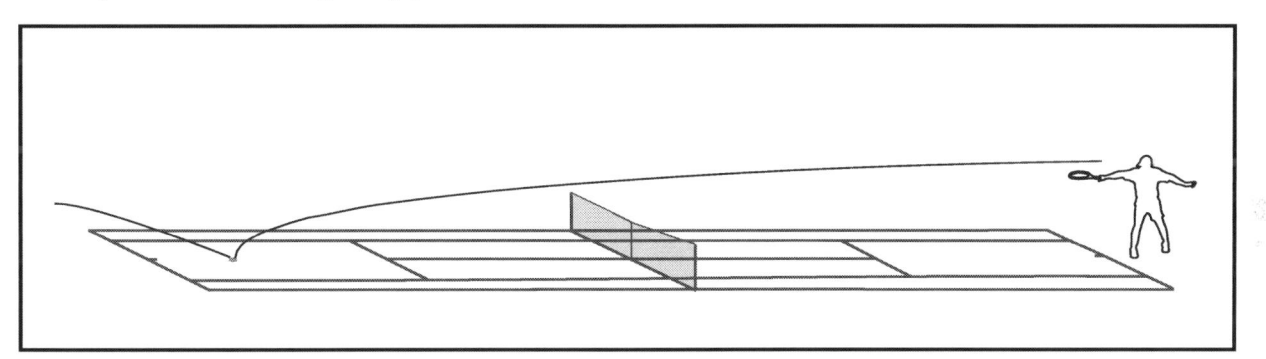

Fig 2 Basic backspin arc

no spin putting pressure on the ball to move in one direction or the other. Gravity is the only thing making the ball drop toward the court. Hard-hit flat shots can have very flat-looking arcs. Because the ball is moving at high speed, it travels straight and level for a long distance before gravity pulls it back into the court. Slow, flat shots will have a round, constantly curving arc. Figure 3 shows a hard-hit flat arc; Figure 4 depicts a slowly hit, high-arcing flat shot.

These illustrations show generic topspin, backspin, and flat shots. You will see infinite variations of these arcs. You will also know what spin is coming at you by the movement of your opponent's racket: a low-to-high stroke produces topspin, while a high-to-low stroke produces backspin. Knowing the general shape of the arc and cueing in to the spin by the movement of your opponent's racket will enhance your ability to see the arcs.

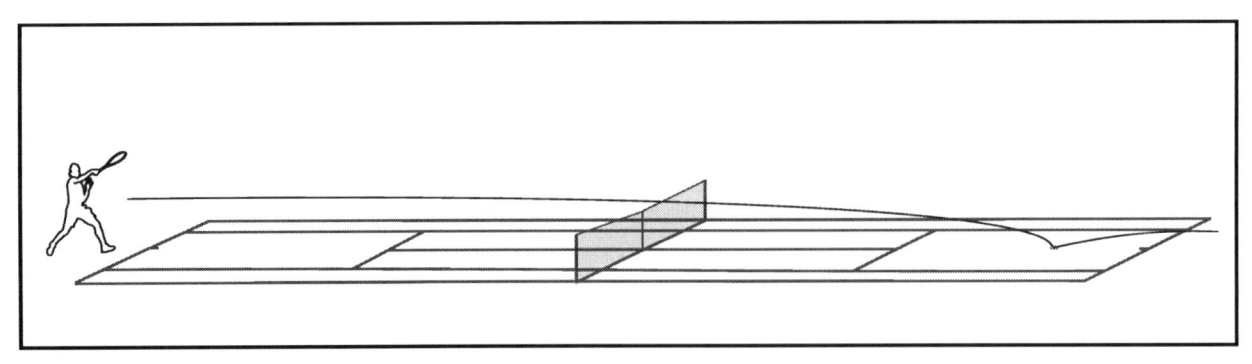

Fig 3 Hard hit flat arc.

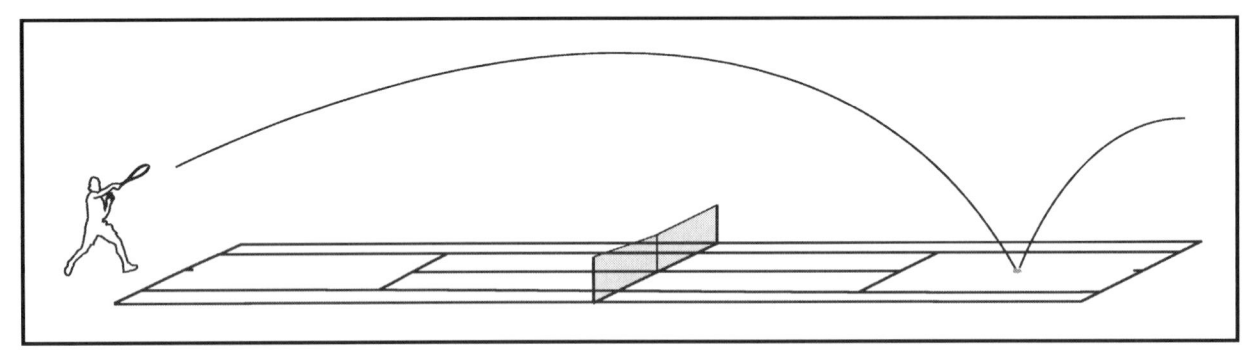

Fig 4 High, slowly hit flat arc.

Open Focus: A New Way of Seeing the Ball

The arc reveals everything about the oncoming shot and is the optimal tool for playing the ball. The good news is that you do not need to analyze the arcs: all you have to do is learn to see them. Seeing the arc and holding it in your mind's eye *is* the analysis. If you see it, you can play it.

To see the arcs, you will first have to adjust how you use your eyes. Most players concentrate on watching the ball as a static thing. Their eyes focus solely on the ball, and not on its path. They might even try to blot out the background of the court. This is wrong thinking and bad technique.

To see the arcs you have to open the focus of your eyes. This means you have to simultaneously see the ball and the background of the court. This allows you to see the ball, perceiving its flight path and capturing its movement as a 3D picture. Seeing the arcs, and holding that perception in your mind's eye, are the skills you need to learn.

Open focus is also a key ingredient to making you a much better player. Open focus will allow you to see the whole court, enabling you to pick out targets in your periphery and enhancing your shot selection. Open focus also enables you to observe where your opponent is and where she is moving. This is an essential skill in advanced tennis play. With this skill, you can choose to run your opponent or hit behind her as the tactical situation dictates. We will go over this in more depth later.

"SEEING THE ARCS" DRILL NUMBER ONE: OPEN FOCUS

Your first step in learning how to see the arcs will be to watch a match or a practice session from the side of the court. Your goal here will be to notice how each ball curves as it travels over the net.

In this first drill, stand by the side of the court. You should place yourself opposite the middle of the court, about twenty-five to fifty feet away. Use the following types of focus while you observe.

Closed focus: For the first part of this drill, watch about ten or fifteen shots using a "closed focus." As the players hit the ball back and forth, focus intently on the ball and try to exclude the background. Working your eyes like this, see if you can judge and record in your mind's eye the shape of each arc. Watch a good number of shots with this incorrect closed-focus method.

Extreme open focus: Now watch another fifteen or so shots using the "extreme open focus" technique. Do *not* focus on the ball. Focus your eyes on an imaginary point above the net. Don't follow the ball with your eyes. Concentrate totally on your peripheral vision. Observe the arc of each ball as you focus on that point over the net. Do your best to see the arcs and record their flight paths in your mind's eye. This is a complete open-focus approach. You will rarely use this focus when you play, but it is an excellent drill. Notice how the arcs appear. Try to trace the arc of each ball as a curved line in the air and record that curve visually. (You will sometimes use this kind of focus in the game: for example, if a slowly hit ball is sitting up in the court, close to the net. As you focus on the ball, you will concentrate on your peripheral vision as you monitor the movements of your opponent. As you get to the moment of hitting your shot, you will choose which side of the court to target based on where your opponent moves.)

Open focus: Now watch another twenty or more shots using the open-focus technique. Focus on the ball following its flight path, but concentrate on the background as much as you can. Use your peripheral vision here. Your concentration on following the ball should be equal to your concentration on peripheral vision and the background of the court. Use this open focus to build a picture of each shot's arc. Once again, judge and record in your mind's eye the shape of each arc. You should find that the arcs are much more apparent now. Watch a bunch of arcs using this open-focus method.

The skill you are building in this drill is the ability to perceive the ball's arcing flight path. You should notice the unique shape of each arc and try to hold it in your mind's eye as a picture. Look for the difference in the shape of topspin arcs and backspin arcs. Look for the shape of flat arcs and low and high arcs. This skill must be nurtured if you want to free up your game and start playing the arcs.

"SEEING THE ARCS" DRILL NUMBER TWO: THE PLAYER'S PERSPECTIVE

In this drill, you stand behind the court (at ground level) and watch a practice session or match. The arcs look different from this "player's perspective."

Because you are looking along the arc, not at the side of the arc, it will be a little more difficult to perceive the arcs from this position. But because this is what you see when you play, you will have to get this picture.

For this drill it is best to stand outside the court, looking through the fence. If the fences at your tennis courts have dense, green backgrounds, you may have to stand directly behind the player, against the fence. This drill is important, however, and so you need to find a way to do it. Watch about twenty-five shots or so using all three types of focus.

Closed focus: Follow the ball and do your best to ignore your peripheral vision. As you use this "incorrect" technique, notice how well you see the arcs.

Extreme open focus: Focus your eyes on an imaginary point over the net. Concentrate completely on your peripheral vision. Once again, try to see the arc shapes, and keep them in your mind's eye.

Open focus: Now try to pick the ball up as soon as it leaves the racket of the player on the opposite side of the court. Focus on the ball as it travels over the net, but concentrate on your peripheral vision as much as you can. Work hard on keeping your focus open. Work to capture in your mind's eye the arc of each shot. Try to see the player on the other side of the court in your peripheral vision as you follow the arc into the court. Do everything you can to hold the shape of the arcs in your mind's eye. Look for topspin shots, backspin shots, and flat shots. This is the player's perspective. You will have this view and use this open focus when you are playing the arcs (see Figure 5).

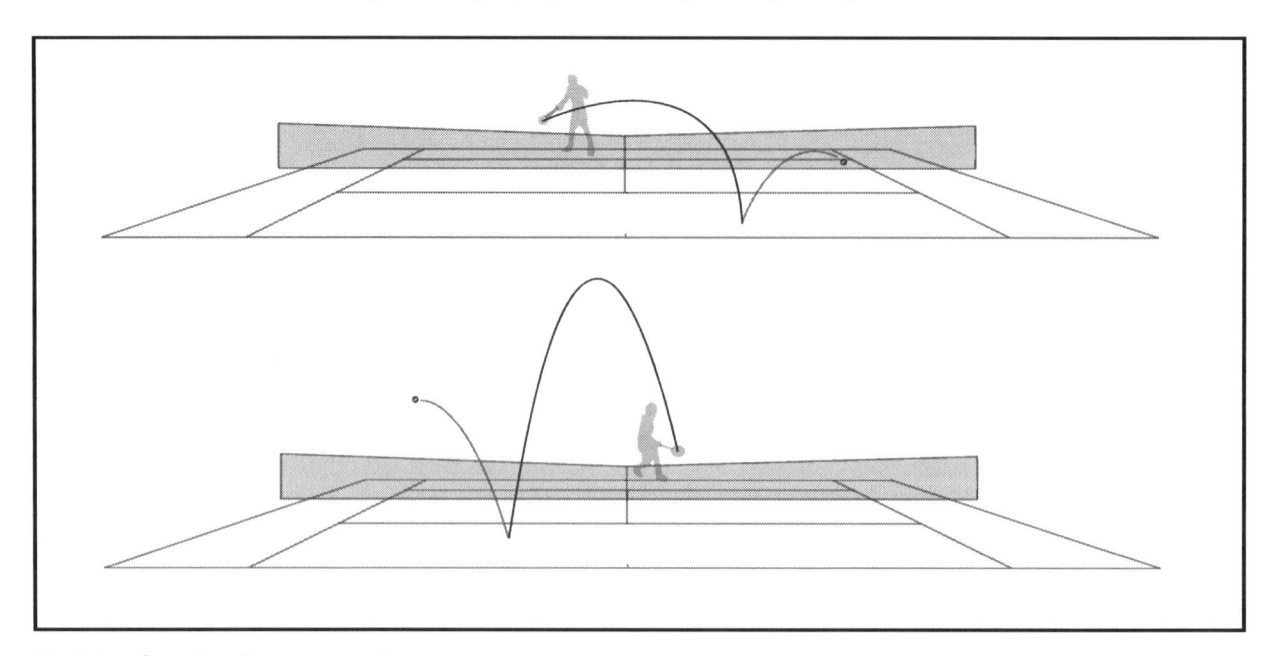

Fig 5 Arcs from the players perspective.

More about Seeing the Arcs

Let's go over the most important things about seeing the arcs.

First, you must have open focus. You cannot focus on the ball in isolation from its movement. You must see the ball and record its flight path in your mind's eye. To do this, you have to use your peripheral vision and develop this visual-memory skill. It may take some time, but after a while you will start to develop your own unique approach to seeing the arcs. Once you begin to capture the entire shape of the arc in your mind's eye, you will produce a distinctive personal way of seeing the ball.

Second, you must concentrate on seeing the ball the moment it comes off your opponent's racket. You need to see the arc of the ball from the moment of its inception. You must achieve the discipline of capturing the movement of the ball the instant it leaves your opponent's racket. This will dramatically improve your shot preparation. The movement of your opponent's racket will also provide a

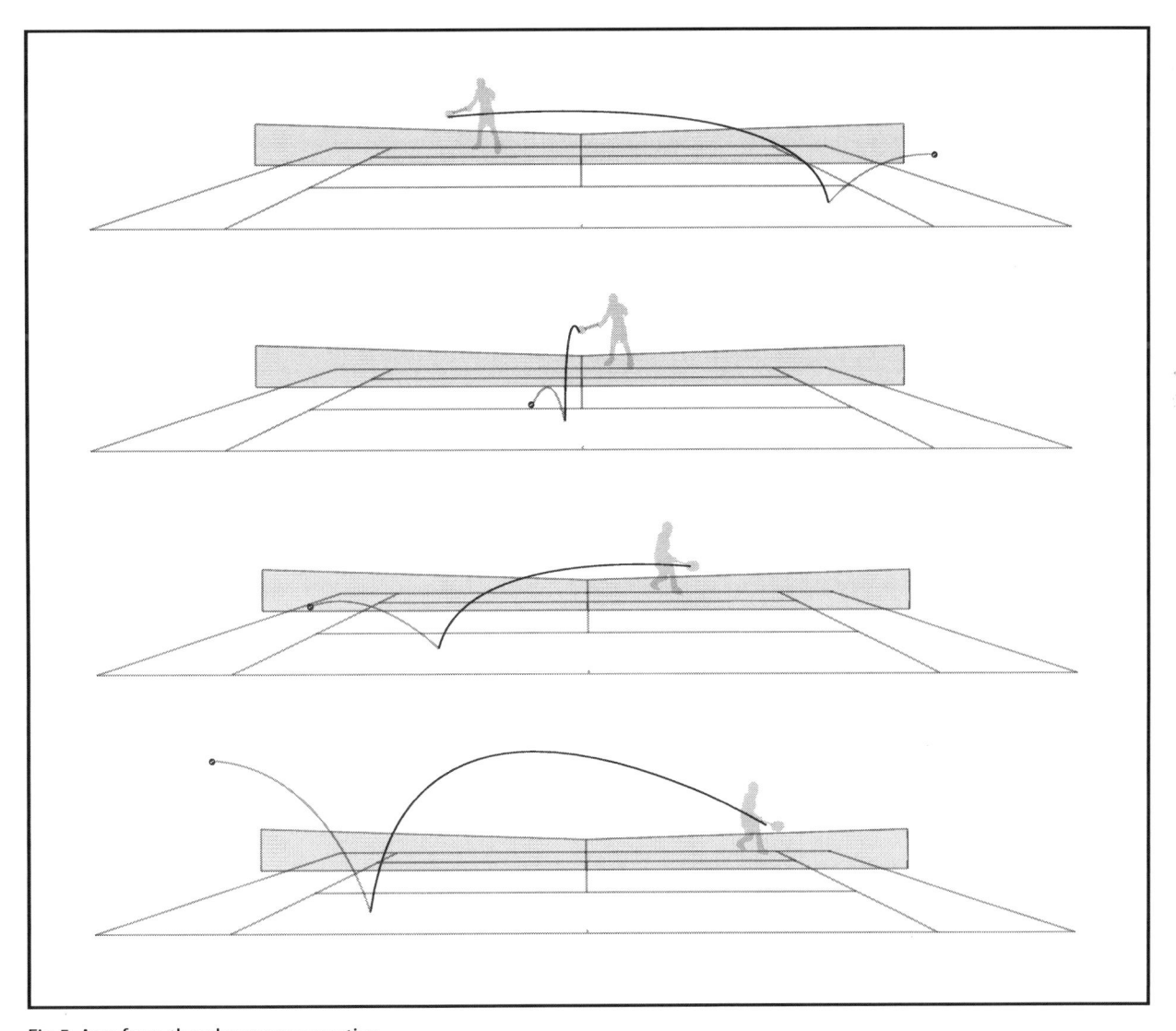

Fig 5 Arcs from the players perspective.

great deal of information about the shot. A low-to-high stroke produces topspin. A high-to-low stroke produces backspin. Seeing the movement of your opponent's racket will enhance your arc awareness. Over time your knowledge of the arcs will build: your mind will act like a computer, building a database of information on possible arcs. As you use this perception technique and your mind builds up its database, you will be able to recognize an arc after only a few feet of travel in the air. This will not be a conscious process. Don't try to make it one. Keep concentrating on seeing the arcs, and your recognition capability will get better and better. As this unconscious process goes on, your game will constantly improve.

What Part of the Arc Do You Play?

Although you have just learned to see the entire arc of the oncoming ball, you do not use the entire arc as a guide for hitting your shot. The portion of the arc that you play is the second half of the arc—that is, from the highest point of the arc to its impact on the ground (or, in the case of a topspin volley, the top of the arc to the point at which your racket strikes the ball). See Figures 6a, 6b, 6c, and 6d. The playable portion of the arc from the player's perspective is shown in Figures 7a, 7b, 7c, 7d, 7e, and 7f.

The shape of the arc, from the top of its trajectory to when it bounces on the court, is the key to unlocking the game. That is the *playable portion of the arc*. From now on, the playable portion of the arc will be the shape your racket will

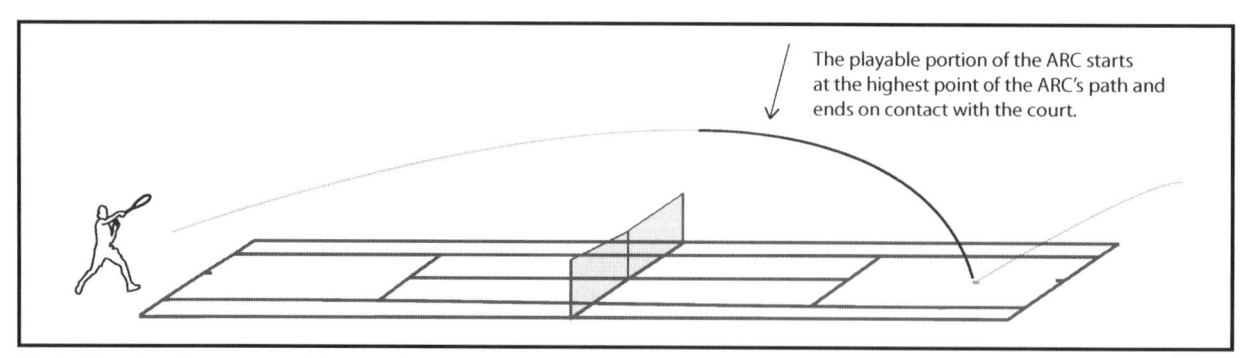

Fig 6a The playable portion of the ARC for a topspin ARC

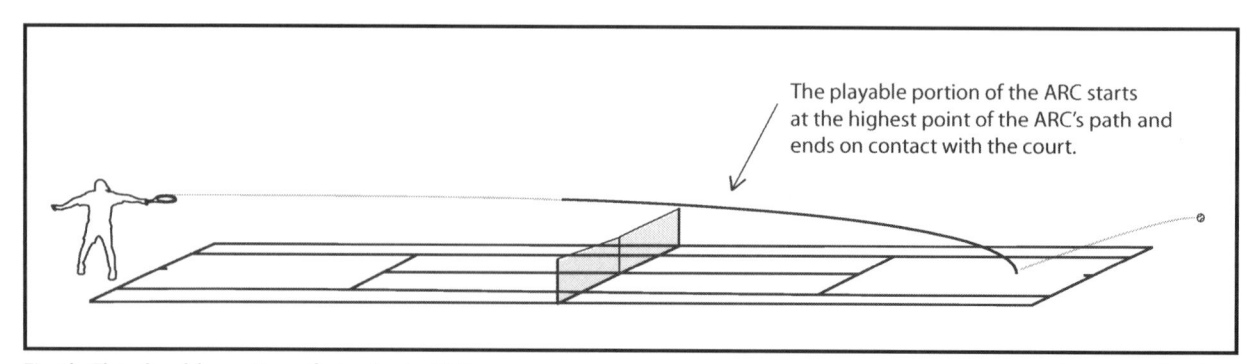

Fig 6b The playable portion of a backspin ARC

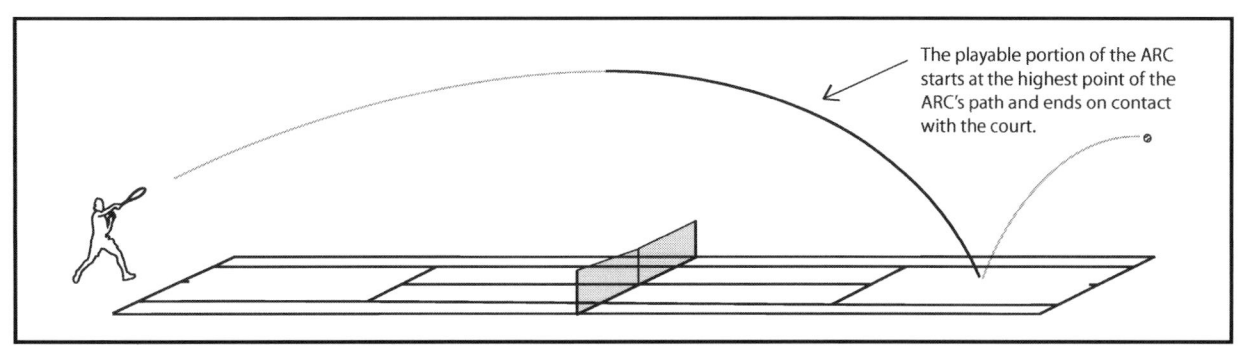

Fig 6c The playable portion of a high flat ARC

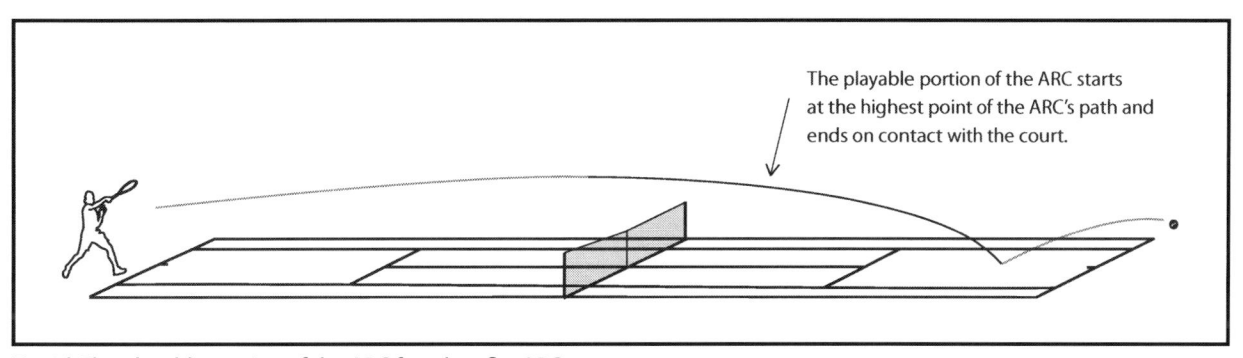

Fig 6d The playable portion of the ARC for a low flat ARC

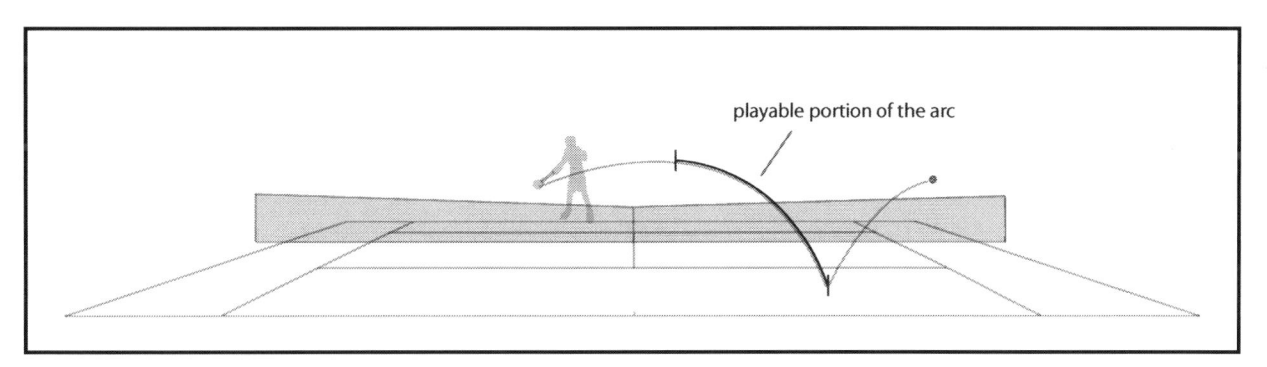

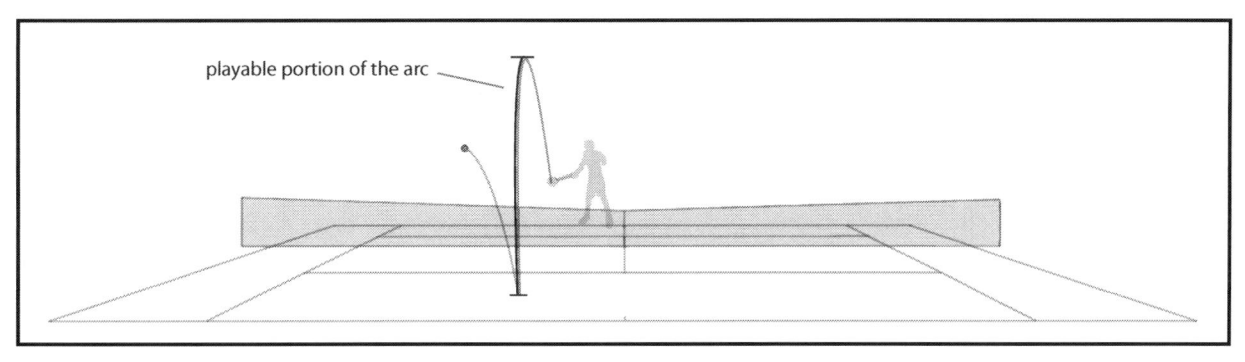

Fig 7a Playable portion of the arc, players perspective. Here is a the playable portion of the arc receiving a shot hit at medium hight, cross court.

Fig7b Playable portion of the arc, players perspective. Here is the playable portion of the arc receiving a high arcing shot with very little spin.

PLAYING THE ARCS | 49

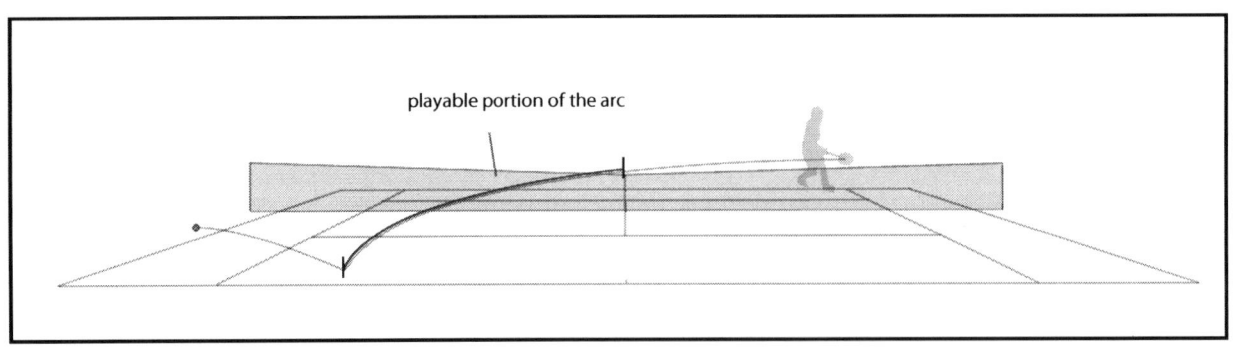

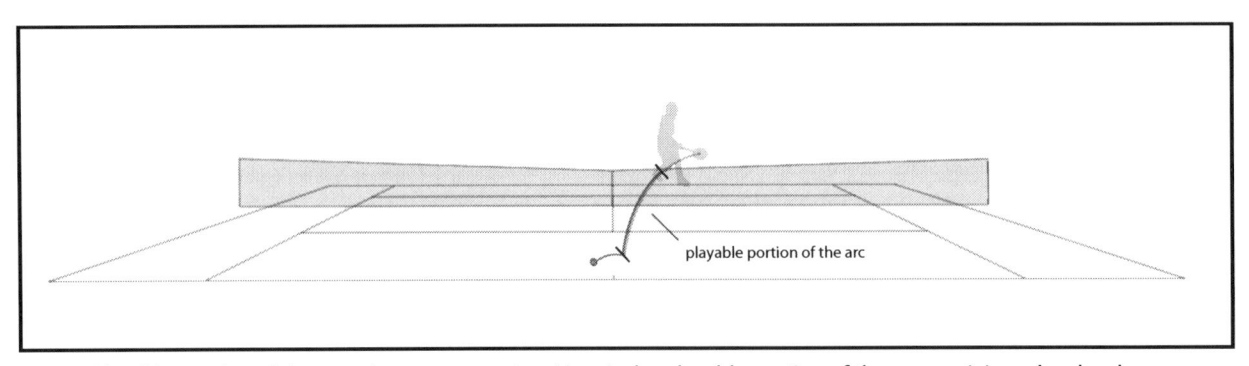

Fig 7c Playable portion of the arc, players perspective. Here is the playable portion of the arc receiving a low cross-court backspin shot.

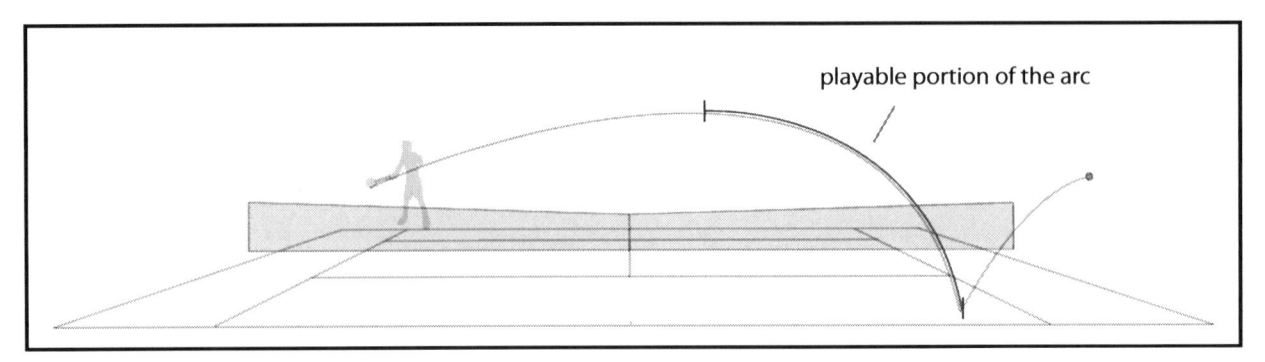

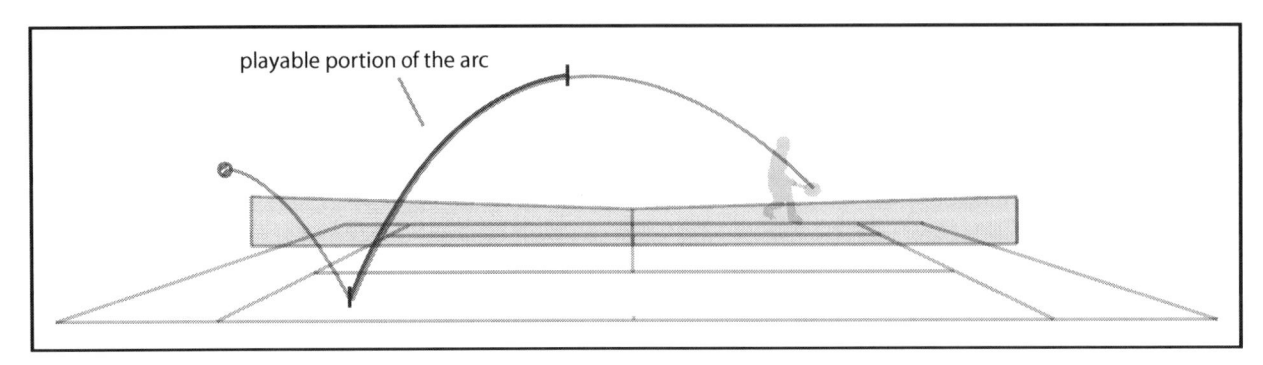

Fig 7d Playable portion of the arc, players perspective. Here is the playable portion of the arc receiving a high cross-court topspin shot.

Fig 7e Playable portion of the arc, players perspective. Here is the playable portion of the arc receiving a low hard hit "flat" shot.

Fig 7f Playable portion of the arc, players perspective. Here is the playable portion of the arc receiving a high, cross-court shot without a lot of spin.

carve as you strike the ball. The shape of the arc, from its highest point to its contact with the court, will be the curved template that will guide the forward swing of your racket as you choose to hit flat shots, ripping topspin shots, or any shot in between. This is the shape you will rip and shred as you create your shots. From now on, when you read the words "play the arc," it will mean playing this portion of the arc.

Don't get confused. It is a common mistake when learning to play the arcs to focus on the ball's path *after* it bounces on the court. Don't do this. The ball's flight path after it bounces off the court is not played. That part of the ball's flight path is completely a result of its arc in the air. As you learn to see the arcs, the resulting bounce of the inbound shot is precalculated. By seeing the arc, the shot's resultant bounce is automatically accounted for. You must rip and ride the playable portion of the arc, which is the arc's shape from its highest point to its contact with the court.

Topspin

To eliminate confusion, at first we will only talk about hitting topspin shots. After the topspin techniques are explained, we will spell out playing the arcs with backspin.

Stroke Essentials

In order to play the arcs with topspin, you must have a couple of things in your stroke when you strike the ball. One is a closed racket face. The second is a basic figure-eight motion to your swing.

Topspin and the Closed Racket Face

A closed racket face means that the face of the racket that strikes the ball is tilted down at the court. If the racket face were tilted up, it would be "open" to the sky. That is where the term "closed racket face" comes from: a closed racket face is "closed" to the sky. See Figures 8, 9a, and 9b for a closed racket face on the backhand and forehand side. Figures 10a and 10b are examples of open racket faces.

Striking the ball from low to high creates topspin shots. The low-to-high movement of the racket spins the ball. The more severe the movement of the racket from low to high, the more spin is imparted.

In the modern game of tennis, most shots are hit with topspin. At the highest level of the game, this spin is extreme. The easiest way to create

Fig 8 Closed Racket Face Forehand Side

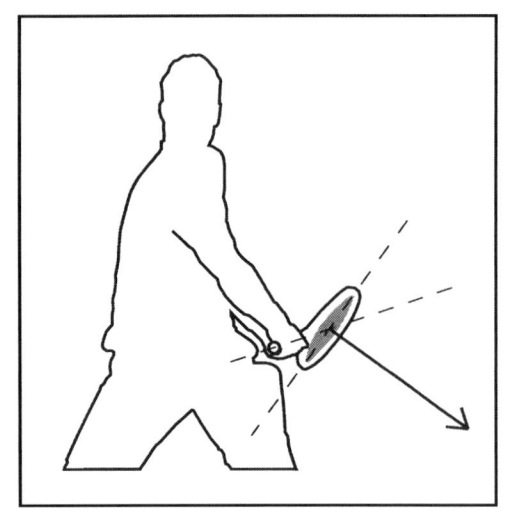

Fig 9a Closed Racket Face Two-handed Backhand.

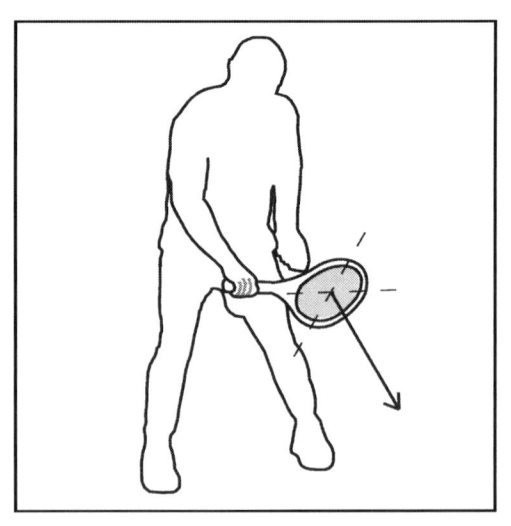

Fig 9b Closed Racket Face One-handed Backhand.

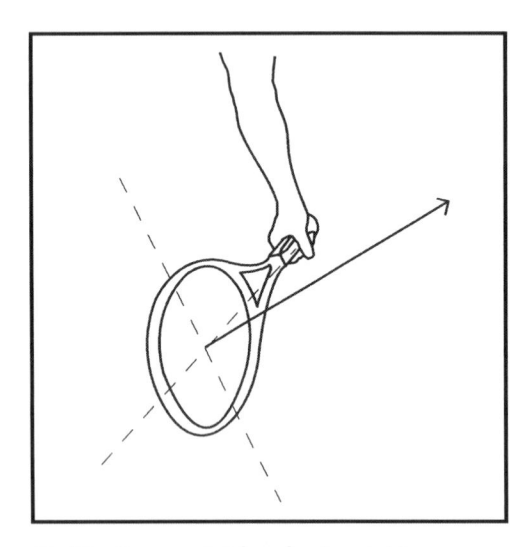

Fig 10a Open racket face forehand side.

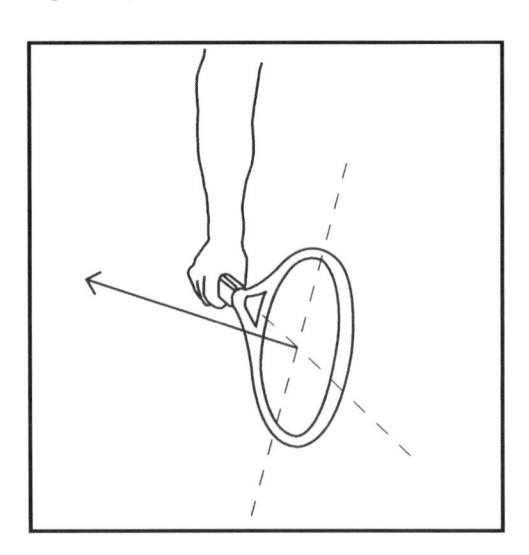

Fig 10b Open racket face, backhand side.

big topspin, like the best players in the world do, is to start your forward swing with a closed racket face. As you initially strike the ball, the racket face may be slightly open, especially on heavy topspin shots. But by starting your forward swing with a closed racket face, the application of topspin is much easier and more consistent.

You can hit topspin shots if you start your forward swing with an open racket face. But this technique requires the racket to be turning as you strike the ball. The racket must be *closing up* as you make contact. This requires excellent timing.

The best way to get a closed racket face as you strike the ball is to adjust your grip. Refer to appendix 5 for more about grips.

Topspin Ground Strokes and the Basic Figure Eight

We have to talk about strokes now. We will not make any hard-and-fast rules. We will describe how your racket should move in a very general way.

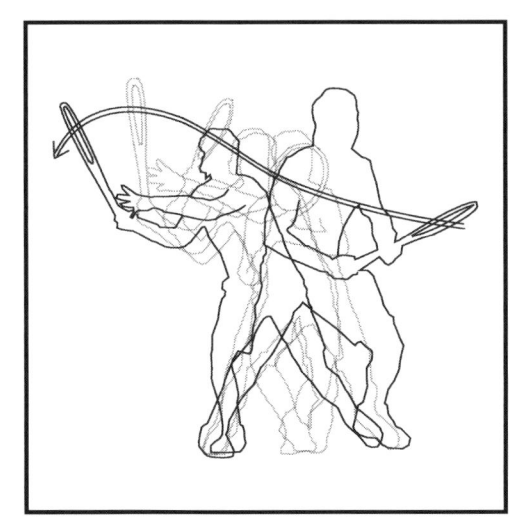

Fig 11a Forehand backswing. First half of the figure 8.

Fig11b Forhand forward swing. Second half of the figure 8.

The shape of your stroke when you hit a topspin shot is a figure-eight lying on its side. Watch your favorite tennis player hit a few balls. Notice the backswing. It will look like a little loop or circle that moves back in a smooth and rolling motion (see Figure 11a). This is the first part of a basic figure-eight motion of the tennis stroke. As the racket travels to the end of the backswing, it moves below the level of the ball. Then, on the forward swing, the racket makes a curved motion around the ball. The curved motion of the forward swing is moved *around* the playable portion of the arc. This is where the arc is ripped. This is where the arc is played (see Figure 11b). The complete motion of the stroke is shown in Figure 11c.

The front side of this figure-eight is open, but we can call it a "figure-eight" to keep things simple. Figures 12a, 12b, 12c and 12d show typical one-handed backhand and two-handed backhand figure-eight strokes.

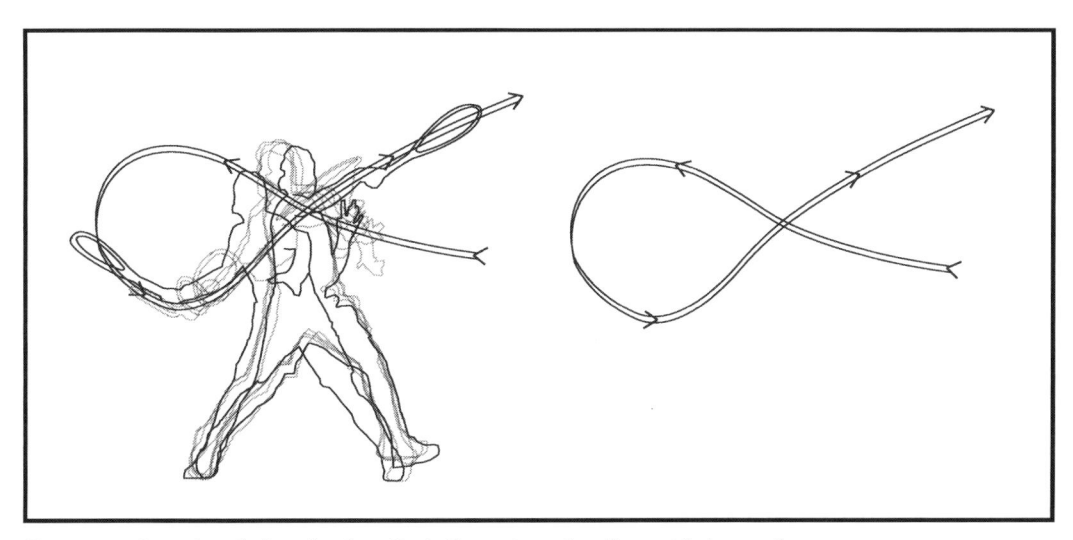

Figure 11c Complete forhand swing. Basic figure 8 motion (front side is open).

PLAYING THE ARCS | 53

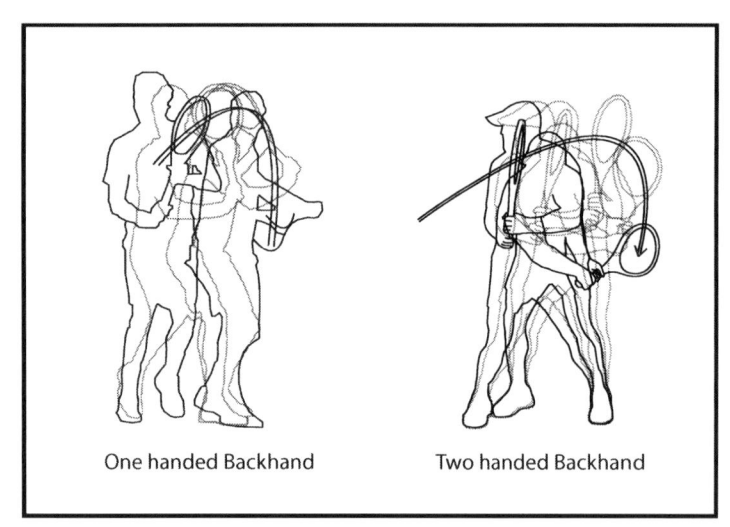

Fig 12a Backhand backswing. First part of the figure 8.

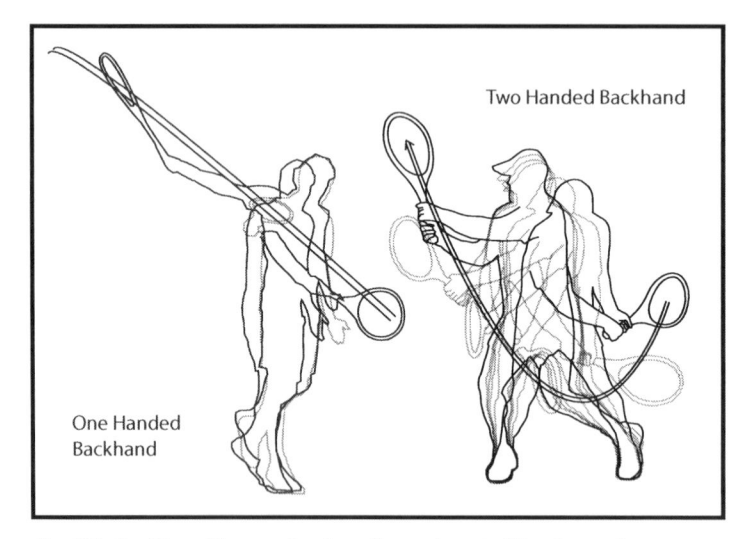

Fig 12b Backhand forward swing. Second part of the figure 8.

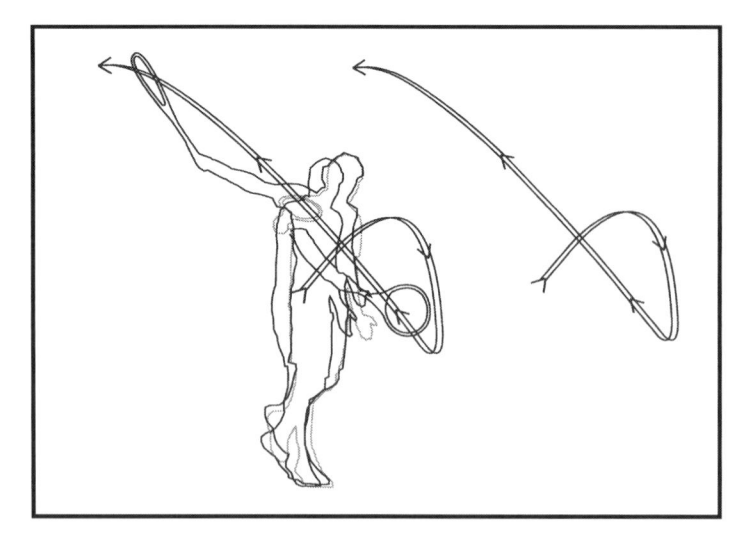

Fig 12c Complete one handed backhand swing. Basic figure 8 motion (front side is open).

Your fluidity and ability to play the arcs will be enhanced if your initial backswing is rounded like the figure-eight shown above. But if you have a really straight, flat backswing, that is okay. Try to round it out a little over time. Don't make this stroke change the focus of your efforts. The focus of your efforts will be on the forward swing of the racket where you play the arc. Choose a favorite professional player and emulate that player. This is a good and reasonable approach to developing your stroke. (For example, Roger Federer's forehand is a near carbon copy of Björn Borg's forehand.)

Preparation = Flowing with the Arcs

It is essential to flow with the arc. That is, when the ball comes off your opponent's racket, your preparation and backswing should start instantly! Your shot preparation should flow back as if pushed by the oncoming ball. Your racket should move as if it were hooked somehow to the ball and is forced back by its movement toward you. Like opposite-polarity magnets, the oncoming shot drives your backswing into motion. Your preparation will improve dramatically if you concentrate on this instantaneous start to your backswing. The backswing of your shot should mirror the arc of the oncoming ball—slightly rounder for high-arcing balls and slightly flatter for low, hard-hit arcs.

The forward swing of the racket should be equally fluid. You should roll up into the ball with smooth

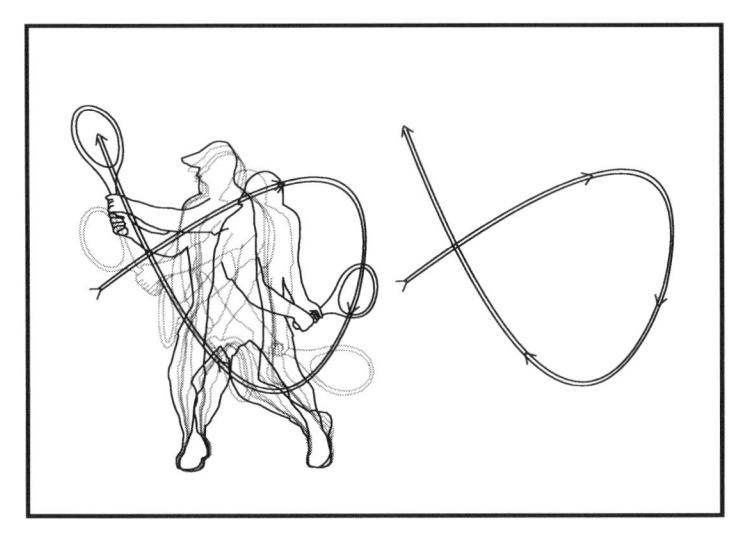

Fig 12d Complete two handed backhand swing. Basic figure eight motion (front side is open).

timing. Watch a really good player hit a few balls and notice the fluidity there. Work hard to make your stroke flow with the ball.

Playing the Arcs

This is where the fun begins. The arc will become your ultimate tool for hitting out: it will enable you to capture the energy of the shot that your opponent hits to you and manipulate that force. By capturing the arc in the movement of your racket, you conserve the shot's energy; your racket uses it like a trampoline to power your shot. You contain and command the energy, speed, spin, and curving force of the ball by playing the arc. Aiming your shot directs the vector of your shot. Playing the arc completes the other half of the ball-control equation by harnessing the energy of the shot that your opponent hits to you.

When you play the arcs, you are playing the energy and physical properties of the inbound arc. You are essentially capturing the energy of that shot. The physics term for this is "conservation of energy." By playing along and around the arc, you are conserving the energy of your opponent's shot in the forward swing of your racket. By using the arc's shape to guide your racket, you harness its power. You will find a new feel for the ball as you experiment with arc play. When you play the arc properly, it feels like you have struck something perfectly square. The weight and pace of the incoming shot rides exactly on your racket as your forward swing moves along the arc. Its power will be captured and will rebound completely off your stroke. By harnessing the energy of the oncoming shot, you control it and use it to your advantage.

Old tennis paradigms called for a same-shaped, unchanging stroke. This technique works if the shape of the arc hit to you is the same every time and the stroke matches the shape of the arc. But if the shape of the arc hit to you changes, this technique falls apart. It does not work. When a constant, fixed stroke impacts changing arc shapes, the result will be an inconsistent shot. The shot is a direct result of the changing arc. The fixed, unchanging stroke works well in a tennis lesson, because the instructor can hit consistently shaped arcs to you. But when match play begins, and the arcs start changing shape, it's all over. No matter how well you manufacture that "perfect," identical stroke, your shot will travel a path that is a consequence of the arc that your opponent hits to you. And

> **BRUSHING UP THE BACK OF THE BALL**
>
> You might hear tennis pundits recommend "brushing up the back of the ball" as a technique. This is the most bankrupt description of the most important action a tennis player makes on the court. Brushing up the back of the ball is a hint about the most critical skill every tennis player should learn. That skill is *playing the arc*. Brushing up the back of the ball is another static concept. It refers to the ball as a nonmoving object. It ignores the shape and energy characteristics of the shot hit to you. It suggests that the ball is just sitting there as if it were on a golf tee. If you "brush up" anything, it is the shape of the arc, not a static, nonmoving ball.

the result isn't truly random. A stroke that encounters an arc that is rounder than its shape will produce a shot that is low—and probably into the net. A stroke that meets an arc that is flatter than its shape will produce a shot that is high—and probably out of the court.

When you play the arcs, your stroke changes with every shot. You move your racket around the oncoming arc. Your racket flows with the shape of the shot your opponent hits to you.

The Forward Swing and How to Play the Arc

The playable portion of the arc is the basis for the forward swing of your racket. This is where the arc is played. This is where the spin is produced. This is where you choose to drive through the arc for a hard-hit, low-spin shot, or flip your racket around the arc for a big topspin shot.

As you play the arc, your racket moves around the shape of the playable portion of the arc. The amount of movement around the arc will vary with the amount of spin you want to produce. When you choose to hit a flat, rolling topspin shot, your forward swing mimics nearly exactly the shape of the arc. To hit more topspin, your racket moves rounder than the shape of the arc. To apply heavy topspin, your racket makes an exaggerated flip around the shape of the arc. The arc is the canvas. Your racket is your brush as you rip your forward swing and create an infinite variety of shots.

You must treat every shot uniquely. You must capture the arc of the inbound shot in your mind's eye. Then the forward swing of your stroke plays that shape. The following figures show how different arc shapes are played for the rolling topspin shot. The spin is called "rolling" because it is not severe. In each example, note how the forward swing of the racket mirrors the playable portion of the arc for each arc shape. (Medium- and heavy-topspin arc play will be explained shortly.) Here are a few examples of playing arcs for rolling topspin shots.

Playing an average-height arc (see Figure 13)

Playing a low, hard-hit flat arc (see Figure 14)

Playing a high arc (see Figure 15)

This symmetric movement around the shape of the arc is the essence of *playing the arcs*. It will unlock incredible shot-making potential for you. Believe me, it is fun to do this. Watch a match on TV and watch the forward swing of the players' rackets. Each forward swing is unique. The forward swing changes as the different arc shapes are played.

The movement of the racket follows the shape of the playable portion of the arc. This "arc play" will produce a rolling topspin shot.

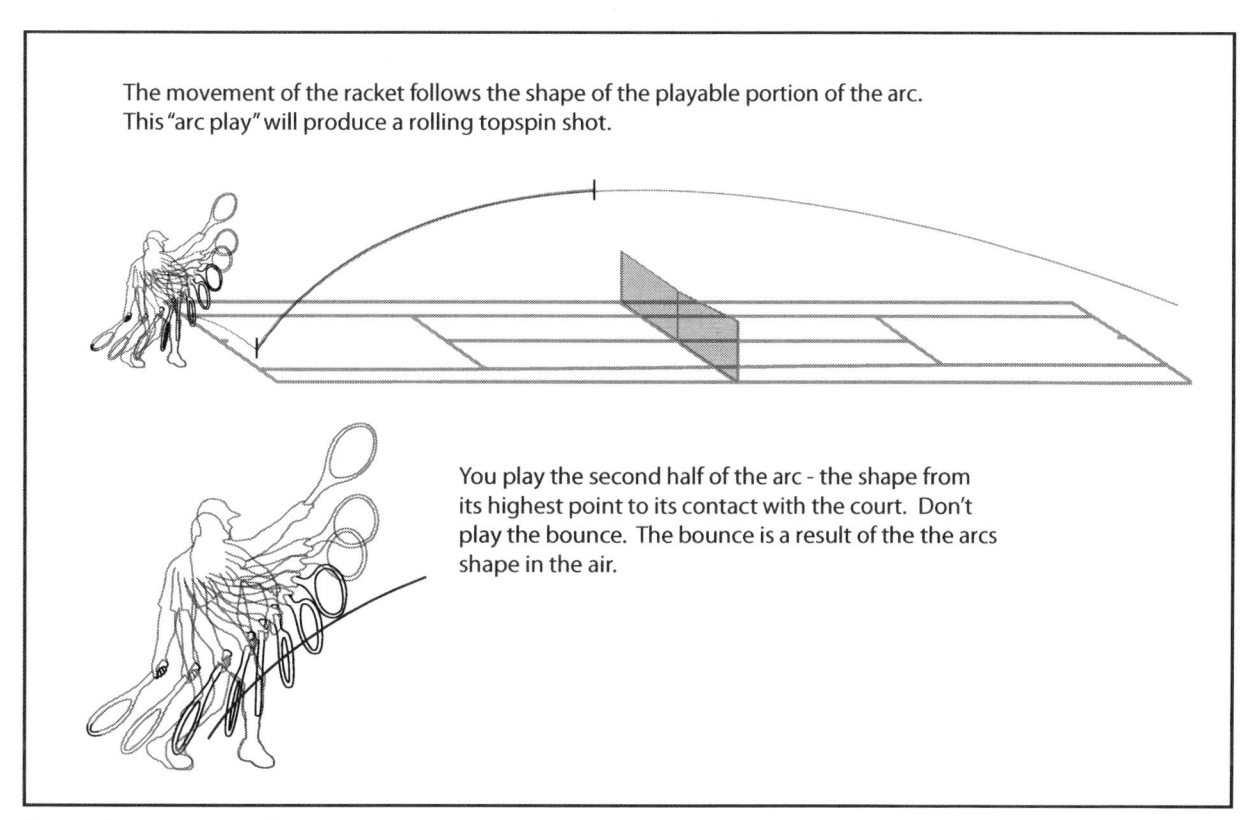

You play the second half of the arc - the shape from its highest point to its contact with the court. Don't play the bounce. The bounce is a result of the the arcs shape in the air.

Fig 13 Playing a average height ARC.

The movement of the racket follows the shape of the playable portion of the arc. This "arc play" will produce a rolling topspin shot.

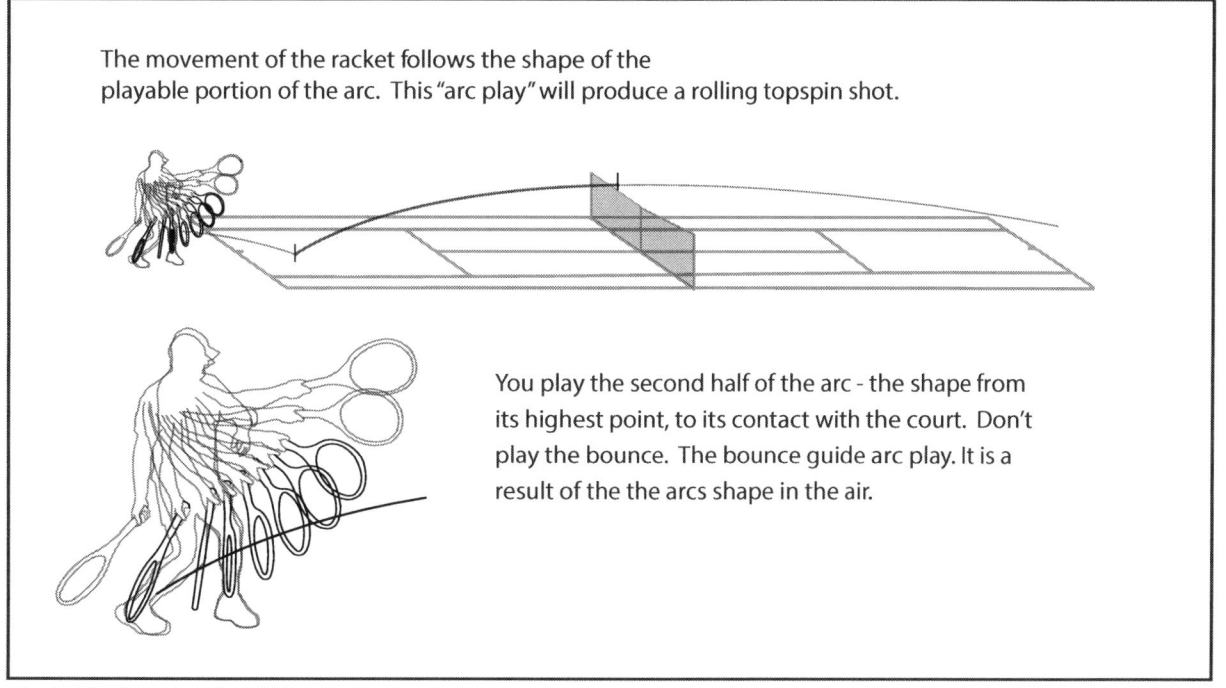

You play the second half of the arc - the shape from its highest point, to its contact with the court. Don't play the bounce. The bounce guide arc play. It is a result of the the arcs shape in the air.

Fig 14 Playing a low flat ARC.

PLAYING THE ARCS | 57

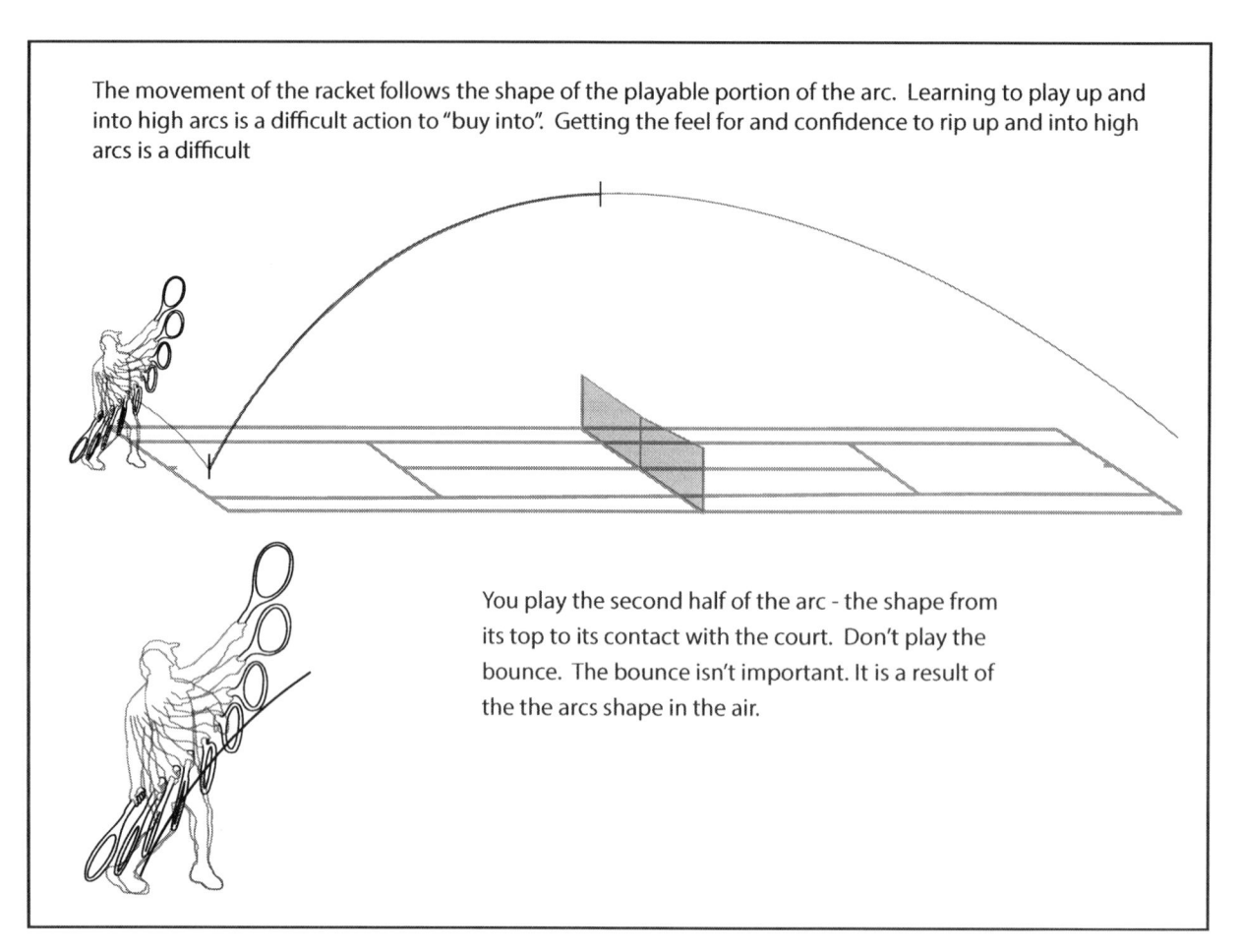

The movement of the racket follows the shape of the playable portion of the arc. Learning to play up and into high arcs is a difficult action to "buy into". Getting the feel for and confidence to rip up and into high arcs is a difficult

You play the second half of the arc - the shape from its top to its contact with the court. Don't play the bounce. The bounce isn't important. It is a result of the the arcs shape in the air.

Fig 15 Playing a high ARC.

DRILL: ROLLING TOPSPIN

We will start your training by hitting easy rolling topspin shots. We are not talking about a ripping, Nadal-type topspin yet. The rolling topspin shot gives you a feel for the arc of the ball. As you play easily up and into the arc, you will develop a feel for the weight of the oncoming shot. You can consider this your warm-up shot, and you should warm up this way every time you play.

You don't need someone to feed you balls for this drill. You can do it in any rally with any partner. For a rolling topspin shot, the forward swing of your racket should mimic, nearly exactly, the shape of the playable portion of the arc. Work hard to capture the oncoming arc in your mind's eye; then, roll your racket up and into that shape. As you strike the ball, your closed racket face will impart the spin. The most important thing is to play each arc individually. You must play up and into each ball uniquely for each and every different arc shape you see. You can hit the ball very hard using the rolling topspin shot. As a matter of fact, all flat shots have a little rolling topspin on them. But in this drill, go easy. Use about 50 percent power as you strike the ball.

Remember, the shapes of the arcs that are hit to you will come in infinite variations. You should do your best to make every forward swing of your racket mirror the unique shape of the inbound arc in this drill.

Turn Up the Power

After you start to get a feel for hitting these easy, rolling topspin shots, start increasing the power of your shot. Go from 50 percent to 75 percent power. Keep playing each arc uniquely. Ensure that your forward swing rolls with the shape of the playable portion of the arc. After you get comfortable hitting at 75 percent power, really go for it. Hit a few shots at 90 to 100 percent of your power. You will miss a few doing this, but you will also find that a lot of these balls will go in the court. Hitting hard and through the arc is how you hit crushing and "flat" power shots.

High-Arcing Balls

The most difficult thing to do as you learn to play the arcs is to hit up and into high-arcing balls. It is a great leap in concept to hit up and into an extremely high-arcing ball if you have never done it before. This is a counterintuitive move for the beginning arc player. Because the ball is so high up, it seems more logical that you should hit down or straight out toward the court. But if you do hit down or straight ahead to the court, you will miss low—and probably into the net (see Figures 16a and 16b).

> **HITTING THROUGH THE BALL VERSUS HITTING THROUGH THE ARC**
> "Hitting through the ball" deceptively implies that the ball is a static thing and that you are driving your racket on a line with reference to nothing but the ball. The appropriate phrase should be "hitting through the arc." The ball is not static. It is moving and dynamic. If you strike the ball without taking the arc into account, your shot will be as random as the variation of the arc that is hit to you.

Here the shooter plays this very high arcing shot along the shape of the playable portion of the arc. The resulting shot is a very effective high arcing return.

Trajectory of your shot when arc is played correctly

Playable portion of the arc

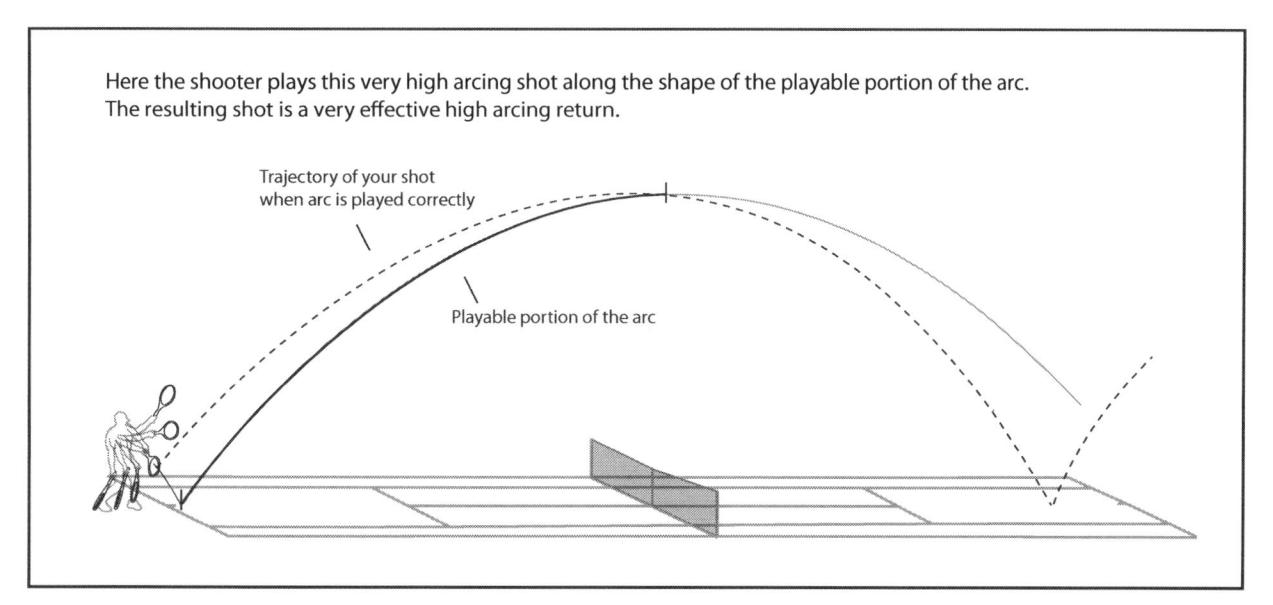

Fig 16a High arcing shot played correctly.

Here the shooter makes the common error of playing a high arcing shot like a normal low arcing ball. The resulting shot will be low and probably into the net. Players who do not understand arc play, make this mistake frequently. They are uncomfortable and unfamiliar with playing up and into high arcing shots.

Playable portion of the arc

When this very high arc is played too flat, out to the court, the resulting shot will be low and probably into the net.

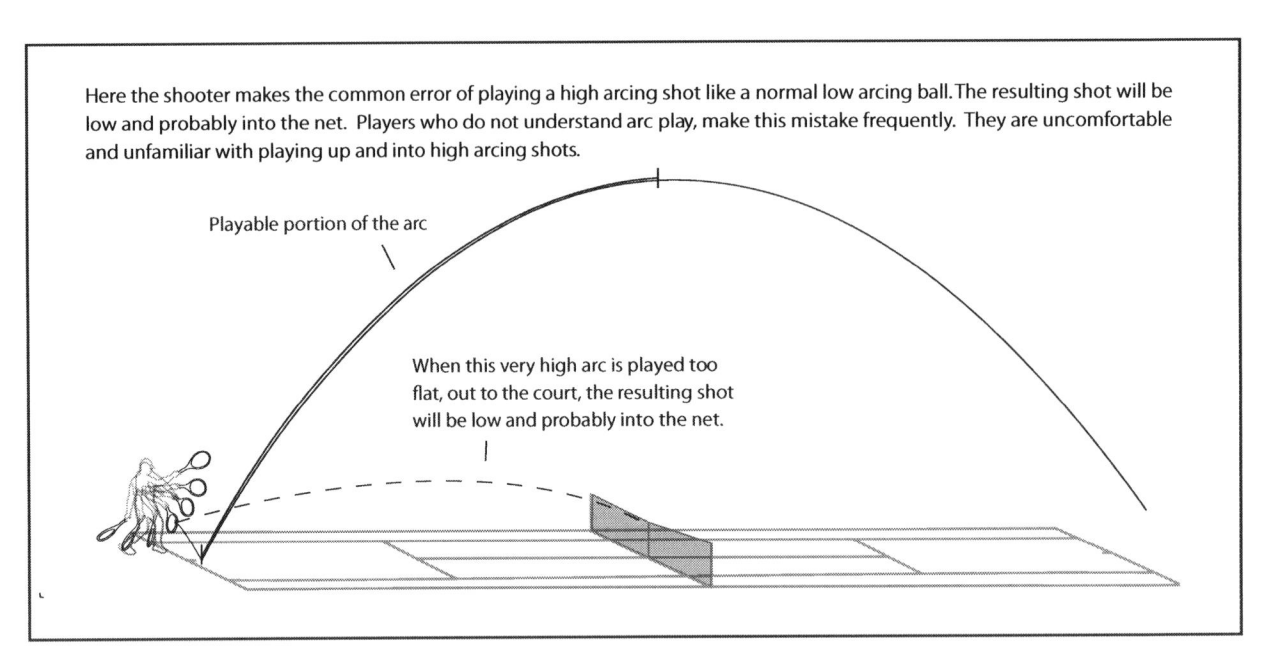

Fig 16b High arcing shot played incorrectly.

Spin Production

To hit big topspin shots, you have to flip your racket around the arc. Your racket moves in a semicircular motion around the ball as you strike it, referencing the shape of the arc. The more extreme the flip, the more spin is produced.

Just as when you played the rolling topspin shot, your racket moves along the arc of the oncoming shot. To impart more spin, the racket moves in a shape that is an exaggerated version of that arc. The most important thing with this technique is that your racket moves symmetrically. That is, the round flip of your racket should be equally below and above the arc. As you experiment with moving your racket around the arc for more spin, you will make a few mistakes. If your shot goes barreling into the net, for example, then your flip is too exaggerated on top of the arc. If your shot sails high, your flip is too exaggerated below the arc.

The following figures show how the arc is played for rolling topspin, medium topspin, and extreme topspin shots. The hitter is playing the same arc in every figure. He is playing around that arc with varying degrees of "flip" in order to impart the spin.

Forehand Spin Production:

For rolling topspin shots the forward swing of the racket mimics the shape of the playable portion of the arc.

Playable portion of the arc

Shape of the playable portion of the arc

Playing the arc exactly along its shape produces rolling topspin.

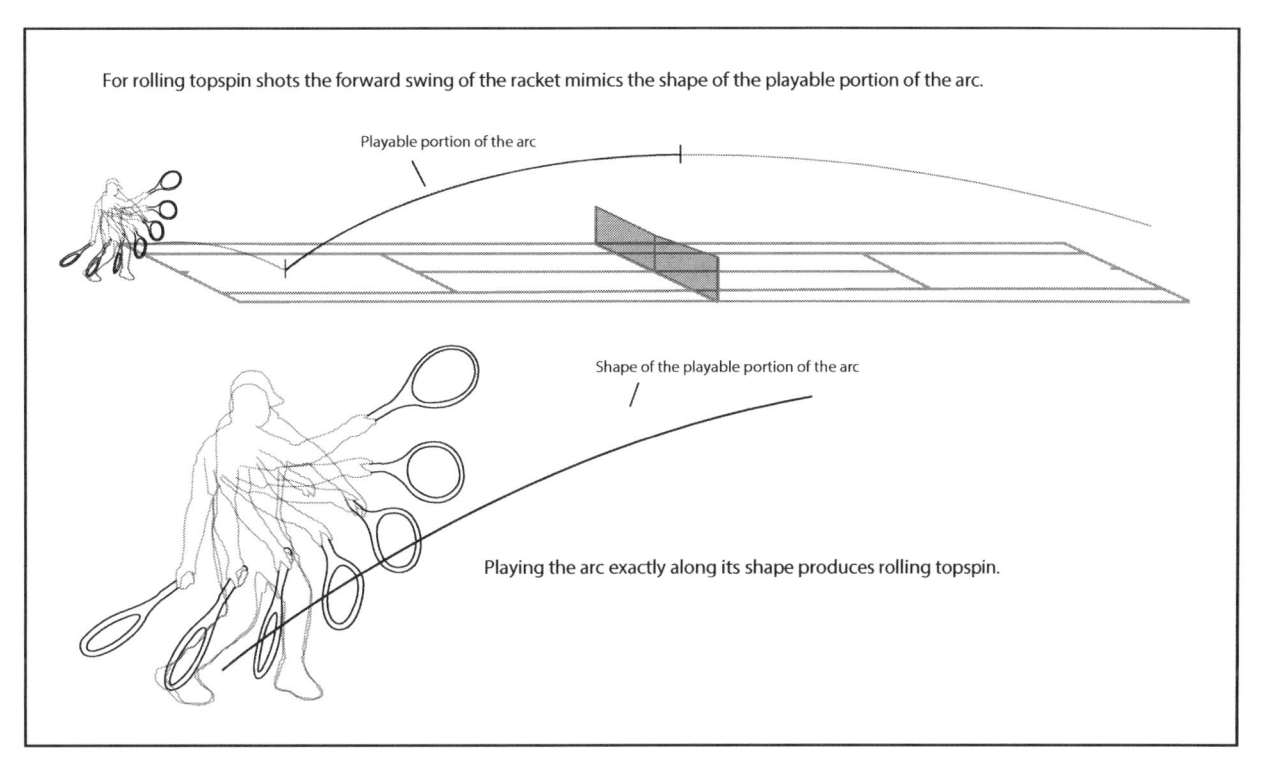

Fig 17 Rolling topspin forehand

This arc is the same shape as the previous illustration. To impart more spin the forward swing of the stroke is played rounder than the shape of the arc. This movement is symetrical around the playable portion of the arc.

Playable portion of the arc

Shape of the playable portion of the arc

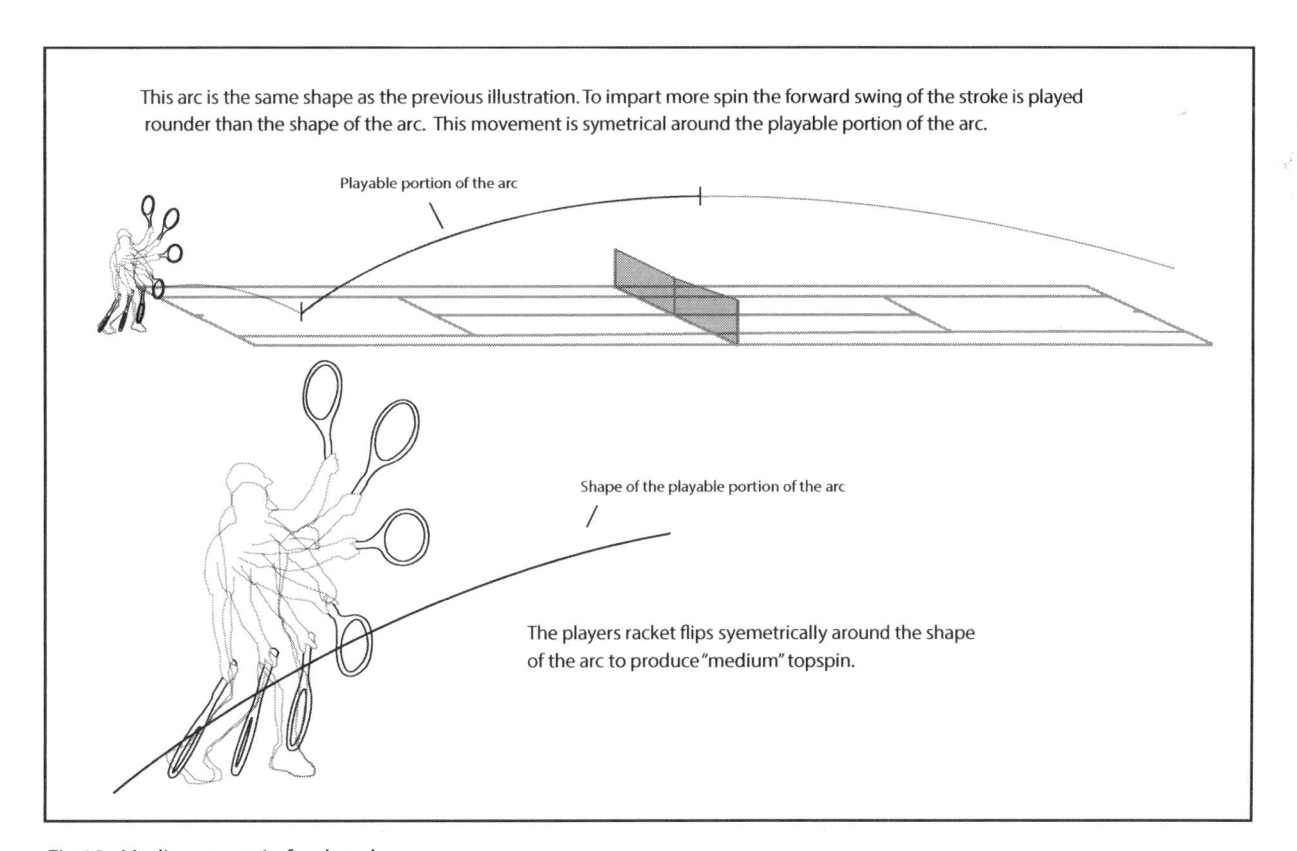

The players racket flips syemetrically around the shape of the arc to produce "medium" topspin.

Fig 18 Medium topspin forehand

PLAYING THE ARCS | 61

This arc is the same shape as the previous illustration. To impart heavy spin the forward swing of the stroke is much rounder than the shape of the arc. The racket is "flipped" around this shape symetrically producing extreme topspin. This is the creative improvisational part of arc play. Enjoy it.

Playable portion of the arc

Shape of the playable portion of the arc

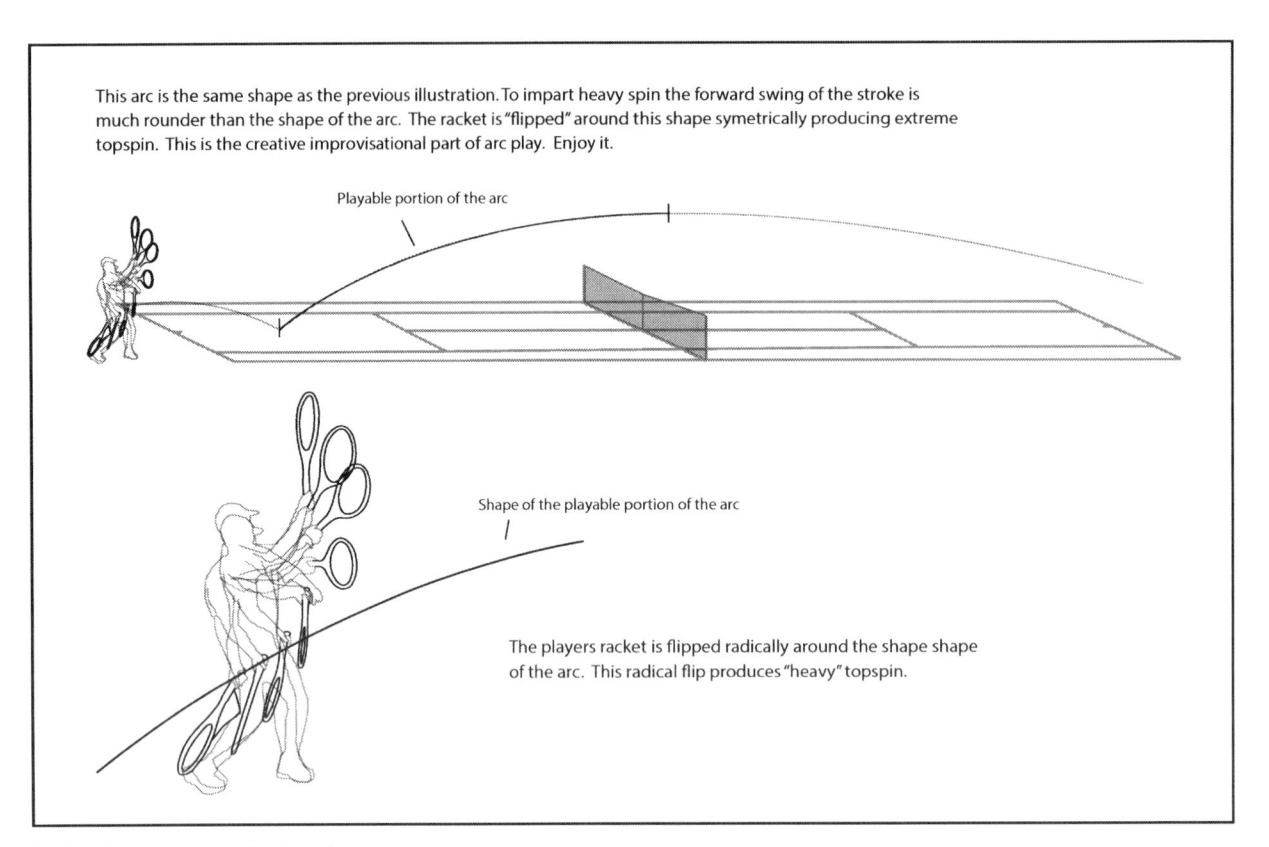

The players racket is flipped radically around the shape shape of the arc. This radical flip produces "heavy" topspin.

Fig 19. Heavy topspin forehand

One-Hand Backhand Spin Production:

For rolling topspin shots the forward swing of the racket mimics the shape of the playable portion of the arc.

Playable portion of the arc

Shape of the playable portion of the arc

Playing the arc exaclty along its shape produces rolling topspin.

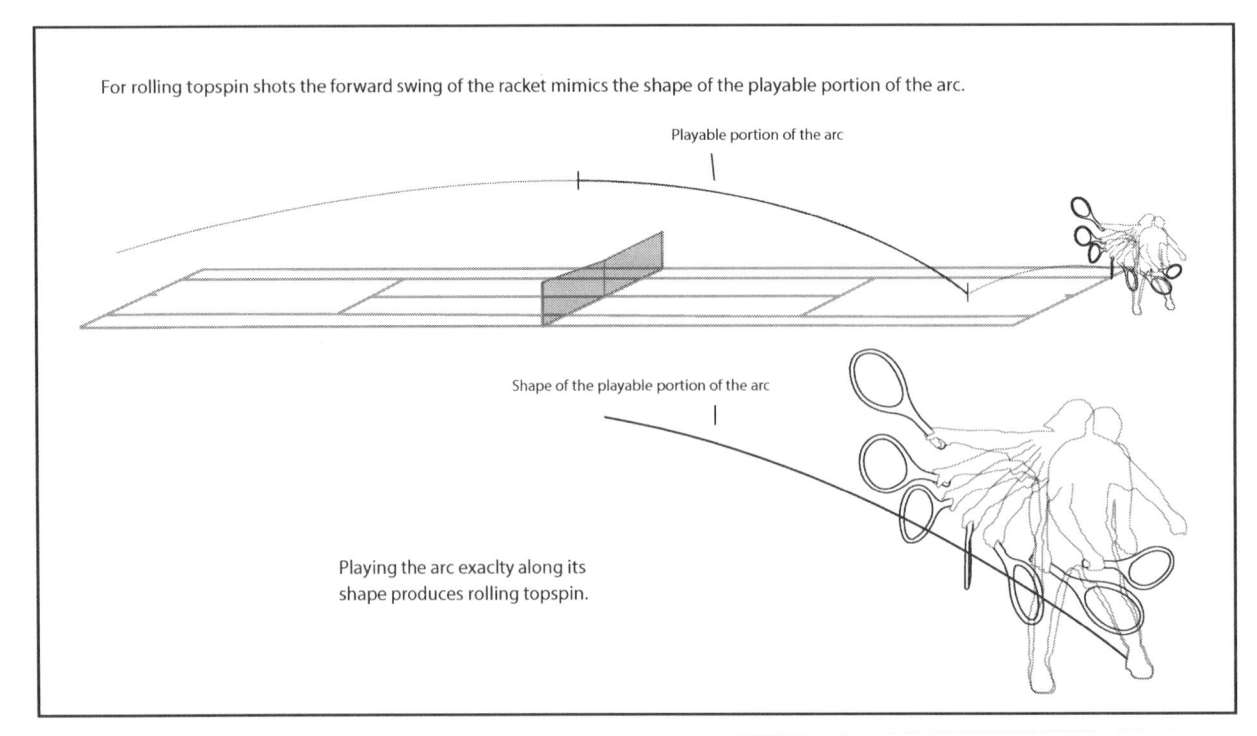

Fig 20. Rolling topspin backhand

62 | HOW TO HIT OUT, GET BALL CONTROL AND PLAY PERCENTAGE TENNIS

This arc is the same shape as the previous illustration. To impart more spin the forward swing of the stroke is played rounder than the shape of the arc producing medium topspin. This movement is symetrical around the playable portion of the arc.

Playable portion of the arc

Shape of the playable portion of the arc

The players racket flips syemetrically around the shape of the arc to produce "medium" topspin.

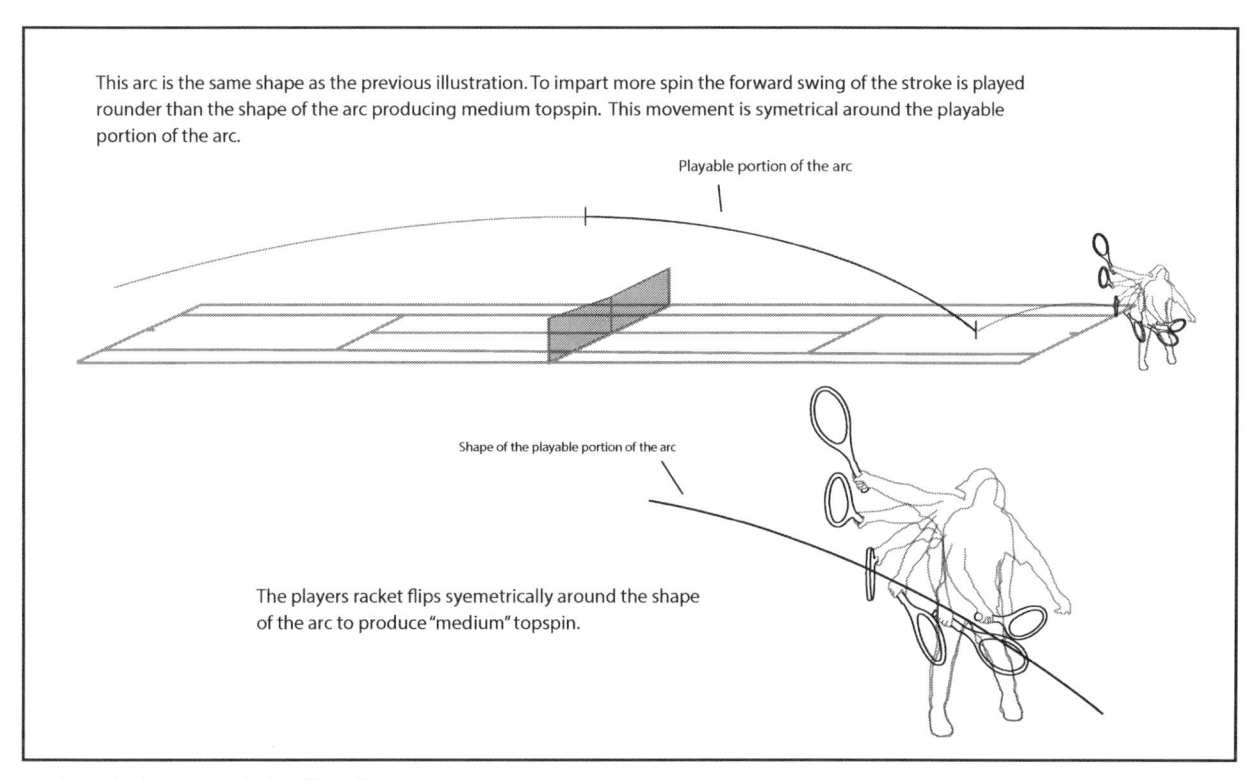

Fig 21. Medium topspin backhand

Playable portion of the arc

Shape of the playable portion of the arc

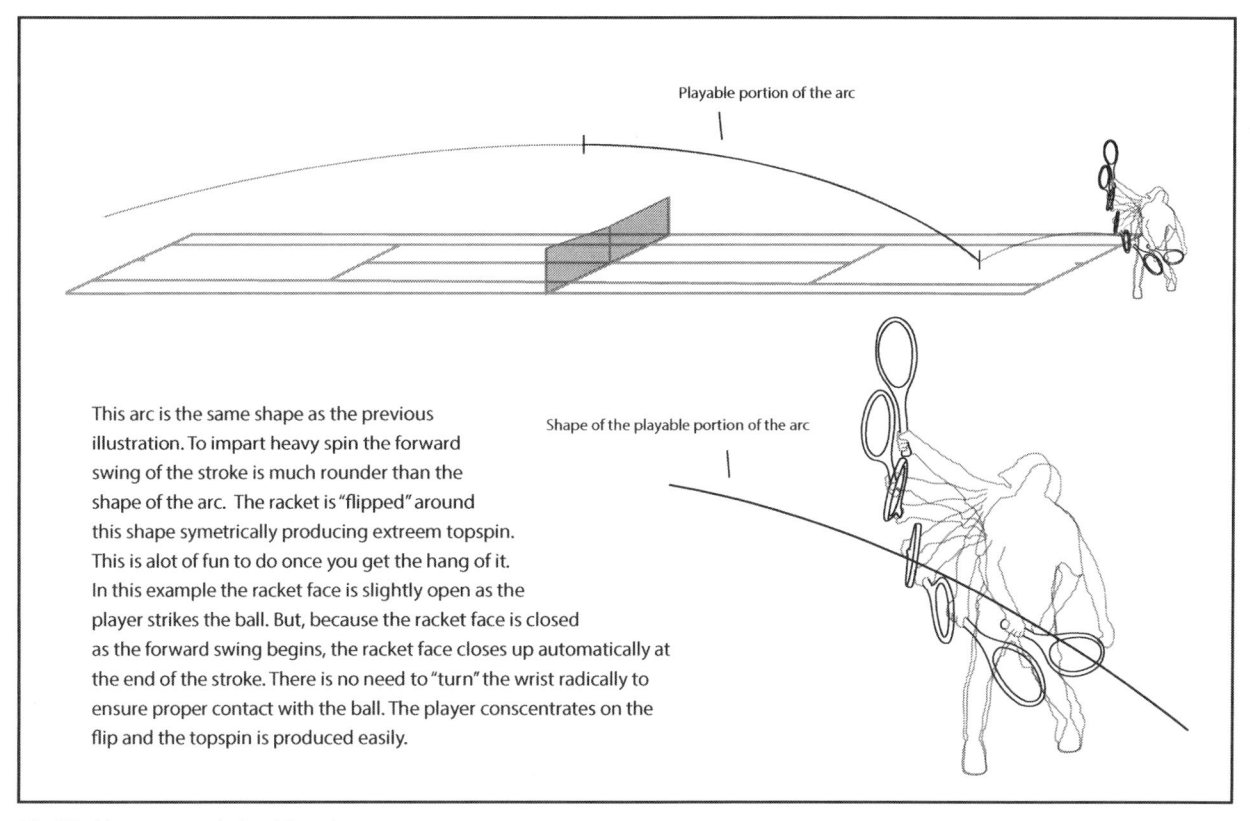

This arc is the same shape as the previous illustration. To impart heavy spin the forward swing of the stroke is much rounder than the shape of the arc. The racket is "flipped" around this shape symetrically producing extreem topspin. This is alot of fun to do once you get the hang of it. In this example the racket face is slightly open as the player strikes the ball. But, because the racket face is closed as the forward swing begins, the racket face closes up automatically at the end of the stroke. There is no need to "turn" the wrist radically to ensure proper contact with the ball. The player conscentrates on the flip and the topspin is produced easily.

Fig 22. Heavy topspin backhand

PLAYING THE ARCS | 63

Two-Hand Backhand Spin Production:

For rolling topspin shots the forward swing of the racket mimics the shape of the playable portion of the arc.

Playable portion of the arc

Shape of the playable portion of the arc

Playing the arc exaclty along its shape produces rolling topspin.

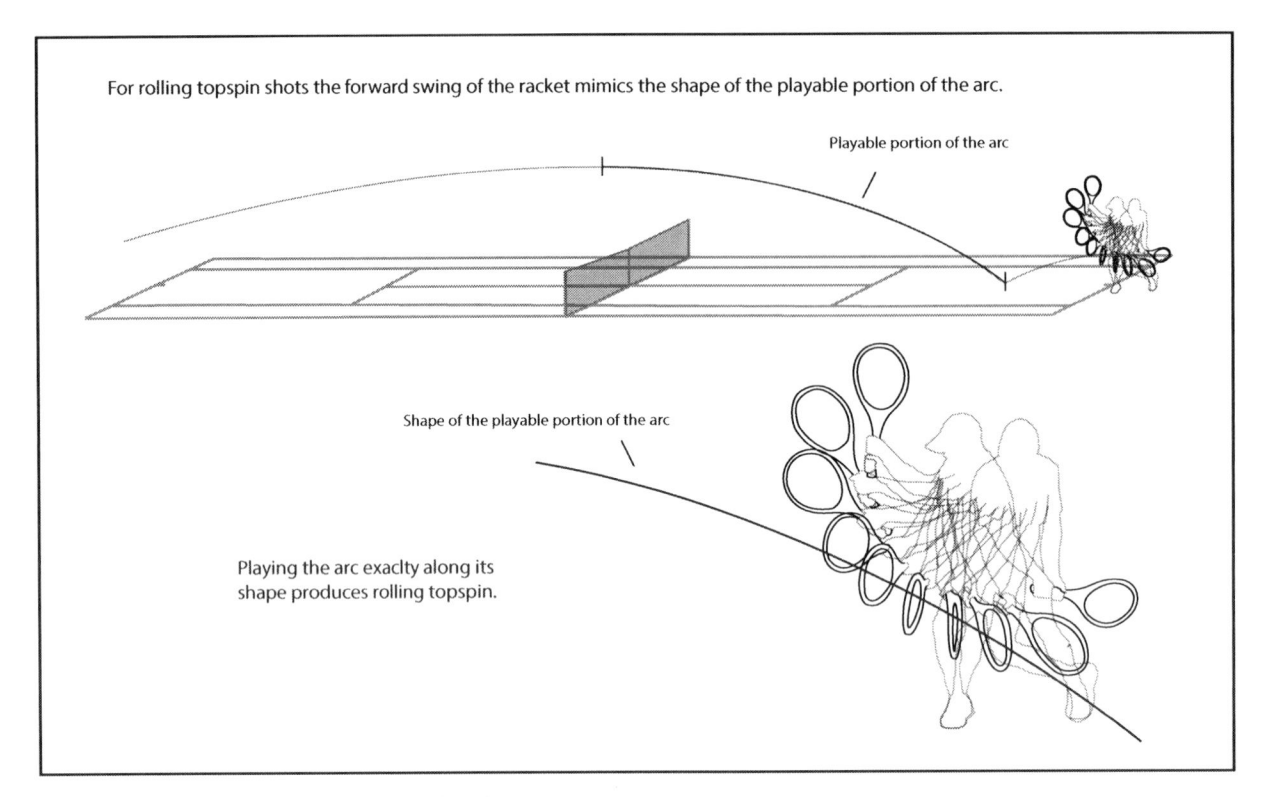

Fig 23. Rolling topspin-two-handed backhand

This arc is the same shape as the previous illustration. To impart more spin the forward swing of the stroke is played rounder than the shape of the arc. This movement is symetrical around the playable portion of the arc.

Playable portion of the arc

Shape of the playable portion of the arc

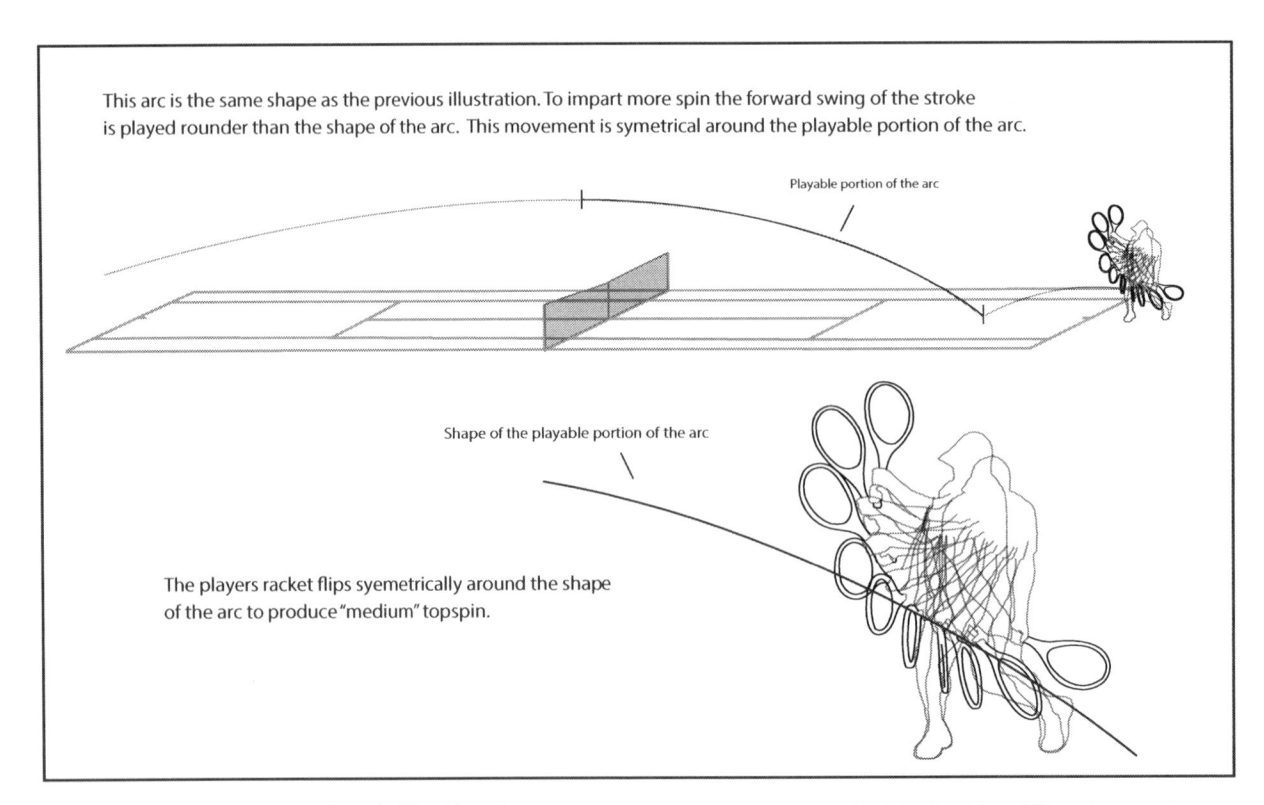

The players racket flips syemetrically around the shape of the arc to produce "medium" topspin.

Fig 24. Medium topspin-two-handed backhand

This arc is the same shape as the previous illustration. To impart heavy spin the forward swing of the stroke is much rounder than the shape of the arc. The racket is "flipped" around this shape symetrically producing heavy topspin. In this example the racket face is slightly open as the player strikes the ball. But, because the racket face is closed as the forward swing begins, the racket face closes up at the end of the stroke. There is no need to "turn" the wrist to ensure proper contact with the ball. The player conscentrates on the flip and the topspin is produced easily.

Playable portion of the arc

Shape of the playable portion of the arc

The players racket is flipped radically around the shape shape of the arc. This radical flip produces "heavy" topspin.

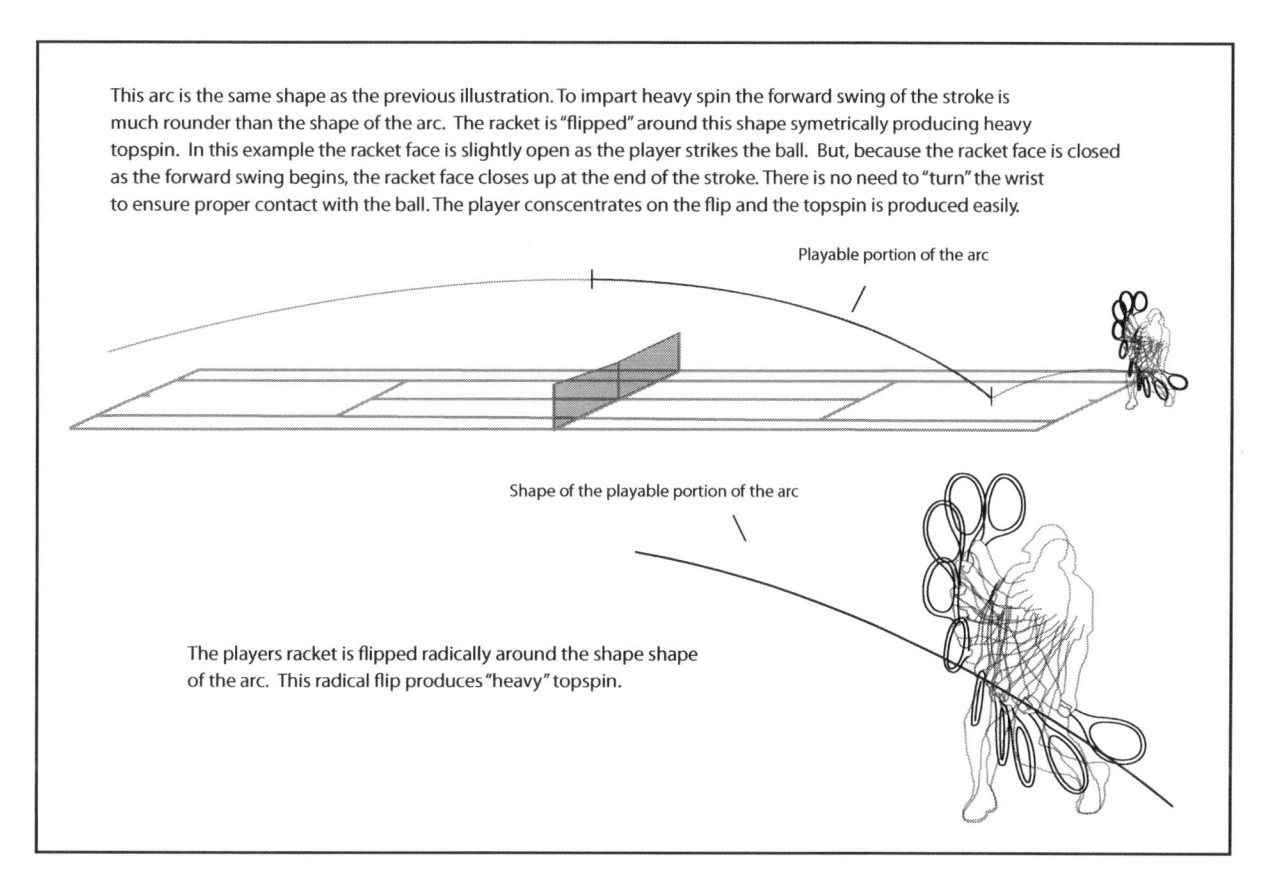

Fig 25. Heavy topspin backhand

More Spin Means Less through the Arc

As you increase the amount of spin on your shot, your racket travels through the arc of the ball less. This is because your racket is flipped in a rounder shape as you strike the ball. So, as you go from a rolling topspin shot to a maximum-flip topspin shot, you drive through the shape of the arc less. The amount this changes is proportional to the amount of spin you impart.

This does not mean that your big topspin shots will have less power. You can really crush a big topspin ball. But a lot of the energy on the shot will be in its spin. Big topspin shots do have a higher probability of going in the court. The spin you put on the ball will drive the ball down into the court, and you will have less of a tendency to miss long. Flatter hard-hit, rolling topspin shots will have more speed and will travel through the court faster. Those shots will have a lower probability of going in the court, however, because there is less spin driving them down into the court. You have to count on gravity and better accuracy in the height of your shot to avoid error.

The important thing to remember is that you now have the tools to choose an infinite variety of shots. You can hit the flatter, rolling topspin shots or the extreme topspin shots—and any shot in between.

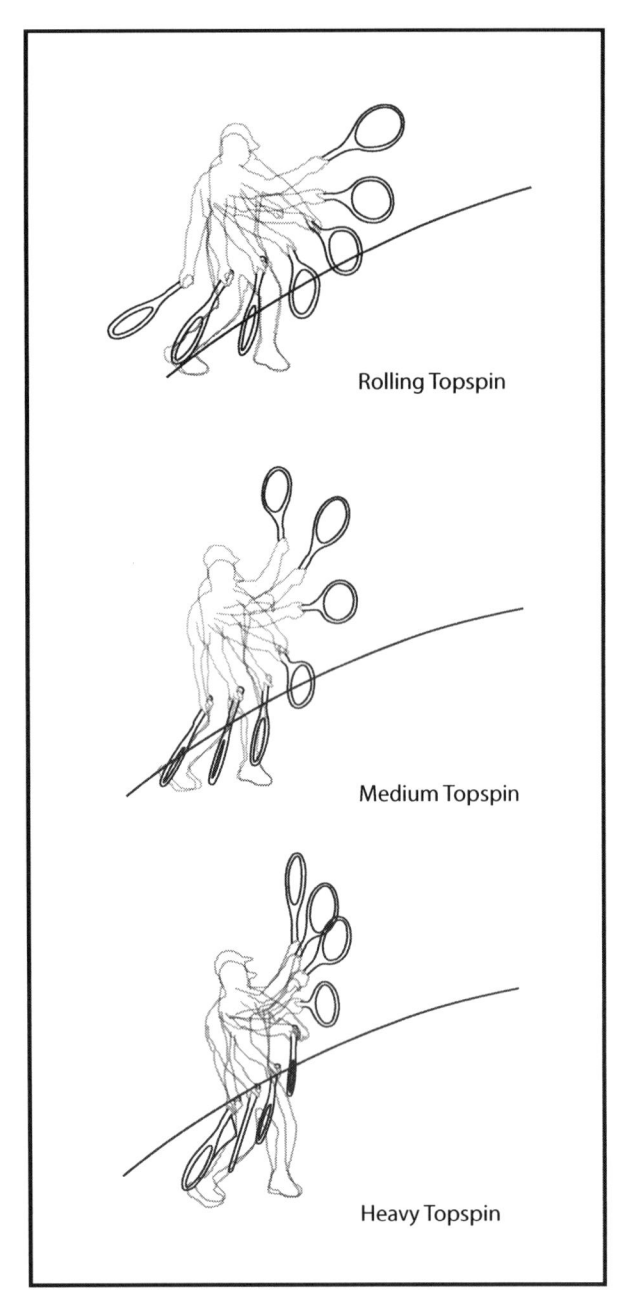

Fig 26. Forehand rolling, medium and heavy topspin forward swings. Here the player is playing the same shaped arc on each shot. The racket is carved around the shape of the arc to produce different amounts of spin.

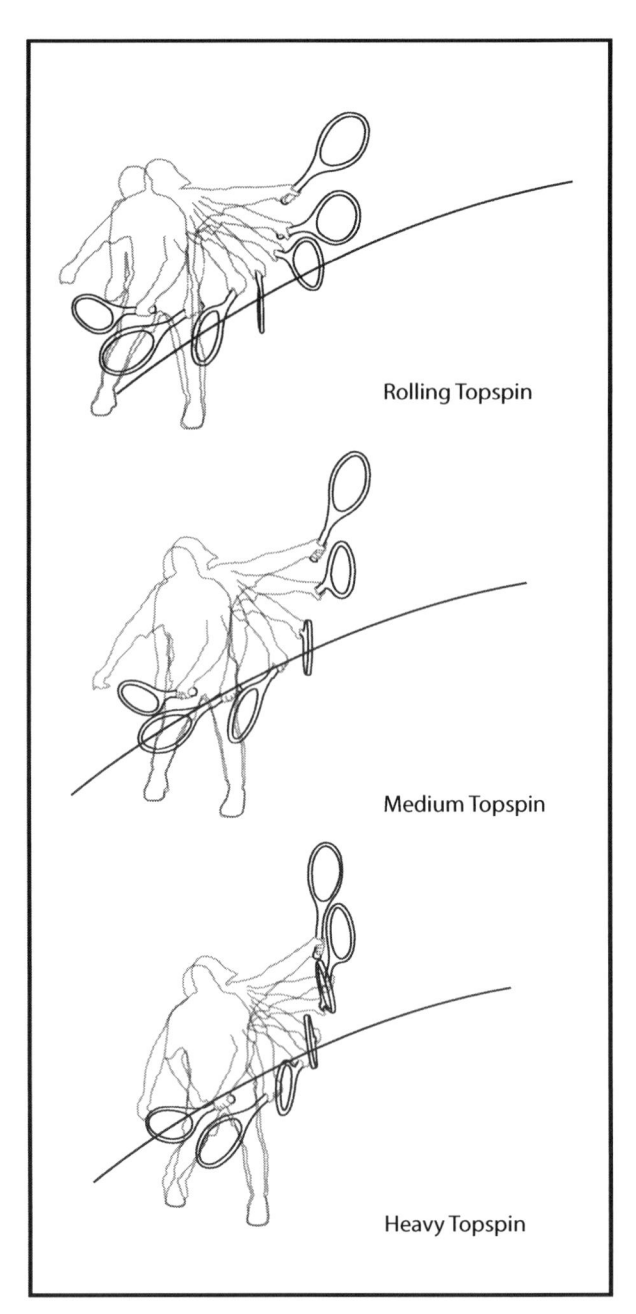

Fig 27. One hand backhand rolling, medium and heavy topspin forward swings. Here the player is playing the same shaped arc on each shot. The racket is carved around the shape of the arc to produce different amounts of spin.

DRILL: WATCH TV

When you get a chance, tune in to a professional match. Watch the fluid figure-eight motion of the backswing and forward swing of the stroke. Pay careful attention to the forward swing. See that each forward swing is unique to the shape of the arc that is played. Look for the movement of the racket as topspin is produced. Notice the curved path the racket takes as the arc is played. Notice

Rolling Topspin

Medium Topspin

Heavy Topspin

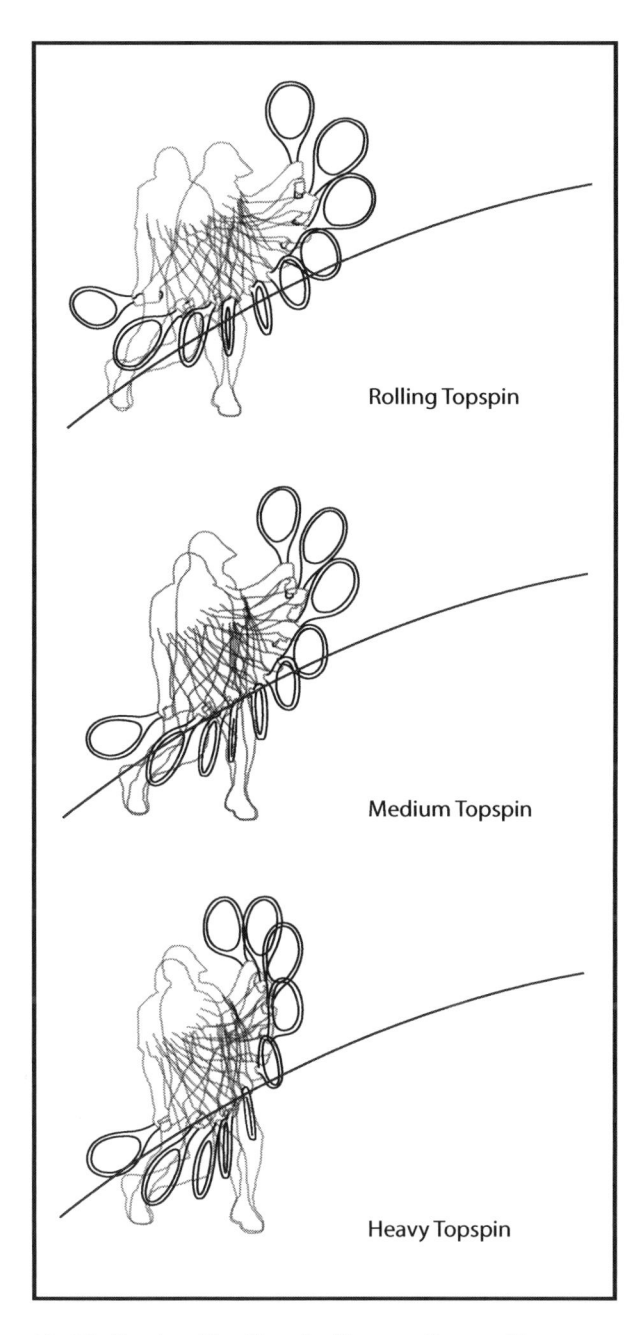

Fig 28. Two hand backhand rolling, medium and heavy topspin forward swings. Here the player is playing the same shaped arc on each shot. The racket is carved around the shape of the arc to produce different amounts of spin.

the different movements of the racket for hard-hit flat shots and big topspin shots.

If you can't find any tennis on TV, remember the last time you watched Nadal, Federer, Djokovic, Williams, or Sharapova play. I hope you have observed the motion of their rackets as they flipped their big topspin shots. Their rackets moved in a half-circle path around the ball. What you probably did not know before is what they were using to guide this round, half-circle move. They were using the shape of the arc. You, too, can make these plays.

Rules of Thumb

The nature of playing the arcs is experimental and improvisational. It is not hard and fast, and it is not rigid. You will need to experiment with the technique and accept that you will make errors as you learn it. Here are a few rules of thumb for playing the arcs:
• The shape of your forward swing is guided by the playable portion of the arc.
• The foundation of arc play is to mirror the shape of the arc with the forward swing of the racket.
• To impart more topspin, the shape of your forward swing must be rounder than the shape of the playable portion of the arc.
• The shape of your forward swing must be rounder equally below the arc and above the arc.

DRILL: SPIN EXPERIMENT

As you go out to the court to experiment and learn to play the arcs, you should always start your session with the rolling topspin drill. Every time you warm up, you should start with easy rolling shots, concentrating on mimicking the playable portion of the arc as exactly as you can. In this drill, you will find that you will get an increased feel for the weight of the arc. You will become more and more fluid with the ball. You'll become attuned to the ball's flight path and the characteristics of the arcs.

After hitting twenty or thirty rolling topspin shots, start increasing the topspin. In the rolling topspin drill, you did your best to mimic the arc exactly. As you start to increase the topspin, roll your racket in a half-circle motion that is rounder than the shape of the arc. Start by making your racket move 25 percent rounder than the arc you are playing. Ensure that you play the arc symmetrically; make sure your racket movement is shaped below and above the arc evenly.

After a good number of these 25-percent-rounder plays, increase the spin again. Flip your racket a little more; work to be about 50 percent rounder than the arc. Once again, your arc play must be symmetrical both below and above the arc.

Expect to make a few errors. You might send a bunch of balls into the net, or you might sail some balls out of the court. (Or both.) Remember, this is okay. You have to make errors if you want to improve. If you are missing low into the net, you are playing too much on top of the arc. In this case, work to play more below the arc. If you are missing high and long each time, then you are playing too much below the arc—with this error, work to play more over the arc.

If you are sailing all your shots long, it might be that you do not have a closed racket face as you strike the ball. If this happens, go back to the rolling topspin drill and concentrate on the closed racket face for a while. Try altering your grip to close the racket a little more.

Playing the arcs is not a robotic, straitjacket technique. It is a free-flowing, creative, and improvisational method. You are carving your racket around the inbound arc like a surfer carves the shape of a wave. Don't be afraid to try a shot. Don't be afraid to miss. Do watch professional players, and do try to emulate what they are doing. They are ripping the arcs, and you can do it too.

DRILL: SWINGING TOPSPIN VOLLEY

This is an advanced drill, but you need to try it. You will definitely need someone to feed you balls during this drill. Stand just inside the service court to receive the ball. The player feeding balls to you should stand inside or on the baseline. Have the server hit you medium- to slow-paced balls that arrive to you in the air. What you will do is hit these balls just like you would on a ground stroke, except you will hit them out of the air, before they bounce.

As you start this drill, work very hard on flowing with the arc. Start your backswing instantly with the oncoming arc. Turn your torso and shoulders as you prepare for the shot. Your basic figure-eight swing should not change. Be as fluid as you can be.

As you strike up and into the oncoming arc, work to roll around it, just as we discussed before. Start with rolling topspin, mirroring the playable portion of the arc. Expect to make a few errors at first. It will be a little difficult to get the timing down, taking the ball right out of the air full-swing. But have fun, be fluid, and you will eventually start rolling some really nice swinging volleys.

As you get more comfortable with the drill, start to experiment with the spin. Try a few medium spin shots. After you do several of these, have some fun and try a few heavy topspin shots. After some heavy topspin attempts, take your spin selection back to medium. Now try hitting the ball harder with medium-spin, just as you might use this shot in the game.

Ensure you hit both backhand and forehand shots. The big purpose of this drill is to learn to flow with the arcs and get a good feel for playing them. It will also introduce the swinging topspin volley as another tool in your match arsenal.

A Word about the Backhand

Ripping topspin shots on the backhand side is challenging; if you hit a one-handed backhand, it is even more difficult. Because you do not have as many muscles working for you when you hit a one-handed backhand, it is harder to control the racket as you flip it around the arc. If you hit a two-handed backhand, the flipping movement of your racket is helped by the second hand, but the range of movement of the racket is constrained by the two-handed stroke.

With this in mind, we will make a couple of caveats about hitting topspin backhands.

Two-Handed Backhands

The two-handed backhand is really a forehand shot with help. The other great power advantage to the two-handed backhand is the torso turn. As you strike the two-handed backhand, your torso turns and your body opens up to the court. This torso turn adds a great deal of power to the two-handed backhand. It is a very effective and strong shot, but it does have its drawbacks. When you play the topspin, two-handed backhand, your racket head does not have the freedom of movement of a one-handed backhand or a forehand shot. It is constrained by the two hands holding the racket, which makes it harder to make exaggerated flips of the racket head around the arc. So if you play a two-handed backhand, you shouldn't try to hit extremely exaggerated topspin shots. You should work on hitting rolling, hard-hit, topspin shots and medium-spin topspin shots. The great advantage of the two-handed backhand is the power that the second hand and the torso turn provide. You should work on driving through the arc with power and take advantage of the added strength. This does not mean you should not apply topspin. You should rip around the arc aggressively and put a good amount of spin on the ball. Just don't go crazy with the flip. Work to produce power and hit through the arc if you do hit two-handed.

One-Handed Backhands

With one-handed backhands, the muscles you have to control your racket are minimal. Compared to the forehand, it is essentially a weak shot. All you have is the back of your shoulder and triceps moving your arm and racket forward. The torso does not have freedom of movement in the one-handed backhand. As you strike a one-handed backhand, the torso must stop its turning movement as the ball is struck. This is the main limiting factor for power on the one-handed backhand. Because of these limitations, the one-handed, topspin backhand requires good timing. To hit a one-handed backhand with ripping topspin takes really good timing. Roger Federer and Stan Wawrinka do this better than anyone in the world today (maybe even in tennis history). Notice that when they strike the topspin backhand, the shoulder does not yank at the ball. The torso stops its movement as the ball is struck. The shoulder is a static pivot for the arm and hand as the forward swing finishes. If you want to hit ripping topspin, one-handed backhands, this is the technique to emulate.

For a beginning arc player, playing a one-handed backhand, you need to rein in your horns a little. Work to hit rolling topspin shots at first. Work to get a feel for the weight of the arc as you play up and into it. As you try to apply more topspin, you will tend to jerk your shoulder across the ball. This is incorrect. As you prepare for the one-handed backhand, your shoulders should be closed to the court. In this closed position, your back is slightly facing the net. As you swing your arm forward, the torso turns. This torso turn should stop with your shoulder pointing to your target. The shoulder now acts as a pivot for the arm to swing forward (watch Federer). As you strike the ball, you flip your racket around the arc, just as we discussed above. This strike of the ball is a release of the wrist and the forearm. The release enables you to flip your racket around the arc. Realize that this is a very tough shot to play; expect to make more than the usual number of errors as you perfect the technique.

The one-handed backhand player should play medium to rolling topspin shots when learning this technique. Work to control the shoulder and torso as you strike the ball. You should *release* your hand and forearm as you strike the ball. Don't yank your shoulder and body.

As you get better at seeing and playing the arcs, experiment with increasing the spin. You need the closed racket face, and you need to flip the racket around the arc, as we have discussed before. With this shot, however, you also need exact timing and a good release of the hand. What I mean here is that when you strike the ball, your forearm and wrist explode at the ball, working around the arc.

Backspin

The arc is also your guide for playing backspin shots. But we have to go over a few basics before you can learn to use the arcs to apply backspin.

Backspin shots are hit by striking the ball from high to low. The racket starts above the ball and finishes below the ball. The ball is hit with an open racket face. To have an open racket face, the side of the racket that strikes the ball is facing slightly up toward the sky.

About the Backspin Stroke

Just as with topspin shots, you start your backswing and shot preparation the moment you see the ball come off your opponent's racket. You should flow with the arc that is hit to you, just as we discussed before. Your racket starts the first half of the basic figure-eight stroke, but as you take your racket back and up, you keep the racket up and above the point at which you strike the ball. The downward strike of the ball imparts the backspin.

How to Use the Arc to Play Backspin

Just as with topspin shots, the arc is the guide for the forward swing of your racket on backspin shots. The difference is that you use a reverse image of the arc to guide the backspin shot. Imagine a reflection of the inbound arc in order to construct this mental picture. The shape of the forward swing of your racket will follow this mirror image. Just as with topspin shots, use the playable portion of the arc to guide your racket. The playable portion of the arc is from its highest point to its impact on the ground. For backspin shots, however, you play the reverse image (see Figure 29).

Your racket curves underneath the arc. For medium spin, it should follow the reverse shape of the arc nearly exactly. The open face of your racket and the

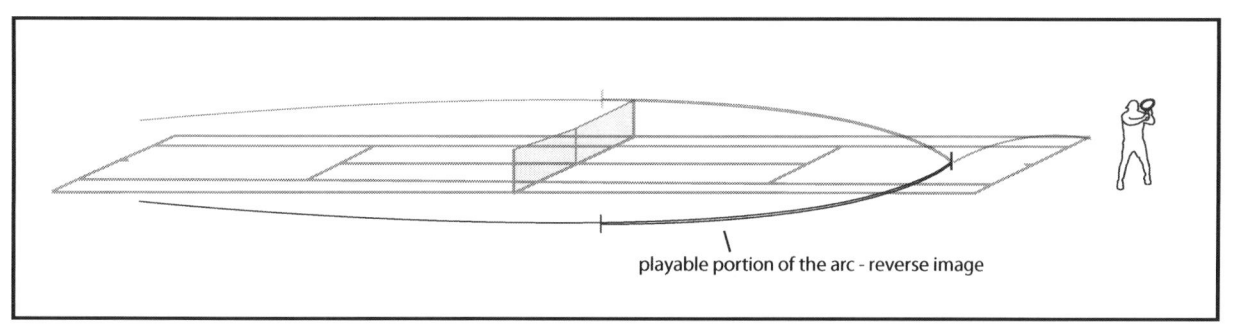

Fig 29. Reverse image of the arc. To play backspin shots you must construct in your minds eye a reverse, mirror, image of the arc. The playable portion of the arc starts at the highest point of the arc and ends where the ball bounces on the court. For backspin shots use the reverse image to guide the forewardswing of your racket.

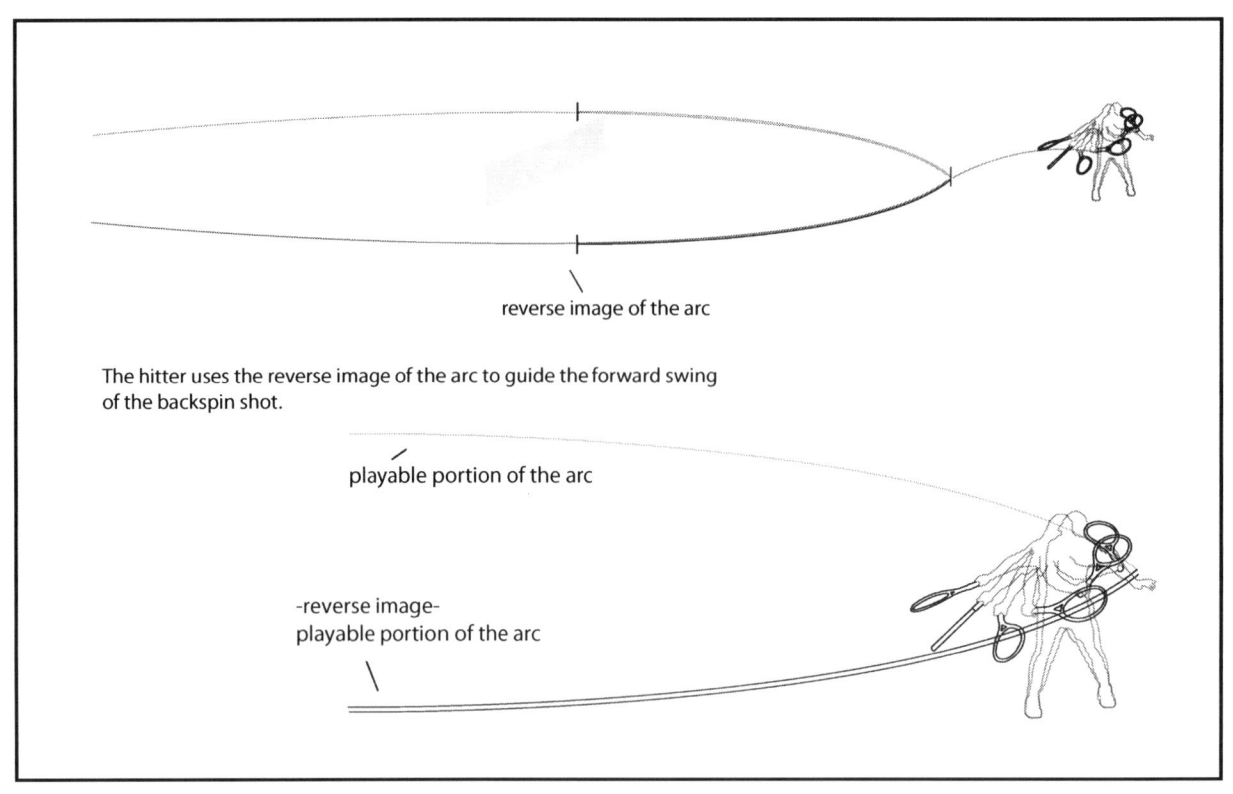

Fig 30. Backspin backhand playing the reverse image of the arc.

high-to-low motion of your swing will apply the spin. To increase spin, your racket moves in a rounder shape than the oncoming arc. Just as with topspin, your arc play must be symmetrical. Your racket will move an even amount above the reverse image of the arc as it does below it (see Figure 30).

Warning: When you start using the arcs to guide your backspin shots, you will have a tendency to apply far too much spin and not hit through the arc nearly enough. Your initial shots may float out in front of you and die before they get over the net. To fix this problem, drive out and through the reverse image of the arc.

Backspin on High-Arcing Balls

When you play a high-arcing ball with backspin, you really need to drive out and through the arc. The reverse image of the arc is the guide for playing spin, but you really have to drive out toward your target. The typical mistake here is to make the forward swing of your racket too curved. This produces too much spin. Your racket will not go through the arc enough. This produces a shot with very little speed and too much backspin. You will have to experiment. Remember: with these higher arcs, you need to drive out toward your target (see Figure 31).

When playing backspin on high arcing incoming shots, you need to drive out and through arc. If you play the reverse image of the arc exactly, the shape of your shot will be weak and too round.

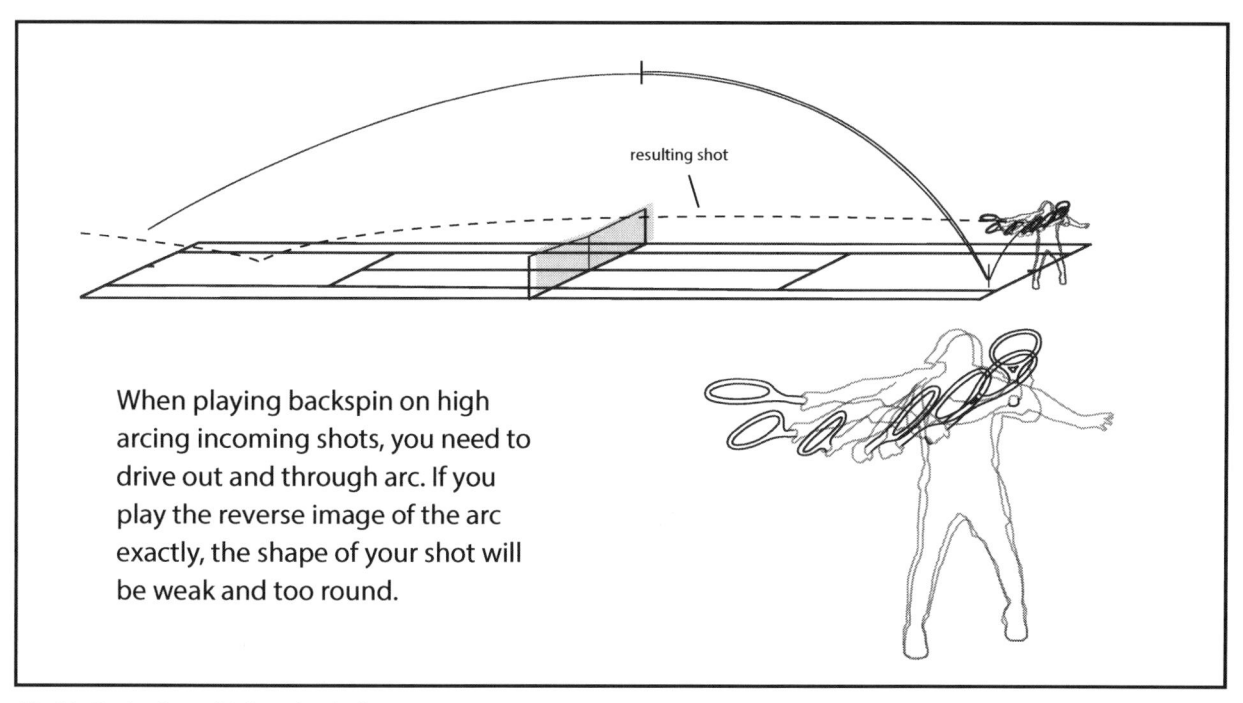

Fig 31. Backspin on high arcing balls.

About Drop Shots

A common error when you start to use the arcs to apply backspin is to move the racket much more roundly than the arc. This produces a shot with a lot of backspin and very little forward movement out into the court. And this is exactly how you hit a drop shot. By making the forward swing of your racket too round—much rounder than the inbound arc—all the speed is taken off your shot, and it produces a drop shot–shaped ball. You can experiment with this as you like. Keep in mind that the drop shot, hit without regard to the position of your opponent, is one of the worst-percentage plays in tennis. But have some fun and experiment (see Figure 32).

Slice backhand foreward swing too round creating dropshot shaped ball.

Foreward swing path much rounder than oncoming arc.

Slice backhand foreward swing played more through the arc creating a shot out and through the court.

Foreward swing path out and through the oncoming arc

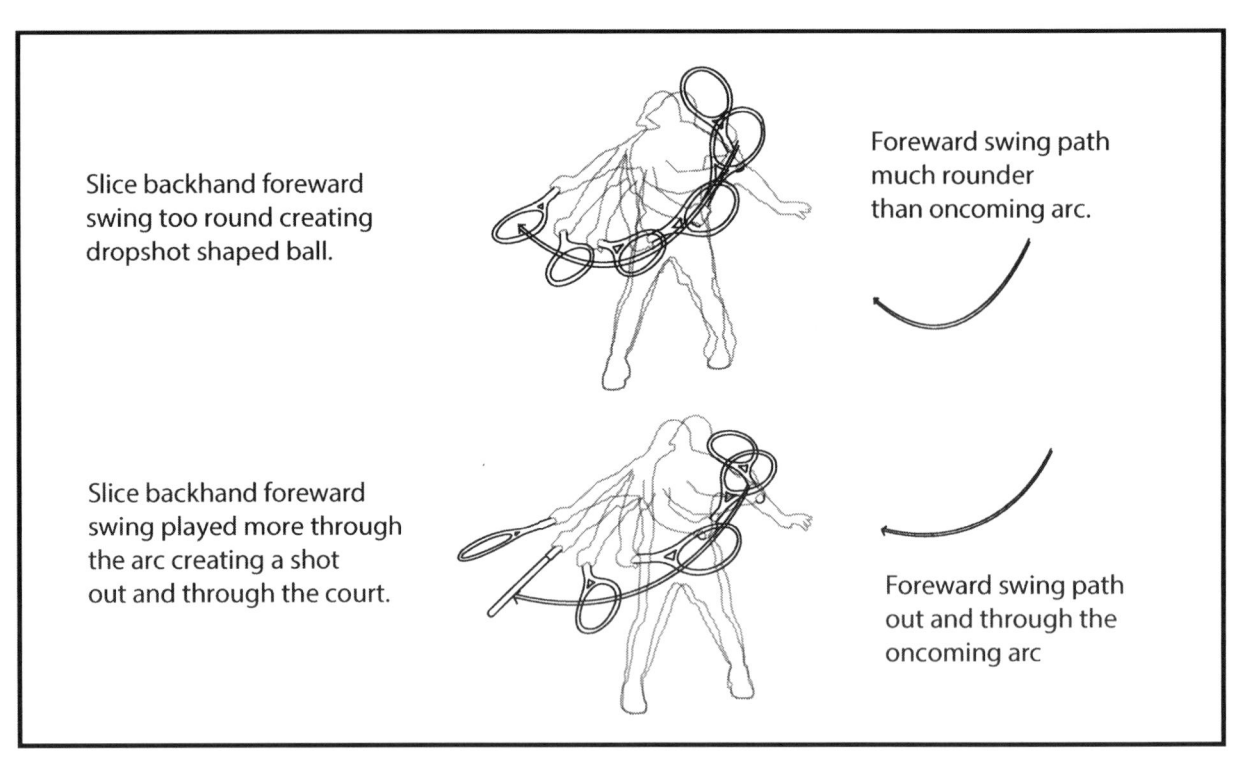

Fig 32. Overplaying arc on backspin shot.

Arc Techniques for Volleys

When you strike a conventional backspin volley, you are playing a punched backspin shot. Since you are applying backspin, your racket needs to start above the point at which you strike the ball. Your racket should start from alongside your body, and your hand should drive out through the reverse image of the arc in a punching motion, finishing way out in front.

This brings us to volley preparation. To get your racket and body in the right position to hit a good punched volley, all you have to do is this: Start with a good ready position with your racket in the middle of your body, pointing out to the court. As soon as the ball comes off your opponent's racket, and you perceive which side the ball is heading for, turn your torso and shoulders, pointing your lead shoulder out into the court. If you make this shoulder-and-torso turn, the racket will be in the perfect position alongside your body to make the aggressive punch out along the arc.

To hit a standard backspin volley, you need an open racket face. The "continental" grip (described in appendix 5) is the preferred grip, as it provides an open racket face for the backhand and forehand shots. As you play the arc on the volley, your racket mimics the reverse image of the arc, applying backspin. To do this, your hand turns underneath the ball, doing the work of playing the arc. The turn of the hand mimics the reverse shape of the arc. The outward punching motion drives through the arc. The punch should be aggressive out to your target.

The turning motion of the hand plays the reverse image of the arc symetrically.
The punching motion of the hand drives out and through the arc.

Reverse image of arc

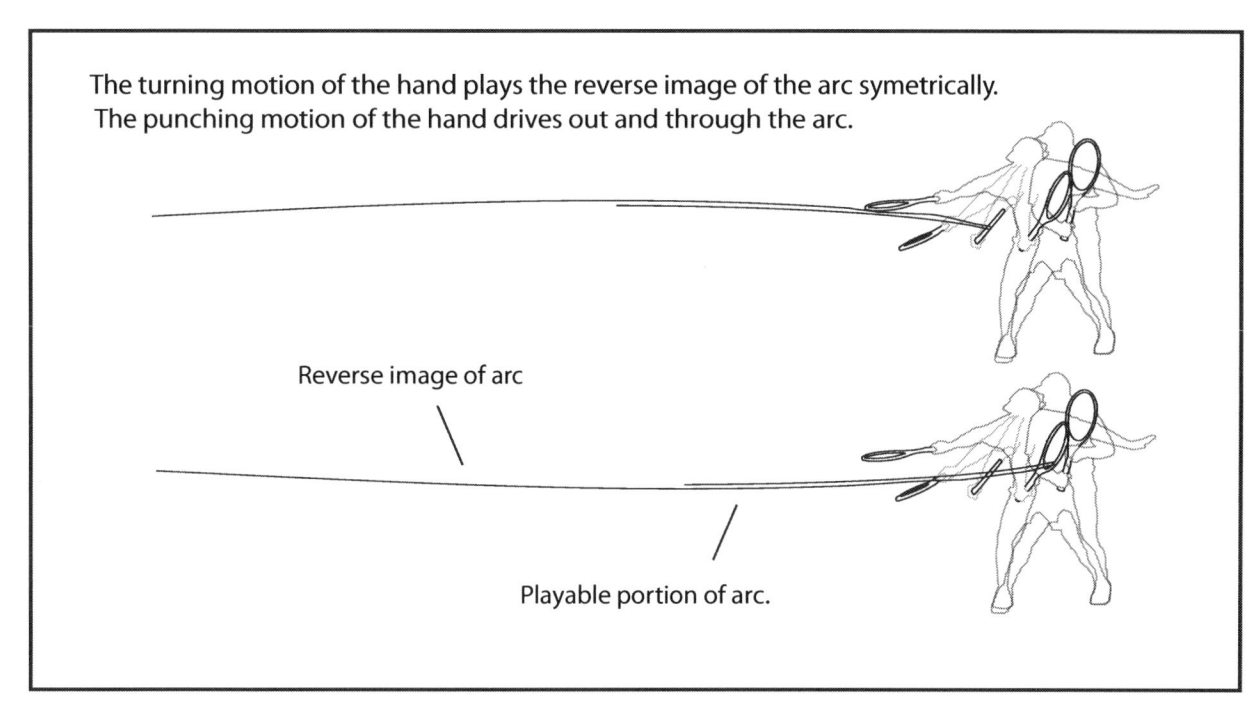

Playable portion of arc.

Fig 33. Backhand volley.

The turning motion of the hand plays the reverse image of the arc symetrically.
The punching motion of the hand drives out and through the arc.

Reverse image of arc

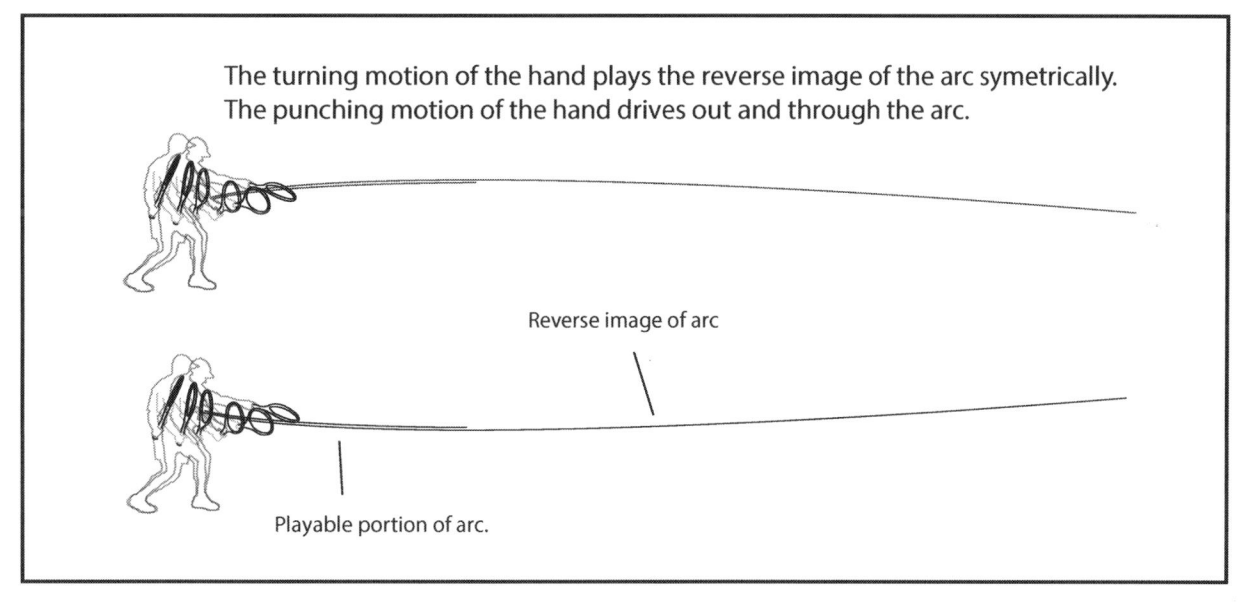

Playable portion of arc.

Fig 34. Forehand volley.

Your hand should turn under the arc of the oncoming shot, playing underneath the shape of the arc and applying the backspin (see Figures 33 and 34).

Like backspin ground strokes, a common error in conventional backspin volleys is to apply too much spin. The tendency for the beginning arc player is to turn your hand and racket under the arc too much. This exaggerated turn under the arc, without an aggressive punch out and through to the target, produces a drop shot–shaped ball. If you find this happening, lessen the turn of your hand underneath the arc. Play the arc flatter, and punch out to your target. As you work this technique, you will get a better and better feel for the arc and will be able to control the amount you play it.

Drop Volley

To hit a drop volley, you embrace the error described above. You play underneath the arc, turning your hand much more roundly than the arc's shape. To absorb the speed of the shot, you reduce the amount of punch out to the target. You might even forgo any punch out to the court, absorbing all of the inbound shots pace, as you turn your hand and racket underneath the shape of the oncoming arc (see Figure 35).

When you first try the arc technique you might inadvertently hit a few shots that are more like drop volleys than hard-hit volleys. Remember, playing the arcs is not hard and fast. These techniques require experimenting and making a few errors. So enjoy experimenting. If your volley drops short and dies, you are playing too much under the arc and not punching through the arc enough. If your volley has no backspin and sails too hard and flat, you are not playing around the arc enough. You must experiment and make a few mistakes to develop good arc play on your volleys.

On this drop volley the hand turns, playing much rounder than the shape of the inbound arc. The punch out to the target is greatly reduced absorbing the energy of the inbound shot.

Playable portion of arc

Reverse image of arc

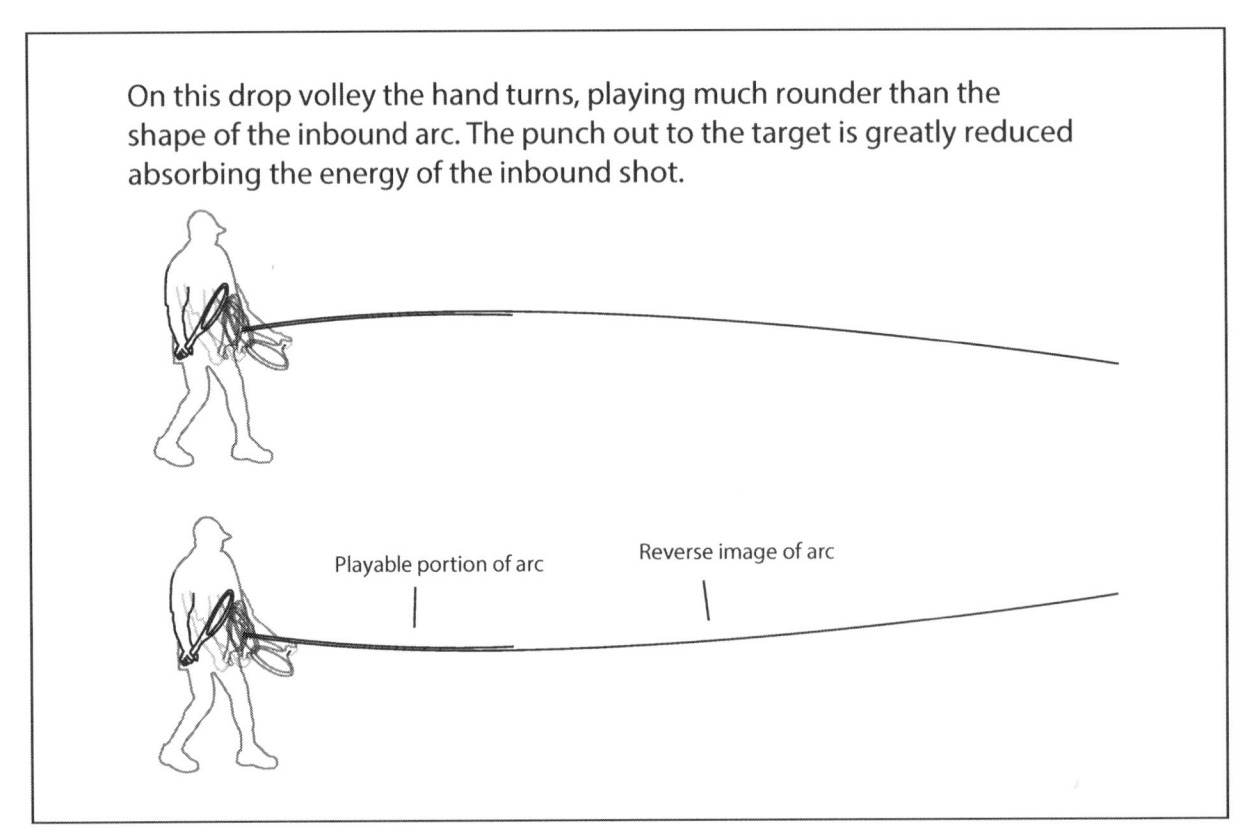

Fig 35. Drop volley.

Low Volleys

Having the ability to hit a volley off a ball that has curved below the net is a difficult skill to acquire. Your knowledge of arcs and how to play them will make this shot a lot easier. The technique remains the same. Hold the reverse image of the arc in your mind's eye, and then play out and underneath the arc. The motion of your hand may be slightly up as you shoot the ball out to your target. Don't be afraid to hit this shot hard. If you choose a target low on the net and play the arc well, the low volley can be hit aggressively with good pace.

The Next Step

So far you have been learning how to play the arcs in a vacuum. The next step in achieving ball control is to combine aiming techniques with playing the arcs. Once these two techniques are married together, your control of the ball will explode. That is the subject of the next chapter.

CHAPTER 3

Arc Projection Combining Two Concepts

Many marriages fail, but the marriage of *aiming for targets* and *playing the arcs* is one that will endure for as long as you play tennis.

When you learned how to use targets, you only learned half of the equation for ball control. Choosing targets, aiming, and adjusting your aim points will enable you to control your shot's direction or vector up, down, left, and right. But this technique does not take into account the energy and characteristics of your opponent's shot.

As you learned to play the arcs, you developed the technique for capturing and using the curving energy of the oncoming shot. Its energy is conserved as you carve your racket around its shape. But in the arc drills, we ignored targets and aiming.

Now we will put these two concepts together and give you the ultimate tool for gaining ball control. Once you use both of these techniques in concert, you will be able to manipulate the flight path of the ball completely. As you fire your shot for your target and rip the arc of the oncoming ball, you command the direction of your shot's flight path and you account for and conserve the energy of the oncoming shot.

DRILL: AIMING AND PLAYING THE ARCS

Start this drill during the warm-up. To start, choose your first target. Make it dead center above the net tape and about four feet above the net. As you'll recall, this is the first target you used while learning the aiming techniques. As you play the arc of the oncoming ball, use rolling topspin, just as when you first learned to play the arc. Hit the ball with medium pace. Now, as you play the oncoming arc, use aiming techniques to correct for errors. If you miss low, adjust your aim point up, the same distance you missed low on your target. If you miss left, adjust your aim point right, and so on. Use all of the aiming techniques you learned in chapter 1.

Work to flow with the arcs as best you can. Work to play every arc as well as you can. Always adjust your aim point around your target. Work to never make the same error twice.

After fifteen to twenty balls, start to increase the topspin and speed of your shots. As you increase the topspin, you will probably need to raise your target; this is because the topspin will drive the ball down and into the court more.

Aiming Techniques Correct Arc Play

Notice that changing aim points fixes incorrect arc play. If you play the arc unevenly, or asymmetrically, it will produce errors high and low. That is, if you play too much over the top of the arc, your shot will miss low, and if you play too much under the arc, your shot will miss high. These arc-playing errors are automatically fixed by manipulating the aim points. Just apply good aiming corrections to your errors. For low errors, adjust your aim point up; for high errors, adjust your aim point down.

As you make these corrections, keep working to play the arc. The up-and-down aiming corrections will instantly correct your arc play. By aiming higher, you will automatically, without conscious manipulation, play more under the arc. By aiming lower, you will automatically play more over the arc of the oncoming ball. This is the magic of marrying these two concepts.

As you work to combine the concepts of aiming and playing the arcs, you should also work to let your shots go. Keep a mind-set of hitting out. As we discussed earlier, keep your focus open; see the entire court and the shape of the arc. Accept your errors and make good corrections.

Experiment with increasing and decreasing spin. Pay close attention to where your errors go as you change the amount of spin on the ball. In general, more topspin needs a higher target, while less topspin requires a lower target.

Experiment with driving through the arc—hard. Hit a few rolling topspin shots with lots of speed. These are usually called flat shots, but you know that flat shots still need some spin. On these shots, you are playing the arc just as you learned before. Know that hard-hit, flatter shots need to be aimed at lower targets. They are lower-percentage shots because heavy spin is not driving the ball down into the court. But hard-hit, flat (rolling topspin) shots are an important tool for winning points. You need to learn where the targets are for these "through-the-arc" shots. You learn this by experimenting and working the targets and aim points. Though the flatter, high-speed, rolling topspin shot is a lower-percentage play, it will produce a lot of winners.

DRILL: USE ALL OF THE TARGETS

Now that you have started to put playing the arcs and aiming together as a joint concept, work all the targets you learned in the aiming chapter. When you are standing in the center of the court, use the center and the left and right targets.

When you are playing your shot from the right side of the court, use the center target for hitting shots crosscourt to the corner. Use the right-of-center target when you want to shoot the ball to the center of the court. And use the target farther to the right to shoot the ball down the line to the right side of the court.

When you are playing your shot from the left side of the court, use the center target for hitting shots crosscourt to the corner. Use the left-of-center target when you want to drive the ball to the center of the court. Use the farther-left target to shoot down the line to the left side of the court.

DRILL: CATEGORIZE YOUR SPIN

Divide your arc play into three categories. Start with rolling topspin shots. As you apply this degree of spin, work on developing a target height that produces a high percentage of shots in the court.

Next, increase the topspin to a medium amount. What do I mean by "medium"? You are going to have to figure this out on your own—it's your game, not mine. Your medium spin is the amount between your rolling topspin or flat shot and your maximum Federer/Borg/Nadal topspin emulation. If you are new to applying big topspin, it might take you a little time and experimentation to get the feel for what medium spin is. In any case, seek to find this medium amount of spin. As you apply this medium spin, work to develop a target height that will produce a high percentage of shots in the court.

After you have worked the medium spin target for a while, increase the topspin. We will call this category "heavy spin." We won't call it "maximum," because maximum implies that you are slightly out of control. To find heavy spin, hit a couple of balls with the maximum amount of spin you can apply, really ripping around the arc. After that, dial it down: reduce the spin by about 10 percent. You can call this your "heavy-spin" shot. Work to find a target height to aim for that produces a high percentage of shots in the court.

The reason I recommend developing these categories is to give you a starting point for building ball control. As you work at the arc concept and become more adept at manipulating your aim points and targets, you will develop your own aiming architecture. You will develop targets and visual cues that are unique to your game. Watch professional tennis; notice where they hit their shots, and where their shots pass over the net. The locations those balls pass over the net are the locations of the targets. Observing this will verify that the targets you learned here are correct.

Getting Out of Control

When you start to experiment with big topspin and hard-hit shots, you will make mistakes. Some might be huge, like hitting a few forehands over the fence, long. Yikes! Remember, it's okay to make mistakes. It is also important to develop these techniques in a safe environment—that is, with someone who understands what you are doing and knows that mistakes are part of the learning process. But keep in mind that you need to be able to dial your experimentation up and down. This is especially true when you are playing a practice match or rallying with someone who doesn't know what you are trying to accomplish. If you are working on aiming and playing the arcs in an unfriendly environment, think "rheostat." A rheostat is the dial on the volume of your radio that goes from one to ten. You can turn it up and down. You can do the same with the speed and spin you apply to the ball.

Always start your warm-up by flowing with the arc and hitting easy, rolling topspin and backspin shots. As you reconnect with the arc, your targets, and your aim points, turn your rheostat up. Increase the spin. Increase the speed of your shots. You will make a few errors, but again, that's okay. Keep turning the rheostat up until your mistakes are happening too frequently. Then turn the speed and spin down. Go back toward your warm-up mind-set. You probably won't have to go all the way back to the warm-up position, but dial it back. Once you gain control again, you can push the rheostat up. Keep experimenting with the "volume."

Hitting Out All the Time

Even when you are bringing the intensity of your speed and spin down, you are still hitting out and going for your shot. Never push the ball, trying to *not* make a mistake. You should strike the ball, crushing it to a target, ripping the arc. This is a very important mind-set to have. Every time you make an error, think of it is a good thing. It is a good thing because you now know how to correct for the error. Simply adjust your aim point and go for the next shot. There is no mystery. If you make a mistake, it is just that: a mistake that can be corrected for. In fact, every mistake builds your aiming database and is one more piece of information for your eye-hand computer that will improve your ball control.

You must go for your shots fearlessly. With the knowledge you have of targets, aim points, and arcs, you now know what to do. It is this knowledge that will enable you to hit out all the time and make the big shots when the pressure is on.

Arc Projection: The Highest Form of Ball Control

Arc projection is the ultimate level of ball control. You project arcs when you shoot for your target and project the shape of the arc you want to produce. You go beyond aiming at targets over the net. You still shoot for those targets and play the incoming arc, but you picture the shape of the shot you want to create. You still use the over-the-net targets to control the vector of your shot and you still play the oncoming arc just as you have learned. But now you project your arc. By visualizing the shape of the arc you want to produce, you create and control the entire flight path of your shot.

This is direct conjuring. You generate your shot by visualizing the shape of the arc you want to make. By visualizing the arc, your hand and racket will be driven to produce the right spin, and the right amount through the arc. If you project a round topspin shape, your hand will comply and rip the topspin. If you project a flat arc, your body will produce the low spin and high-speed arc. You are bending reality to your will. Go for it.

When you start with arc projection, you can begin to be more and more specific with your accuracy. You should project your arc through your over-the-net target

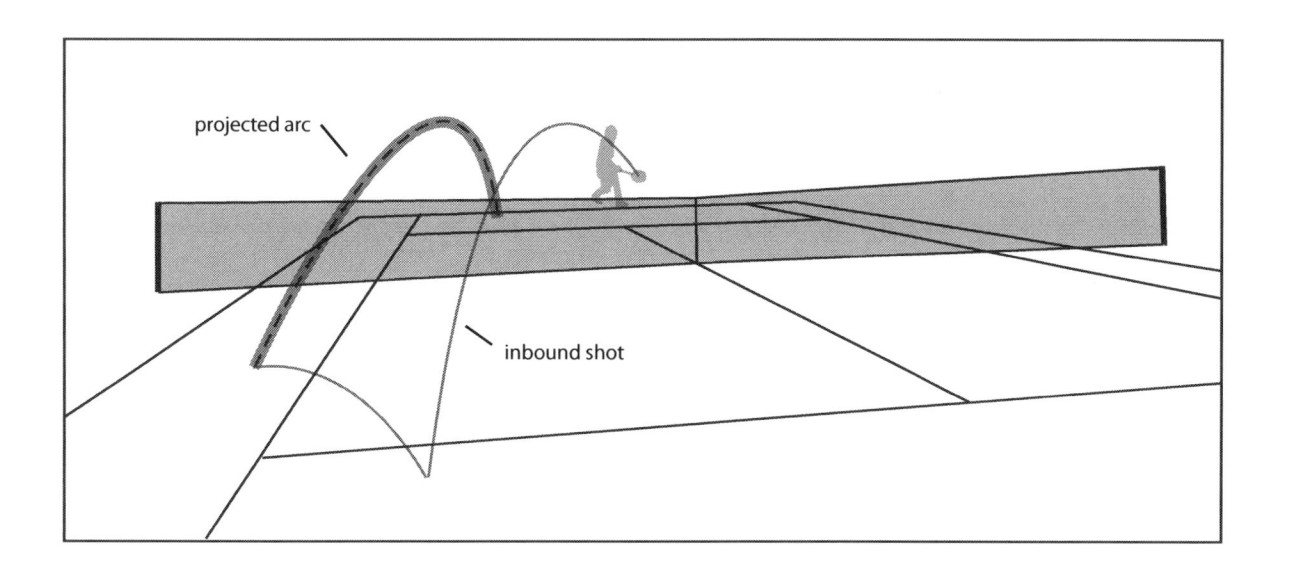

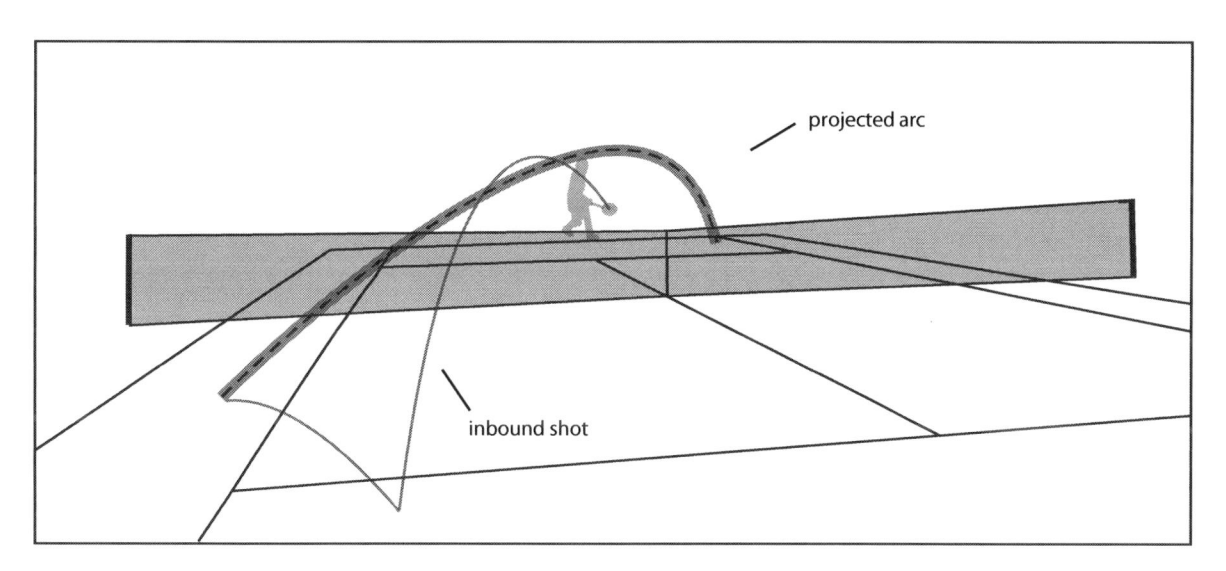

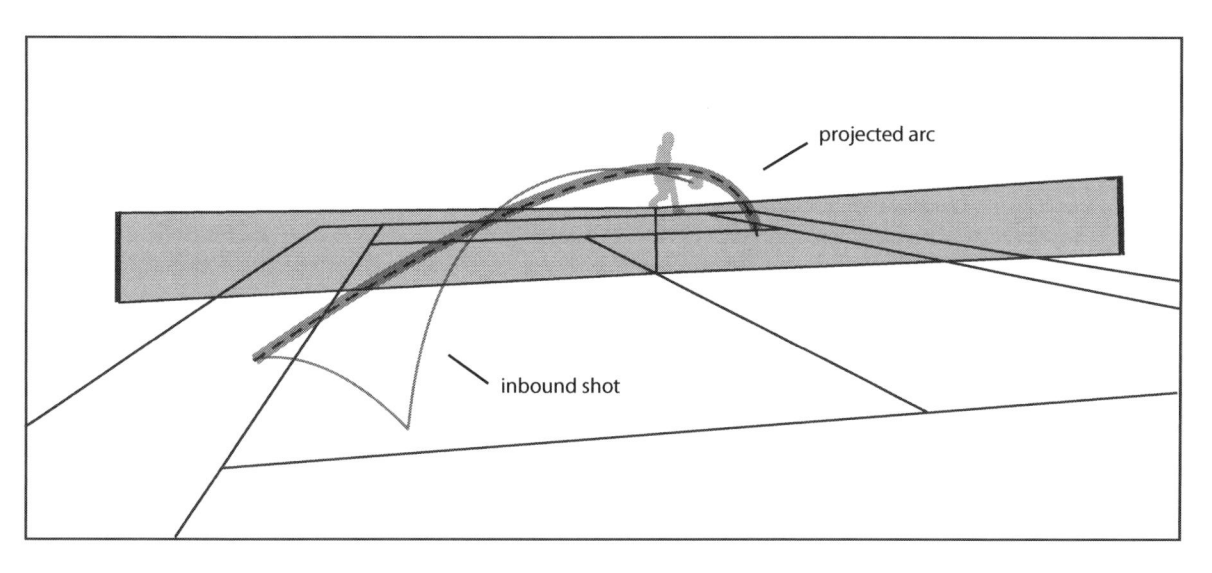

Fig.1 Arc projection examples

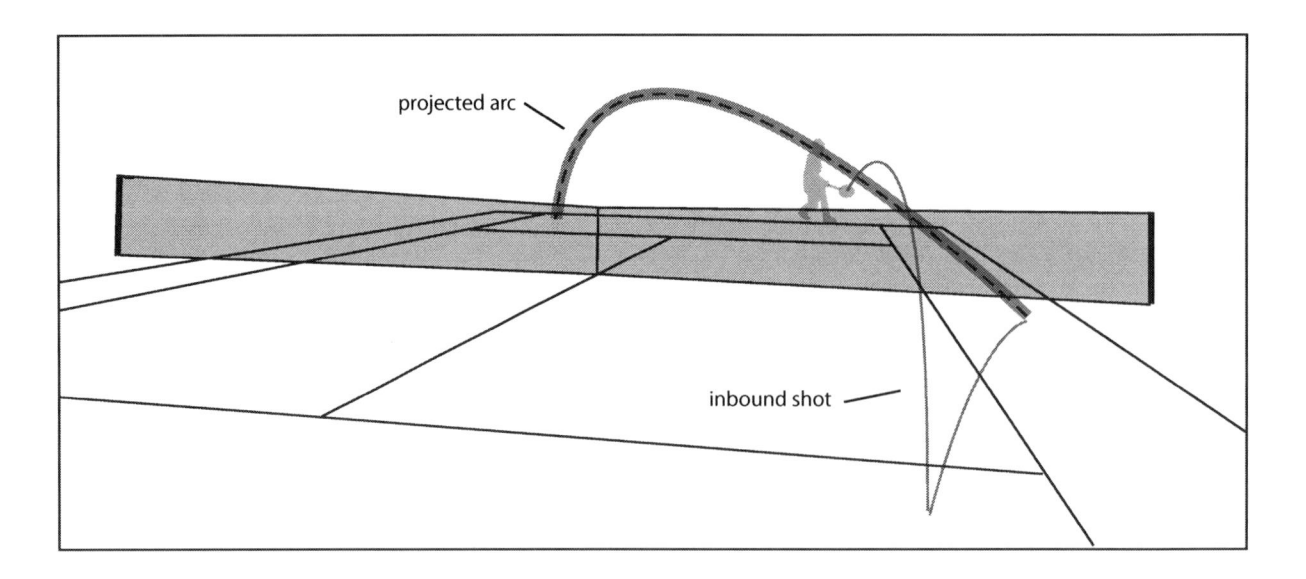

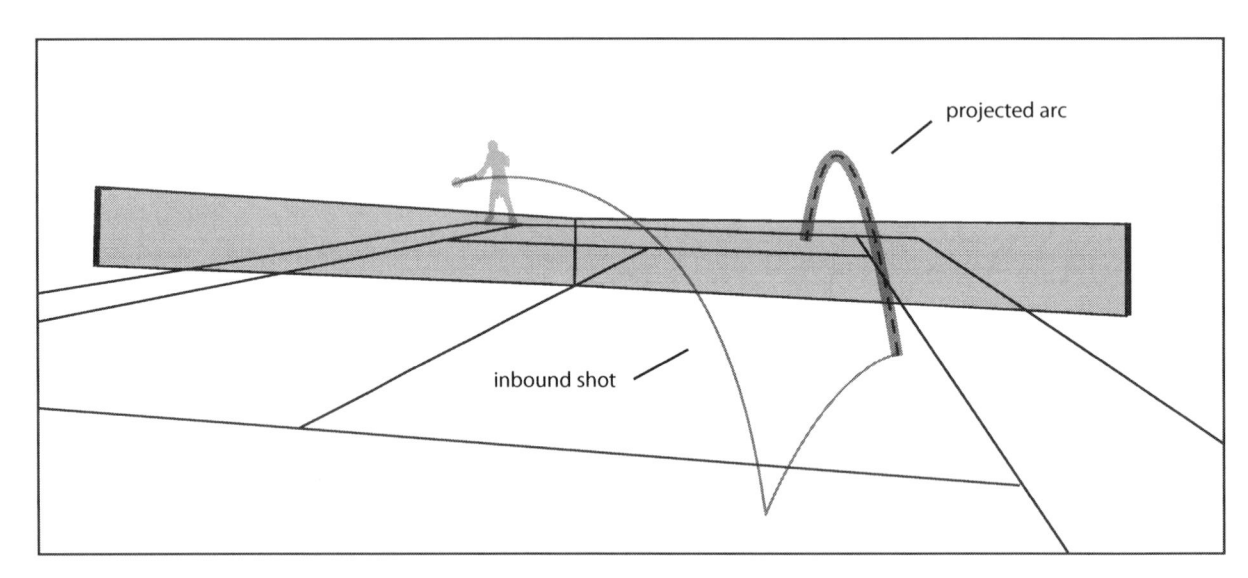

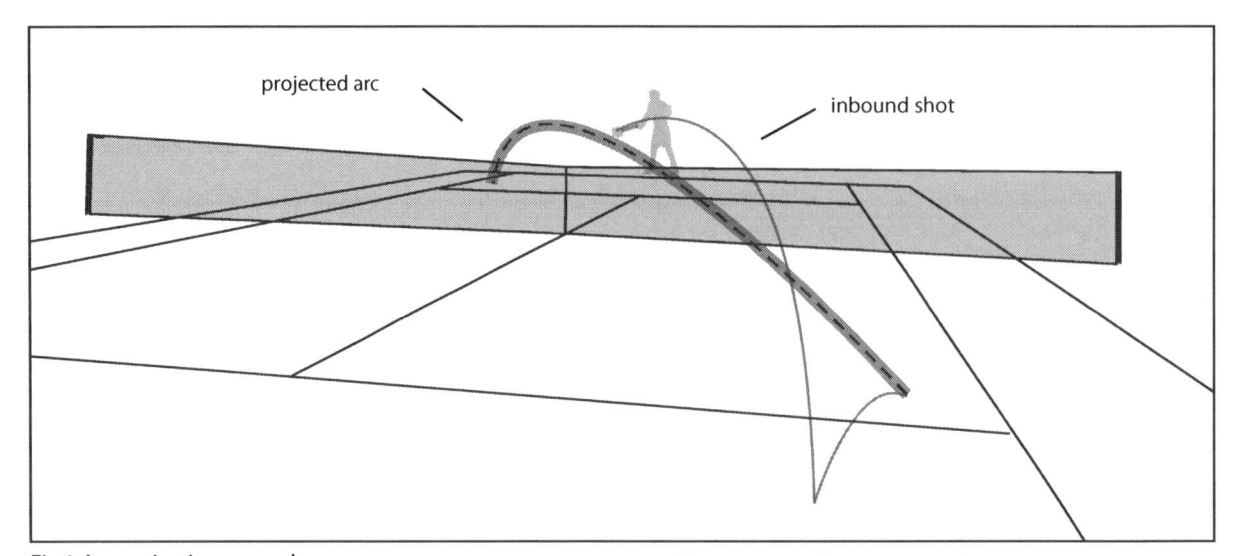

Fig.1 Arc projection examples

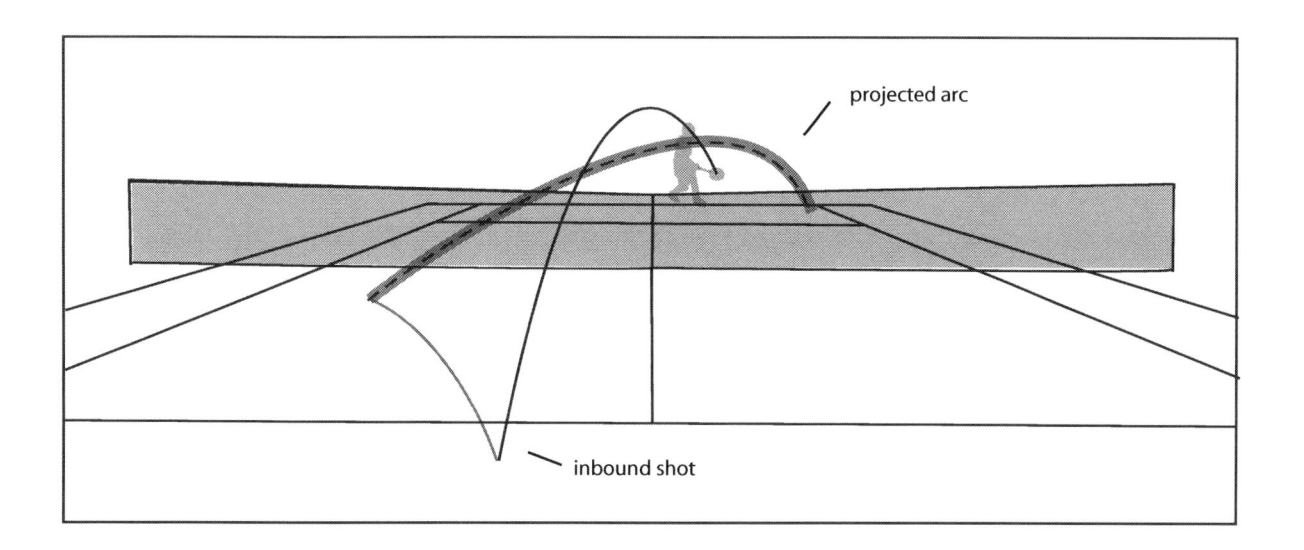

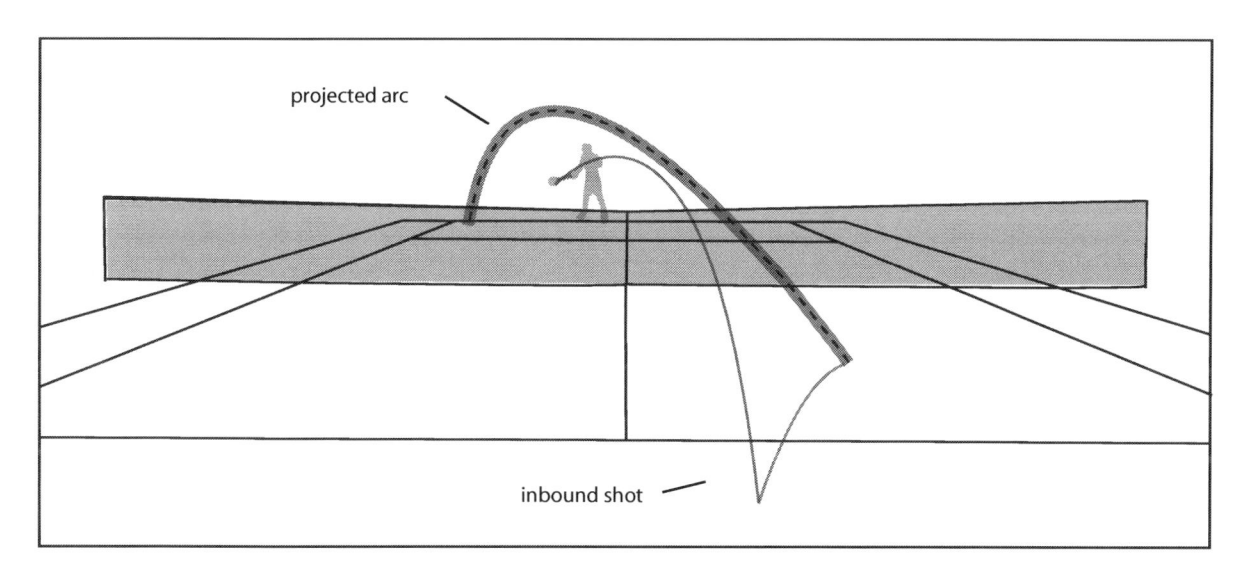

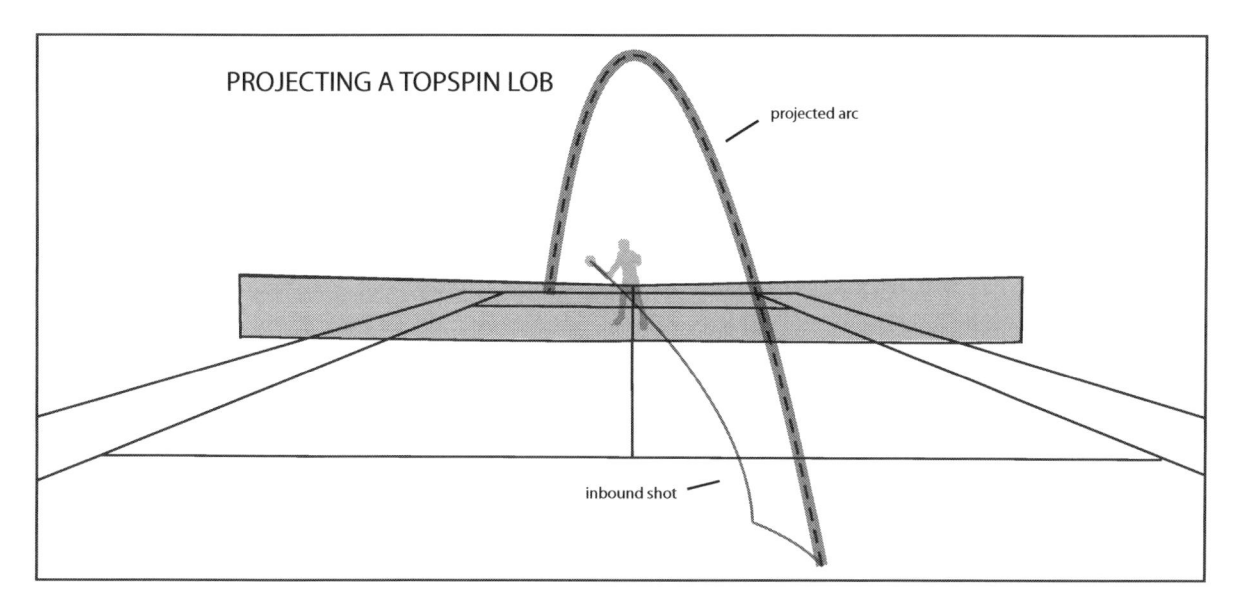

Fig.1 Arc projection examples

and onto a specific spot on the court. As you become accustomed to projecting your arcs, and you get more specific about where you want your shots to land in the court, the over-the-net targets will begin to fall away. This is because you are creating the entire shot visually. Here you transition from indirect targets above the net to a more complete manipulation of the ball that encompasses the entire flight of the shot.

Keep in mind as you make this transition to arc projection that the over-the-net targets still hold. That is, to get the ball to go to the left, right, and center of the court, you still have to project the arc through the same spots over the net. If you begin to lose accuracy, go back to focusing on the three targets and shoot your arc through those spots. You know where they are and can go to them anytime (see Figure 1).

Changing Shapes

Playing the oncoming arc perfectly produces a shot very near the shape of that oncoming arc. As you experiment with arc projection, you can start to alter the shape of your shot away from the shape of the oncoming arc. You can take a low inbound arc and project a high-topspin arcing shot. This is how a topspin lob is created. You can take a deep, high, inbound arc and go for a flat, lower arc. Keep this in mind: The more you make your shot's shape differ from the inbound arc, the more likely you are to make an error. Do some experimenting here. Try making a big, arcing, topspin shot off a low, inbound arc. See how much you can change the shape. Find out when the errors increase. With a high, inbound arc, shoot for a lower, flatter arc. See when the errors start to multiply. You have to experiment to learn your limits and get ball control.

Even when you project an arc shape that is very different from the oncoming arc, you still have to play the arc. The arc is always the basis for making your shot. You rip around the oncoming arc and project the shape of your shot out into the court. Your racket and hand will make the necessary move to produce the shot you project.

Getting Closer to the Line When Shooting Down the Line

By projecting arcs, you get more specific with your accuracy. With this in mind, you can start to shoot closer to the line when shooting down the line. Remember, this is a high-risk shot and you will tend to miss wide of the sideline much more than when pulling the ball crosscourt. The reasons for this will become clear in the chapter on strength and position.

High-Angle Shots

You can also create higher-angle shots. When you shoot a ball crosscourt, on a sharp angle, you need to produce more topspin to get the ball to drop down into the court. By projecting this tighter arc, your hand will produce the increased spin automatically. You manipulate the movement of your racket by projecting the arc in your mind's eye. It is an unconscious thing. You aren't making your hand and racket move in some straitjacketed, preconceived way. Rather, by projecting the arc, your stroke will alter to make the shot happen. If you did not get your arc to dip down onto the court the way you wanted, then project a more exaggerated curve to your arc. Experiment. Conjure different shapes. You will be amazed at what you can create using your mind's eye to bend reality to your will. This is where the game really gets fun.

DRILL: ARC PROJECTION

You can do this drill anytime: during your warm-up, when hitting with a practice partner, or during a match. Make the figure-eight motion of your stroke flow with the arc of the oncoming shot as best you can. Choose your target over the net. As you rip around the arc, picture in your mind's eye the shape of the arc you want to produce. Work to directly engender the shape of your shot. Picture and project out into the court the arc you want to generate. Use your mind's eye to create your shot.

You still work the aiming technique as before. If you miss low, correct high by projecting a higher arc. If you miss high, project a lower arc. If you miss right, project your arc to the left. If you miss left, project your arc farther to the right.

First, picture the rolling topspin arc. Work to see the arc you want to produce in your mind's eye. After you have produced about twenty rolling topspin arcs, imagine a very round, heavy-topspin arc. Project that arc out over the net and into the court. You will find that your racket and stroke will change to comply with your visual command. After you make a few heavy-topspin arcs, picture a hard-hit flat (rolling-topspin) arc. See in your minds eye that flatter arc strike out over the net. Your racket and body will comply. Experiment with high-angled shots. Project a few arcs with tight topspin shapes and shoot for a target farther to the right or left of your normal crosscourt shot. Have fun going for these high-angled shots. If your shot doesn't curve with enough shape, project an even tighter arc. *Very important note*: You don't have to move your target too far to the right or left of your normal crosscourt target to get a high-angle shot.

Arc Projection: A Final Word

First, you need to master aiming techniques and playing the arcs. As these concepts become integral to your game, you will complete the process by projecting arcs. Arc projection will allow you to carve shots through targets over the net to certain spots on the court. If your accuracy degrades as you transition to arc projection, step back to playing the arcs and shooting for over-the-net targets. As you regain your accuracy, start conjuring the shape of your arcs again. Look to project the entire shape of your shot.

This is the purest and highest form of ball control. You directly conjure in your mind's eye the shot you want to produce. You picture the arc of your shot and generate it through visualization. This visualization will command your body to do the right thing. Have fun bending reality to your will.

CHAPTER 4

Strength and Position: The Foundation of Percentage Play

A tennis match is like a game of chess. In chess, each piece can only move a certain way. A queen can move in any direction on the chessboard, the bishop can only move on the diagonal, and the rook can only move in straight lines. In tennis, your ability to choose your shot is constrained like a chess piece's movements. Sometimes you can hit your shot in any direction and have a high-percentage chance of success; in this situation, you are like the queen. Sometimes you can only shoot across the court on an angle; here, you are like a bishop. At times you can only choose a shot straight up the court; in this case, you are like a rook. The trick is to know when you can choose shots like a queen, a bishop, or a rook. When you understand this, you can make high-percentage shot selections.

Three things define your high-percentage shot selections. They are your strength, your position, and the vector of the oncoming shot. Once you understand these concepts, you will know when you can choose shots like the queen, a bishop, or a rook. This knowledge will make you a complete percentage-tennis player.

Strength

Throughout the targets and aiming chapter, I hinted about strength and pulling the ball. Now it is time to learn exactly what your strength is and how to use it. To understand the strength concept, we will use a forehand example with a right-handed player (see Figure 1).

When the player in our example shoots for a target to the left side of his body, he "pulls" the ball into his "strength." Targets on that side of the body are "in strength." When the player in our example shoots for a target to the right side of his body, he "pushes" the ball away from his strength. Targets on that side of the body are "out of strength." The location of your strength is defined by an imaginary line extending out from the shoulders, through the other side of the court. We will call this line your "line of strength" (see Figure 2).

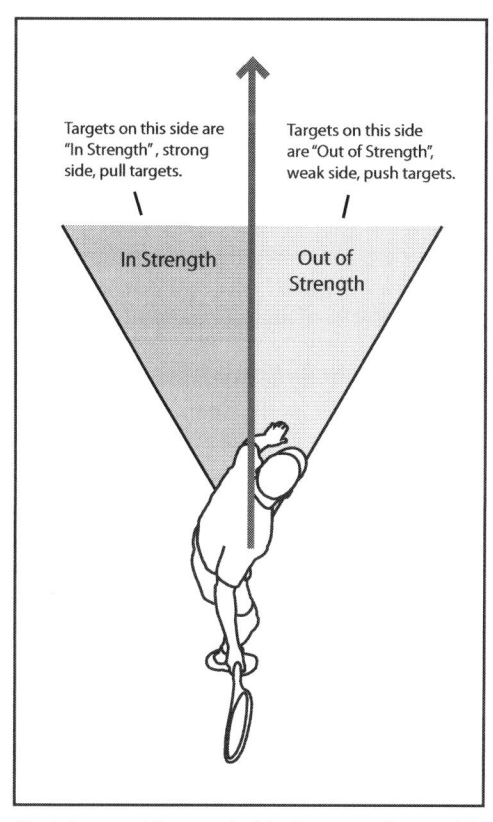

Fig 1 Strong side - weak side. In strength - out of strength

Line of strength

Targets on this side are "in strength" strong side targets.

Targets on this side are "out of strength" weak side targets.

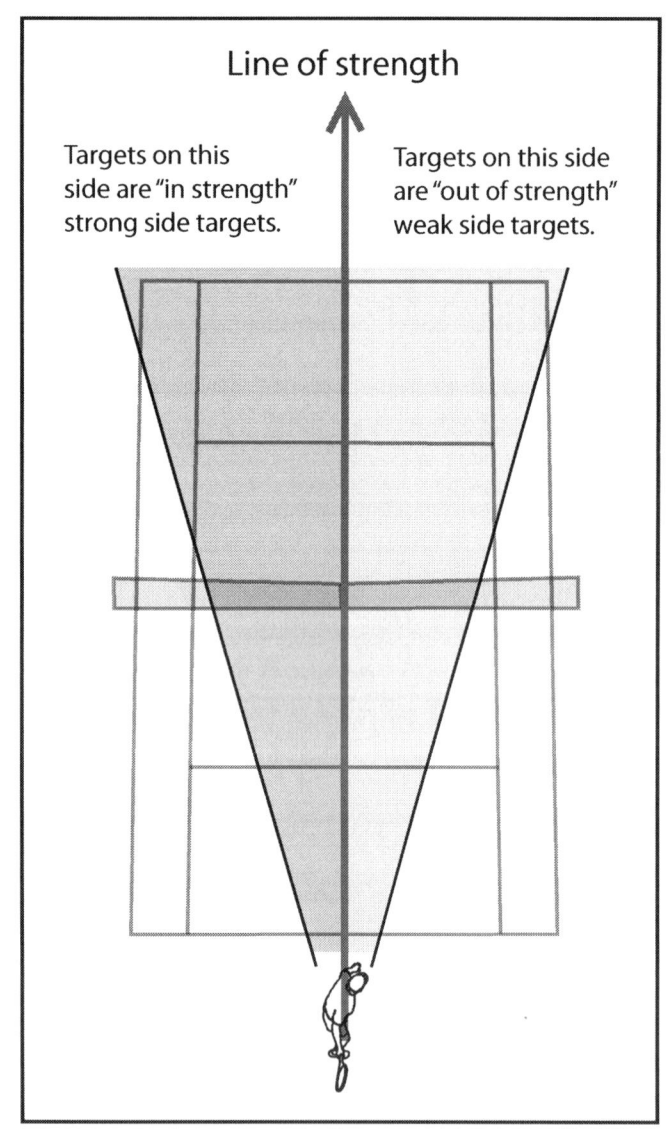

Fig 2 Line of strength

Shots that are aimed to targets on the strong side of your line of strength are always higher-percentage shots. Here's why: When you shoot for targets on the strong side of that line, your racket pulls across your body. When you hit a shot to the strong side, the ball stays on the racket's strings for a longer period of time. This is because of the pulling path of the racket. Because the ball is on the strings for a longer time, you influence the ball's flight path more. When you hit a shot to the strong side, the muscle groups controlling the racket are used longer and more fully. On the forehand, the biceps, forearm, pectorals, and the torso turn drive the racket for a greater period of time. For one-handed backhands, the shoulder, triceps, and forearm drive the racket for a greater duration. For two-handed backhands, the strength of both arms, the shoulders, and the torso turn have more effect on the ball's direction. Because of all of these factors, you are able to dominate the ball's direction when you aim for targets in your strength. Shots aimed to targets on the strong side of your body will always be higher-percentage shots. We will call this area your *strength* and we will talk about *in-strength targets* in the future.

Conversely, shots that are aimed at targets on the weak side of your line of strength are always lower-percentage shots. Here's why: When you shoot for targets on the weak side, you are essentially pushing the ball. When you shoot a ball to the weak side, the ball stays on your strings for a shorter period of time. As you push the shot away from your body, the ball leaves the racket sooner as it is released to the target. Because the ball is on the strings for a shorter period of time, you influence its flight path less. The muscles driving the racket go away from the body. Because of this pushing movement away from your body, the stroke influences the ball's direction less. Because of these factors, the movement of your racket has less effect on the flight path of the ball. Shots that are aimed to targets on the weak side of your body are always lower-percentage shots. Targets on this weak side are *out of strength*, and we will talk about *out-of-strength targets* going forward.

Position

Your "position" is not where you are located on the court. Position is how your body is oriented to the court as you prepare to strike the ball. Your position is defined by where your shoulders and line of strength are pointing as you start the forward swing of your stroke. Your line of strength is controlled as you move your feet and make your shoulder and torso turn during your shot preparation.

How well you can position yourself depends on how much time you have for shot preparation. As you move your feet and make your shoulder-and-torso turn in preparing for the shot, you change your position on the court. As you change your position, your line of strength moves, covering more or less of the court with your strength. When you have lots of time to prepare for the shot, you can position your body so that the whole court is covered by your strength. If you are rushed or are on the run, you will not be able to control your position as well. If you're in a poorer position, only part of the court will be in your strength.

Strength and Position: How They Work Together

You change your shooting capability as you prepare for the shot. Your strength, or your strong side, is where you can target your shots with a high-percentage chance of success. If your body is positioned so that your strength covers the entire court, then you can shoot at targets anywhere on the court with a high-percentage chance of success. Conversely, if your body is positioned so that only one side of the court is covered by your strength, you can only aim to that side with high success. Those targets are "strong side" and in strength; they are high-percentage shots. In contrast, shots to targets on the other side are "weak side" and out of strength; they have a lower chance of success.

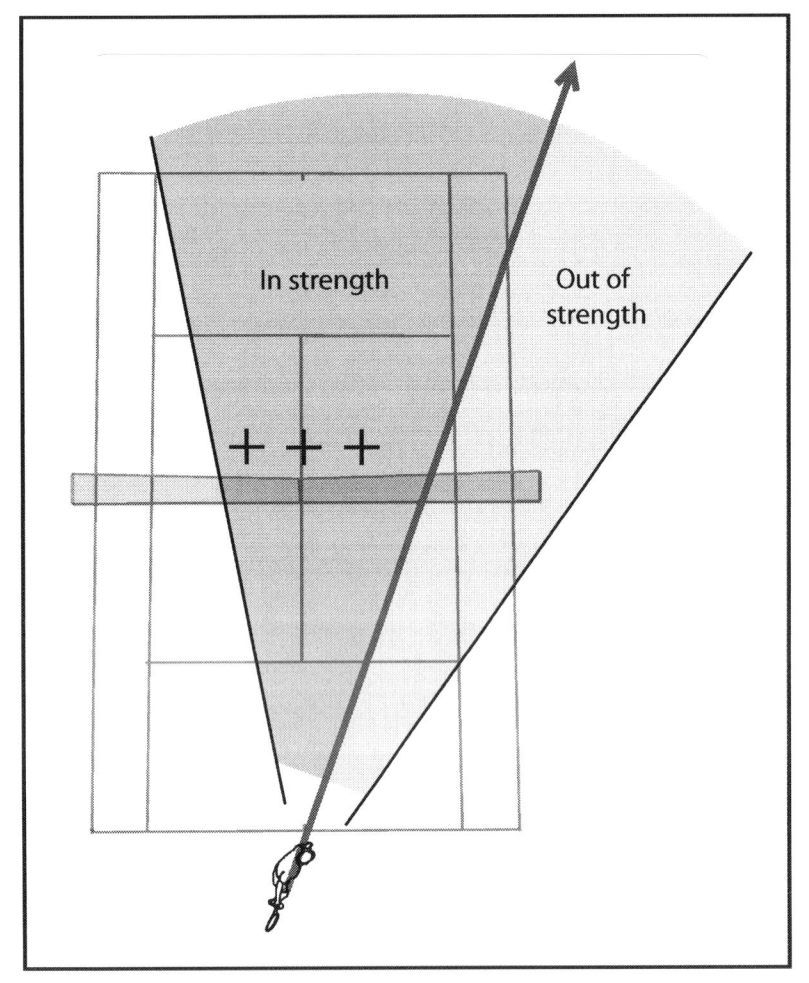

Fig 3 QUEEN. In this "position" the players strength covers all the targets. He is like the Queen in chess and can shoot the ball anywhere on the court.

Going back to the chess example: If your position is such that your strength covers the entire court, then you are like the queen in chess. You can shoot with a high probability of success to either side of the court (see Figure 3). If your position places your line of strength across the court, so that only one side of the court is covered by your strength, you are like a bishop: you can only shoot at the crosscourt target with a high probability of success (see Figure 4). If your position places your line of strength so that it covers only the shot down the line, you are like the rook: you can only shoot at the down-the-line target with a high probability of success (see Figure 5).

PREPARATION

Shot preparation is a combination of your backswing, foot movement, and, most importantly, the turning and control of your upper torso and shoulders. As you flow with the arc, preparing for your shot, you need to emphasize the turning of your upper body. By exaggerating this turn, you will control and direct your line of strength. Control of your strength is the most important part of shot preparation. It defines which targets you can choose as you place your "strength" out over the court. The shoulder and torso turn will get your backswing started. This turn is more important than foot movement. A good torso turn will substitute for late footwork if you are rushed. The initial rotation of your shoulders and torso is the most important move you make on the court. You need to emphasize it and make it an integral part of your shot preparation.

Strength and position work together. How your body is oriented to the court controls how much of the court is in strength. Shot preparation is the critical factor here. Good footwork, combined with an aggressive torso turn, moves your strength around the court. Shots to targets in the strong side are always higher percentage than shots to targets out of your strength, which are always lower-percentage shots.

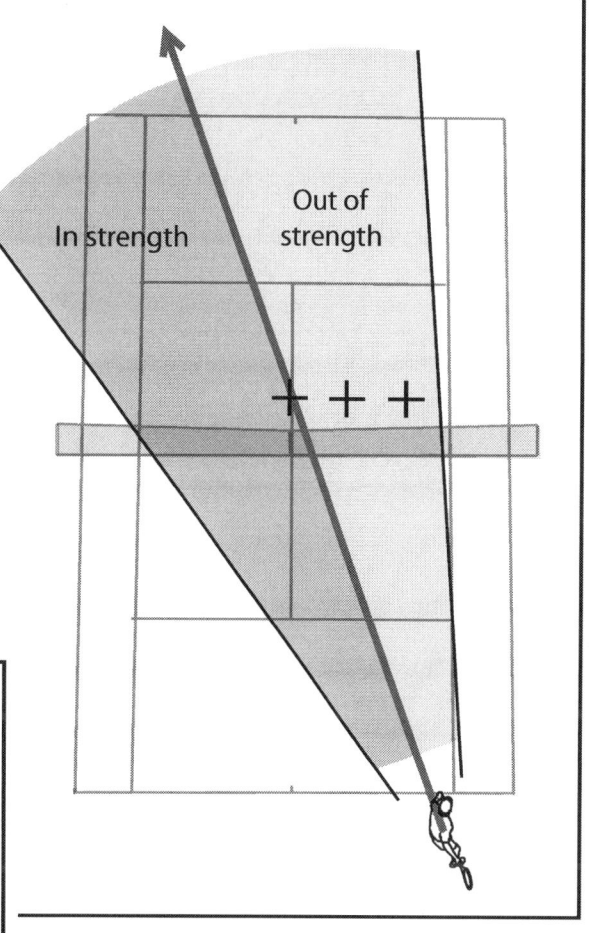

Fig 4 BISHOP. In this "position", the players strength only covers the cross court target. He is like a Bishop in chess and can only shoot the ball on an angle cross court.

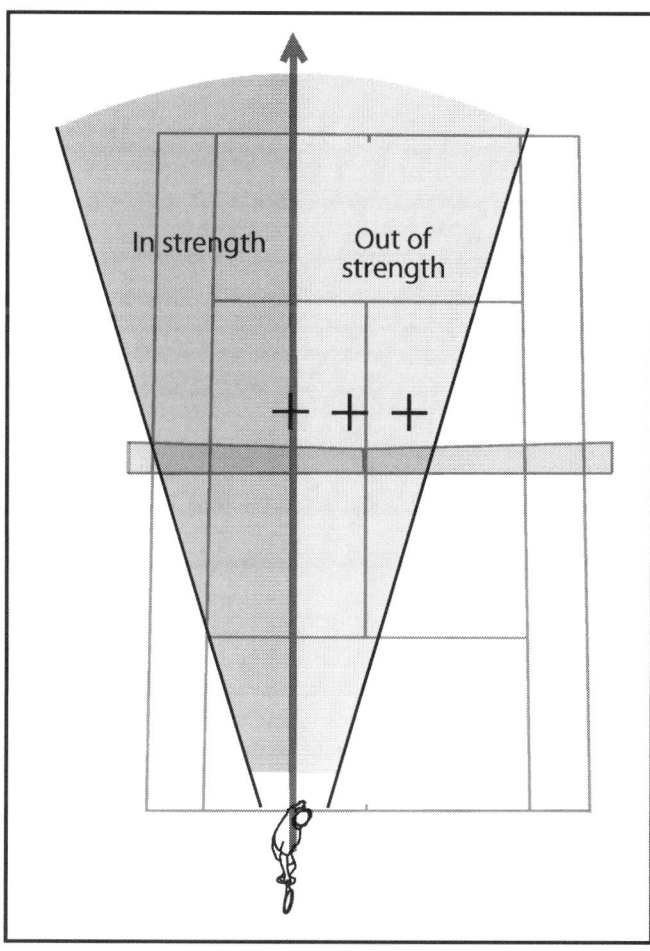

Fig 5 ROOK. In this "position" the players strength only covers the up the line target. He is like the Rook in chess and can only shoot the ball "up the line".

STRENGTH AND POSITION: THE FOUNDATION OF PERCENTAGE PLAY | 93

Two Ways to Control Position

Footwork and the torso turn during shot preparation are the two ways to control your position and move your strength around the court. In the queen, bishop, and rook illustrations, the player's feet are aligned with the shoulders. His line of strength projects along the shoulders and along the feet out into the court. When the feet are aligned with the shoulders, the player is in a "closed stance." In the closed stance, the player's lower body is turned away from, and is closed to, the court.

Shots can also be hit using an "open stance." When a player is in an open stance, his feet are positioned so that his lower body is facing the court. The open stance gets its name because the lower body is open to the court. When using the open stance, the position and location of your strength are controlled by the shoulder and torso turn.

The Open Stance and Expanding Your Strength

Björn Borg was the first player to use the open-stance forehand as a dominating weapon. In fact, Roger Federer's forehand is nearly a mirror image of Borg's open-stance forehand. All the top players use the open-stance forehand today.

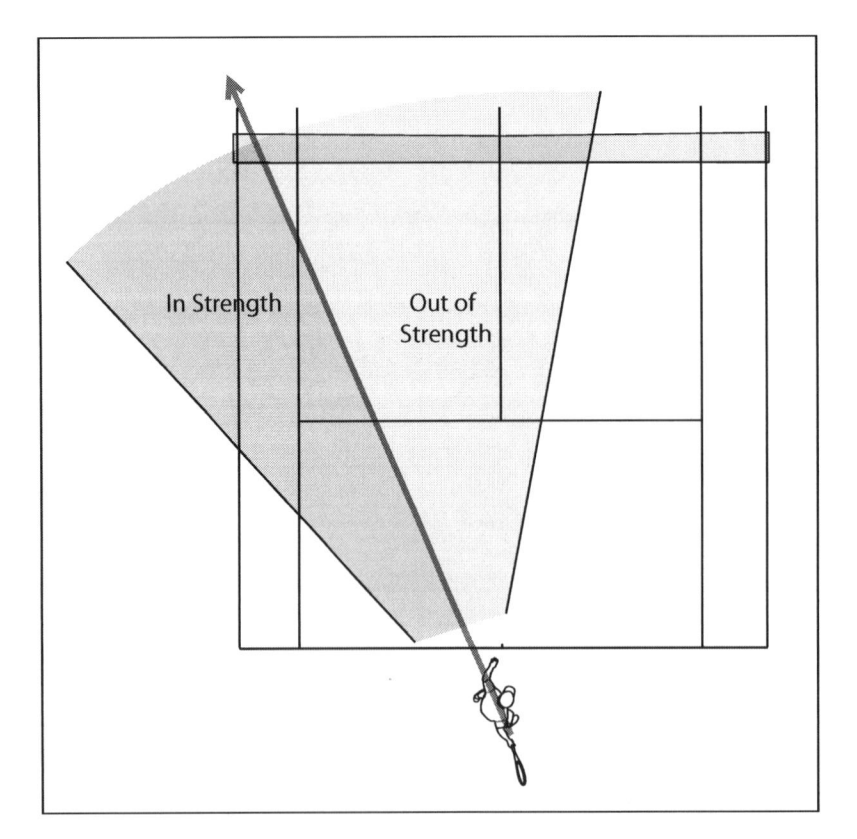

Fig 6a OPEN STANCE FOREHAND. Here the player is in an open stance but has not made a good shoulder and torso turn. Virtually none of the court is in strength.

If a player using the open stance has his shoulders aligned with his feet, virtually none of the court is in strength (see Figure 6a). If you draw a line of strength along the feet of the player, the line points way over to the forehand side of the court (assuming a right-handed player). In this position the player would have only one target to choose from. He would have to shoot to the strong side, crosscourt, nearest his strength. If he chose another target, he would be pushing the ball, making a low-percentage shot.

To control your position using an open stance, you must make an aggressive shoulder-and-torso turn during your shot preparation. By making this aggressive turn, you move your line of strength to cover more of the court with your strong side. By exaggerating this turn, you "expand your strength" over more of the court. By expanding your strength you give yourself more high-percentage shot selections and more tactical options. The turning of the torso and shoulders is *the* critical move in shot preparation, especially when using the open stance. It is the most important part of your tennis stroke (see Figure 6b).

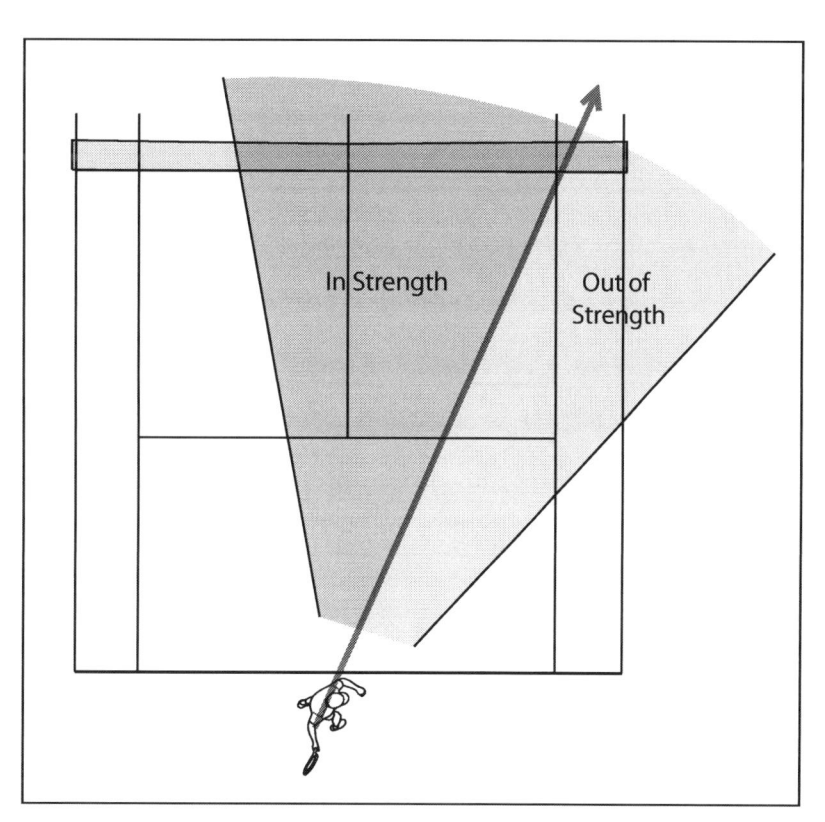

Fig 6b OPEN STANCE FOREHAND Here the player is in the open stance and has made an aggressive torso turn. This places his strength over the entire court.

STRENGTH AND POSITION: THE FOUNDATION OF PERCENTAGE PLAY | 95

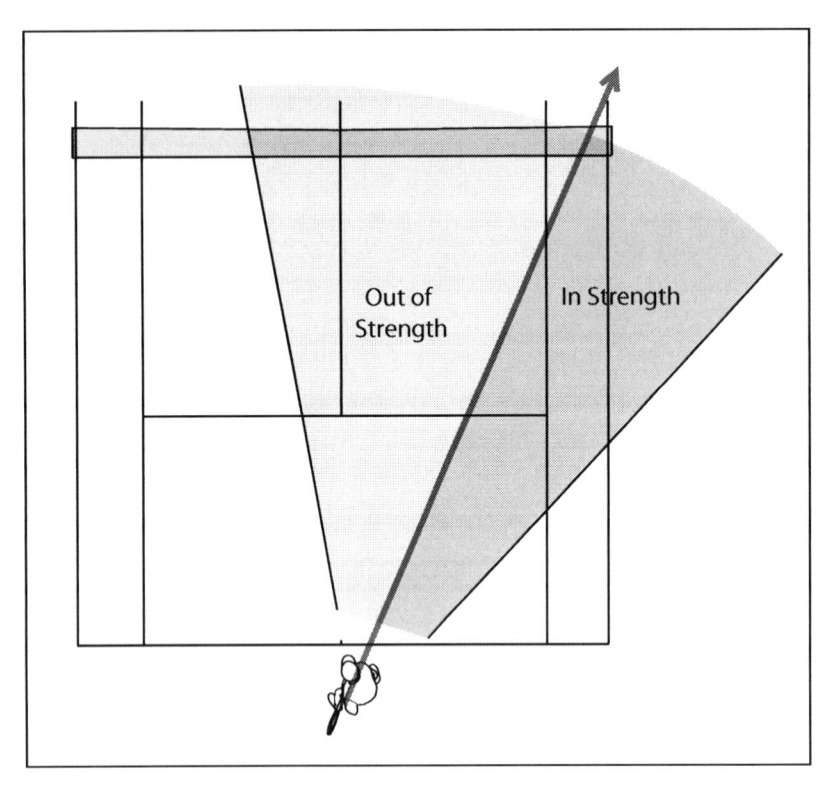

Fig 7a OPEN STANCE TWO HANDED BACKHAND Here the player is in an open stance but has not made a good shoulder and torso turn. Virtually non of the court is in strength. He must choose the cross court target to make a marginally high percentage shot.

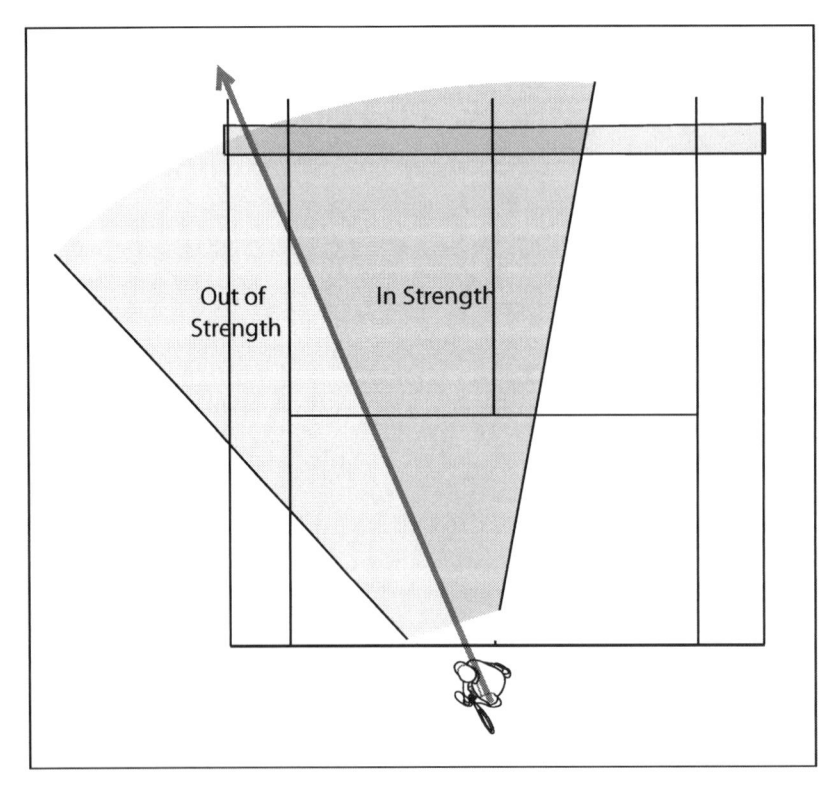

Fig 7b OPEN STANCE BACKHAND Here the player is in the open stance and has made an aggressive torso turn. This places his strength over the entire court.

Open-Stance Backhands

Two-Handed Backhands

The two-handed backhand can be hit with an open stance. This is because, during the forward swing, the torso rotates as in a forehand. The two-handed backhand hitter can prepare for the shot with an open stance and then make an aggressive torso turn, placing her strength out over the court. As the two-handed backhand is hit, the torso turns with the forward swing, adding power and strength to the shot. The ability to rotate the torso fully as you strike the two-handed backhand makes it a more powerful shot than the one-handed backhand. The uncoiling torso turn makes the two-handed backhand nearly as powerful as a forehand (see Figure 7a and 7b).

One-Handed Backhands

Hitting an open-stance, one-handed backhand generally produces a weak shot. This is because the torso must stop its rotation as the ball is struck. The need to stop the torso turn is the greatest weakness of the one-handed backhand. It is better to use a closed stance on one-handed backhands. Good footwork is essential here. When hitting a one-handed backhand, your line of strength will usually project out along your feet into the court. So in order to control your line of strength and move your strong side around the court, you have to move your feet. Don't ignore the torso turn on your one-handed backhand. You need to turn so that your shoulder closed to the court as you start your forward swing. If you don't, your shot will be weak and control will be difficult.

The Vector of the Oncoming Shot

The third component to understanding high-percentage shot selection is the vector of the oncoming shot. Adding this logic to strength and position will enable you to choose high-percentage targets in all situations on the court.

A vector is the direction or course followed by an airplane, missile, or the like. "The like," in our case, is the tennis ball that your opponent hits to you. The vector of the oncoming shot is its direction and speed: that is, where it is coming from, its line of travel, and its velocity. It is the linear energy of the oncoming arc. The arc of the shot is its curving flight path; the vector of the shot is its direction and pace.

A Few Facts about Vectors

When you shoot at a target directly along the vector of the oncoming shot, you have a high-percentage chance of success. You have a good probability of success at hitting that shot accurately.

When you shoot at a target away from the vector of the oncoming shot, you have a lower-percentage chance of success. You have a lower probability of success at hitting that shot accurately.

As you move your target farther away from the vector of the oncoming shot, your probability of success gets lower.

Why are these things true? Because of this physics law: *angle of incidence equals angle of deflection*. The best way to understand this concept is to roll a ball up against a flat surface. You can use a wall and a tennis ball. If you roll the ball up to the wall, straight on, the ball will bounce straight back toward you. In this case, the ball strikes the flat surface with zero angle of incidence. The ball deflects straight back, with zero angle of deflection (see Figure 9).

Now try rolling the ball up to the wall on an angle. Notice that the ball will deflect off the wall on an angle. The angle it deflects is equal to the angle that it approached the wall. The angle of approach is the angle of incidence. The angle the ball deflects off the wall is the angle of deflection. These two angles are equal (see Figure 10).

Try rolling the ball against the wall at greater angles. Notice that as you increase the angle, the ball bounces off the wall at a greater angle. A greater angle of incidence produces a greater angle of deflection (see Figure 11).

Here is how this relates to making a tennis shot. The vector of the oncoming shot is like the ball approaching the wall. Your racket, as you make your forward swing, approximates the wall. The direction your shot takes off your racket is akin to the ball bouncing off the wall.

However, the ball doesn't just bounce off your racket. You are driving through the arc of the ball. You are influencing the ball's direction with the

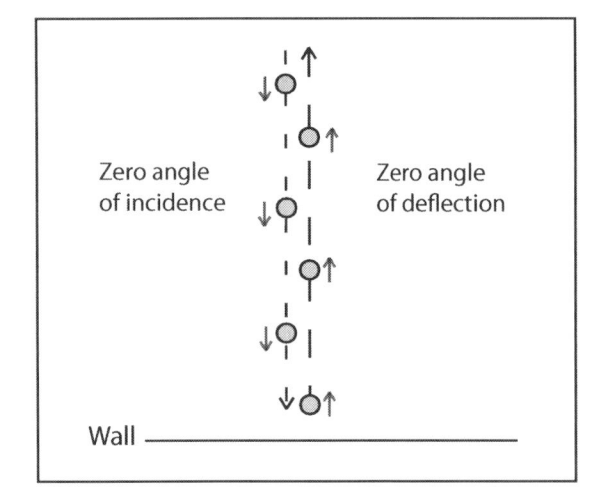

Fig 9. Here ball strikes the wall straight on (zero angle of incidence) and and bounces straight back (zero angle of deflection).

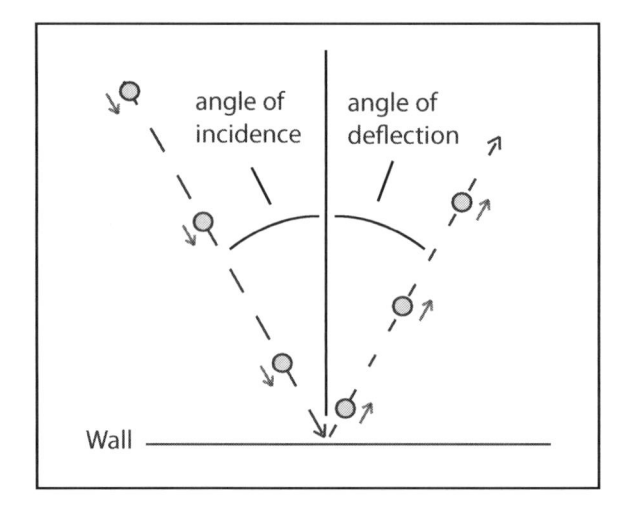

Fig 10. Here the ball strikes the wall on and angle (30 degrees angle of incidence) and bounces off on the same angle (30 degrees angle of deflection).

forward movement of your stroke. Even so, the rule that angle of incidence equals angle of deflection still holds.

Your resulting shot will tend to deflect away from your target as follows. If your target is directly along the vector of the oncoming shot, it is like rolling the ball straight on to the wall. Here, there is zero angle of incidence, so there will be zero angle of deflection. Your shot will have no tendency to deflect away from the target. Your shot will have zero "deflection factor" (see Figure 12).

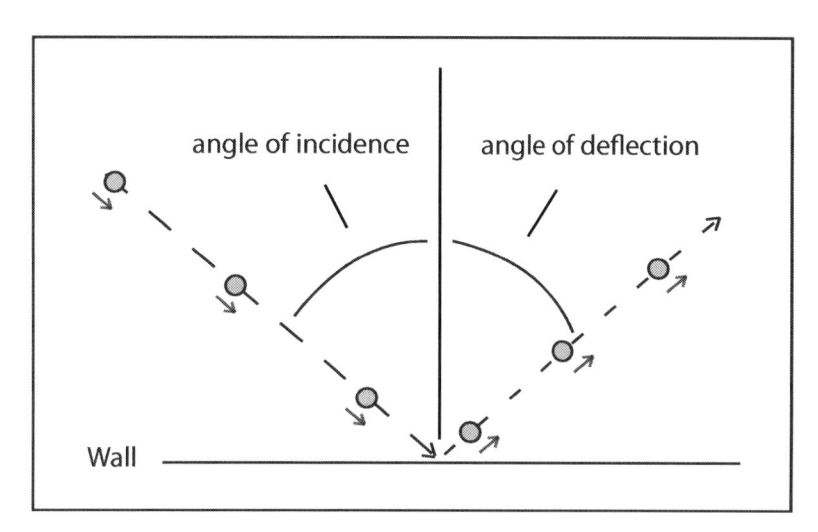

Fig 11. Here ball strikes the wall on a greter angle (45 degrees angle of incidence) and bounces off on the same angle (45 degrees angle of deflection).

If your target is away from the vector of the oncoming shot, it is like rolling the ball against the wall on an angle. Here, there is an angle of incidence. Because of the angle of incidence, your shot will tend to deflect away from your target according to the rule. Because your target is off vector, there is a deflection factor (see Figure 13).

As you move your target farther away from the vector of the oncoming ball, your shot will have a tendency to deflect farther away from your target. As your target moves farther off vector, the deflection factor will increase (see Figure 14).

The amount your shot will deflect away from your target also depends on the speed or power of the oncoming shot. If you are playing a slow, softly hit shot, there will be very little tendency for the ball to deflect off target. The motion of your racket overcomes the vector energy of the ball. Your shot will pretty much go where your racket drives it—that is, at the target.

If the oncoming shot is a hard-hit, fast-approaching ball, on the other hand, your shot will have a greater tendency to deflect away from your target. This is because the movement of your racket doesn't overcome all of the ball's vector energy. The harder and faster the oncoming shot, the more your shot will tend to angle off, deflecting away from your target.

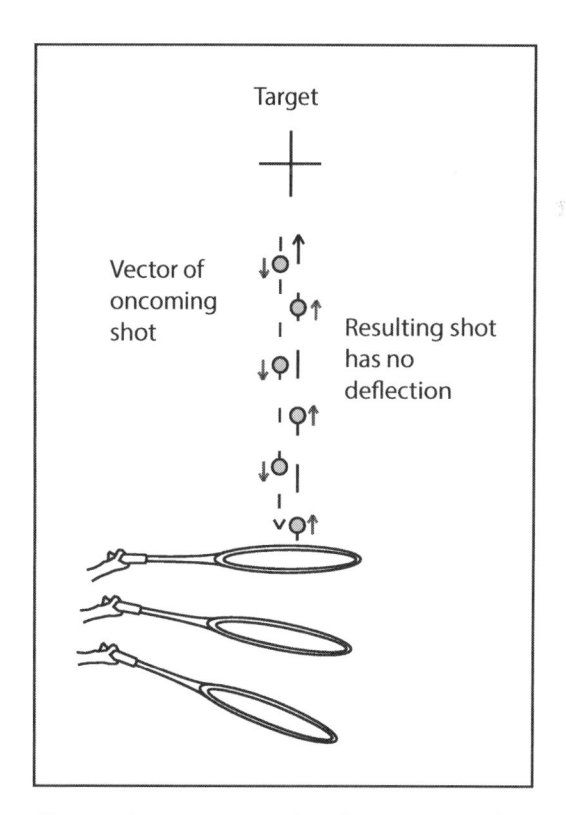

Fig 12. Here the target is directly over vector of oncoming shot so the angle of incidence is zero. The resulting shot has no tendency to deflect - there is zero "deflection factor."

STRENGTH AND POSITION: THE FOUNDATION OF PERCENTAGE PLAY | 99

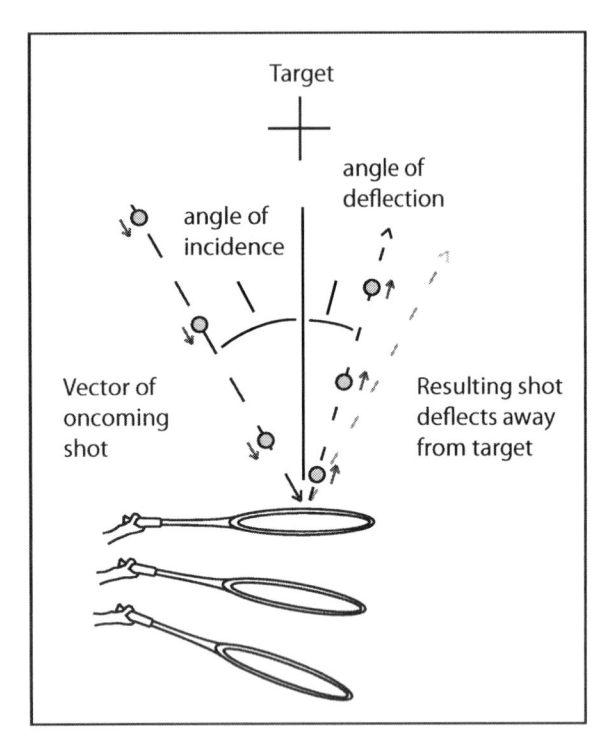

Fig 13. Here the target is away from the vector of the oncoming shot creating an angle of incidence. The resulting shot tends to deflect away from the target because of the angle of incidence equals angle of deflection rule. But, the deflection is less, because the force of the racket overcomes part of the deflection.

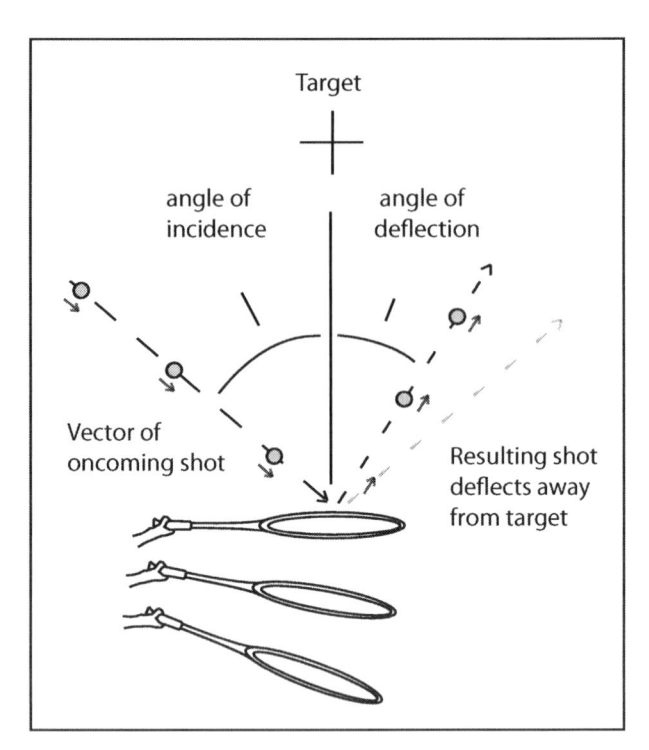

Fig 14. In this figure the target is farther away from the vector of the oncoming shot. This creates a greater angle of incidence and a bigger shot deflection. But, once again, the amount of deflection is reduced by the force of the racket driving out to the target.

Changing Direction? Make That "Shooting Off Vector"

Changing direction? Every time you hit a shot in tennis, you change the direction of the ball. The ball is coming at you. You shoot the ball in nearly the opposite direction to the other side of the court. But "changing direction" is the common name for shooting for a target off vector, especially when shooting down the line off a crosscourt shot. You have just learned why this is hard to do: it is difficult because of the ball's tendency to deflect away from the target. The reason the ball deflects is because of the vector energy of the ball and the physics law that the angle of incidence equals the angle of deflection. It is also difficult to do because the court is shorter and the net is higher when shooting down the line. In chapter 5, we combine strength and position with shooting for targets off vector, and you learn when this off-vector target is a high-percentage shot. "Changing direction" is a poor name for this shot selection on the tennis court: it is better described by the term "shooting off vector."

All the Tools Required

You now have all the tools you need to play percentage tennis. You know where the strong and weak sides of the court are. Your strong side is the pull side of your line of strength: that side of the court is *in strength*. The weak side is the push side: that side is *out of strength*. The location of your strength is a result of your position on the court. Your position is defined by the orientation of your body to the court as you prepare to strike the ball. You control your position by moving your feet and making an aggressive torso turn during shot preparation.

You also know how the vector of the oncoming shot affects your accuracy. As you move your target away from the vector of the oncoming shot, your shot tends to deflect away from your target. The farther your target is from the vector of the oncoming shot, the more the shot tends to deflect. With these three tools, we can construct a few rules of thumb for percentage play. Here comes the most important rule of thumb.

Strength Overcomes Deflection

When you shoot at targets in strength, the pulling motion of your stroke and the time that the ball is on your strings dominate the direction of your shot. When you shoot at a target off vector but in strength, your strength overcomes the deflection. The domination of strength over deflection enables you to shoot off vector with excellent control when shooting at targets that are in strength. This rule is the core concept in percentage tennis. Understanding it is a huge part of high-percentage shot selection.

The Truth about Crosscourt and Down-the-Line Shots

Some pundits define percentage tennis as this: crosscourt shots are high-percentage shots, because when you hit a crosscourt shot, the court is longer. So the crosscourt shot is high percentage because you have more court to shoot at and a greater distance to miss. And when you hit a crosscourt shot, your ball will pass over the lowest part of the net, so you have a lower chance of missing into the net. This is true!

They also say that down-the-line shots are lower percentage for the opposite reasons. When you hit down the line, the court is shorter: you have less distance to miss. And when you hit a down-the-line shot, the net is at its highest, so you have a higher chance of missing into the net. This is also true.

Why aren't these truths the most important part of our percentage-tennis discussion? Here is the reason: even though these facts are true, and they will affect your shot's chance of success, the most important factors for shot selection are *strength*, *position*, and the *vector of the oncoming shot*. These factors are more important and they dominate the crosscourt and down-the-line logic.

But as we discuss high- and low-percentage targets, keep in mind that the down-the-line and crosscourt logic still holds: the length of the court and the height of the net will affect your chances of success. What is more important is that you understand strength and position and the vector of the oncoming shot, and that you use these as the controlling factors in your shot selection.

Strength and Position Rules of Thumb

Choosing high-percentage targets in different situations during a point depends on your position and the vector of the oncoming shot. If you can get your feet, shoulders, and torso positioned so that your strength covers the entire court, you will have more high-percentage targets. High-percentage targets are always in strength. When your target is in strength and on vector, that shot will be a very high-percentage shot. When you shoot for targets off vector, your strength must cover that target. This is when you can successfully "change direction." The crosscourt and down-the-line facts (see side box) also affect your shot's chances of success. Crosscourt shots have more court to shoot for and pass over the lowest part of the net. Down-the-line shots cross the highest part of the net and have less court to shoot for. But the keys to understanding when down-the-line targets are high percentage are strength and position and the vector of the oncoming shot.

Anticipation: Strength and Position, the Double-Edged Sword

Anticipation in tennis is the ability to know where your opponent is shooting her next shot. If you know where the next ball is going, you can move into position early and make a great play.

Is anticipation the same as guessing? Or is there some logic to it? The intuitive reader will already realize that everything we have just discussed about choosing high-percentage shots applies to both you and your opponent.

Strength, position, and the vector of the oncoming shot are a double-edged sword. By analyzing your opponent's strength and position, you will know where her high-percentage shots are. If your opponent's strength is covering only one side of the court, you move to cover that side of the court early. You "give" your opponent the low-percentage play. Uneducated players will choose those shots and make a lot of errors as a result.

As a rule of thumb, if your opponent's strength only covers one side of the court, move slightly into that side of the court. Stand over toward that side. Be ready to pounce on any balls pulled to strength by your opponent. By moving into your opponent's zone of strength, you are giving her the low-percentage play. This will do two things. First, you will bait ignorant players into choosing the low-percentage shot. Second, if your opponent does choose the smart shot, you will be in a better position for your next play.

If your opponent's strength covers both sides of the court, move to the center of her strength. From this position, you can cover her shot options best. It may even encourage your opponent to go for a target too close to the line and make the unforced error.

Faking and Baiting

Sometimes you can fake your opponent by initially standing away from her high-percentage shot. Then, as she makes the correct play, move early to cover this shot. This tactic does have its risks, depending on the quality of your opponent, but it can work. If you are at net and have to defend against a passing shot, this fake to the weak side combined with an early move to your opponent's strength can be quite effective.

Guessing

Sometimes you do have to play the guessing game. This is especially true if you are very defensive and your opponent is playing a sitter in the middle of the court. If your opponent's strength covers the entire court, you know he or she can shoot to either side. Here you have to get a feel for what your opponent has done in the past. When in doubt, move to the middle of his strength and defend from there. Or you can attempt to bait your opponent by moving to cover one side of the court. In this case, you are hoping to bait him to shoot to the more open side of the court. It is also possible that your opponent has constantly tried to hit behind you as you have moved to cover the open court in strength. In this case, you can fake a move to the open court, anticipating his attempt to wrong-foot you. At the last minute, you can move to cover the shot behind your faked run. Or, if your opponent consistently shoots for strength, you can hesitate near the edge of his strength and then move to the strong side.

The Jam Shot

When your opponent is playing a ball that is jammed into his body, there is only one target he can choose. He has to hit the ball to the strong side. Now it is time to fully use your knowledge. You can wait on the edge of his strength and then move aggressively to his strong-side target. This is most effective when you are at net, and your approach shot or your volley is jammed into your opponent's body. Hesitate near the middle of the court and then move aggressively to his strong-side target. There is nowhere else your opponent can hit the ball. Crush the volley for a winner.

Summary

Shot selection is choosing where to hit your shot. High percentage shot selections are defined by your strength and position and the vector of the oncoming shot. When you understand how these concepts work together, defining your choices on the court, you will become an excellent percentage tennis player. Winning points will get easier. Your ability to solve tactical problems on the court will improve dramatically. You will constantly put pressure on your opponent by making high percentage shot selections.

Your anticipation should also improve significantly with your new knowledge of strength, position, and the vector of the oncoming shot. The rules of high percentage shot selection apply equally to you and to your opponent. You will be able use your knowledge to anticipate the next shot and win points quickly and efficiently.

Chapter 5 is very important; it includes a detailed description of high and low percentage targets in different situations on the court. This chapter shows shot probabilities as the result of your position on the court and the vector of the oncoming shot; it sorts oncoming shot vectors into three simple categories:

- Vector down the middle of the court
- Vector crosscourt
- Vector down the line

Situations on the court are defined by these three simple conditions. A usable template for decision-making is presented for each. Once you understand this logic, making high-percentage shot selections during a point will be easy. It is critical to read and understand this section to fully understand how strength and position and the vector of the oncoming shot work together. This knowledge will make you a complete percentage tennis player

CHAPTER 5

How to Make High-Percentage Shot Selections

We are going to break down situations on the court into three simple conditions. These conditions depend on the vector of the oncoming shot—that is, where the ball is coming from and its path of travel. The three conditions are:

1. vector down the middle of the court
2. vector crosscourt
3. vector down the line

With our understanding of strength and position, and the fact that your shot deflects away from your target when shooting off vector, we will be able to define where the high-percentage targets are in each of these conditions. We will use the three targets we developed in the aiming chapter with one addition. This target is the "high-angle target" crosscourt and will be explained in the examples. Remember, the goals for the three targets are to shoot the ball to the middle of the court, the right side of the court, and the left side of the court. The high-angle target goal is to produce a sharply angled shot crosscourt.

Note that we will show a right-handed player in these examples. If you are left-handed, make the forehand/backhand inversion.

We will also classify how "high percentage" each target is. We will use the following terms: very high percentage, high percentage, dependent, low percentage, very low percentage, and good risk.

Very high percentage: This means that shooting to this target will yield nearly 100 percent success. Shots to a very-high-percentage target can be crushed with confidence.

High percentage: Shots to high-percentage targets have a good chance of success and can be taken with low risk.

Dependent: Shots to dependent targets are high percentage in some situations and low percentage in others. The shot's probability of success is a function of three things: the speed and depth of the shot you are receiving and how long you have to prepare for the shot. Fast oncoming shots have more vector energy and deflect off target more than slowly hit shots. It is also harder to get into position and control your strength when playing shots that land deep in the court. Shooting for targets off vector when playing these hard-hit, deep balls will produce more errors. So shots to dependant targets will be high percentage when the oncoming shot lands shallow in the court or is slowly hit. If the oncoming shot is deep and hard hit, and you have good position shooting into your strength, this shot will be a good risk. There will be a chance of error but making the shot will pay off big, possibly winning the point. Time for preparation also affects the quality of your position for your shot. You generally need a little time in position to truly cover a target with your strength. This is especially true when shooting down the line and off vector. Shots to a dependent targets are low percentage if you are rushed getting into position. If you are in position early your chance of success goes up regardless of the depth and speed of the oncoming shot.

Low percentage: Shots to low-percentage targets are high risk and have a high probability of failure.

Very low percentage: Shots to very-low-percentage targets are straight-up bad shot selections. They should never be taken.

Good risk: A shot is considered to be a "good risk" when going for the target produces a good chance of winning the point along with an acceptable chance of making an error. The shot must pay off big to risk making the mistake.

Now let's take a look at those three simple conditions, broken down into twelve components. Below is a chart to help you keep track of all this information.

The three main conditions and their permutations:

Condition 1A: Vector of the oncoming shot is down the middle of the court
Forehand shot / Position: strength covers *only part of the court*

Condition 1B: Vector of the oncoming shot is down the middle of the court
Forehand shot / Position: strength covers *the entire court*

Condition 1C: Vector of the oncoming shot is down the middle of the court
Backhand shot / Position: strength covers *only part of the court*

Condition 1D: Vector of the oncoming shot is down the middle of the court
Backhand shot / Position: strength covers *the entire court*

Condition 2A: Vector of the oncoming shot is crosscourt
Forehand shot / Position: strength covers *only part of the court*

Condition 2B: Vector of the oncoming shot is crosscourt
Forehand shot / Position: strength covers *the entire court*

Condition 2C: Vector of the oncoming shot is crosscourt
Backhand shot / Position: strength covers *only part of the court*

Condition 2D: Vector of the oncoming shot is crosscourt
Backhand shot / Position: strength covers *the entire court*

Condition 3A: Vector of the oncoming shot is down the line
Forehand shot / Position: strength covers *only part of the court*

Condition 3B: Vector of the oncoming shot is down the line
Forehand shot / Position: strength covers *the entire court*

Condition 3C: Vector of the oncoming shot is down the line
Backhand shot / Position: strength covers *only part of the court*

Condition 3D: Vector of the oncoming shot is down the line
Backhand shot / Position: strength covers *the entire court*

Condition 1A: Vector of the Oncoming Shot Is Down the Middle of the Court

Forehand shot

Position: strength covers *only part of the court* (see Figure 1).

Here, the oncoming shot is hit right down the middle of the court, and you are hitting a forehand. In Figure 1, your strength covers half of the court. Your shoulders and feet are positioned so that only the left side of the court is in strength. In this condition, there are two high-percentage targets.

Crosscourt Target to the Left Side of the Court: Very High Percentage

The target to the left side of the court is your best shot selection. This target is very high percentage because it is right in the center of your strength. The target is off the vector of the incoming shot, but the deflection factor will be overcome as you drive the ball into your strength. Because you are shooting crosscourt, you have more "miss distance" long in the court. All of these factors make this shot very high percentage.

Middle-of-Court Target: High Percentage

The target right up the middle of the court, directly on the vector of the oncoming shot, is high percentage. This target is at the edge of your strength. It is still in strength, though, which makes it high percentage. Because the target is directly on the vector of the oncoming shot, there is no deflection factor. Since this target is in strength and has no deflection factor, it is a high-percentage shot.

Crosscourt Target to the Right Side of the Court: Low Percentage

The low-percentage target is to the right side of the court, on the weak side. Because the target is out of strength, you will be pushing this shot. The target is also off the vector of the oncoming shot, so it will deflect away from the target. Because you are aiming out of strength, the deflection factor will be significant. This is a bad play and a low-percentage shot.

Line of strength

The middle of the court target is high percentage. It is on the edge of your strength and on vector.

In Strength | Out of Strength

The cross court target to the left side of the court, is very high percentage because it is deep in strength and you have more court to shoot for.

The target to the right side of the court is low percentage. It is out of strength and off vector.

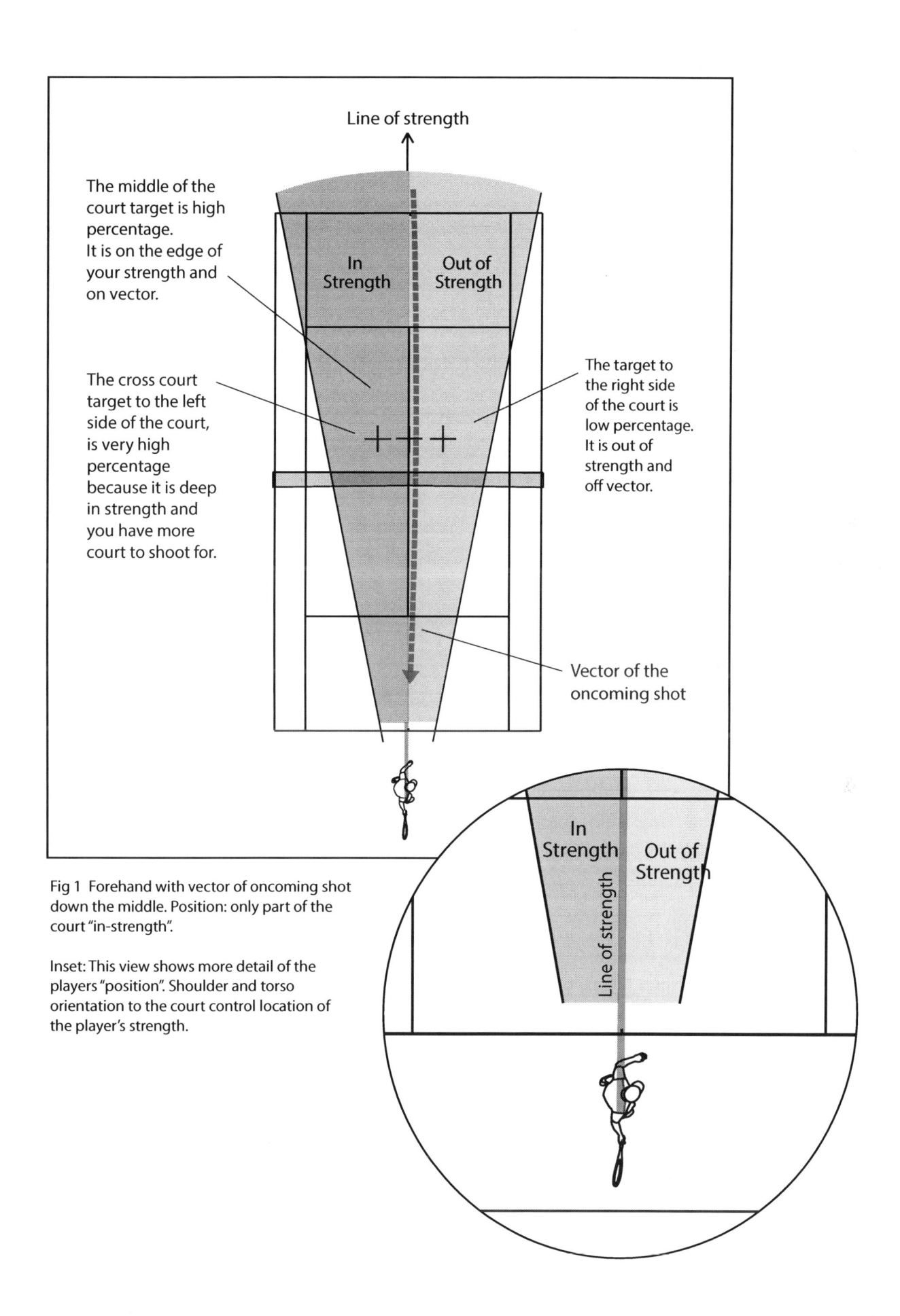

Vector of the oncoming shot

Fig 1 Forehand with vector of oncoming shot down the middle. Position: only part of the court "in-strength".

Inset: This view shows more detail of the players "position". Shoulder and torso orientation to the court control location of the player's strength.

In Strength | Out of Strength

Line of strength

HOW TO MAKE HIGH PERCENTAGE SHOT SELECTIONS | 109

Condition 1B: Vector of the Oncoming Shot Is Down the Middle of the Court

Forehand shot

Position: strength covers *the entire court* (see Figure 2).

In figure 2, you are playing another forehand. Your feet and shoulders are positioned so that your line of strength is pointing to the right side of the court. Here, your strength covers the entire court. This position offers more high-percentage shots.

Crosscourt Target to the Left Side of the Court: Very High Percentage

The target to the left side of the court is now deep in your strength. Even though it is off the vector of the oncoming shot, the pulling power of the racket will overcome deflection. Also, because the shot is on a crosscourt angle, there is more court to shoot into. This is a very-high-percentage shot in this position. You can hammer this shot with confidence.

Middle-of-the-Court Target: Very High Percentage

This target is now in the middle of strength, giving you excellent control. Since the target is directly on the vector of the oncoming shot, there is no tendency for your shot to deflect. This target is now very high percentage. You can hit this shot hard with success.

Crosscourt Target to the Right Side of the Court: High Percentage

The target to the right side of the court is now a high-percentage shot. By moving your feet and shoulders, your strength now covers this target. Although there will be the tendency for the shot to deflect (because the target is off vector), remember that strength overcomes deflection. It is now a high-percentage shot because it is in strength.

Also remember that in the aiming chapter, we chose targets that were very conservative. We used three targets. Our goal was to shoot the ball to the middle, to the left side, and to the right side of the court. Those targets are very close to the center tape, near the middle of the net, and they produce shots that land well inside the court. The reason for this is the deflection factor. In each case, when you are aiming off the vector of the oncoming shot, your target needs to be conservative due to your shot's tendency to deflect. This applies to all off-vector targets.

Your goal is to approach zero errors. You want to hit almost every shot in the court. With these conservative targets, your errors and misses will go in the court for winners, and not out for errors. This is commonly called hitting shots with good "margin." This means shooting for conservative targets with a good amount of court to miss into.

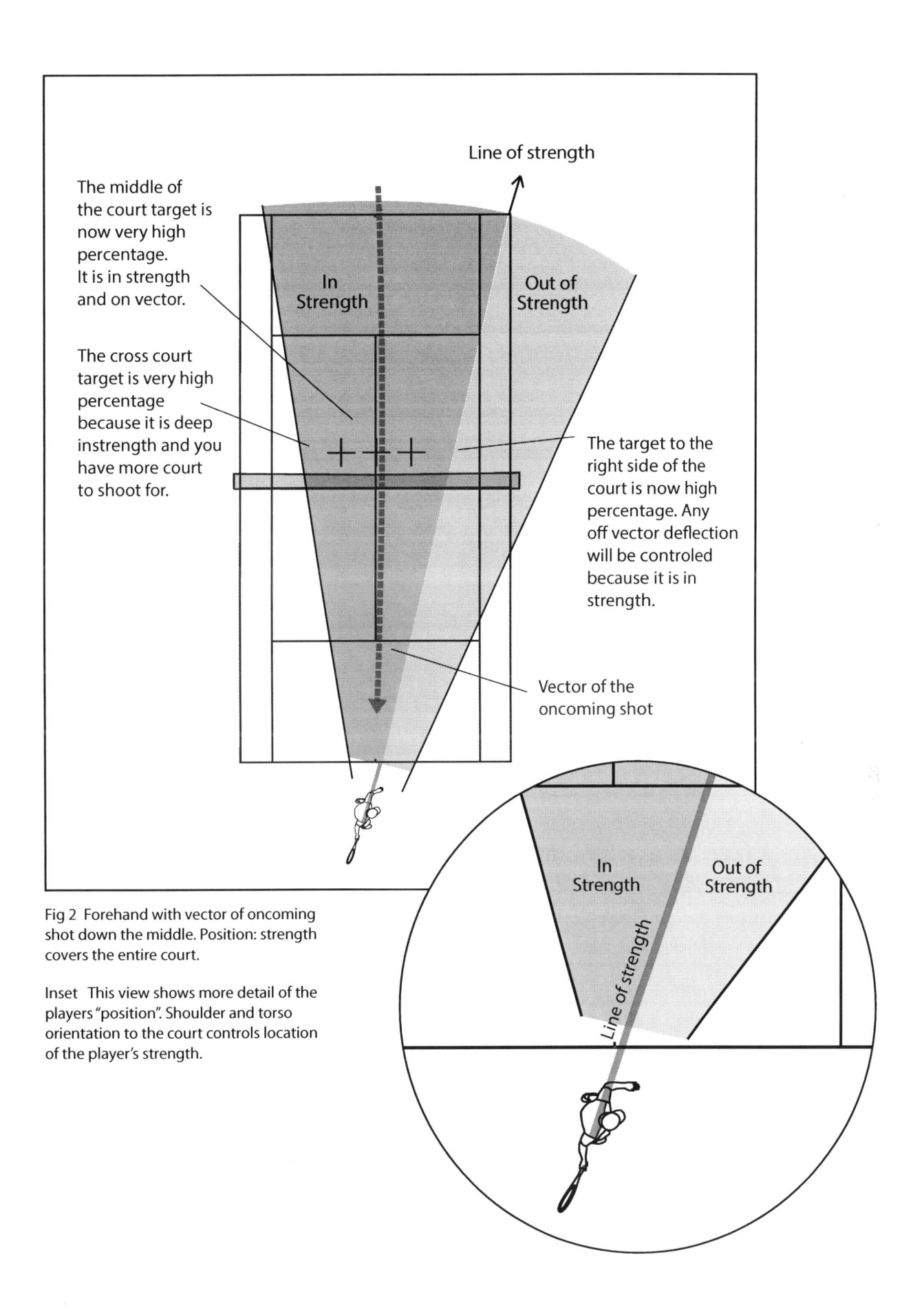

Line of strength

In Strength

Out of Strength

The middle of the court target is now very high percentage. It is in strength and on vector.

The cross court target is very high percentage because it is deep instrength and you have more court to shoot for.

The target to the right side of the court is now high percentage. Any off vector deflection will be controled because it is in strength.

Vector of the oncoming shot

Fig 2 Forehand with vector of oncoming shot down the middle. Position: strength covers the entire court.

Inset This view shows more detail of the players "position". Shoulder and torso orientation to the court controls location of the player's strength.

In Strength

Out of Strength

Line of strength

HOW TO MAKE HIGH PERCENTAGE SHOT SELECTIONS | 111

Condition 1C: Vector of the Oncoming Shot Is Down the Middle of the Court

Backhand shot

Position: strength covers *only part of the court* (see Figure 3).

In Figure 3, the vector of the ball is up the middle of the court, and you are hitting a backhand. Your shoulders and line of strength are pointed straight up the middle of the court. In this position, your strength only covers one side of the court. Just as in the forehand example, there are two high-percentage targets, as follows.

Crosscourt Target to the Right Side of the Court: Very High Percentage

This target is well into your strength, making it a very-high-percentage target. There is a some deflection factor, but the pulling power of your stroke will control the deflection. Also, because you are shooting crosscourt, you have more miss distance long in the court. This also makes the shot high percentage.

Middle-of-the-Court Target: High Percentage

The target straight up the middle of the court is a high-percentage shot. It is on the edge of strength, but still in strength. The target is directly on the vector of the oncoming shot, so there is no deflection factor. This shot can be hit hard with confidence.

Crosscourt Target to the Left Side of the Court: Low Percentage

The target to the left side of the court is a low-percentage shot. It is out of strength, so you are pushing the ball. The ball is on your strings for a short period of time, and you have less influence over its flight path. The target is also off vector. Shots to this target will deflect, and the deflection will be more significant because you are shooting for a target out of strength. Shots to this target are low percentage.

Line of strength

Out of Strength | **In Strength**

The middle of the court target is high percentage. It is on the edge of your strength and on vector.

The target to the left side of the court is low percentage. It is out of strength and off vector.

The cross court target is very high percentage because it is deep in strength.

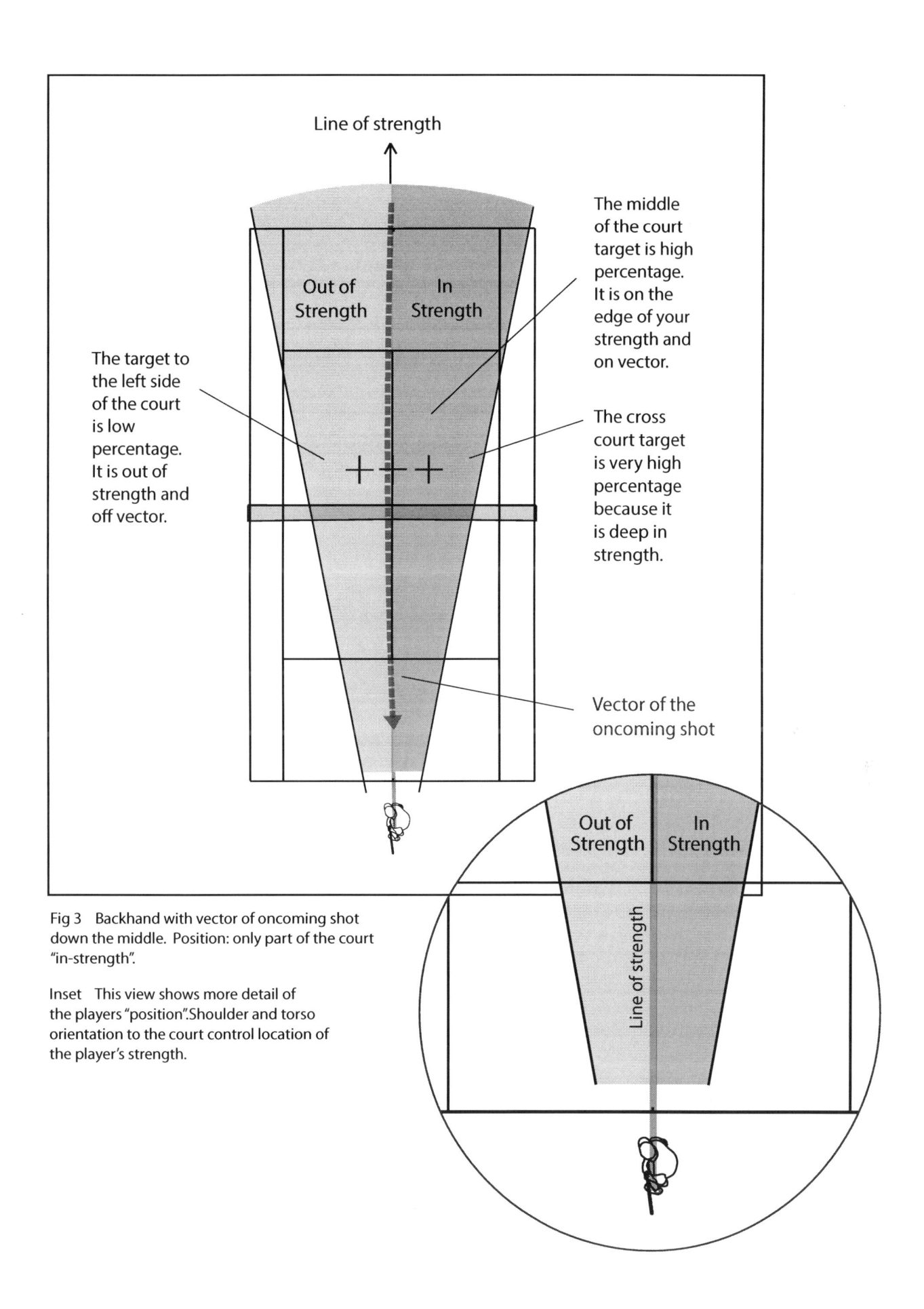

Vector of the oncoming shot

Out of Strength | **In Strength**

Line of strength

Fig 3 Backhand with vector of oncoming shot down the middle. Position: only part of the court "in-strength".

Inset   This view shows more detail of the players "position". Shoulder and torso orientation to the court control location of the player's strength.

HOW TO MAKE HIGH PERCENTAGE SHOT SELECTIONS | 113

Condition 1D: Vector of the Oncoming Shot Is Down the Middle of the Court

Backhand shot
Position: strength covers *the entire court* (see Figure 4).
In figure 4, your strength covers the entire court. This position is achieved by moving your torso, shoulders, and feet. They are placed so that the line of strength is pointing to the left side of the court.

Crosscourt Target to the Right Side of the Court: Very High Percentage

The shot to the right side of the court is a very-high-percentage shot. This target is deep in strength. The target is off vector, but deflection off vector will be minimal because the target is in strength. Because you are shooting crosscourt, you have more miss distance long in the court. This also makes the shot high percentage. You can crush this shot.

Middle-of-the-Court Target: Very High Percentage

The target straight up the middle is now very high percentage. This target is well in your strength. It is also on vector, producing zero deflection factor. You can hammer this shot with a high rate of success.

Crosscourt Target to the Left Side of the Court: High Percentage

The target to the left side of the court is now a high-percentage shot because it is in strength. There is a deflection factor, but the deflection should be controlled by the placement of strength to that portion of the court. Because you are well positioned, you can shoot for this target with confidence.

Line of strength

Out of Strength

In Strength

The middle of the court target is now very high percentage. It is in strength and on vector.

The cross court target to the right side of the court is very high percentage because it is deep in strength.

The target to the left side of the court is now high percentage. Any off vector deflection will be controlled because it is in strength.

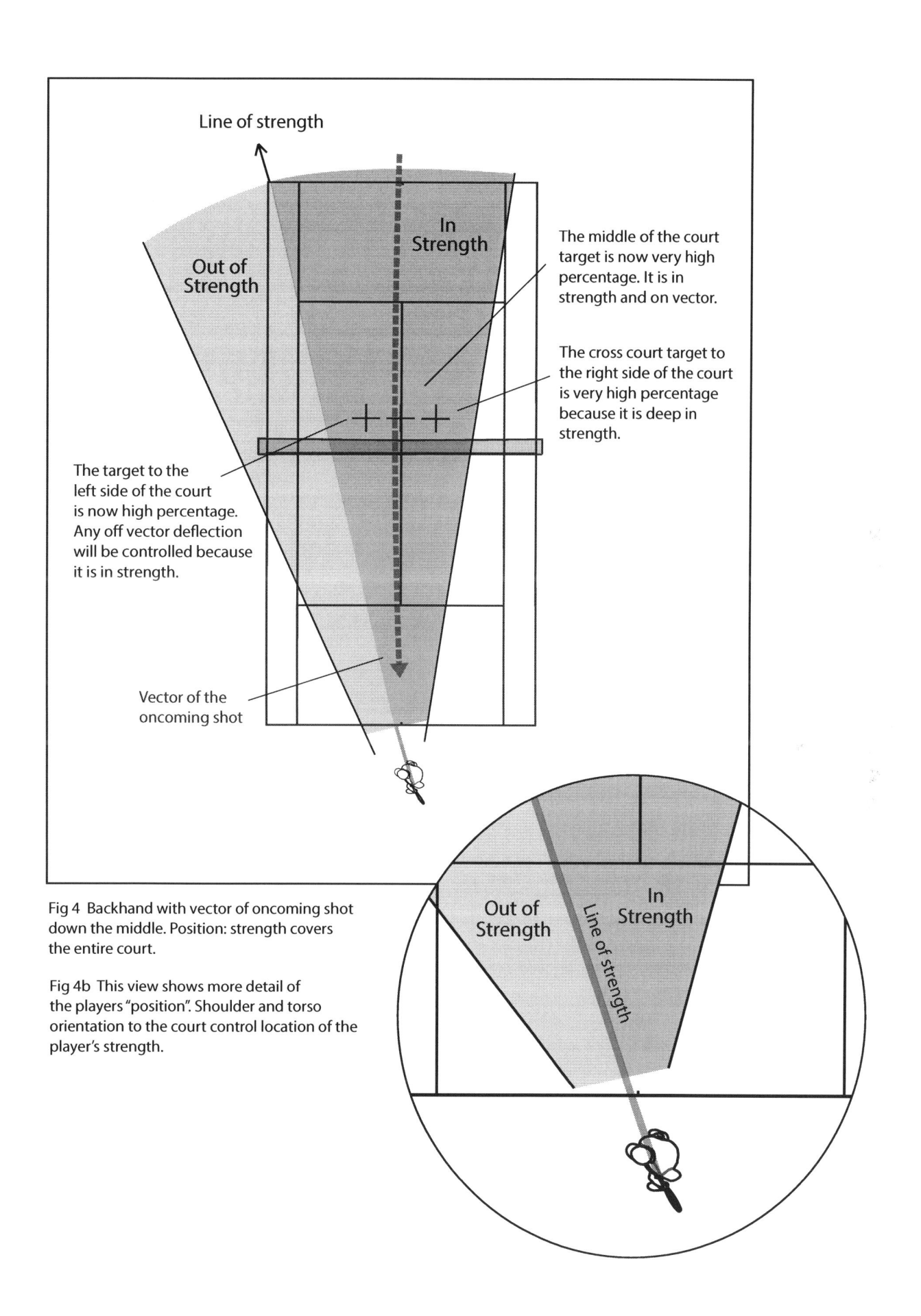

Vector of the oncoming shot

Out of Strength

In Strength

Line of strength

Fig 4 Backhand with vector of oncoming shot down the middle. Position: strength covers the entire court.

Fig 4b This view shows more detail of the players "position". Shoulder and torso orientation to the court control location of the player's strength.

HOW TO MAKE HIGH PERCENTAGE SHOT SELECTIONS | 115

Condition 2A: Vector of the Oncoming Shot Is Crosscourt

Forehand shot
Position: strength covers *only part of the court* (see Figure 5).

In the second condition, the oncoming shot vector is crosscourt. The shot is coming from the left side of the court, and the ball's vector is to the opposite corner, crosscourt.

In Figure 5, you are receiving the ball on your forehand side. Your shoulders and feet are positioned so that your line of strength is directly on the vector of the ball. This position is common, especially when players are rushed and don't have much time to prepare for the shot.

Crosscourt Target: Very High Percentage

Playing this ball in this position, the crosscourt target to the left side of the court is a very-high-percentage target. This target is in strength and on vector. Because this target is directly along the vector of the oncoming shot, there is zero deflection factor. And since you are pulling to strength, you will dominate the direction of your shot. Finally, because you are shooting crosscourt, you have more miss distance long in the court over the lowest part of the net. This also makes the shot high percentage. This shot can be hit really hard, with very high confidence.

High-Angle Target: Good Risk

There is another target to choose in this situation: the high-angle target we talked about earlier. You can choose a target slightly to the left of the crosscourt target, deeper in strength. One caveat here is that you are running out of court. The angle is extreme, and with less real estate to shoot for, you will tend to miss wide of the court. But this target is very much in your strength. You can take a good risk here and go for this shot, increasing the angle of the play. In order to be successful with this shot, however, you have to play the arc with a lot of topspin. You need to flip your racket rounder than the arc to get your shot to dip into the court. This is a fun shot to go for. Go ahead and rip some of these to see what it takes to get the ball down and into the court when you take this chance.

Important: The high-angle target is very close to the crosscourt target. You don't have to move your target very far to the left to get the extreme angle. This is critical for success with this shot.

Line of strength

The cross court target right over the center of the net is very high percentage. It is in strength and on vector. You can crush this shot.

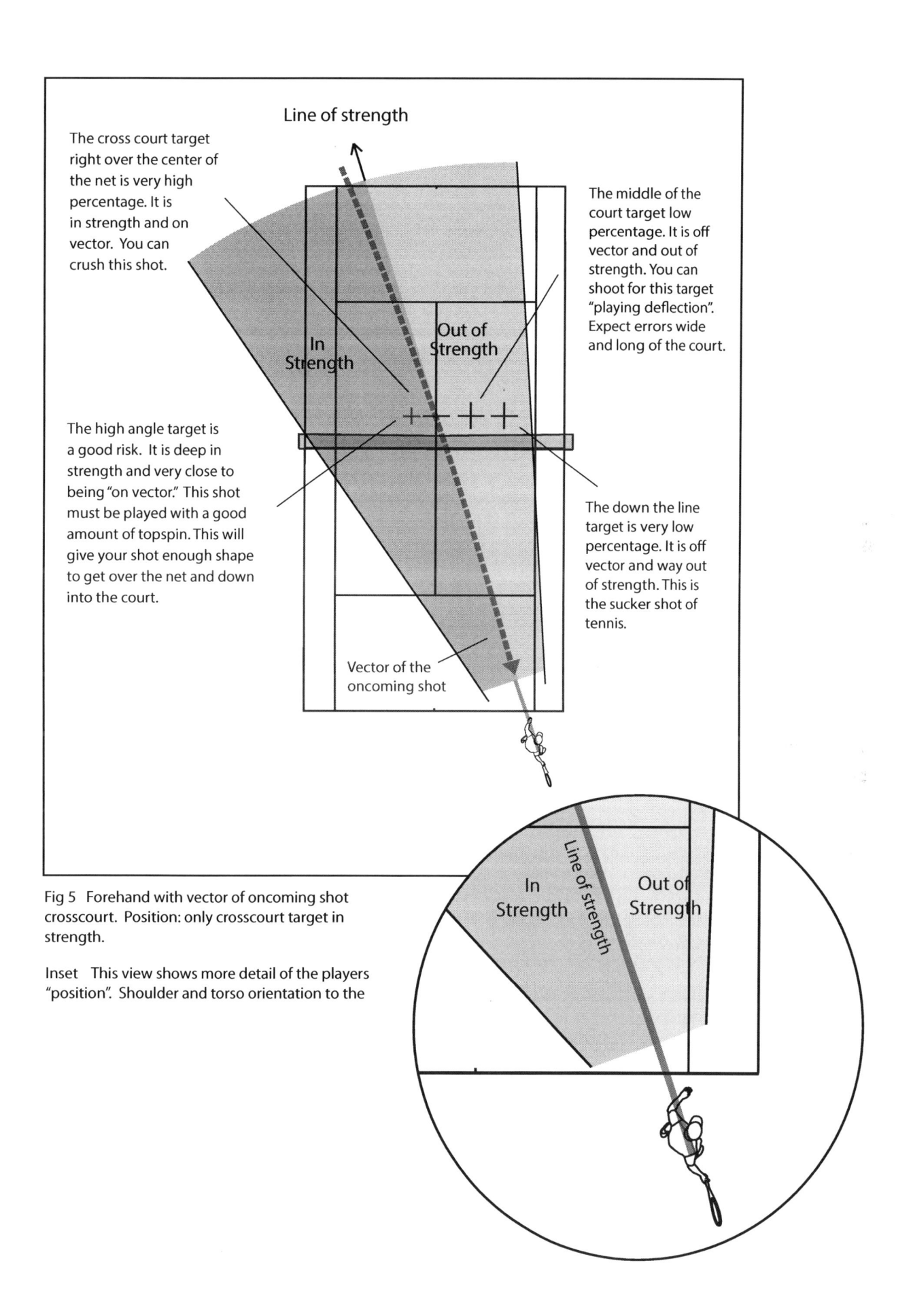

The middle of the court target low percentage. It is off vector and out of strength. You can shoot for this target "playing deflection". Expect errors wide and long of the court.

In Strength

Out of Strength

The high angle target is a good risk. It is deep in strength and very close to being "on vector." This shot must be played with a good amount of topspin. This will give your shot enough shape to get over the net and down into the court.

The down the line target is very low percentage. It is off vector and way out of strength. This is the sucker shot of tennis.

Vector of the oncoming shot

Fig 5 Forehand with vector of oncoming shot crosscourt. Position: only crosscourt target in strength.

Inset   This view shows more detail of the players "position". Shoulder and torso orientation to the

Line of strength

In Strength

Out of Strength

HOW TO MAKE HIGH PERCENTAGE SHOT SELECTIONS | 117

Condition 2A, *continued*

Middle-of-the-Court Target: Low Percentage

The target to the center of the court, just to the right of the tape, is out of strength and off vector. Because of this, it is a low-percentage play. This shot will definitely deflect toward the open court. This is especially true if you are playing a ball that is a deep, high-speed, hard-hit shot. You can take this shot, but expect some large errors wide of your target and/or long of the court. This is an acceptable risk at times if you really need to change the angle of play when you are being dominated on the crosscourt angle.

Playing Deflection

Taking this risk is called "playing deflection." When you choose this target out of strength and off vector, you know it will deflect; in this case it deflects into the open court. You can make this shot selection, looking for deflection to produce a good shot nearly down the line. Just know that there is a high risk of error, long and wide of the court.

Down-the-Line Target: Very Low Percentage

The shot for the right side of the court, down the line, is very low percentage. It seems like the right side of the court is wide open, and you should be able to choose a target there and find success, but this is one of tennis's "sucker shots." When you are in this position and you go for a target well out of strength and off vector, you are showing bad judgment. In the aiming chapter, we talked about the circle of error being elliptical when you shoot down the line. This is the condition where the circle of error gets very elliptical. A lot of wide misses happen when players shoot for a target in that gaping open court, out of strength and way off vector; this is especially true if they are playing a ball that is a deep, high-speed shot.

Strength against Strength

When you are in this position, with your strength covering only the crosscourt, on-vector target, it is imperative that you shoot for the very-high-percentage target right on the vector of the oncoming ball. You can crush this shot. It is better to make this play and wait for another inbound shot that is weaker and easier to play. The weaker inbound shot will give you more time to get your strength positioned toward the open court. Watch a professional match. You will see a lot of plays on this line crosscourt—strength against strength. To the uneducated, it looks like the players should be shooting for the open court. If you know about strength and position and the vector of the oncoming shot, though, then you know the players are making the high-percentage plays and biding their time. They are waiting for a weaker inbound shot. They are waiting for the chance to get better positioned. They are waiting for the chance to get their torso and shoulders set so that their strength will cover the open court. When in position, they take the shot down the line to the open court with success.

Condition 2B: Vector of the Oncoming Shot Is Crosscourt

Forehand shot
Position: strength covers *the entire court* (see Figure 6).

In Figure 6, you are receiving the crosscourt ball to your forehand again. Your shoulders and feet are set so that your strength is covering the open court. In this position, you have more high-percentage targets.

Crosscourt Target: Very High Percentage

The target that is crosscourt, dead center over the net, and directly on the vector of the oncoming shot is a very-high-percentage target. This target is deep in strength, and the pulling power of your racket will fully control the ball. Because it is right on the vector of the ball, there will be zero deflection. And because you are shooting crosscourt, you have more miss distance long in the court. This also makes the shot very high percentage. This shot can be hammered. You can hit this shot with maximum power and with high confidence of success.

High-Angle Target: Good Risk

The high-angle target is a good risk in this position. It is deep in strength, so your stroke's power and the amount of time the ball is on your strings is maximized. The target is slightly off vector, but your strength will dominate this deflection. The only limiting factor on this shot is that you are running out of court. Because of the extreme angle, you have a higher chance of hitting the shot wide of the sideline. It is still a good-risk shot, though. This shot will work better and better for you as you learn to play the arcs and apply greater topspin to curve this ball down into the court. As your arc play improves, you will be able to strike this shot with extreme topspin and increase the angle of play dramatically.

Middle-of-Court Target: High Percentage

The target for the center of the court is now high percentage. Your strength covers this target, and deflection will be minimized. You can crush this shot with confidence. The only problem with this shot selection is that it may not challenge your opponent. It is a good option if you are trying to jam her, but it will probably be one that she will easily play.

Down-the-Line Target: Dependent

With your strength covering the entire court, the target down the line, to the right side of the court, is dependent. This target, in all cases, is a lower-percentage shot, because the net is higher and the court is shorter when going down the line. But your probability of success depends on other factors. They are the depth and speed of the oncoming shot and how much time you have prepare to get into position. This shot is low percentage if you are rushed getting your strength out

Line of strength

In Strength

Out of Strength

The cross court target, right over the center of the net, is very high percentage. It is deep in strength and on vector. You can crush this shot.

The high angle target is a good risk. It is deep in strength and near the vector of the oncoming shot. This shot must be played with a good amount of topspin. This will give your shot enough shape to get over the net and down into the court.

Vector of the oncoming shot

The middle of the court target high percentage. It is in strength and near the vecto of the oncoming shot. You can hit this hard with high confidence.

The down the line target is now dependant. It is in strength but way off vector to the shortest part of the court over the highest part of the net. If the oncoming shot is:
- slowly hit, it is high percentage.
- shallow in the court, it is high percentage.
- hard hit and deep in the court is a good risk. If you are rushed getting into position this shot is low percentage. If you are in position early your chance of success goes up regardless of the depth and speed of the oncoming shot.

Fig 6   Forehand with vector of oncoming shot

Inset   This view shows more detail of the players "position". Shoulder and torso orientation to the court control location of the player's strength.

In Strength

Out of Strength

Line of strength

HOW TO MAKE HIGH PERCENTAGE SHOT SELECTIONS | 121

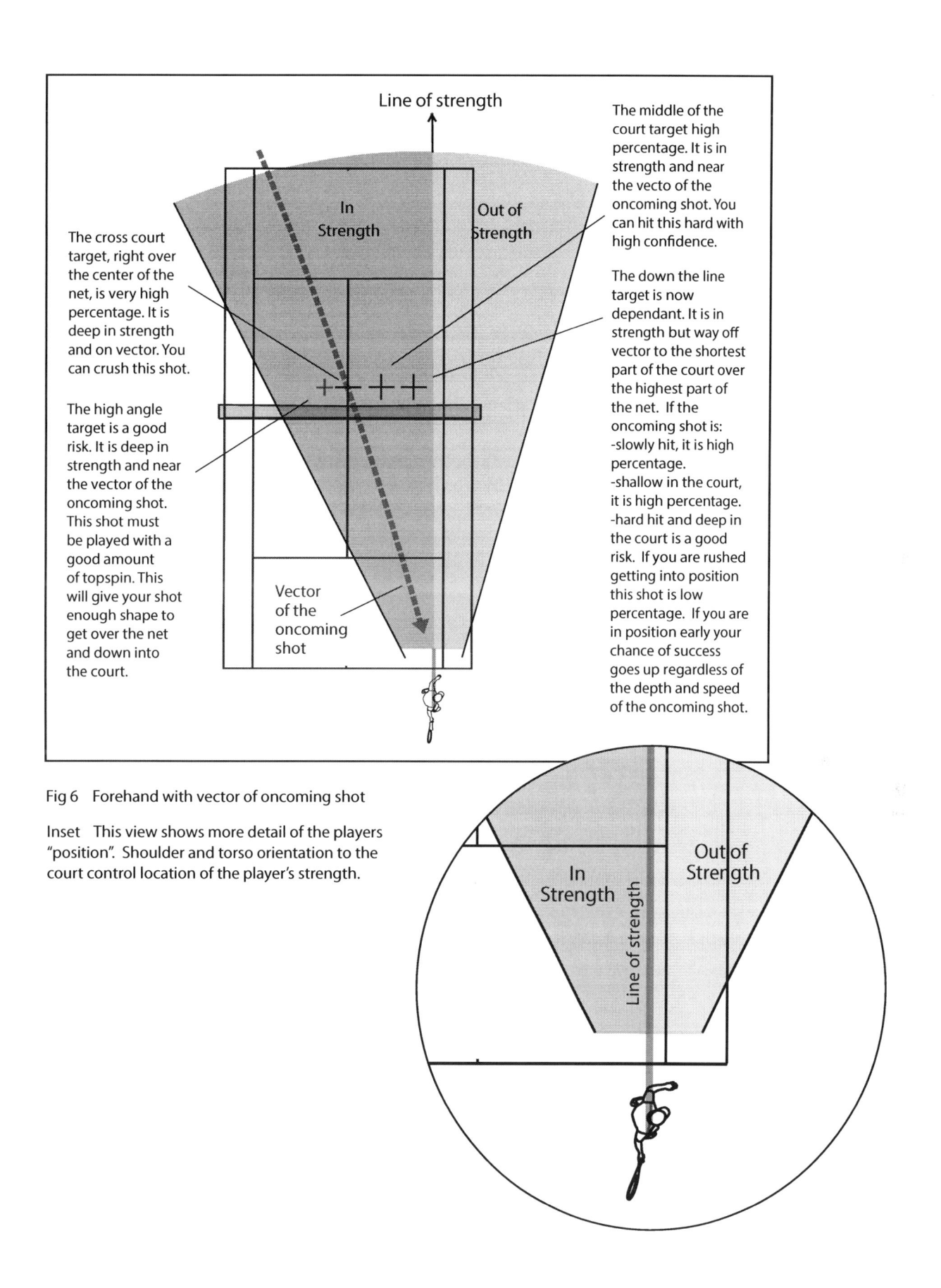

over that portion of the court. If you are in position early controlling your strength well, your probability of success goes up dramatically. If the oncoming shot lands short in the court and you are in good position, this shot is high percentage. If the oncoming shot is slow paced and you are in good position, this is a high-percentage shot. If your are in position early and are playing a hard-hit shot deep in the court, this shot is a good risk. There will be a chance of error but making the shot can pay off big, possibly winning the point. This is when you take the risk of "changing direction" and shooting down the line, off vector.

Notice that this target does not direct the ball directly at the sideline. If you hit your target dead on, your shot will actually land in the middle of the right side of the court. The reason for this conservative target is the deflection factor. Remember, your circle of error becomes elliptical when you shoot off vector. Even when your target is in strength, your shot will tend to deflect to the right of the target, near the sideline. This is especially true if you are playing a hard-hit, fast-moving ball. If you choose a target that is very close to the sideline, you will miss a lot of shots wide of the court. That is why we choose a target that shoots the ball to the middle of the right side of the court. Let deflection take your ball near the sideline for a winner.

Shooting Closer to the Lines

In certain circumstances, you can choose a target farther off the vector of the ball, closer to the sideline. If you look back at Figure 6, you have great position, with your strength covering the entire court. If the shot that is hit to you is a sitter, with little pace, you can move your target farther off vector toward the sideline. Because the ball has very little speed, the deflection factor will be minimal, and your strength will completely direct your shot on-target. It is important to note that this is a risky shot. As you improve your understanding of strength and position and get better at ripping the arcs, you will learn when you can take this risk. Even if the ball is a sitter and your position is excellent, the target you select should still give you at least some margin of error. Remember, you're going to make errors. We want our errors to go in the court for winners, and not out of the court for a lost point.

Condition 2C: Vector of the Oncoming Shot Is Crosscourt

Backhand shot
Position: strength covers *only part of the court* (see Figure 7).

Here, the oncoming shot is received on the backhand, and the ball's vector is crosscourt from the opposite corner. Your position is not great here. Your line of strength is right along the vector of the oncoming shot.

The middle of the court target low percentage. It is off vector and out of strength. You can shoot for this target "playing deflection". Expect errors wide and long of the court.

The down the line target is very low percentage. It is off vector and way out of strength. This is the sucker shot of tennis.

The cross court target right over the center of the net is very high percentage. It is in strength and on vector. You can crush this shot.

The high angle target is a good risk. It is deep in strenght but you are running out of court. This shot must be played with a good amount of topspin. This will give your shot enough shape to get over the net and down into the court.

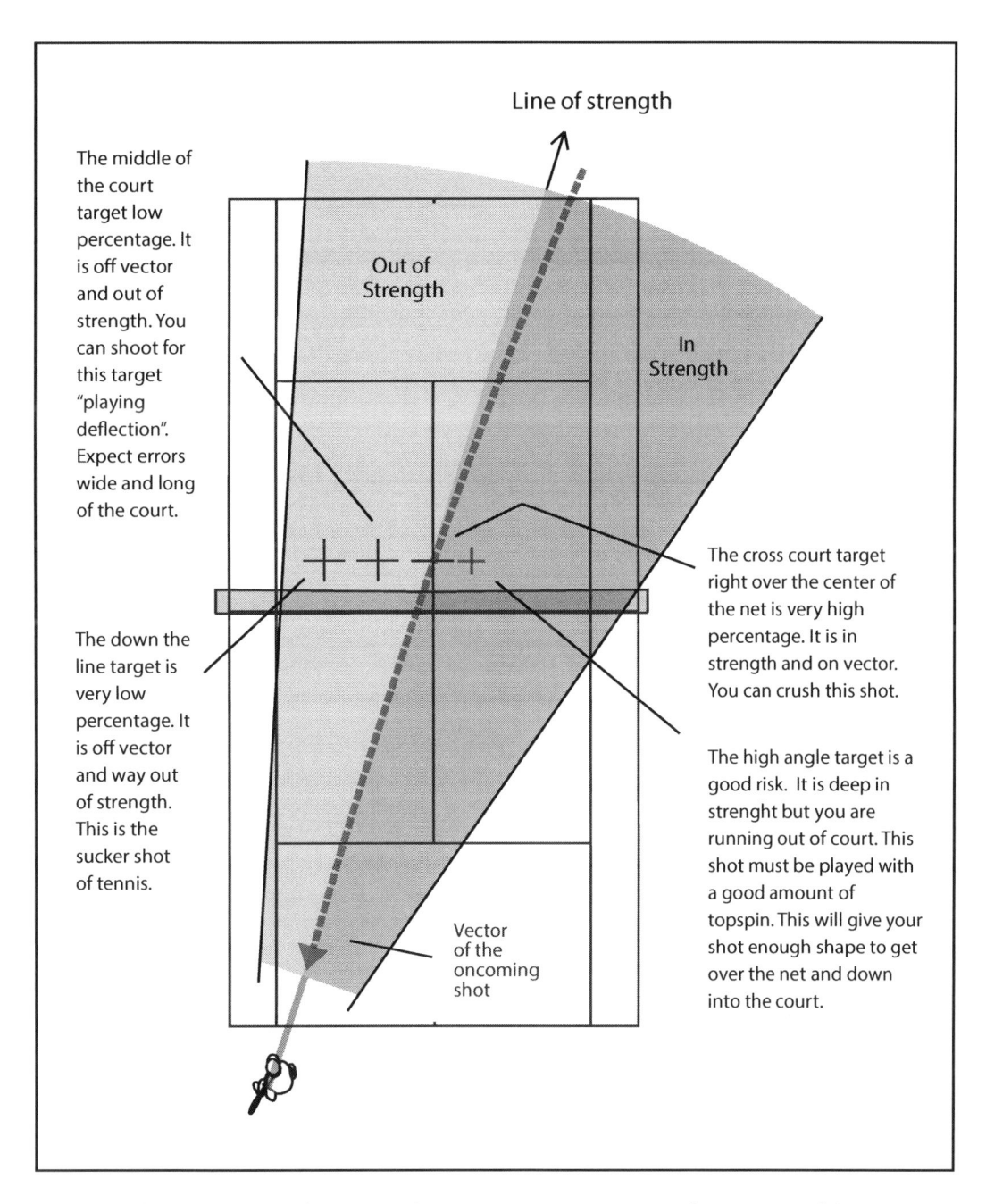

Fig 7   Backhand with vector of oncoming shot crosscourt. Position: strength covers part of the court.

HOW TO MAKE HIGH PERCENTAGE SHOT SELECTIONS | 123

Crosscourt Target: Very High Percentage

Just as in the forehand example, for the same reasons, you have only one very-high-percentage target with this condition. That target is right on the vector of the ball, directly over the center of the net. This target is in strength and on vector, so the pulling path of your racket will control your shot. Because the target is on vector, there is zero deflection factor, thus increasing your chances of success. Because you are shooting crosscourt, you have a lot of miss distance long in the court. This shot can be crushed with low chance of error.

High-Angle Target: Good Risk

You can also choose the high-angle target as a good risk. This increased angle is deeper in strength, but you are running out of court, and there will be some deflection. To have success with this high-angle shot, you must play the arc with more topspin to get it down into the court. This can be a challenge for one-handed backhand players. If you do play a one-handed backhand, and you have not gotten the hang of flipping over the arc, it is more prudent to choose a target that is directly on the vector of the ball. If you are a one-handed backhand player, you can try this high-angle shot with less pace. Shooting a slower shot with more finesse may give you more success at getting the ball down and into the court. Two-handed backhand players will find more success with this high-angle target. Because of the added power of the second hand and the full-torso turn, they will be more successful in controlling this shot. If you are a two-handed backhand player, you need to get this shot into your arsenal. It is very effective for you, and it will win you a lot of points. Both one-handed and two-handed backhand hitters should use this target. You will learn through experimentation when to choose this shot. *Remember, the target for this shot is just to the right, very close to the crosscourt target.*

Center-of-Court Target: Low Percentage

The target for the center of the court in this condition is a low-percentage shot. If you shoot for this target, your shot will deflect toward the open court. The circle of error is elliptical in this case. You should also expect errors long of the court. You can choose this shot playing deflection. Know that your shot will deflect off-target toward the open court. Expect errors wide and long of the court.

Down-the-Line Target: Very Low Percentage

In this condition, the down-the-line target, to the left side of the court, is a very low-percentage shot. This target is way out of your strength, which reduces your control. There is a big deflection factor as you are shooting at a target way off vector. You also have less court to shoot for, and the net is higher here. All these factors make this shot very low percentage.

Condition 2D: Vector of the Oncoming Shot Is Crosscourt

Backhand shot
Position: strength covers *the entire court* (see Figure 8).

In Figure 8, you are receiving the crosscourt shot to your backhand again. But here, you are well positioned. Your shoulders and torso are positioned so that your line of strength points up the sideline, and your strength covers the open court. Just as in the forehand example, you have a lot of high-percentage targets.

Line of strength

Out of Strength

In Strength

The middle of the court target high percentage. It is in strength and near the vecto of the oncoming shot. You can hit this hard with high confidence.

The down the line target is now dependant. If the oncoming shot is:
- slowly hit, it is high percentage.
- shallow in the court, it is high percentage.
- hard hit and deep in the court it is a good risk.
If you are rushed getting into position this shot is low percentage.
If you are in position early your chance of success goes up regardless of the depth and speed of the oncoming shot.

The cross court target, right over the center of the net, is very high percentage. It is deep in strength and on vector. You can crush this shot.

The high angle target is a good risk. It is deep in strength and near the vector of the oncoming shot. This shot must be played with a good amount of topspin. This will give your shot enough shape to get over the net and down into the court.

Vector of the oncoming shot

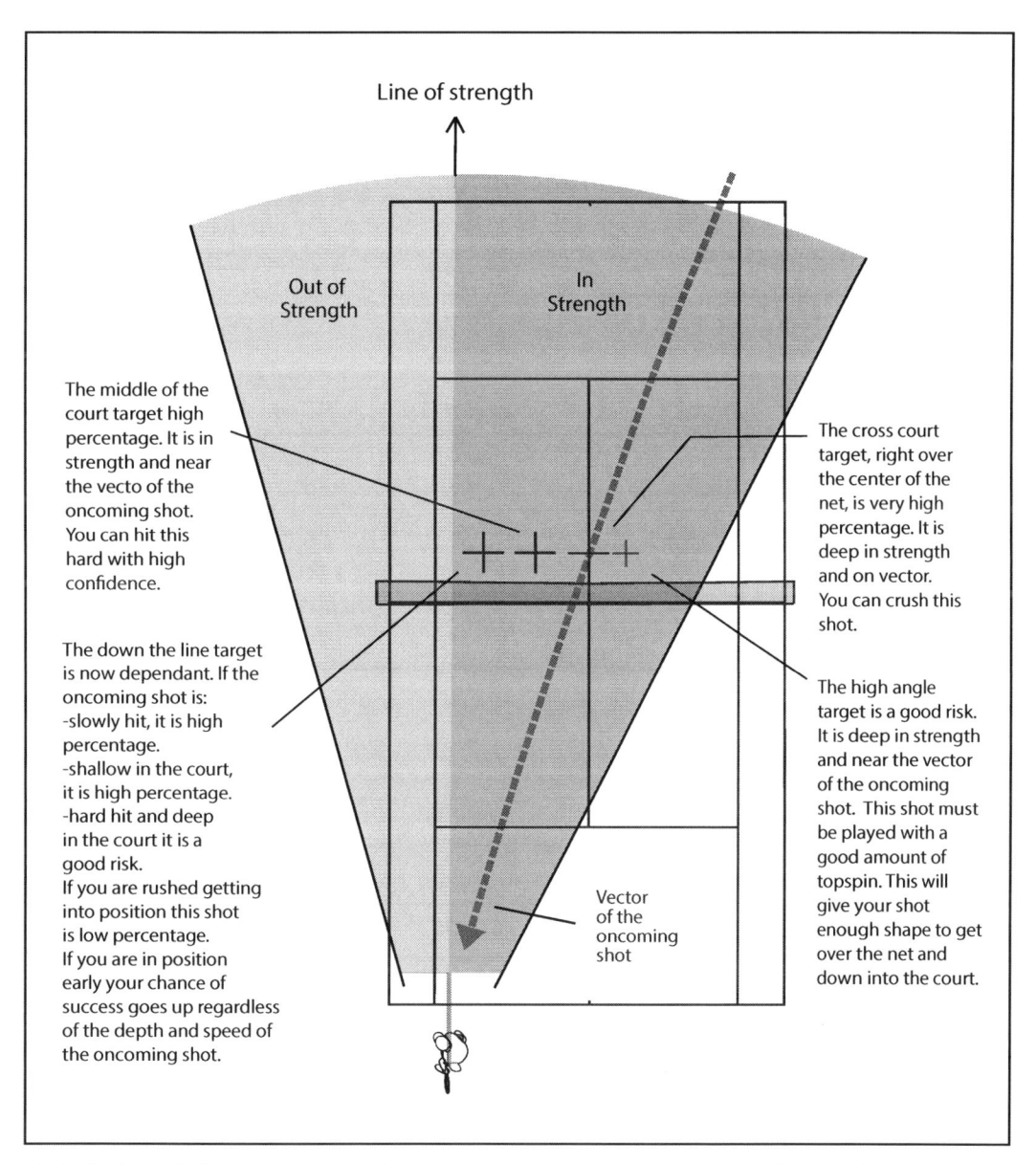

Fig 8 Backhand with vector of oncoming shot crosscourt. Position: entire court in strength.

Crosscourt Target: Very High Percentage

The very-high-percentage target is crosscourt, directly along the vector of the oncoming shot. This target is deep in strength and has no deflection factor. You can crush this shot at your maximum power.

High-Angle Target: Good Risk

The high-angle target is a good risk. There is some deflection factor to deal with, but since the target is deep in strength, it will be minimal. The only problem with this shot is that you are running out of court; the chance of missing wide is therefore increased. You need to experiment with the high-angle shot and learn where to target and aim it so that it will become a real weapon for you. The arc must be played with more topspin to ensure that it dips down into the court. This shot is easier for a two-handed backhand, as we discussed above. Most players miss this high-angle shot because they shoot for a target that is far too wide of the center tape. *The target for this shot is just to the right of the crosscourt target.*

Center-of-the-Court Target: High Percentage

The target for the center of the court is now a high-percentage shot. It is in the middle of your strength. You do have some deflection factor to deal with, but your strength should overcome this, and you have a lot of court to miss into if the ball deflects wide. The only problem with this shot is that it may not challenge your opponent, since it lands in the center of the court, but it is a good option if you are attempting to jam your opponent.

Down-the-Line Target: Dependent

With your strength covering the entire court, the down-the-line target is dependent. If the oncoming shot is slow paced, it is high percentage. If the oncoming shot lands short in the court, the down-the-line target is also high percentage. If the oncoming shot is deep and hit hard, on the other hand, then this shot is a good risk. If you are rushed getting into position, this shot is low percentage. It is important to have quality position when taking this shot. In order for you to be successful here, you need to be well set, with your strength covering the down-the-line target. This down-the-line shot always carries inherent risk, since you have less court to shoot for and the net is higher; if you have quality position, however, this shot is high percentage, and you will enjoy success shooting off vector, "changing direction."

Whenever you shoot for the down-the-line target off an oncoming crosscourt ball, your shot will tend to deflect. This is true even when your strength covers the target. Because of this deflection factor, the target is not right at the sideline. This allows for the deflection and the elliptical circle of error. Keep this target conservative, and your errors will "paste" the line for winners.

"The next point—that's all you must think about"

—Rod Laver

Condition 3A: Vector of the Oncoming Shot Is Down the Line

Forehand shot

Position: strength covers *only part of the court* (see Figure 9).

In Figure 9, you are receiving a shot that your opponent hits from the side of the court up the line at your forehand. Here, your shoulders and line of strength are pointing to the opposite corner of the court. You have not had the time to get your shoulders turned and your feet positioned to cover more of the court with your strength.

Crosscourt Target: Very High Percentage

The only true high-percentage target here is dead center over the middle of the net, shooting for the left side of the court. This crosscourt target is in strength, and you have a lot of court to shoot at. Since the target is off vector, there will be some deflection, but since the target is in strength, that deflection will be minimal. You can hit this shot really hard with a high level of confidence.

High-Angle Target: Dependent

With this position, the high-angle target to the left of the center of the net is dependent. The target is deep in strength, but there is a big deflection factor to deal with. You are also running out of court, and the chance of missing wide is increased. If the shot you are playing is slow and shallow, this shot can be a good risk. If you are playing a hard-hit and deep ball, however, the high-angle shot is low percentage.

Middle-of-the-Court Target: Low Percentage

The target for the middle of the court is now a low-percentage shot. It is off vector and out of strength. The shot will deflect. With this position it is better to choose cross-court target in strength.

Down-the-Line Target: Dependent

The down-the-line target to the right side of the court is dependent. It is way out of your strength, so your control over the shot is degraded. But the target is directly on the vector of the oncoming shot, which means zero deflection. This out-of-strength / on-vector condition is the only circumstance in which you can successfully shoot for a target out of strength. For this shot to be a good risk, you need to have exact timing: you need to flow perfectly with the oncoming shot. If you are flowing on time, the shot is a good risk. If you are rushed and uncomfortable with your timing, on the other hand, then it is a low-percentage shot. It can be used as a high-risk surprise play to try to wrong-foot an opponent who is moving to cover your strength. Expect errors when you take this chance to win the point.

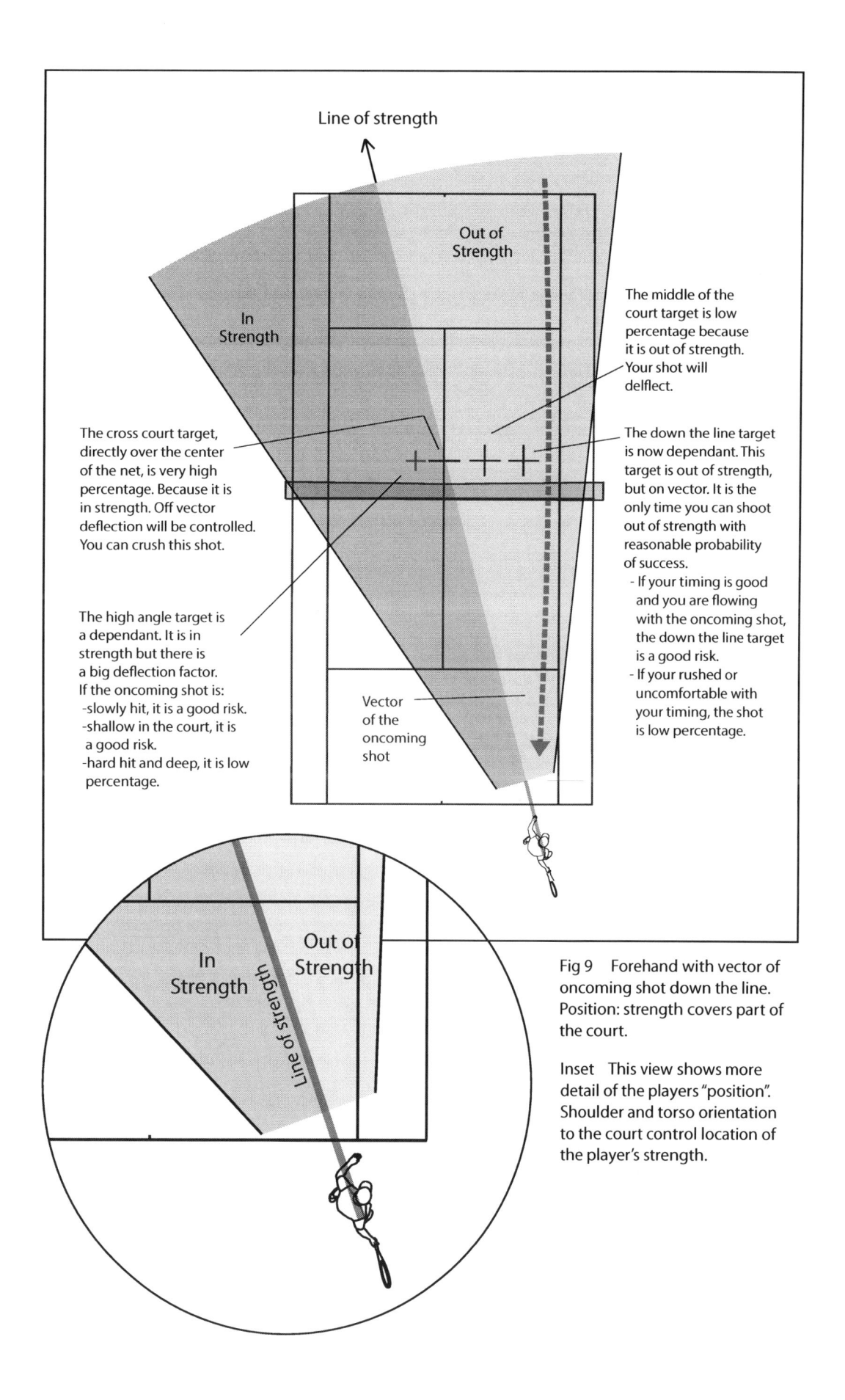

Line of strength

Out of Strength

In Strength

The cross court target, directly over the center of the net, is very high percentage. Because it is in strength. Off vector deflection will be controlled. You can crush this shot.

The middle of the court target is low percentage because it is out of strength. Your shot will delflect.

The down the line target is now dependant. This target is out of strength, but on vector. It is the only time you can shoot out of strength with reasonable probability of success.
 - If your timing is good and you are flowing with the oncoming shot, the down the line target is a good risk.
 - If your rushed or uncomfortable with your timing, the shot is low percentage.

The high angle target is a dependant. It is in strength but there is a big deflection factor. If the oncoming shot is:
 -slowly hit, it is a good risk.
 -shallow in the court, it is a good risk.
 -hard hit and deep, it is low percentage.

Vector of the oncoming shot

In Strength

Out of Strength

Line of strength

Fig 9   Forehand with vector of oncoming shot down the line. Position: strength covers part of the court.

Inset   This view shows more detail of the players "position". Shoulder and torso orientation to the court control location of the player's strength.

HOW TO MAKE HIGH PERCENTAGE SHOT SELECTIONS | 129

Condition 3B: Vector of the Oncoming Shot Is Down the Line

Forehand shot
Position: strength covers *the entire court* (see Figure 10).

In Figure 10, you have your shoulders and line of strength pointing up the line toward the right corner of the court. Your strength now covers the entire court, and you have several high-percentage options.

Crosscourt Target: Very High Percentage

The crosscourt target, over the center of the net, is very high percentage. This target is now deep in strength. It is off vector, but your strength will overcome the deflection factor. You also have a lot of court to shoot for. You can crush this ball with confidence.

High-Angle Target: Dependent

The high-angle target is dependent. The target is deep in strength, but you are shooting far off vector, so you have a big deflection factor to cope with. You are also running out of court, and the chance of missing wide is increased. If the oncoming shot is slow paced, this play is a good risk; if the oncoming shot lands short in the court, this play is also a good risk. If you are playing a hard-hit, deep ball, though, the shot is low percentage and should be avoided.

Middle-of-the-Court Target: High Percentage

The target in the middle of the court, just to the right of the center tape, is now a high-percentage target. There is some deflection factor to deal with, but this target is in the middle of your strength and can be hit hard with confidence. This shot may not challenge your opponent, as it will land in the center of the court. It is a good jam option if your opponent is moving to cover the open court.

Down-the-Line Target: High Percentage

The down-the-line target is now a high-percentage play. The deflection factor is nearly zero, and the target is in your strength. You can take this shot with confidence. The only caveat here is that the net is high, and you don't have much court to shoot for, so you will need to play the arc with a lot of spin and shape to get it over the net and down into the court. This target shoots the ball to the middle of the right side of the court, not directly at the sideline. It gives you a good margin of error, because your circle of error becomes elliptical when you shoot down the line.

Line of strength

In Strength

Out of Strength

The cross court target, right over the center of the net is very high percentage. The target is off vector but it is deep instrength. You can crush this shot.

The middle of the court is target high percentage. It is in strength and near the vector of the oncoming shot. You can hit this shot hard with high confidence.

The high angle target is dependant. It is in strength but there is a deflection factor because you are shooting way off vector. If the oncoming shot is:
- slowly hit, it is a good risk.
- shallow in the court, it is a good risk.
- hard hit and deep, it is low percentage.

The down the line target is now high percentage. It is on vector and in your strength. You can take this shot with confidence. You will have play the arc with more topspin or shoot slightly lower to get the your shot down and in to the court.

Vector of the oncoming shot

Fig 10 Forehand with vector of oncoming shot crosscourt. Position: entire court in strength.

Inset: This view shows more detail of the players "position". Shoulder and torso orientation to the court control location of the player's strength.

In Strength

Out of Strength

Line of strength

HOW TO MAKE HIGH PERCENTAGE SHOT SELECTIONS | 131

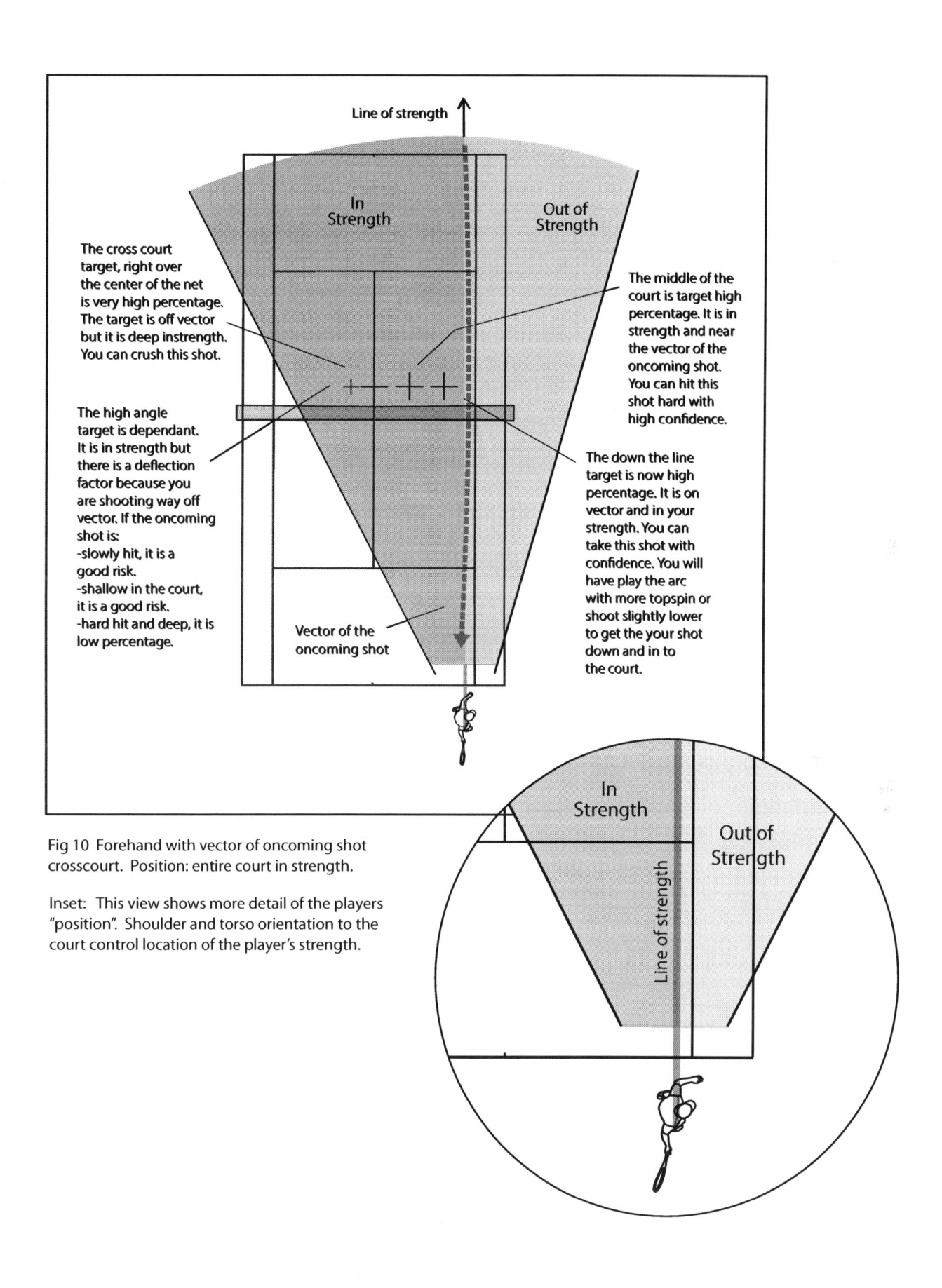

Condition 3C: Vector of the Oncoming Shot Is Down the Line

Backhand shot

Position: strength covers *only part of the court* (see Figure 11).

In Figure 11, the oncoming shot is received from the left side of the court, and the ball's vector is up the line to your backhand. Here, your shoulders and line of strength are pointing to the opposite (right) side of the court. You have not had the time to get your shoulders turned and your feet positioned to cover more of the court with your strength.

Crosscourt Target: Very High Percentage

The crosscourt target, dead center over the middle of the net, is very high percentage. This target is in strength, and you have a lot of court to shoot at. Because the target is off vector, there will be a deflection factor, but it will be minimal since the target is in strength. You can hit this shot very hard with high confidence.

High-Angle Target: Dependent

In this position the high-angle target is dependent. This target is deep in strength, but you are shooting way off vector. Deflection can be significant when you're shooting at this angle off the down-the-line oncoming shot. If the shot you are playing is slow, this shot is a good risk. If the oncoming shot lands shallow in the court, this shot is also a good risk. If you are playing a deep, hard-hit ball, on the other hand, then the shot is low percentage and should be avoided. You are also running out of court. You have to play the arc with more topspin to give your shot enough shape to get down into the court. Know that taking this shot, when it is a good risk, will produce a few errors.

Middle-of-the-Court Target: Low Percentage

The target for the middle of the court is now a low-percentage shot. It is off vector and out of strength. The shot will deflect. With this position it is better to choose cross-court target in strength.

Down-the-Line Target: Dependent

The down-the-line target is now dependent. It is on-vector, so there will be no deflection, but it is way out of strength, which makes it a risky play. The only time it is a good risk is when you are flowing with the ball with perfect timing. At all other times, it is a low-percentage shot. Expect a lot of errors if you take this risk.

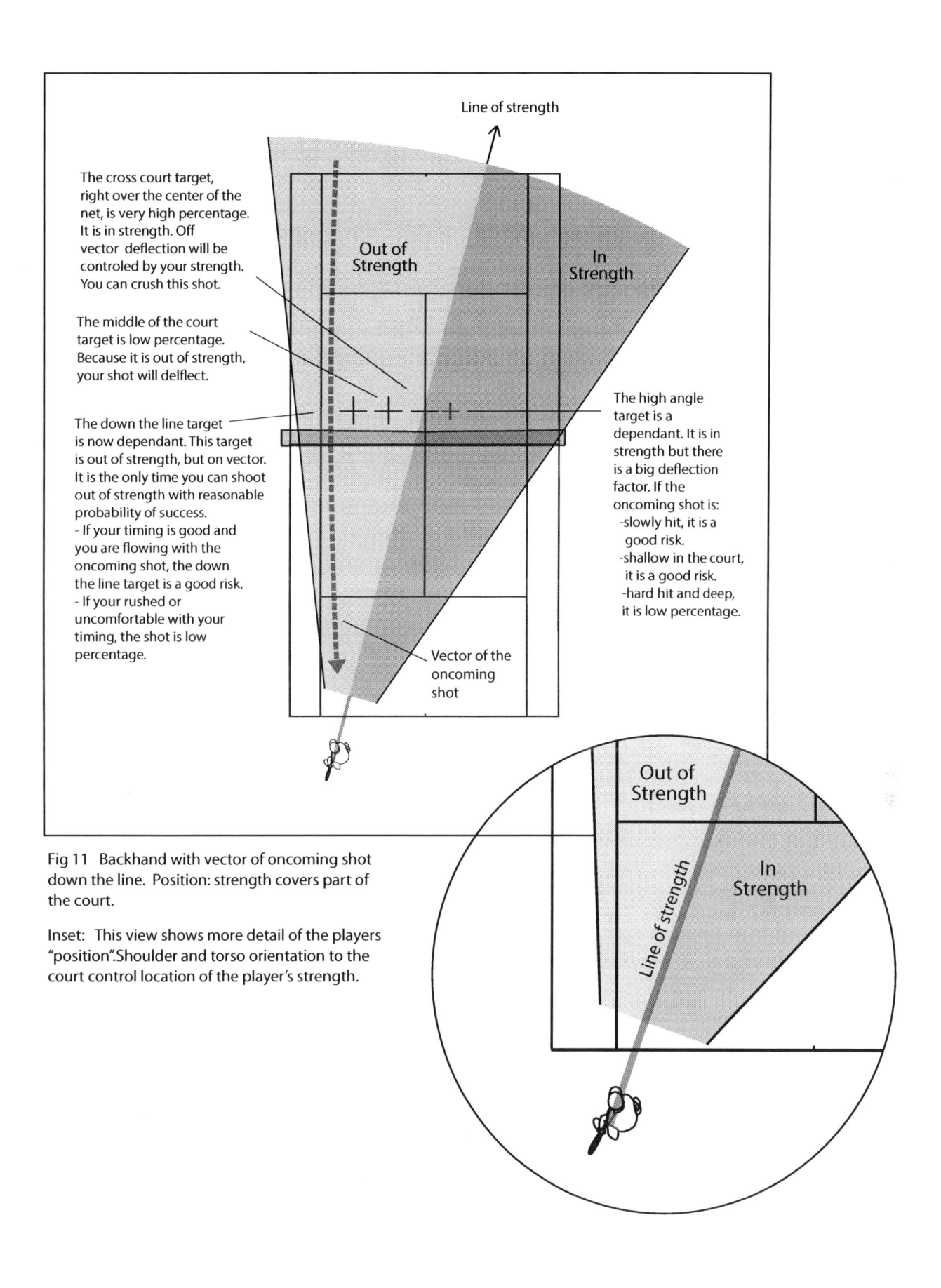

Line of strength

Out of Strength

In Strength

The cross court target, right over the center of the net, is very high percentage. It is in strength. Off vector deflection will be controlled by your strength. You can crush this shot.

The middle of the court target is low percentage. Because it is out of strength, your shot will delflect.

The down the line target is now dependant. This target is out of strength, but on vector. It is the only time you can shoot out of strength with reasonable probability of success.
- If your timing is good and you are flowing with the oncoming shot, the down the line target is a good risk.
- If your rushed or uncomfortable with your timing, the shot is low percentage.

The high angle target is a dependant. It is in strength but there is a big deflection factor. If the oncoming shot is:
 -slowly hit, it is a good risk.
 -shallow in the court, it is a good risk.
 -hard hit and deep, it is low percentage.

Vector of the oncoming shot

Fig 11 Backhand with vector of oncoming shot down the line. Position: strength covers part of the court.

Inset: This view shows more detail of the players "position". Shoulder and torso orientation to the court control location of the player's strength.

Out of Strength

In Strength

Line of strength

HOW TO MAKE HIGH PERCENTAGE SHOT SELECTIONS | 133

Condition 3D: Vector of the Oncoming Shot Is Down the Line

Backhand shot

Position: strength covers *the entire court* (see Figure 12).

In Figure 12, you are receiving the shot hit up the line to your backhand again. In this case, you have had time to move into a better position. Your shoulders and line of strength are pointing up the line, and your strength dominates all the targets.

Crosscourt Target: Very High Percentage

The very-high-percentage target here is still directly over the middle of the net, crosscourt. This shot is deep in strength. The target is off vector, but your strength will dominate the deflection. You can confidently rip this crosscourt shot hard at maximum power.

High-Angle Target: Dependent

The high-angle target is dependent. The target is deep in strength, but a big deflection factor. If the oncoming shot is slow, it is a good-risk shot. If the oncoming shot lands short in the court, it is also a good risk. If you are playing a hard-hit, deep ball, though, the shot is a low-percentage shot and should be avoided.

Middle-of-the-Court Target: High Percentage

The middle-of-the-court target is high percentage. This target is nearer the vector of the ball and is well in your strength. The low deflection factor and target in strength make this shot a high-percentage play. Your shot may not challenge your opponent, though, since it will go toward the middle of the court. It will be a good shot if your opponent has moved to the center of the court and you want to jam the ball right at her. In general, it is a neutral tactic: it will not force the angle of the play or generate a change to the momentum of the point. It is still a high-percentage shot.

Down-the-Line Target: High Percentage

The down-the-line target is now a high-percentage play. The deflection factor is nearly zero, and the target is in your strength. You can take this shot with confidence. The only caveat is that the net is high, and you don't have much court to shoot for. You will have to shoot your shot low or with a lot of topspin and shape to keep it in the court. With your strength covering this target, however, it is still a high-percentage shot and a good play.

Line of strength

Out of Strength

In Strength

The middle of the court target high percentage. It is in strength and near the vector of the oncoming shot. You can hit this hard with high confidence.

The cross court target, right over the center of the net, is very high percentage. It is deep in strength and you have a lot of court to shoot for. You can crush this shot.

The down the line target is now high percentage. It is on vector and in your strength. You can take this shot with confidence. You will have play the arc with more topspin or shoot slightly lower to get the your shot down and into the court.

The high angle target is a dependant. It is in strength but there is a deflection factor because you are shooting way off vector.
If the oncoming shot is:
-slowly hit, it is a good risk.
-shallow in the court, it is a good risk.
-hard hit and deep, it is low percentage.

Vector of the oncoming shot

Fig 12 Backhand with vector of oncoming shot crosscourt. Position: entire court in strength.

Inset: This view shows more detail of the players "position". Shoulder and torso orientation to the court control location of the player's strength.

Out of Strength

Line of strength

In Strength

HOW TO MAKE HIGH PERCENTAGE SHOT SELECTIONS | 135

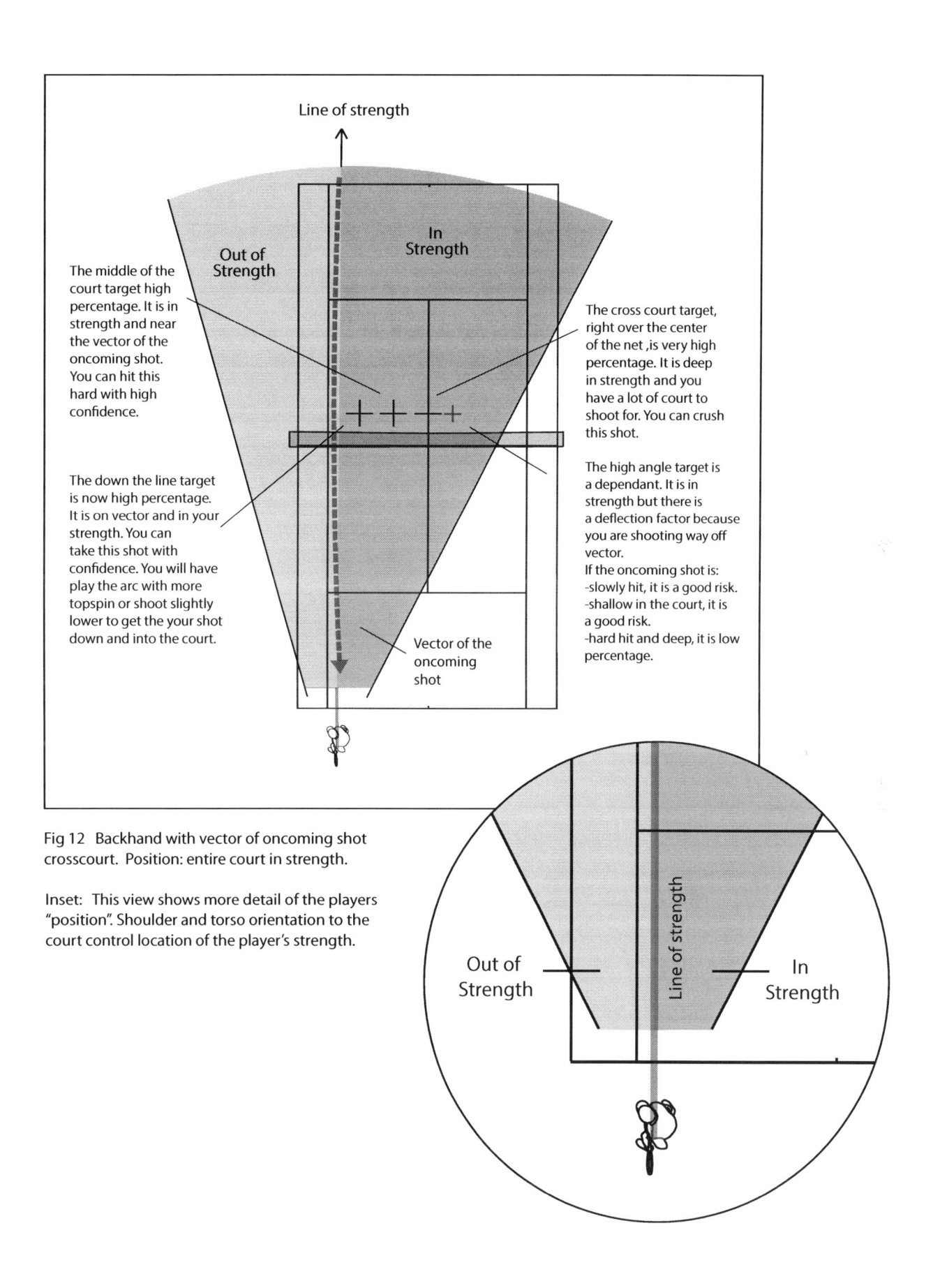

What to Do When You Are Jammed

Forehand shot

Sometimes when you receive a shot into the middle of your body, you are unable to move your feet or get a good shoulder-and-torso turn to control your strength. As we've discussed, this is called being "jammed." In Figure 13, you are hitting a forehand off a ball down the middle of the court. You have no time to get your body into a good position. Because of this, your feet and shoulders are pointing off to the side of the court.

Your strength is now off the court and covering none of the targets. The crosscourt target to the left of the center of the net is closest to your strength. It is the only target you can choose that will use the pulling path of your stroke to control the ball. In this situation, it is the only high-percentage shot.

The target over the center of the net is now "dependent." The target is on vector, so there will be no deflection factor. But a shot to this target will be pushed even more out of strength. This out-of-strength and on-vector conflict makes the target dependent. If well timed, you can find some success in shooting at this target. But it is more likely, because you are pushing the ball out of strength, that you will make an error or a weak shot. When your opponent has jammed you, this target is not recommended.

The crosscourt target to the right is a very low-percentage shot. It is way out of strength and off vector. Your chances of success with this shot are very low. Don't choose this shot if you are jammed.

Backhand Shot

If you are jammed into your backhand, the same applies, but in reverse. Choose the shot closest to your strength to the right side of the court. It is a high-percentage shot. The on-vector target is dependent, as previously discussed. The off-vector, out-of-strength target is very low percentage. It is a terrible shot selection. Don't choose this shot. See Figure 14, on page 142.

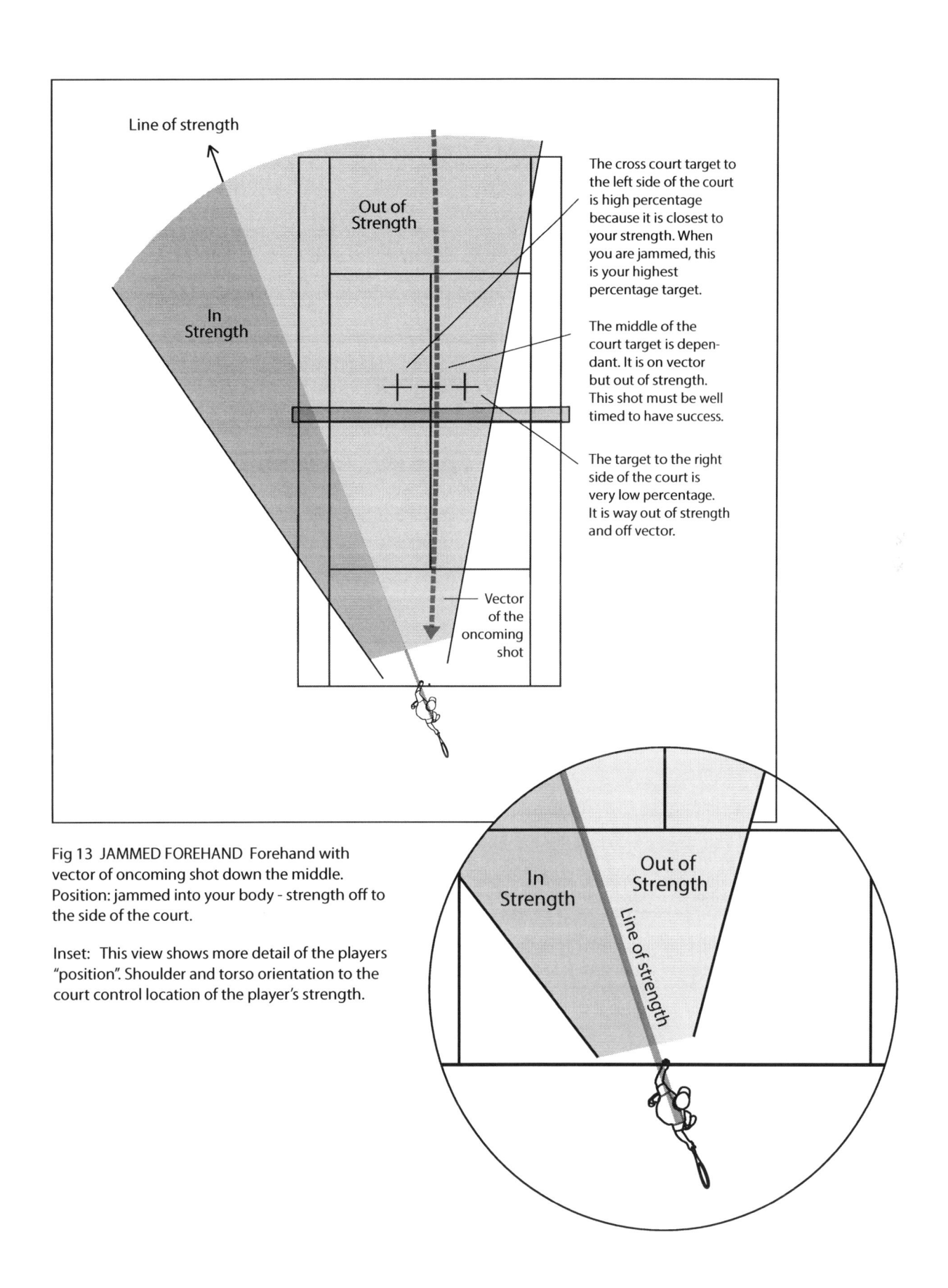

Line of strength

Out of Strength

In Strength

The cross court target to the left side of the court is high percentage because it is closest to your strength. When you are jammed, this is your highest percentage target.

The middle of the court target is dependant. It is on vector but out of strength. This shot must be well timed to have success.

The target to the right side of the court is very low percentage. It is way out of strength and off vector.

Vector of the oncoming shot

Fig 13 JAMMED FOREHAND Forehand with vector of oncoming shot down the middle. Position: jammed into your body - strength off to the side of the court.

Inset: This view shows more detail of the players "position". Shoulder and torso orientation to the court control location of the player's strength.

In Strength

Out of Strength

Line of strength

HOW TO MAKE HIGH PERCENTAGE SHOT SELECTIONS | 137

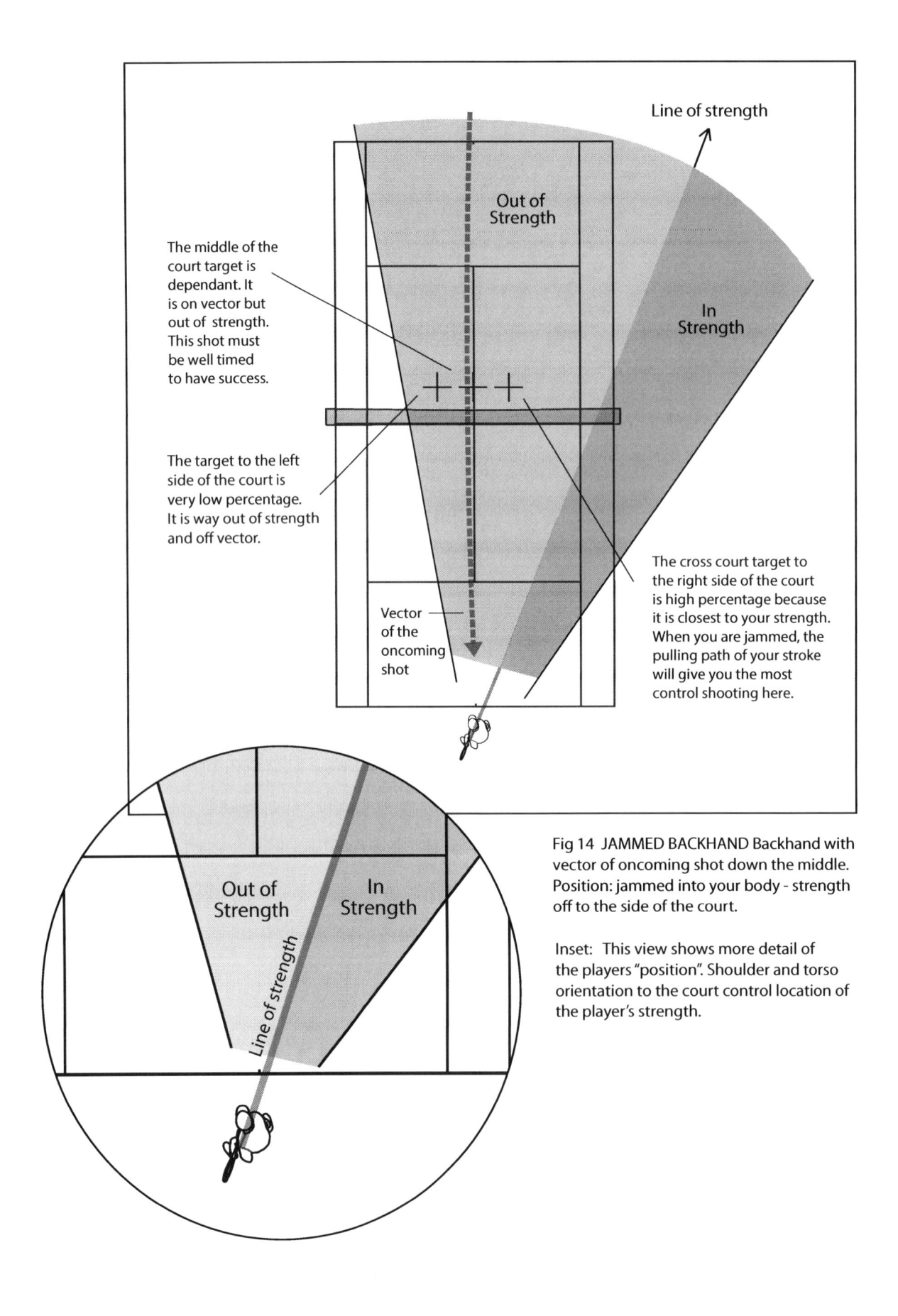

Line of strength

Out of Strength

In Strength

The middle of the court target is dependant. It is on vector but out of strength. This shot must be well timed to have success.

The target to the left side of the court is very low percentage. It is way out of strength and off vector.

Vector of the oncoming shot

The cross court target to the right side of the court is high percentage because it is closest to your strength. When you are jammed, the pulling path of your stroke will give you the most control shooting here.

Out of Strength

In Strength

Line of strength

Fig 14 JAMMED BACKHAND Backhand with vector of oncoming shot down the middle. Position: jammed into your body - strength off to the side of the court.

Inset: This view shows more detail of the players "position". Shoulder and torso orientation to the court control location of the player's strength.

138 | HOW TO HIT OUT, GET BALL CONTROL AND PLAY PERCENTAGE TENNIS

False Position

Sometimes when you are playing a deep, hard-hit, oncoming shot, your position and control of your strength may be false. This happens when your preparation for the shot is rushed, and you have very little time to turn your shoulders and torso to control your strength. It usually happens with very deep, high speed, oncoming shots. The general rule is that you need a little time with your shoulders and torso in position to control the location of your strength. This is especially true when you shoot at targets that are near the edge of your strength and off the vector of the oncoming shot. When in doubt, choose a target that is deep in strength. Wait for an oncoming ball that will allow you sufficient time to prepare for your shot. Then you can confidently choose a target that is off vector near the edge of your strength.

Strength and Position When You Are on the Run

We will put hitting on the run into two categories: out-of-control and in-control runs.

The Out-of-Control Run

When you are running hard for a ball and you can barely reach it to make the play, you are in an out-of-control run. Your arms will be extended, and you won't be able to drive through the arc. When you are playing the ball on an out-of-control run, your shoulders and line of strength may not exactly define where the high-percentage targets are. This is especially true if you are running hard for a backhand; this is even more true for one-handed backhand players. You will notice that when you make the hard run for a ball to your backhand, your line of strength can point quite a bit wide of the court. If we were to use the logic in the previous examples, your strength would cover the entire court. If that were true, you could then choose any target and shoot wherever you want. But this is not the case. When you are running hard, and you do not have the time to get set and to control your shoulders and torso, your shot-selection options are limited. The out-of-control run gets you to the ball in an outstretched position. It does not provide you with real position to control your strength and choose your shot. Your high-percentage shot in this extended condition is usually the target over the middle of the net, pulling the ball crosscourt.

This situation also applies to a hard run to the forehand side. If you are in an out-of-control run and you barely make it to the ball, the highest-percentage target will be over the middle of the net, pulled crosscourt.

The In-Control Run

You can be on the move for a ball, running hard, and still be able to control your strength. You make an in-control run when you are moving to the ball and you can control your shoulders and torso as you prepare for the shot. You also have to arrive at the ball in control of your body and not in an outstretched position. With these two factors managed, you can use your shoulders and line of strength to choose the high-percentage targets. If your strength covers the target, then you can choose that target. You'll get a feel for just how well you can control your strength with your shoulders as you experiment with this concept. If you are making an in-control run, the rules of strength and position apply, as we have discussed in detail.

Your running shots will vary from 100 percent in control to completely outstretched and barely getting to the ball. You have to experiment and get a feel for making the running shot. If you use the strength, position, and vector logic, you will get a feel for when you can make big plays down the line near the edge of your strength. Get out on the court and experiment using these tools. You will get better and better.

Move Your Targets Higher When You Are on the Run at Maximum Reach

If you are on the run for a shot near your maximum reach, you need to bring your target up. The tendency here is to miss low and into the net. Your in-strength target will look good and doable, but because you are outstretched and on the run, the normal-height target will not work for you. Next time you watch a match, notice how many balls are shot into the net when players are outstretched, on the run, and shooting crosscourt into their strength. You can fix this. Always raise your target significantly higher when you are in this situation. You will learn through experimentation how high to raise the target. Start by doubling the height of your target over the net.

Volley Shot Selection

All of the lessons you have just learned about shot selection also apply to volleys in spades. Watch a tennis match. Wait for a player to approach the net. Look for shot selections out of strength. The best players in the world will come to net and choose targets way out of strength and off vector to the open court. They will often miss these shots badly. These glaring errors are the best example of the validity of the strength-and-position shot-selection logic.

When you hit a traditional volley that is punched with backspin, your racket stays on the ball a much shorter time than with a ground stroke. Because of this, the movement of your racket influences the ball's direction less than with ground strokes. This fact means that when you hit a traditional volley, you must always choose targets that lie well within your strength. Don't clown around and push the ball out of strength toward the open court. It is best to crush your volley to a target deep in strength—usually crosscourt and on vector—than to impatiently shoot for the open court out of strength. By smashing your volley deep in strength, you will not make an error. You will either win the point or will force your opponent to hit a weak shot. The weak shot will give you time to position your strength over the entire court. Once you are holding the entire court in your strength, you can confidently choose any target and win the point.

Summary

The examples we have gone through don't cover every situation you will face on the court. The oncoming shot might not be right down the middle, exactly crosscourt, or directly down the line. Your strength won't always just cover one target or all the targets. And as you play oncoming shots farther off the court, the targets will slide over, farther away from the center tape. But you can use these examples as a decision-making template and apply it to almost every shot selection you make on the court. You are building your own personal aiming-and-targeting architecture. You will have to go out there and experiment. You also need to watch a few professional tennis matches. Look at how the players prepare for their shots. Watch for the vector of the oncoming shot and how the player's strength is positioned. Notice what shots they choose. You will be pleasantly surprised to see how strength and position and the vector of the oncoming shot drive shot selection. You will also notice that almost all errors occur when shots are taken out of strength and or off vector.

CHAPTER 6

How to Play a Point

Tennis has changed from a finesse, all-court, serve-and-volley game to a power backcourt contest dominated by hard-hit, topspin ground strokes. The transition started with Björn Borg, who created the template that the great players follow today.

Before Borg, almost all male tennis players hit one-handed backhands. Most pre-Borg players used serve-and-volley as a mainstay of their attack. The last great practitioner of the serve-and-volley tactic was Pete Sampras. He was a power player with a great serve and great ground strokes, but he was the last champion to use the serve-and-volley as a mainstay of his game. After Sampras came Agassi and Courier and the like. Both hit two-handed backhands and relied on winning points from the baseline. This "Borg style"—big forehand and two-handed backhand—has subsequently dominated the game. Federer is an exception, with his great one-handed backhand. But he, too, won—and still wins—most of his points from the backcourt.

There are many reasons serve-and-volley tennis has gone by the wayside. The most important is the new-technology racquets that enable players to hit ground strokes and passing shots so well. What used to be an adequate approach shot is now a sitter for a killer passing shot. Approaching the net frequently has become a losing, low-percentage tactic at the highest level of the game. The bigger sweet spot, enhanced stability of the new rackets, and high-tech strings make possible passing shots and service returns that were simply not possible before.

So what is the plan in the modern power game? How is it played—and how can you play it, too? It's pretty simple, really. The power game revolves around strength and position. A player's strength and position, along with the vector of the oncoming shot, define where the high percentage targets are. You crush your ground strokes to high percentage targets. When you have multiple high percentage targets you make your opponent move. When your opponent is forced to move his position will be degraded. His shot will become predictable. You will be able to anticipate and get into even better position for your next shot. With great position you have multiple high percentage targets. Now you hammer your next shot to the target of your choice using the tactical game plan described below. You keep doing this on every shot until the point is over.

What follows is a guide to playing points. A tennis match is played one point at a time, which is how you should approach the game: one point at a time.

Three Essential Concepts for Tactical Success

Expanding Your Strength: Your high-percentage shot selection options are determined by how much of the court is covered by your strength. How much of the court you cover with your strength is a result of your shot preparation. Shot preparation is a combination of your backswing, footwork, and—most importantly—the turning and control of your upper torso and shoulders. As you flow with the arc, preparing for your shot, you need to emphasize the turning of your upper body. By exaggerating this turn, you "expand your strength" over more of the court. By expanding your strength you give yourself more high-percentage shot selections and more tactical options.

Holding the Court: When your strength covers the entire court, you "hold the court" in your strength. This gives you the option to hit to all the targets. When you are holding the court in your strength, your opponent will be unable to anticipate your next shot. You will have the option to shoot to either side of the court or right up the middle. This is the path to winning points. You won't always be able to achieve this dominating position, but you should make it your number-one priority. Your goal on every shot is to position your body so that you dominate the entire court with your strength. Integrating the torso turn into your shot preparation is the key to achieving this goal.

The Killer Position: You are in the "killer position" when you are playing a weak ball that lands near the middle of the court and you hold the entire court in your strength. Because you are playing a weak, slowly hit ball short in the court, you have time to hesitate before you choose your target. Because you hold the court in your strength, you can shoot to the left or right side of the court at will. Your opponent will be forced to choose which side of the court to defend. In this position you wait for your opponent to make a move, and then shoot behind or in front of your opponent, winning the point. Always work to achieve this killer position on weak balls to the middle of the court (see Figures 1 and 2).

Putting It All Together

As a newly minted percentage-tennis player, you know where the high-percentage targets are. They depend on your strength, position, and the vector of the oncoming shot. Sometimes you have only one high-percentage target. Sometimes you have more. There are really only three targets with this new paradigm: you can shoot to the left side of the court, to the middle of the court, or to the right side of the court. That's it—it's really simple. You crush shots to these conservative targets. When you make errors, your errors go in the court for winners, not out for lost points. If you have only one high-percentage target, you shoot for that target. Even if your opponent is standing right there on your target, you still pound that target. But this begs the question: What shot do you choose when you have multiple high-percentage targets? This is where tactics come into play. The tactical plan I will give you is simple.

Killer Position Forehand

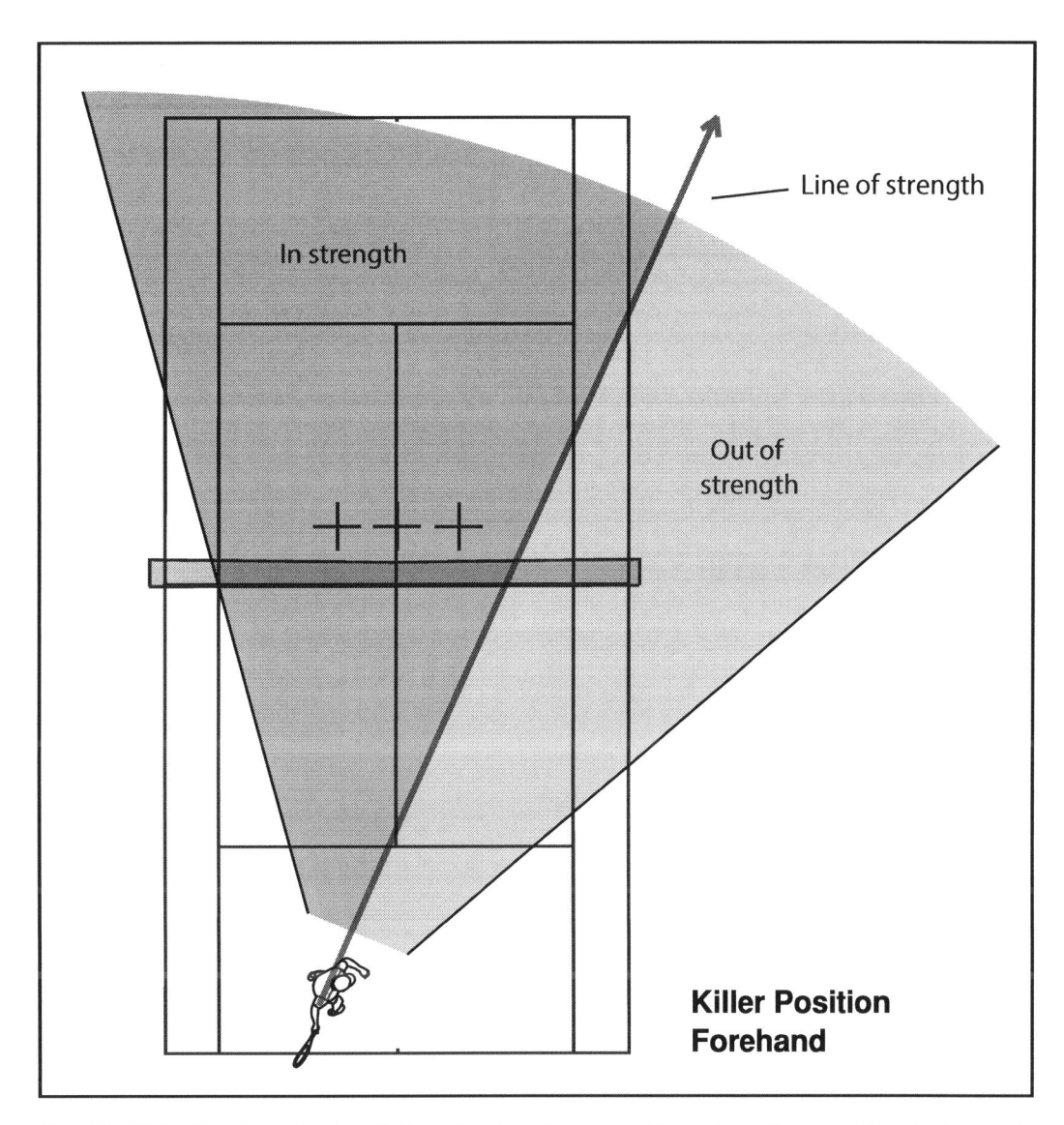

Fig 1 The **Killer Position - forehand**. Here the player has moved in to play a short weak ball. He has made a good shoulder and torso turn covering the entire court with his strength. He can shoot to any target. This is the killer position. As he holds the court in his strength, he waits for his opponent to make his move and hammers the winner.

When you have multiple target options, you have three tactical choices. They are: to run your opponent, wrong-foot your opponent, or jam your opponent. When you run your opponent, you choose the target that shoots the ball farthest from her position. When you wrong-foot your opponent, you choose the target behind your opponent's run: that is, your opponent is running to cover the open court, and you shoot the ball where she came from. The third choice is to jam your opponent. When you do this, you choose the target that shoots the ball right at your opponent's body.

Wait a minute. All of these tactical shot selections assume that you can see where your opponent is. How do we do that? Remember the idea of open focus? Let's discuss this further.

Killer Position Backhand

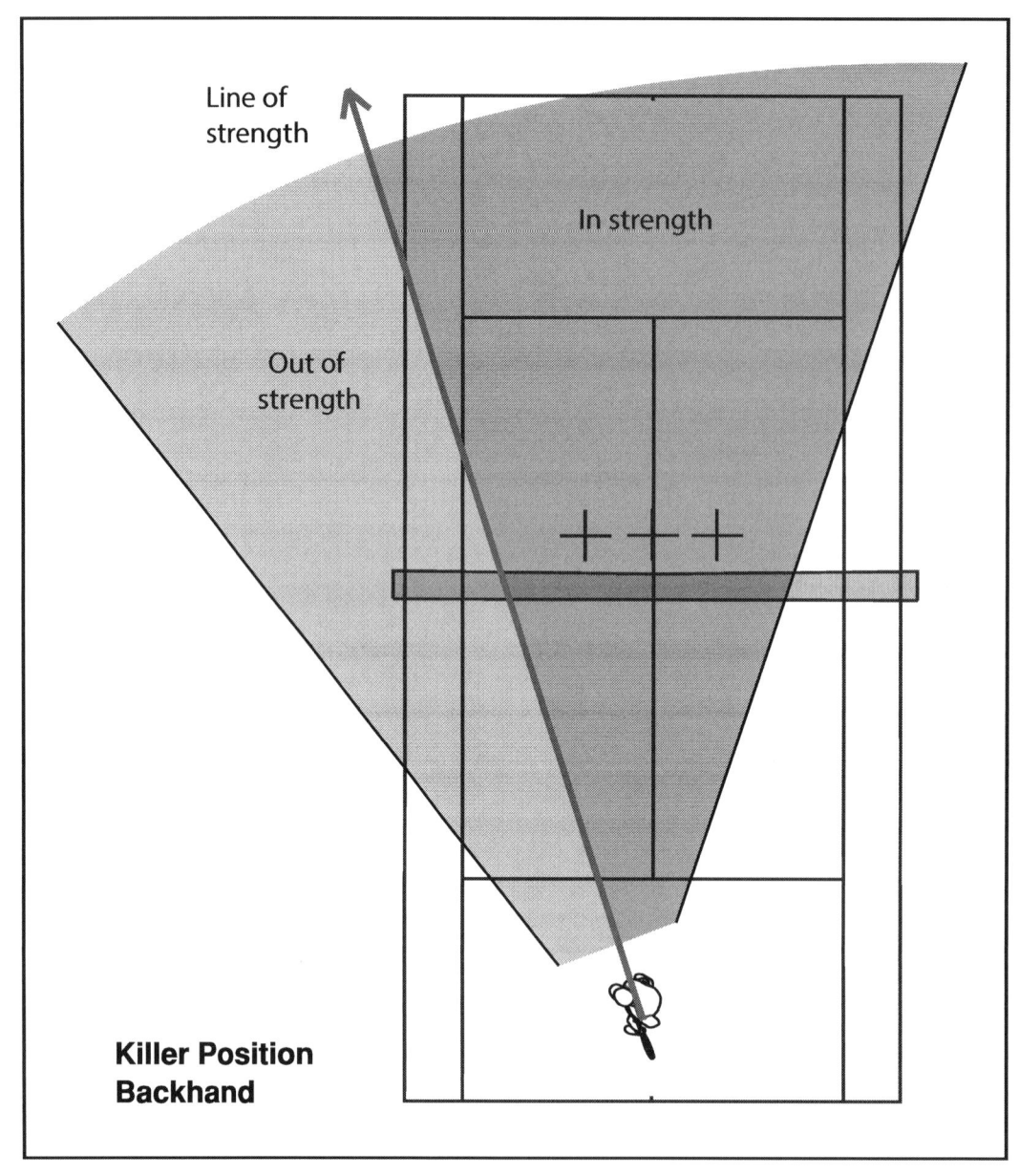

Fig 2 The **Killer Position - backhand**. Here the player has moved in to play a short weak ball. He has made a good shoulder and torso turn covering the entire court with his strength. He can shoot to any target. This is the killer positin. As he holds the court in his strength, he waits for his opponent to make his move and hammers the winner.

How to Use Open Focus During Points

When you learned to see the arcs, you learned the open-focus concept. The ability to see the arc and capture its shape in your mind's eye requires a different way of watching the ball. You have to notice the ball's travel through the space of the court in 3D. By doing this, you increase the use of your peripheral vision. The wider, more open focus of your vision provides a huge benefit to your game, besides just being able to see the arcs. It enables you to see your opponent at the same time you are seeing the arc. You will be able to notice her movement and position on the court while you are watching the ball. Of course, there will be times when you lose sight of your opponent's position; this happens if you are pulled wide in the court or you are running back for a ball. But when you have good position on the ball, you should be able to keep your opponent in your field of view. You will definitely be able to keep your opponent in sight when you play balls short in the court, well in front of you. You will use this vision to choose shots that win you points quickly and efficiently.

The Point-Playing Game Plan

Always choose a high-percentage target in strength. If you only have one high-percentage target, shoot for that target. Even if you hit your shot right back to your opponent, you choose that target. Here, seeing your opponent is not a factor in choosing your shot. You are now a percentage-tennis player, and you will choose the high-percentage target—even if your opponent is standing right there. You are patient and will wait until you have more high-percentage choices before you shoot to the open court.

If you have multiple high-percentage targets, you can choose to run, wrong-foot, or jam your opponent. The default tactic is to run your opponent.

Option One: Run Your Opponent

Running your opponent is the fundamental game plan. When you choose to run your opponent, you choose the target that will shoot the ball farthest away from him. This play makes your opponent physically exert himself to the maximum. Also, since your opponent is on the run, his position will be poorer when he gets to the ball. Since his position is compromised by his run, he will have fewer high-percentage targets to choose from. He will most likely be forced to hit to only one side of the court; with your knowledge of strength and position, it will be easy for you to anticipate this shot. This is usually the "pull" target in his strength. If your opponent's position is compromised enough, this pull shot will go toward the middle of the court. It will also land short in the court, near the service line.

The choice to run your opponent should be your default shot selection. You must establish the fact that you will run your opponent by hitting to the open court whenever you can. This will set up options two and three: wrong-footing and jamming your opponent.

Option 2: Wrong-Footing Your Opponent

When you wrong-foot your opponent, you are hitting behind your opponent's run. She is already moving to cover the open court; her momentum is going in one direction, and you hit the ball behind her. The opportunity for this wrong-footing play will occur when your strength dominates the entire court. Since you have shown your opponent that you will run her by hitting to the open court, she is forced to move to cover that side. This is when you put your expanded vision and open focus to use. You are in a good position, with the choice to hit to either side of the court. Your open focus enables you to see your opponent make her early run to cover the open court. You now hold the court in your strength. When you see your opponent move, you choose the target that will shoot the ball behind her. A winner or a very tough shot to return will be the outcome.

Don't fall in love with this tactic. The wrong-foot play should be used judiciously. If you consistently hit behind your opponent, she will eventually catch on and start anticipating your shots. It is important to go for this play only after you have first established that you will shoot to the open court and run your adversary. Your opponent should be desperate to move to the open court to cover your vicious, hard-hit shot. Once you have established that you will run your opponent, you can wrong-foot with discretion—and big success.

Option 3: Jamming Your Opponent

When you jam your opponent, you choose a target that shoots the ball right into her body. For this to be effective, your shot needs to land deep in the court. When you jam your adversary well, she will only be able to choose one shot. You can anticipate the shot to her strong side because she will be unable to move her feet or shoulders into position to cover the entire court with her strength, You can move there early, baiting her to make a low-percentage shot. Or you can hesitate until she makes her shot to the strong side, moving aggressively to strike the anticipated ball. This is an effective shot if you are approaching the net; it is also effective if you can catch your opponent on the run, jamming her while she is moving. Your opponent's body will be open to the court, and she will have to hit to strength or make a very low-percentage shot selection.

Work for the Killer Position

By running your opponent, you compromise his position. As he makes his out-of-control run for the ball, he will be forced to pull the ball to his strength. This on-the-run pull shot will often go toward the middle of the court and will land short, near the service line. This will give you a chance to get into the killer position for your next shot. You are in this position when you are playing a short, weak ball near the center of the court and you have enough time to cover the entire court with your strength. Because you are forward in the court, your shot travels a shorter distance, and your adversary will have less time to react and get to your ball. As you hold the court in your strength, your opponent is "hung out to dry" on one side of the court or the other; he must then move or stay put to counter your next shot. You now have all the tactical options at your disposal. You use your expanded vision to make the decision to run, wrong-foot, or jam your opponent. From this killer position, the point is in your hands; a winning shot is a very likely outcome.

More on Holding the Court

You hold the court when your position places your strength over the entire court, and you have time to wait before you choose your target.

As you hold the court in your strength, you use your expanded vision to see both the ball and your opponent. In this situation, play is slowed down, and your opponent will be forced to make a move to one side of the court or the other. She may stand on the edge of your strength, then at the last minute make a run to the open court. Or she may move near the center of your strength. Her other option is to start the run early to the open court. The important thing for you as the offensive player is to wait until the last moment to choose your target. If your opponent moves early, then you can wrong-foot her. If she chooses to stay put, you can run her by driving the ball to the open court.

If you are playing a hard-hit ball, the vision principle still works. As long as you can position your body so that your strength covers both sides of the court, you can use the location of your strength and your expanded vision to optimize your shot selection. Play here is at a quicker pace: you won't have time to hesitate and hold the court in your strength. You might be on the move, or your opponent might strike the ball hard enough so that you will not have any time to "lord" over the court, waiting for your opponent to make her run. During this faster-paced part of the point, you still can monitor the movement of your opponent and choose your target based on her position and movement. If your opponent is on one side of the court, way out of position, she will have to move toward the open court. If she starts her run early and aggressively, you can use your expanded vision to wrong-foot her. Or if she is hesitating, not moving to cover, you can shoot your shot to the open court, choosing to run your opponent.

When to Approach the Net

You will also have the option to come in to the net and volley as you play forward in the court. In today's game, few players choose to come in to the net. Instead, they wait for the ball to bounce and then play the ground stroke. They do this is because the new-technology rackets make it a lot easier to hit effective passing shots. It is also because most players are incompetent at net play.

A good rule of thumb is to move to the net to play the volley when your opponent is making an out-of-control run and will be well out of position when she gets to your shot. In this situation your opponent will be forced to shoot toward the center of the court. Move to the middle of the court and close in on the net. By closing in on the net, you cut off passing-shot angles. Get close. Work to hit your volley when the ball is above the net. Make your opponent hit a great lob to beat you. Crush your volley toward your strength; don't push your volley weakly out of strength. Do this even if you hit the ball right back to your opponent. If you hit your volley hard, she will be rushed and will then give up an easier ball to volley. Now you can make an aggressive torso turn on your next volley, covering the court with your strength and giving yourself more target options. The tactical choices are the same: run, wrong-foot, or jam. Start by running your opponent, which will then set up the wrong-foot option.

It is also a good option to move in to volley if you are forward in the court and your opponent hits a high, deep ball that will make you retreat. Don't be afraid to hit the swinging topspin volley in this situation. You know how to do it now. You have to try it and make a few mistakes if you want to own this shot. Choose a high-percentage target in your strength, and rip the topspin volley. It is a lot of fun!

Point-Tactics Summary

It is a simple game plan:
1. Always choose a high-percentage target in strength. If you only have one high percentage target shoot for that target even if your opponent is standing right there.
2. Run your opponent. Establish that you will run your opponent when you have multiple high-percentage targets.
3. Wrong-foot your opponent judiciously. After your opponent is desperate to cover the open court chasing your run shot selections, wrong-foot her intermittently. Make the wrong-foot play a surprise. Use it when your opponent is anticipating your run shot selection.
4. Jam when prudent. This play is a good change-up when your opponent is well positioned to the middle of your strength. You can also use it effectively when you are approaching the net.
5. Hold the court in your strength. Make a good shoulder-and-torso turn a part of your preparation for every shot. This will enable more tactical options.
6. Play forward in the court. Seek the killer position. Take advantage of short balls. Move in, and cover the entire court with your strength. This is when you can hold the court and use your expanded vision to make winning shot selections. Work the run game plan. Work to push your opponent back in the court. This will open up the wrong-foot and jam options.

Changing Pace = Changing Arc Shapes

During a point a good tactic is to "change pace." This is usually thought of as changing the speed of your shot. You need to take this concept one step further. To challenge your opponent and throw him off rhythm, you should think of changing pace as changing the shape of your shots arc.

Most players make their stroke without reference to the shape of the oncoming shot. They don't understand how to "play the arcs". You can take advantage of this by varying the shape of the arc you hit. Firing a hard flat shot, followed by a high arcing topspin shot can generate errors. Shooting a high topspin arc followed by a low backspin arc will challenge your opponent skill set and win you points.

If you opponent is crushing every one of your hard hit topspin shots its time to change things up by changing arc shapes. Throw in a high, low speed arc deep in the court. Rip some high arcing topspin shots. This is particularly effective against a player who hits mostly hard flat shots.

Playing different arc shapes is one of the hardest skills to learn in tennis. And most players you face will not have an "arc playing" concept to deal with different shaped shots. To throw your opponent off rhythm during a match, project different arc shapes. To change pace, combine changing the arc of your shot with changing the speed of your shot.

The Björn Borg Square

I named this tactic after Björn Borg because he pioneered its use. I am not sure why I choose to call this tactic a "square." I think it's because you play angles on the court, and you kind of "square up" to the ball as you strike it. It doesn't really matter. It's just a name to hang on this very important tennis tactic.

Prior to Borg's entry into the tennis world, players pretty much played forehands when the ball went to their forehand side and backhands when the ball went to their backhand side. Some professionals occasionally "ran around their backhand" as part of their game plan, but nobody did it like Borg. He did his best to work each point so that he was standing in the backhand side of the court smashing open-stance forehands anywhere he wanted. He would leave the other side of the court open, daring his opponents to hit to his forehand side. He would hit shot after shot from this position, his opponents seemingly unable to change the angle of play. Since his performances during his great career, the advent of new-technology rackets, and the dominance of backcourt play, every great player now uses this tactic to win points. Federer, Nadal, Djokovic, Sharapova, and Williams, to name a few, all move into this Borg square—standing in the backhand side of the court and dominating play with their forehands.

Why is this tactic so effective? How did Borg get away with this game plan? Why didn't his opponents just shoot for the open court? Strength and position and the vector of the oncoming shot explain why the "Borg square" is so effective.

The Tactic

The basis of the Borg square tactic is to run around weakly hit shots to your backhand side. Once there, the plan is to pound "inside-out" forehands, crosscourt, to your opponent's backhand until you get a slowly hit ball landing

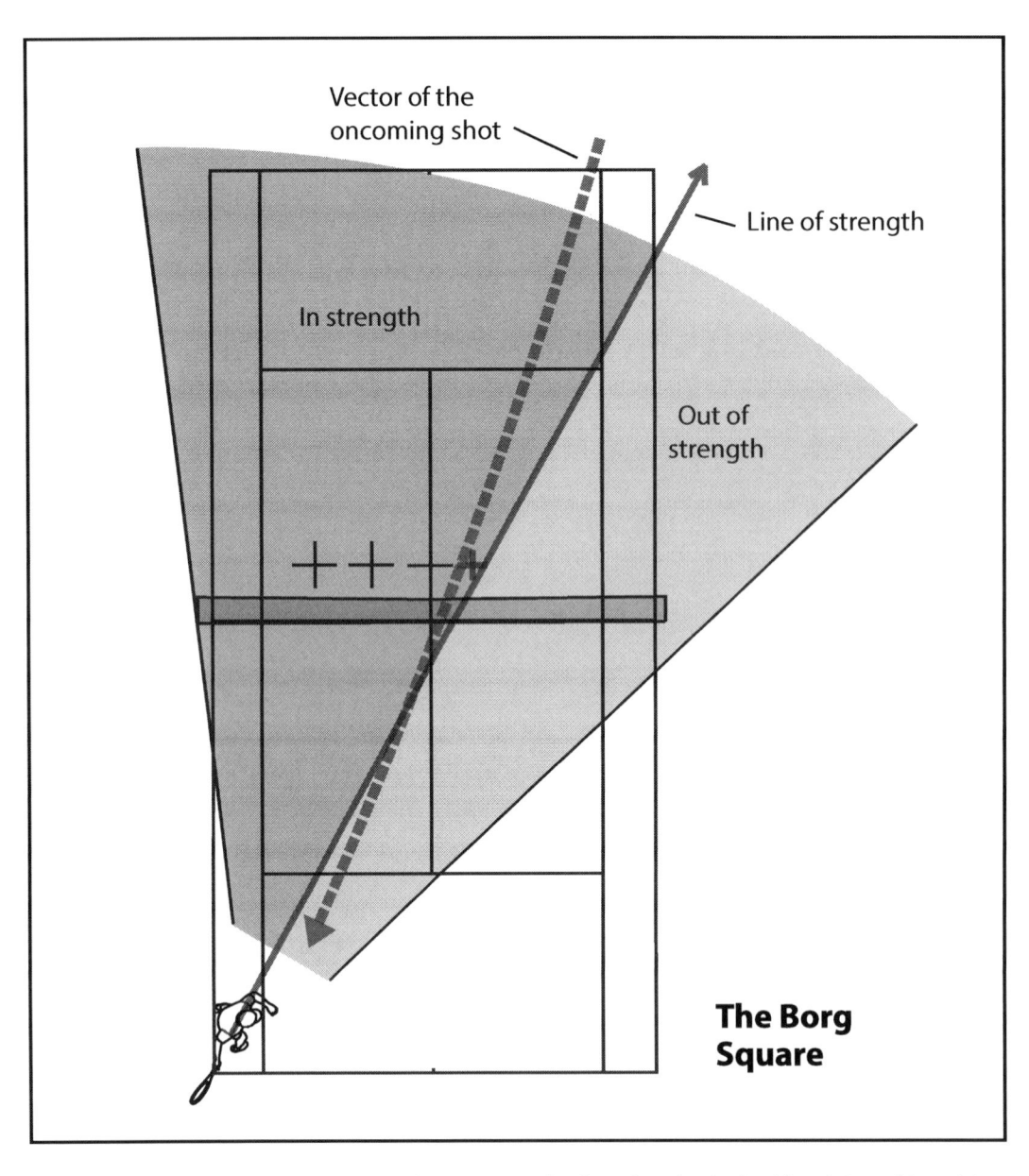

Fig 3 **The Borg Square**. Here the player has run around a shot played to his backhand. By making a big shoulder and torso turn he covers the entire court with his strength. He can rip his shot on vector cross court seeking a weaker ball. Or, he can crush his shot to the left side of the court to the target deep in strength.

near the center of the court. Once you get this sitter, you move into position with your strength covering the entire court. Now you hold the court in your strength. In this killer position, you can shoot the ball to either side of the court. Your opponent must commit to covering one side of the court or the other and you can crush the ball for a winner.

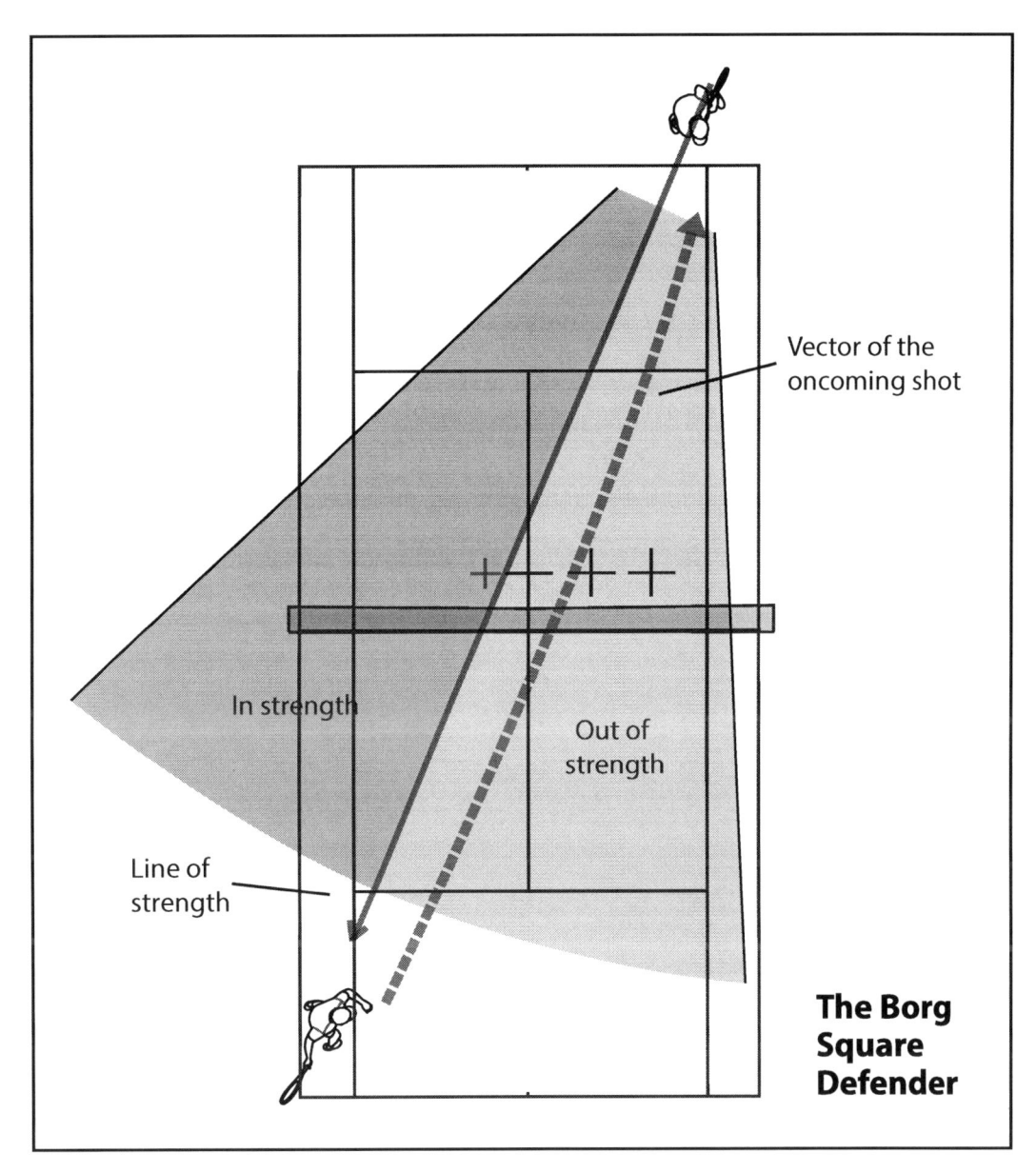

Fig 4 **The Borg Square Defender**. Here the defensive player, recieving the shot crosscourt, has limited options. The target down the line to the open court is very low percentage. It is out of strength - off vector - over thehighest part of the net - and into to the shortest part of the court. He must shoot crosscourt, near his strength, to make a high percentage shot selection.

Why the Borg Square Works

Now let's understand why this tactic works so well, and why your opponent is made so defensive by it. Figure 3 shows a player in the Borg square. He is standing in the backhand side of the court. He is receiving a ball crosscourt from his opponent's backhand side.

First, why doesn't the opponent just shoot the ball into the open court? Here's why: this tactic is based on hitting hard, fast shots, deep in the court, on a crosscourt angle to the opponent's backhand side (assuming a right-handed opponent). If your opponent chooses a target down the line into the open court, he is choosing a shot way off vector. His deflection factor will be high. That makes the shot to the open court a low-percentage shot. Also, if your shot is hard hit, deep in the court, on an extreme angle, your opponent will not be able to get his strength into position to cover the open court. If your opponent's strength isn't covering the open court, his shot to that side will be even lower percentage. The down-the-line shot is also over the highest part of the net into the shortest part of the court. This, too, makes it lower percentage. So you are "giving" this shot to your opponent because you know it is a very low-percentage shot on three counts: it is out of strength, it is off vector, and it is over the highest part of the net into the "short" court. You are essentially saying, "Go ahead, make my day. Choose a really low-percentage shot." If your opponent takes you up on this challenge, he will have a high probability of missing or will hit a weak shot into the middle of the court that you can then crush for a winner (see Figure 4).

Second, how do you get into this dominating position on the court? When can you do it, and what do you have to do to get there? Borg was able to get into this position for a couple of reasons. One was that his forehand was so good that his opponents did everything they could to keep the ball away from that side. So a lot of balls were hit weakly to his backhand side. He simply moved around those weakly hit, short balls and crushed his forehand. You can do the same thing. If your opponent hits a ball weakly to the middle of the court or to your backhand side, you can quickly move into position to hit the open-stance forehand crosscourt to your opponent's backhand side. This is commonly called an "inside-out" forehand. The other reason Borg was able to get into this position was his very effective two-handed backhand. He was one of the first modern-era men's player to use the two-handed shot effectively: Borg hit very hard, deep, crosscourt shots off his backhand side. He was also able to increase the angle on his two-handed backhand, crosscourt, very effectively. The high-angle play does carry some risk, but it is very effective, and it is more effective if you hit a two-handed backhand. This shot will produce a lot of weakly hit crosscourt shots near the middle of the court. These weak oncoming shots are perfect for running around to get into position for the open-stance forehand. Borg played against a lot of one-handed backhand players, and they were hard-pressed to cope with this hard-hit, sharply angled ball. So, like Borg, you can get into this position by moving around a weakly hit ball to your backhand side or to the middle of the court. This ball usually comes after you hit a really hard shot on a crosscourt angle to your opponent's backhand.

The third question is: Why is this such a dominating position? Part of the answer is the effectiveness of the inside-out crosscourt forehand. It is a very high-percentage shot for a several of reasons. One reason is the vector of the oncoming shot (see Figure 3). You are receiving a ball that is hit crosscourt. The ball's vector is coming on an angle from the backhand side. We know from previous discussions that when you choose a target right on the vector of the oncoming shot, there is zero deflection factor. Having zero deflection factor makes the inside-out crosscourt forehand a high-percentage shot. The other reason is that with an aggressive shoulder-and-torso turn, the crosscourt target is in strength, making the shot very high percentage. You are also shooting crosscourt, which means that the net is at its lowest and you have a huge amount of court to shoot into. This makes the inside-out crosscourt forehand a very high-percentage shot. So the player in the Borg square fires a shot right back to his opponent's backhand, on vector, in strength, over the lowest part of the net, and into the longest part of the court. The target for this shot is just about over the center tape, on vector.

The other reason this position is tactically dominating is due to your expanded strength. Our player has turned his shoulder and torso so that the line of strength is pointing along the vector of the oncoming shot (see Figure 3). In this position our player holds the entire court in his strength. A player using the Borg square can choose any target he wants, left side, right side, or middle of the court. He can drive his shot hard, back on the vector of the ball. This will produce an even weaker shot from his opponent's backhand. Or he can rip the ball to the left side of the court to his opponent's forehand side. This shot is deep in strength and can be crushed, forcing his opponent to run the maximum distance to retrieve the shot. These hard-hit shots will produce a lot of winners or weak balls to the center of the court. From here, making the transition to the killer position is quick and easy.

So here is the game plan: Once you are in the Borg square, you drive the ball on vector to your opponent's backhand side until you have a weak ball sitting for you near the middle of the court. You then make your aggressive shoulder-and-torso turn, covering the entire court with your strength. Here, you are in the killer position. You hold the court in your strength and you have all the options. You can choose any target; you can shoot to either side of the court. Now your opponent must do one of two things. He can stand in the backhand side of the court, waiting for another hard-hit ball on vector. Or he can run to cover the open court to defend against your shot deep-in-strength.

Now it is time to use your open focus to see what your opponent is doing. If he is staying put near the backhand side, it is time to rip the ball to the target on the left side of the court, deep in strength, and make him run. Or, if you see him moving to cover the open court, you can fire on vector, inside-out, to the backhand side behind your opponent's run, wrong-footing your opponent.

When Borg used this tactic, he pounded inside-out shots to the backhand side of his opponent until he got a weak sitter to crush. Once he got his sitter, he moved into the killer position, assessed his opponent's movement, and crushed his forehand for a winner.

Watch the top players use this Borg square tactic. It is both very effective and easy to incorporate into your game. You will be able to use it to win many points in the future.

Drop Shots and Other Wrongheaded Game Plans

I hope you saw the 2013 Wimbledon Women's Final. Sabine Lisicki lost to Marion Bartoli in a low-quality, disappointing match. Lisicki had played brilliant tennis until the final, vanquishing Serena Williams and other higher-ranked players on the way. Excellent ball striking, power tennis, and smart risk taking had characterized her play. In the final, however, she was a completely different player.

The occasion obviously weighed heavily on Lisicki, and nerves affected her performance. But what can be most instructive to you as a tennis player is the way Lisicki changed her tactical approach—and why she changed it. She had played great points in her previous matches. She ran her opponents and wrong-footed them judiciously. Lisicki chose targets in strength and took chances near the edge of her strength when appropriate. She went for her shots with courage. She hit out all the time. Lisicki used the same point-playing game plan we discussed earlier. But, in the final, all of that disappeared. She abandoned playing her game. Lisicki tailored her point-playing tactics and shot selection completely to avoid Bartoli's strengths and to take advantages of her weaknesses.

Bartoli hit two-handed off both sides, just like Monica Seles did. (In fact, she modeled her game after Seles.) Because of her double two-handed style, Bartoli chose shots that were deep in strength, almost always on extreme angles crosscourt. She shot to the edge of strength, down the line, only when she was in a perfect position, with her strength dominating both sides of the court. This game plan is essentially very conservative strength-and-position shot selection. It is enhanced because both shots are hit two-handed, with the other hand providing extra force toward the strong side. These were Bartoli's strengths.

Conventional tennis wisdom has it that a two-handed player should be move as wide as possible in the court, forcing the two-handed hitter to stretch. This takes advantage of the lesser reach of the two-handed shot. Since Bartoli hits two-handed off both sides, this tactical plan says to hit sharp angles to work against the lesser reach. Bartoli is also weak moving forward and not much of a volleyer. Conventional tennis wisdom also says that if your opponent does not volley well, you should try to draw her into the net to force her to hit her weaker shot.

Great ball striking and good shot selection are what got Lisicki to the finals. But she traded that excellent approach for a wrongheaded game plan in the finals. She changed her tactics to take advantage of Bartoli's weaknesses and avoid her strengths. Instead of crushing her shots to high-percentage targets and making smart shot selections as the points unfolded, she tried to shoot for extremely high-angle forehands to "stretch" the two-handed player. Because Lisicki doesn't have a big flip, topspin forehand, she was unable to make this high-angle shot; as a result, she missed that shot wide almost every time she attempted it. Lisicki also unwisely chose to hit multiple drop shots to draw Bartoli into the net and force her to hit her weak volley. This resulted in farcical points in which Bartoli, hip to the tactic, moved easily to play the drop shot and then crushed the high volley that was meant to be a lob.

Lisicki returned to her brilliance for a moment in the middle of the second set. She went back to crushing the ball to high-percentage targets. She went for her shots and made smart shot selections. This got her a service break and a couple of held serves, but it was too little, too late.

The lesson of this tennis tragedy is not that you should ignore your opponent's strengths and weaknesses. It's that your opponent's strengths and weaknesses are *not* the most important factor in shot selection and point-playing tactics. You play *your* game. You shoot *your* shots. You always choose targets in strength. You always start by running your opponent and then wrong-footing prudently. You jam your opponent to change the flow of a point. If your opponent has a weakness (such as a weaker backhand), you choose shots to that side when you have the option. You don't choose shots to that side when it does not follow the rules of playing a point. You only choose the drop shot when conditions are right (more on this below). You are playing your game using right shot-selection logic. Never let your opponent's strengths and weaknesses take you out of that logic. You can avoid those strengths and attack those weaknesses, as long as you make shot selections that follow the rules of playing a point, which are, one more time: *Always choose high percentage targets in strength; when you have the option to hit to either side of the court, run your opponent first, then wrong-foot judiciously, and then jam your opponent to alter the flow of a point and change things up.*

As long as you remain inside that logic, you can choose shots that will stay away from your opponent's strengths or take advantage of her weaknesses when the choice presents itself. Don't let a contrived game plan take you out of your shot-selection logic.

In summary, you have your game, and your opponent has hers. You know how to play a point. Crush the ball to well-selected targets. Play your game. Hit your shots. When you have the option to choose multiple shots, you can shoot to your opponent's weakness. Don't let playing your opponent's weaknesses, or staying away from her strengths, drive you into low-percentage shot selections.

When to Hit a Drop Shot

The drop shot is a good shot selection under certain conditions. It is best employed when 1) your opponent is deep in the court behind the baseline; 2) your opponent is already moving to cover the open court; and 3) you are forward in the court, with your strength covering both sides of the court. In this situation you have the option to strike the ball hard to either side or jam your opponent; here, the drop shot becomes a fourth shot selection. Because you are in a position to crush the ball to either side of the court, the drop shot should completely wrong-foot your opponent as she moves to cover the open court or anticipate a shot behind her. You should choose the drop shot infrequently: only as a surprise.

Vision is a key component of the drop shot. Given the above conditions, you are forward in the court, with your strength dominating. Your preparation should be exactly like your hard-hit topspin or backspin shots. Make a good torso turn with a fluid figure-eight start to the backswing. As your open focus shows you your opponent's move to anticipate your shot deep in the court, you play underneath the arc. The arc play is far rounder than the shape of the incoming arc. You purposely do not hit through the arc. You play around it, producing big backspin. Your target should be about a foot above the net.

Some Drop Shot Don'ts

Don't hit the drop shot when you are deep in the court. The drop shot is slow, and your opponent will have time to see, react, and move to play the shot.

Don't hit the drop shot if your opponent is in a good position to receive your shot: that is, standing in the middle of your strength, ready to move in any direction.

Don't hit the drop shot on big points. If you do, it is a desperation shot. The chance of making a nervous error on this shot is very high.

Don't hit the drop shot out of frustration. You often see players hit drop shots because they can't figure out how to win a point. Avoid this hopeless move. Keep with your point-playing logic. Choose the drop shot only when the conditions are right. If your opponent is beating you, hang in there; at some point he will come out of the zone. Making good high-percentage shot selections will keep the pressure on. It will get your opponent out of the zone sooner than by showing your desperation with poorly chosen drop shots.

The drop shot is a good shot to choose under the right conditions. Use it as a weapon—infrequently, and with the element of surprise—to win points.

The Error Sine Wave

During a match your accuracy and ball control will travel a performance sine-wave pattern. A sine wave travels up and down in a horizontal direction (see Figure 5). Just like a sine wave, your accuracy will go from very high to very low. During a match, there will be times when you can't miss; there will also be times when you are unable to hit your targets. When you start to make lots of errors out of the court, it is important to have a technique to get yourself back into the match, hitting a high percentage of shots inside the lines.

The technique here is to use the rheostat concept on your targets. As you improve and start to project arcs, you will tend to choose targets that put your shots closer to the lines. Your improved ball control will encourage you to shoot for those lower-percentage targets because you can. When you start to make an unacceptable number of errors, however, you need a fix. The fix is to dial the rheostat down. You need to go back to more conservative targets. You should

| Hitting all targets with accuracy: Okay to shoot closer to the sidelines. |
| Missing targets you normally hit consistently: Bring your targets in towards the center of the court. |

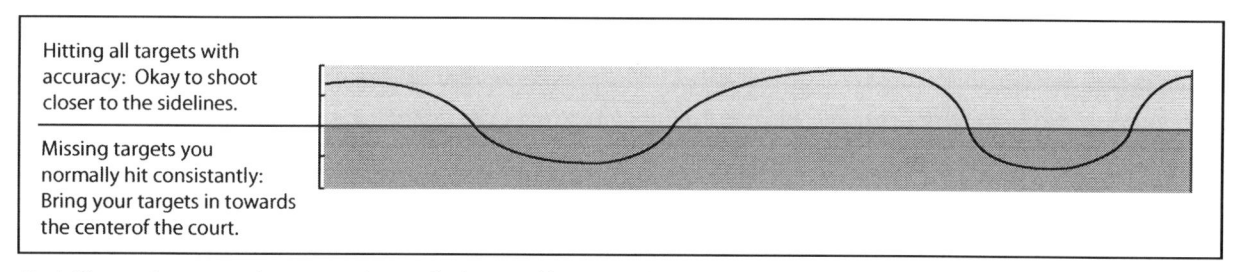

Fig 1. The performance sign wave. As you find yourself missing shots you normally make easily bring your targets in towards the center of the court, nearer the center of the tape target. As you reduce your errors you can move your targets out nearer the sidelines. If and when your performane degragdes again bring your targets back to the center of the court near the center tape target.

bring your targets back toward the center of the court. Use the three targets you learned in the aiming chapter. These targets are very near the center of the net and will produce shots that land well inside the court. As you bring your targets in toward the middle of the court, you will bring your errors back to near zero. Depending on how badly you are doing, you may have to shoot only for the center of the court for a while. Once you start hitting balls in the court, your confidence and your feel for the targets will return.

After you start shooting a high percentage of balls in the court, you can dial the rheostat back up. You can start shooting for targets farther left and right of the center of the net, producing shots wider in the court, closer to the lines.

The important thing is to stop missing. You need to stop giving away free points. Tennis is a game of errors. As you move up in skill level and competition, giving away free points becomes very costly. You have to make your opponent play the ball. Give the other player a chance to miss. Don't let the match get away from you. Avoid dropping points (and even games) by continuing to go for shots and targets that you just can't get a handle on. The trick is to recognize what is happening. Be in control of your game; dial your ambition up and down.

Summary

Tennis can be a very simple game. Instructors and coaches often grossly complicate it. Players brains are chock full of tips and techniques that create more confusion than competence. The techniques you learned here are simple. You crush shots to targets. You shoot to the middle, the left side, and the right side of the court. You learned where the high percentage targets are. You know which shot to select for a given situation.

The tactical plan is simple. You run your opponent. Once your opponent is on the run her shot selection options will be compromised. You will be able to anticipate the next shot and get into a great position hammer your next shot. That will give you the option to wrong foot, jam, or run your opponent again. The game couldn't be simpler.

Tennis is played one point at a time. The better you can drive your focus to this incremental, one point at a time mindset, the better your mental focus will be. Your goal should be to win every point. Yes, every point. Approach your next match with this attitude.

CHAPTER 7

How to Control Your Brain During Competition

"Anybody who has played sports and says they have never choked is lying to you."
—Pete Sampras

"We all choke. Winners know how to handle choking better than losers."
—John McEnroe

Tennis is a stratified game. There is a pecking order: a hierarchy of perceived and real capabilities. As you get better and face players who are considered better than you, you must face up to and overcome the expected outcome—that is, beat people who are supposed to be better than you. We will now address this problem and provide you with a few tools to achiever success in that endeavor.

"Clueless" versus "Logical"

It is important to approach tennis with a dispassionate, unemotional logic, but if you are out there making "strokes," this is difficult to do. If you expect good, accurate shot making to be the result of perfect, uniformly reproduced strokes, you will be frustrated and confused by your errors. Outcomes will be random. Anger and frustration will dominate. You will be living in Einstein's definition of insanity: doing the same thing over and over again while expecting a different outcome. This is what I like to call the "clueless" approach.

You can approach tennis dispassionately and unemotionally if you think logically.
And you have learned this logic: it is ball control and percentage tennis. Ball control—knowing how to aim for targets and make corrections for errors—is the opposite of doing the same thing over and over while expecting a different outcome. Ball control is the continuous application of a system, reacting to errors in a logical way. Percentage tennis is the knowledge that some shots have a better chance of going into the court than others. It is a logical template for decision-making. A tennis match is a long-run game of chance. By choosing high-percentage targets you give yourself the best possible opportunity to be victorious at the end of the day. This logic enables an unemotional approach to the game.

Going Forward

As a percentage-tennis player, you go out to the court and fire away at targets. You choose targets based on your knowledge of strength, position, and the vector of the oncoming shot. You know that you almost always make a small error every time you make a shot. You know that making errors is okay. You know how to correct for any error. The game is not mysterious; it is logical. If you miss a shot, it's because you missed. It is not because you did not make a good stroke or your grip was wrong. If you miss your target, you adjust your aim point, rip the arc, and fire away at your next shot. You keep shooting for targets and making adjustments. You keep going for it. You hit out with confidence and without fear of missing. You continue to apply the aiming logic, making adjustments for every error, until the last shot of the match.

It does not matter who you are playing. It could be your sister or Roger Federer. You still do the same thing. You fire away at targets and rip the arcs. You play a tennis match one point at a time. You play a point one shot at a time. Because you know where the high-percentage targets are and how to adjust for mistakes, you know that over the course of the match, you are going to hit a huge number of balls in the court. This should produce success. If you don't win, then the other player just played better than you. It is not an emotional or personal thing. It is simply applying the logic, taking high-percentage risks, and letting the chips fall where they may.

Zoning and Choking

Tennis is a stand-alone, single-combat game. You are out there solo against another competitor. You make every play, every decision. You're under lots of pressure. Amazingly, it is possible to miss *any* shot in tennis. From the first serve of the match to the easiest sitter, nothing is really guaranteed. This possibility is ever present and looms like a specter in the consciousness of every player. Sometimes the possibility of missing is as far away as another country. Sometimes it suffocates and strangles the brain, dominating thought and visualization. How can you control the demon of self-destruction and failure? How can you prevent your mind from being your own worst enemy? How can you keep from—yes, I'll say it—*choking*?

Everyone chokes. It's important to know this and not to be too hard on yourself, or to think that you are unique and incapable of overcoming it. From the average club player in a match against his local nemesis to the world's number-five player against the world's number-one player, everyone chokes at times. Choking can't be eliminated completely. It must be managed and kept to a minimum. The player who chokes less, wins.

Competitors make nervous errors because they cannot control their thoughts and mental imagery. This usually occurs when the player is in a position to win. Here, expectation colors the thinking. If the player believes he should *not* be winning, then those thoughts will come up. As those ideas register in his conscious mind, thoughts of losing and thoughts of failure will emerge. These thoughts then create negative imagery. The player might even visualize himself missing. This negativity feeds the subconscious mind. Those thoughts and images act like commands. Once those orders are issued, the body does what the mind has inadvertently directed—miss the easy sitter, or double fault—choke when you are in a position to win.

The great champion (and excellent analyst) Chris Evert accurately observed that most tennis players play better when they are behind. Why is this? It doesn't make much sense. It is counterintuitive that tennis players would hit more freely and better when they are behind. When you are behind, you could lose. It seems that this would put pressure on, not take it off. When you are ahead, you can win. The other player has to make the shot or lose. Intuition says that the player who is ahead should be under *less* pressure, not *more* pressure. But this is not the case. It is always the same story: When you are ahead and in a position to win, *belief* or *disbelief* enters your mind and affects your play. The player who believes she should win is less likely to miss. The player who doesn't believe that she should win will choke big-time. This happens at the highest level of the game. So if it happens to you, do not despair.

Negative thinking and negative belief are unavoidable. Many times those beliefs are based on fact. If you are about to beat someone whom you have never beaten before—someone who is supposed to be really good, someone who is supposed to be better than you—then those negative "truths" will come up. These "facts" about your status in the tennis hierarchy will hover about in your mind. When you become conscious that you are actually in a position to win, you confront those beliefs and your mind will replay this preconceived reality. The internal conversation might go something like this: "This guy is supposed to be much better than me. I have never beaten this player before. This player is ranked much higher than me." You must expect this kind of thinking to occur. What you need is a way to drive your mind clear of those thoughts and produce positive action thoughts and positive mental imagery.

The secret to controlling negative thinking and purging nervous errors is twofold. First, you need to understand why this kind of thinking happens and you need to expect it. Second, you must develop technique to control your mind when this self-doubt occurs during competition. A lot of scientific research has been conducted on how the mind works when athletes compete and when regular folks are subjected to stressful situations. The research shows that the mind has two operating systems. One is calculating, verbal, judgmental, and "conscious." This is called the *explicit system*. The other is intuitive, noncalculating, spontaneous, and "unconscious." This system is called the *implicit system*. Choking occurs when the explicit, conscious, system is operating. Free-flowing performance— being "in the zone"—occurs when the implicit, unconscious, system is at work.

What follows is a discussion on managing your brain during competition. You will learn to understand and recognize which mental operating system is at work. You will learn techniques to move your brain from the explicit, judgmental, "choking" system to the implicit, unconscious, "zoning" system. Try these techniques and ways of thinking as you go forward. It can take your game to a place where, when you are under pressure, belief and disbelief will no longer enter into the equation. Instead of being dominated by expectation, you will just play points—clinical, unemotional, cutthroat, and precise.

Understanding Your Brain: The Implicit and Explicit Operating Systems

Let's look more closely at the explicit and implicit mental operating systems. In Steven Kotler's great book *The Rise of Superman: Decoding the Science of Ultimate Human Performance* (which all of you should read), the author writes (page 34):

> The brain has two systems for processing information. The first, the *explicit system*, is rule-based, can be expressed verbally, and is tied to conscious awareness…But when the cold calculus of logic is swapped out for the gut sense of intuition this is the *implicit system* at work…This system relies on skill and experience, is not consciously accessible, and cannot be described verbally. These two systems are often described as "conscious" versus "unconscious" or left brain versus right brain…

Let's take a look at these two operating systems in more detail.

Explicit Operating System = Conscious = Judgmental = Choking

When your brain is using the explicit system, you are talking to yourself. You are internally verbalizing. The conversation is judgmental and calculating. You are aware of your surroundings and are concerned about possible outcomes. For example:

> "What if I miss my second serve?"
> "My dad is over there, and he doesn't look happy."
> "How could I miss that last shot?"
> "If I don't hold my serve, this match is over."

I could go on. The explicit operating system uses the brain's prefrontal cortex. The explicit system is working when analytical and judgmental thinking occurs.

Implicit Operating System = Unconscious = Playing Out of Your Mind = Zoning

You have also experienced the implicit operating system while playing tennis.

When your brain is using the implicit operating system, the prefrontal cortex is quiet. You are not talking to yourself. Your brain is nonthinking. You are acting spontaneously. You are ripping your shots automatically. You are going for it without having to drive your brain anywhere. You have no idea whom you are playing or who else is around. You don't have to consciously make yourself produce shots. When you are in this mental state, you play "out of your mind." You are "unconscious." You are in the zone. The implicit system uses multiple parts of the brain at the same time. While using the implicit system, those parts of the brain work together; connections are fluid and spontaneous.

Steven Kotler also quotes Dr. Arne Dietrich about a "hypofrontality," or quieting of the thinking part of the brain (page 49 in *The Rise of Superman*): "In flow [read zone], parts of the prefrontal cortex [the calculating part of the brain] are temporarily deactivating. It's an efficiency exchange. We're trading energy usually used for higher cognitive functions for heightened attention and awareness."

When you are using the implicit mental operating system—when you are in the zone—the calculating part of your brain is inactive. This state is also called "hypofrontality." *Hypo-* means under or beneath, so *hypofrontality* means that the thinking, front part of your brain (the prefrontal cortex) is quiet and inactive. Great competitors are able to control their minds and drive their prefrontal cortex quiet while competing. By doing this, they access the unconscious, zoning mental state. That is the trick. That is the key to achieving high performance under pressure. You must develop the ability to quiet the front part of your brain and allow your mind to access all of its experience, intuition, and capabilities.

The Zone

Scientists call the unconscious, zoning state *flow*. But the term is interchangeable with *zone*. The psychology professor Mihaly Csikszentmihalyi coined the term *flow*. Here is how he defined it. Flow/zone means:

> …being so involved in an activity, nothing else seems to matter. The ego falls away. Time flies. Every action, movement, and thought follows inevitably from the previous one. Your whole being is involved, and you're using your skills to the utmost.

Other basic properties of the flow/zone state are mental clarity, emotional detachment, and its automatic nature. Dr. Csikszentmihalyi identified ten components of the flow/zone state:

1. *Concentration*: A high degree of concentration on a limited field of attention.
2. *Clear goals*: Expectations and rules are discernible, and goals are attainable and align appropriately with one's skill set and abilities. The challenge level should be high.
3. *Direct and immediate feedback*: Successes and failures are apparent, so behavior can be adjusted as needed.

4. *Control*: The subject has a sense of control over the situation.
5. *Balance between ability level and challenge*: The activity is neither too easy nor too difficult.
6. *Absorption*: There is a narrowing of awareness down to the activity itself.
7. *Loss of self-consciousness*: Action and awareness merge.
8. *Distorted sense of time*: One's subjective experience of time is altered.
9. *Intrinsic reward*: The activity is intrinsically rewarding, so action is effortless.
10. *Awareness*: The subject has a lack of awareness of bodily needs.

Well, there it is. It is nice to have the zone explained so succinctly. But what is even nicer is how zone-friendly ball-control techniques are. Let's go over how ball control meshes with the zoning state.

Concentration on a limited field of attention: Using ball control, the only thing you focus on is where you want the ball to go. It is very limited and very compatible to focus and concentration.

Clear goals: There is no clearer goal than shooting a shot at a specific target.

Direct and immediate feedback: Aiming techniques provide instant feedback about your behavior. Your successes and failures are apparent and measurable every time you make an error. And, most importantly, by correcting for your errors, you have the perfect method to adjust your behavior when you miss.

Control: By directly manipulating the flight path of your shots, you have ultimate control over your game. There is no mystery about what is happening while you play. You are not trying to make some movement with your body (read: *stroke*) that will indirectly produce a shot. You directly command the ball to go where you want it to go. Ball control gives you the ultimate sense of control over the situation.

Absorption: Ball-control techniques—shooting at targets and projecting arcs—are simple and uncomplicated, so the mind can easily limit its focus to these very specific activities. You can become absorbed with ease.

Loss of self-consciousness: When you use ball-control techniques, your focus is not physical. You are not trying to control your body's actions. This reduces self-consciousness. Your awareness can become one with the action you are performing. That is direct conjuring; bending reality to your will by making the ball go where you want it to go.

Ball control is zone/flow-friendly. It removes all the rubbish and manifold points of focus that can clutter your mind. Your mind does not have to reach for and retain multiple techniques. Using ball-control techniques, your mind is instead like a magnifying glass, focusing your thoughts into one unifying theme, the way the sun's rays can be focused into a burning, hot light. Because of its simplicity and clarity, ball control will be the key to quieting your calculating prefrontal cortex. Ball control will be your hall pass to the implicit, zoning mental state.

"Flow/Zone Hacking"

Steven Kotler coined the term "flow/zone hacking" in *Rise of the Superman*. Zone hacking is a technique for transitioning from the explicit, conscious mental state to the implicit, unconscious, mental state—the zone. It refers to a method or means to get the mind into the zone. *Rise of the Superman*'s main focus is on extreme athletes who perform extraordinary, truly death-defying, feats. Many of the flow/zone hacks Kotler describes have to do with one's environment and are really not germane to competitive tennis. Here, we will focus solely on controlling your brain within the competitive tennis environment.

The Observer

Now that you understand how your brain works, the verbalizing, explicit system should be easy to recognize. And that is what you must do. You need to be able to recognize when your brain is verbalizing and being judgmental. You need an internal observer that is displaced from the self to scrutinize your thinking. The observer can only be active when you are conscious and out of the zone. When your brain is in the zone, using the implicit system, you are not conscious, and your internal observer will be as inactive as your quieted prefrontal cortex. But when you come out of the zone, you need to use the internal observer to recognize this new state and help quiet the front of your brain.

Verbalization Leads to Visualization

Competition-induced, internal conversation produces haphazard and random visualizations that accord with your inner monologue. Fear is an integral part of the talking, implicit system. As your prefrontal cortex blabbers to itself, all the fears and concerns you have kick off little videos in your brain. These visualizations lurk just below the talk. The videos are manifestations of your fears. They act like commands, and your body will obey them. In general, your body follows whatever you visualize.

For example, you might be in a big point, about to hit a second serve. Your internal conversation may be telling you, "I can't miss this serve, or I'll be out of the match." This talk will produce visualization. And that visualization will probably be very negative and fear-based. What you fear in this situation is missing your second serve. That fear will produce a mental video of you missing the second serve. You actually see yourself making the error. If you shoot that second serve in this condition, you will most likely miss it—just as you visualized it. This is the quintessential choke. This is when your internal observer must intervene before you shoot that second serve.

*The Reset: Using Your Internal Conversation
to Produce Desired Visualizations*

The implicit, zoning state is not consciously accessible, so you can't just stomp your feet and demand that the front part of your brain shuts up. You can't have a hissy fit and make the negative videos go away. What you must do instead is gain control of your internal conversation and use it like a tool. Once your observer recognizes explicit self-talk, you make a mental reset. You halt the random talk. You drive your internal conversation. This driven conversation will produce wanted, positive visualizations. Once you conjure the positive visualization, you focus only on that visual. Transitioning from self-talk to visualization quiets the prefrontal cortex. This is the skill that great competitors have.

   The problem most players face when they are out of the zone, making internal conversation, is that they do not know what to think about. They don't have a path from self-talk to visualization because they don't know what to visualize. They can't quiet their prefrontal cortex because they have no holistic concept to focus on. Is it grip or follow-through? Is it watching the ball or footwork? When they attempt to concentrate and control their mind, they are like a mosquito on a pond. Their mind flits from concept to concept. In this confused condition, fear-based visualizations are rampant. They confront beliefs about the possible outcomes. Visualizations inspired by their worst fears of failure come emerge. Those visualizations act like commands, and the choking begins.

   Visualizations *are* commands. Your body follows what your mind pictures. You conjure outcome through mental imagery. This truth acts in your favor now that you use ball-control techniques. Once your internal observer recognizes the explicit self-talk, you take charge. You recognize and accept that the fear-based, negative videos are a result of your beliefs about possible outcomes. And then you make your mental reset. You drive your self-talk to the heart and center of ball control. You talk about *where* you want your shot to go. You make conversation about your target and projecting the arc of your shot. As you make that conversation, your mind will begin to visualize your shot. Once that video starts to play, you hold that in your mind's eye. You burn that picture into reality.

   In our second serve example, things might go something like this. Your internal observer recognizes the negative talk and the visualization of missing the second serve. Now, you reset and start driving your brain. You make a conversation along these lines: "Okay, I'm going to rip this second serve right there. I'm going to go for it. I'm going to smash this f——ing serve, and it's going to go through my target and into the corner right there." As you make this conversation, your mind will start to visualize. Once the visualization of your scorching second serve is summoned, you hold it and amplify it. Then you let it rip.

   When you transition from verbalization to visualization, you quiet and control your conscious mind. This is the "hack." Moving the mind from talk to visualization is what quiets the calculating prefrontal cortex. The process of using self-talk to produce wanted, positive visualizations, and then focusing on those visualizations, is the entry point to the zone. This is the skill that great competitors have. You can nurture and develop this skill using this process:

1. Use your internal observer to recognize random, fearful self-talk and imagery.
2. Make a mental reset to halt the random talk.
3. Make driven, positive self-talk, focusing on ball control.
4. Transition from verbal talk to visualization.
5. Hold those wanted visualizations in your mind's eye.
6. Then let it rip.

Positive-Action Thoughts

Thoughts are a combination of talk and visualizations. They occur when the mind is using the explicit mental system. Use your observer to analyze what occurs when you have a thought. Try this, for example: "I really want to see my best friend." The conversational part of the thought—"I really want to see my best friend"—will bring up a few visualizations. The video might be about what that person looks like, or where he lives. Try something else. Try something that bothers you. For example, "I don't like going to the dentist." If it's true that you don't like going to the dentist, you might visualize the dentist's drill or your mouth being uncomfortably numb. All explicit thoughts bring up visualizations. You can use this fact about thoughts to your advantage.

The Tool Kit

A positive-action thought is a thought that is directed at a desired outcome. It is made up of self-talk and visualization. It is something you use to generate a desired result. Your job is to develop a "tool kit" of positive-action thoughts for your tennis game. They will all center on ball control. These thoughts must produce shot-making visualizations. This "thought tool kit" is what you go to when your internal observer notices the explicit mental state. The verbal part of these thoughts must be fearless. The talk needs to be bold and warlike. The visual part of these thoughts must summon targets and project arcs. You must conjure the image of your shot firing out through your target and into the court.

As you build your tool kit, you should focus first on serving and the service return. The period between points is when most explicit self-talk occurs. This period between the action of the game is when you are most susceptible to pressure. It is when you confront your fears and beliefs. Your internal observer must be vigilant during these breaks in the game. You must learn to make the mental reset as soon as possible.

For your service, build a known and driven thought package that will conjure the targets in your aiming architecture. The talk should revolve around manifesting your service arc and going for it. You can't give a damn about missing. The thoughts should be vibrant with the visualization of your projected shot. Once that projected shot is created in your mind's eye, focus only on the visualization and let the talk fall away. Now you can serve.

For service returns, create a set of thoughts that see you exploding into the arc of the inbound serve. Your thoughts should be bright with imagery of your return striking out over the net and through your target. Once you conjure this visualization, focus, and ride it as you bounce in preparation. Now you are ready.

For general point play, your positive-action thoughts must be very simple. If you fall into explicit thinking in the middle of a point, you're in trouble, so these thoughts have to be very straightforward. They have to center on ripping the inbound arc and pounding the three targets: left, right, and center of the court. Don't get complicated here. These thoughts must be raging with abandon. They must be explosive, with a daring indifference about missing. This is where you go for it—and let the chips fall where they may.

Ball-control techniques are about bending reality to your will. You conjure your shot. You fire the ball at a target and make it go there. You project your arc out into the court on the path you create. Ball control is visual. The emphasis on the visual enables you to easily transition from talk to visualization. Going from the talk to the visual is what quiets the front part of your brain and opens the door to the zone.

Meditation and Mantra

When your mind is in the zone, using the implicit operating system, it produces low-alpha brain waves. Low-alpha brain waves are associated with REM sleep, meditation, and insight. So the implicit, zoning mental state has meditation-like brain waves. Getting into and out of the "unconscious zone" of tennis play is much like the meditation process.

Meditation refers to any of a family of practices in which practitioners train their minds to self-induce a mode of consciousness in order to realize some benefit. A *mantra* is a sound, syllable, word, or image that is considered capable of transformation.

The meditator focuses on a mantra. As the meditator focuses on the mantra, his brain moves from the mantra to other conscious thoughts. When the meditator notices this, he focuses again on the mantra. Through this process, the mind quiets, and conscious thoughts eventually disappear, exorcised by the meditation process. After these unwanted thoughts are purged, the meditator achieves an altered state of consciousness. This new level of consciousness is not permanent. Eventually, the meditator becomes aware, and the mind surfaces to focus on conscious thoughts again. When this happens, the meditator restarts the process. He focuses on the mantra and seeks to achieve the beneficial mental state. The movement from conscious extraneous thoughts, to conscious focus on the mantra, to the altered state of consciousness, and then back to conscious thought is a kind of mental sine wave.

The mental part of a tennis match follows a similar sine wave. Your mind travels from the conscious state to the unconscious, zoning state and then back to the conscious state. The zone is usually exited when under pressure, when in a position to win.

Take stock of your mental state the next time you play. Notice how your mind moves from a conscious—explicit—state to an unconscious—implicit—state. You will ride this mental sine wave every time you play. Watch a professional match. See if you observe the same mental undulation in great players. I recommend Serena Williams, Djokovic, Sharapova, and Federer. These players are some of the best at managing their brains during competition. But even they experience periods of play in which nerves and explicit thinking get in the way of great shot making. Notice that for extended periods of time, they play almost perfectly. Then, for short periods of time, they make errors that seem unreasonable and out of character. At times, even they are affected by the pressure of the situation. They too get nervous. Notice how they gather themselves and reenter the zone. Watch some lesser players compete against these greats. Notice that the pressure of the situation usually drives the exit from the zone. Notice that the exit usually occurs when they are in a position to win.

For most players, the movement from the conscious to the zoning state is a haphazard event. They occasionally achieve the zone for a random duration of time. But now you know what is happening in your brain. You know the difference between the explicit, thinking state and the implicit, zoning state. You can take control of this process. The meditation paradigm is one approach to gaining that control.

Your tennis mantra will be the visualization of your shot. You will get to this visualization using positive-action thoughts that bring up the visualization of your projected arc. Like the meditator, you focus and hold the mantra. As you focus on the visualization, your conscious thoughts will begin to fall away. As your mind quiets, you enter the implicit, zoning, mental state. This is the beneficial altered consciousness you are seeking. But the unconscious, zoning state is fragile. Your brain will inevitably resurface; you will come out of the zone and start thinking. Once you notice conscious thoughts, you make the mental reset. Refocus on your mantra—the visualization of your next ripping shot. It may take a few attempts to purge the conscious thinking from your brain and quiet the prefrontal cortex. Be patient. Focus on the visualization of your next projected arc. That is your mantra. With practice, you will be able to use it to quiet your conscious thinking and reenter the zone.

Your job as a tennis competitor is to constantly work on managing your brain. Understand that you can't stay in the zone all the time. Your mental state will follow a sine wave from the conscious state, to the zoning state, and back to the conscious state. The goal is to recognize your exit from the zone quickly and minimize your time out of it. Work to develop your tennis mantra. The mantra is visual. It is the conjuring of your next ripping shot. Use positive-action thoughts to bring up those visualizations. Then use those same thoughts to summon the reality of your next shot. Those visualizations are your tennis mantra. Focusing on that mantra will quiet the prefrontal cortex and will enable reentry to the zone.

Conclusion

Being out of body, playing "out of your mind," zoning, shooting, ripping arcs, hitting out all the time: that is where you want your game to be. The concepts you have learned here will enable you to do it. Ball control is a liberating approach. It embraces errors. Having the knowledge that making errors is an essential, integral part of improving will give you the freedom to miss. Shooting shots using mind's-eye targets will permit you to explode when you hit the ball. Creating different arc shapes through visualization will open a treasure chest of possibilities. It will free you to improvise. You, too, can make all those amazing shots you see great players create. Direct conjuring—bending reality to your will by force of mind—is gratifying and intrinsically satisfying. And that is what you do when you use ball-control techniques: you bend reality to your will.

You should have fun experimenting with the concepts you have learned. Be sure to give yourself the freedom to miss, and always go for your shots. Every mistake you make will put another pixel in the picture, making it clearer. Every error will add another detail to the blueprint of your aiming architecture. Every point you lose while you are hitting out, smashing your shot to your target, will make you a better player. Keep going for it out there with courage and abandon.

Glossary

Aiming architecture: The structure of visual targets you develop on the court to control the ball. The architecture uses the net as a visual reference and the mind's-eye targets over the net and out over the court to manipulate the flight path of your shots. This architecture will start with the generic targets shown in the text and illustrations but will become unique to your game as you progress.

Arc: The curved flight path of the ball as it travels over the net and into the court. It is the signature of the shot's energy: its speed, spin, and direction.

Arc projection: Creating, in the mind's eye, the entire arced shape of your shot, and using this mentally created, visual shape to direct your shot out into the court. It is the highest form of ball control.

Ball control: Using targets and aiming to control the ball without direct manipulation of the body or stroke.

Center tape target: The target that is located directly over the center of the net, above the tape holding the net to the court.

Circle of error: The circle encompassing a grouping of misses as you shoot for a certain target.

Flat shot: A shot hit with very little spin. Usually driven hard and low over the net.

Flow:
   1. The fluid movement of the tennis stroke as if connected with the movement of the oncoming shot.
   2. Synonym of zone (see below).

Hitting out: Fearless striking of the ball with no concern about missing.

In-Strength: The "pull" side of the body, defined by the line of strength (see below) projecting out from your shoulders. Shots directed toward your strength are higher-percentage shots.

Jam *(tactical shot selection)*: Directing your shot into the body of your opponent.

Line of strength: An imaginary line projecting out along your shoulders into the court. This line defines the "in-strength" and "out-of-strength" areas of the court.

Out-of-strength: The "push" side of the body, defined by the line of strength (see above) projecting out from your shoulders. Shots directed out-of-strength are lower-percentage shots.

Percentage tennis: Making shot selections that have a high probability of going into the court.

Rolling topspin: A shot hit will a moderat topspin. This shot is not aggressively flipped. This is the same amount of topspin that should be applied to "flat" shots.

Run *(tactical shot selection)*: Directing your shot at the target that will make your opponent run the farthest distance.

Shot: Firing the ball at a specific target. It is akin to pulling the trigger on a gun that is directed at a certain location.

Shot selection: Choosing where to shoot your shot. In its highest form, this means choosing the direction and arcing shape of your shot.

In-Strength: The "pull" side of the body, defined by the line of strength (see above) projecting out from your shoulders. Shots directed toward your strength are higher-percentage shots.

Winner: An unreturnable shot.

Wrong-foot *(tactical shot selection)*: Directing your shot behind your opponent's run. This compels your opponent to change the direction of his or her movement.

Zone: A mental state of consciousness in which the mind is acting intuitively and spontaneously, using multiple parts of the brain to perform tasks. When in this state the thinking calculating part of the brain is not active.

APPENDIX 1

Volley Targets

Your targeting goals will be the same for volleys. You will drive the ball to the middle of the court and the left and right sides of the court The target goals are conservative and take into account the circle of error (see Chapter 1) that is inherent with all your shots. You will also learn where the high-angle volley targets are. Many points are won using a very simple, high-angled volley. Volley-aiming architecture will use the net as the visual reference point for constructing your targets.

Volley targets will be slightly different from ground-stroke targets. You will need to move your targets lower, closer to the net, for volleys. Start with your targets about a foot above the net (see Figure 1).

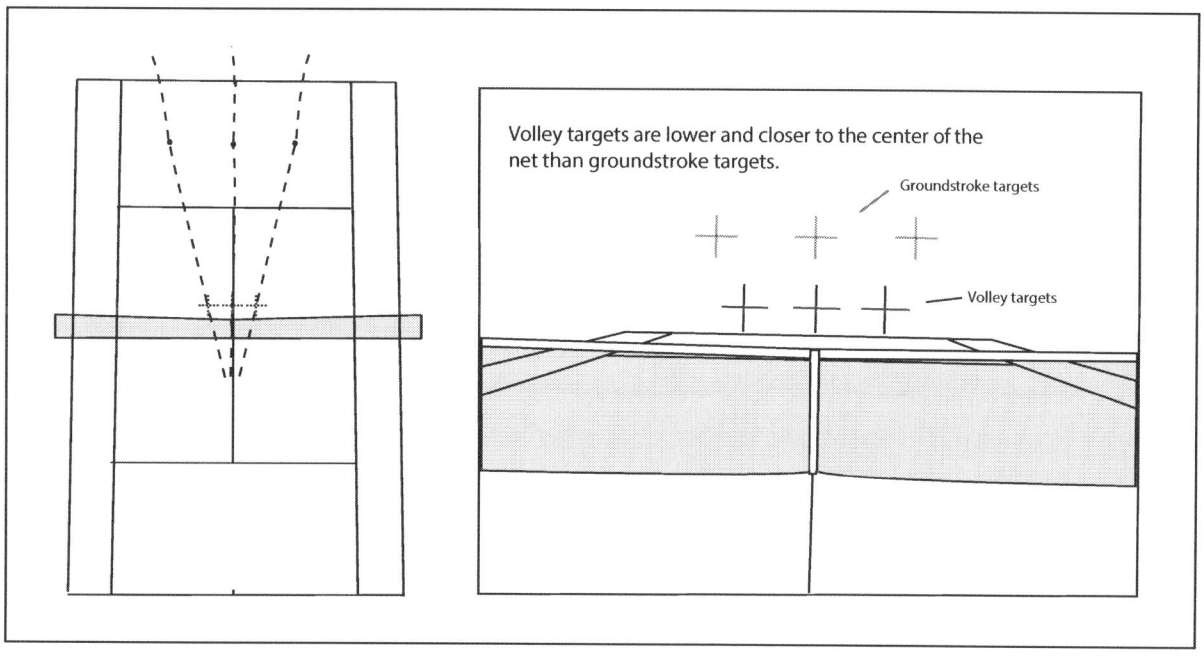

Fig 1 Volley targets from the center of the court.

Also, your targets for shooting to the right and left sides of the court will be very close to the center tape when volleying from the center of the court. Since you are closer to the net when you volley, the angle created by aiming left and right will be much greater. If you use ground-stroke targets for your volleys, you will shoot the ball wide of the court most of the time (see Figure 2).

Volley targets contract even more as you get closer to the net. The targets for the left and right sides of the court will be very near the center tape from this close-in position. This is because the angle required to shoot the ball to the left and right sides of the court gets smaller and smaller as you get closer to the net (see Figure 3).

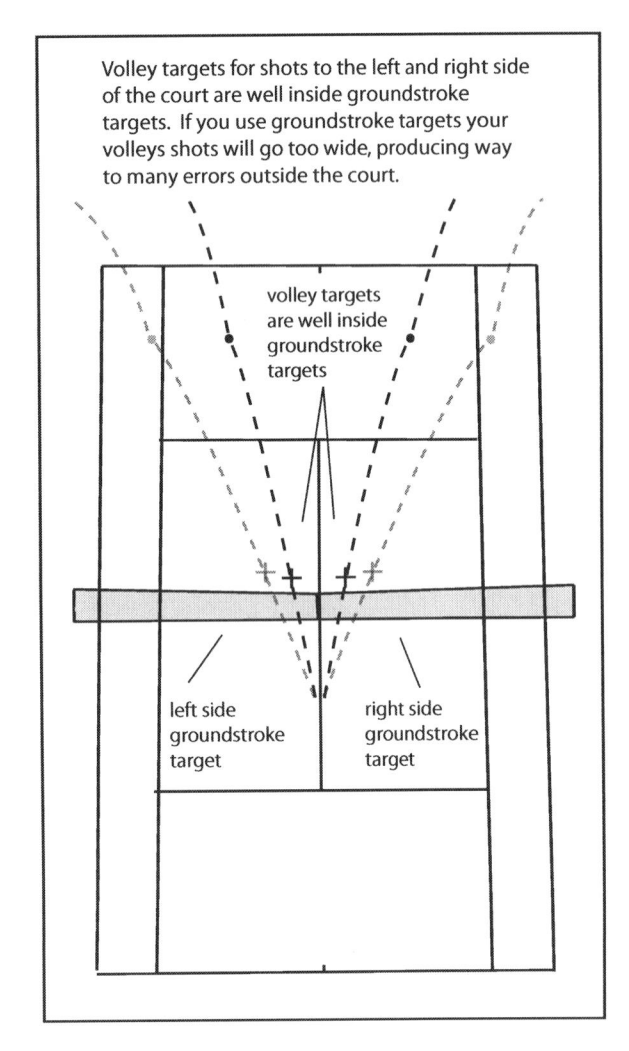

Fig 2 Volley targets to the left and right side of the court from the mid-court position.

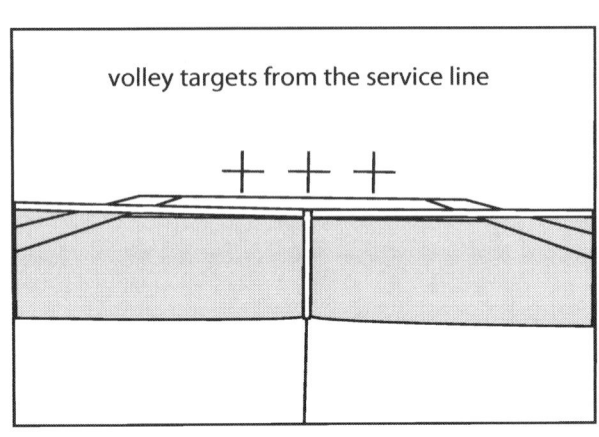

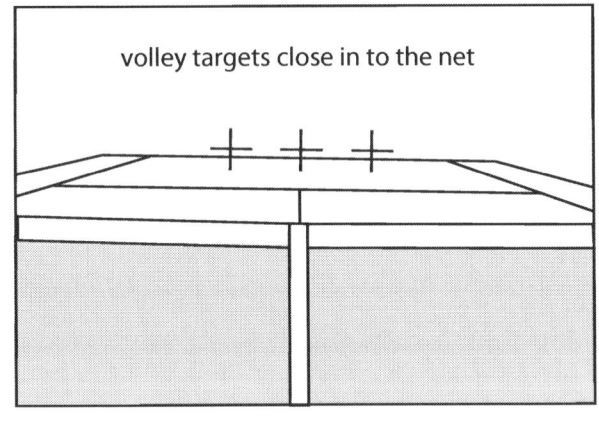

Fig 3 Volley targets compress as you get closer to the net. As you move in closer to the net the volley targets for the left and right side of the court get closer to the center tape. The closer your are to the net the less agle is required to shoot the ball to the left and right side.

When you are shooting volleys from the right or left side of the court, your volley targets will change. They will slide over, just as they did on the groundstroke targets. But volley targets will slide over even more. All three targets will be between the center tape and the sideline. To shoot the ball crosscourt from this position, you must choose a target to the right of the center of the net. As you get closer to the net, your volley targets will contract, drawing closer together. Figure 4a shows the targets from the right side of the court when volleying from the service line; Figure 4b shows the targets from a position close to the net. Figures 5a and 5b show volley targets from the left side of the court. Notice that the volley targets get closer together as you close in on the net.

Volley Target from the Right Side of the Court

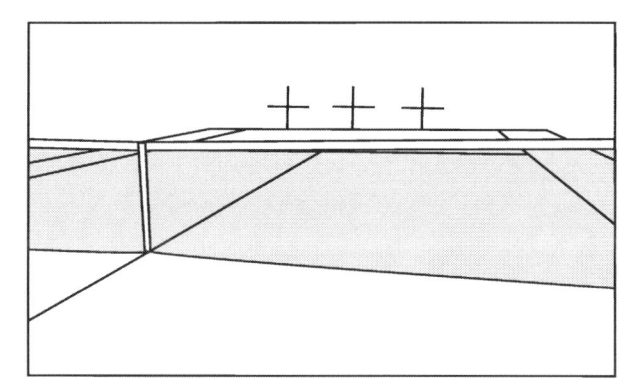

Fig 4a Volley targets shooting from the right side of the court when shooting from the service line.

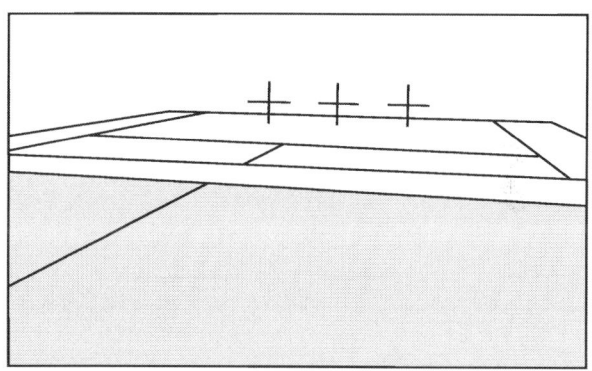

Fig 4b As you close into the net the volley targets get even closer together. The angle required to shoot the ball to left and right side of the court is smaller the closer you are to the net.

Volley Target from the Left Side of the Court

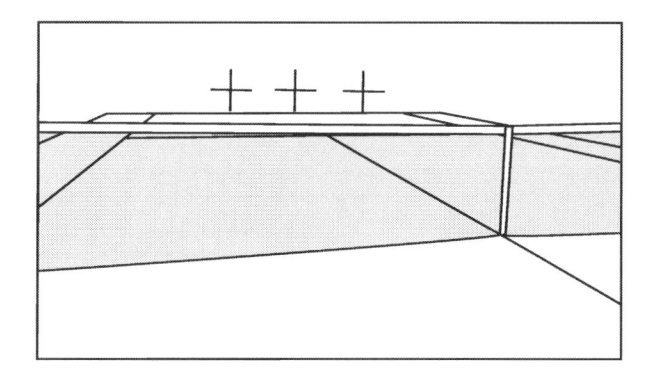

Fig 5a Volley targets shooting from the left side of the court when shooting from the service line.

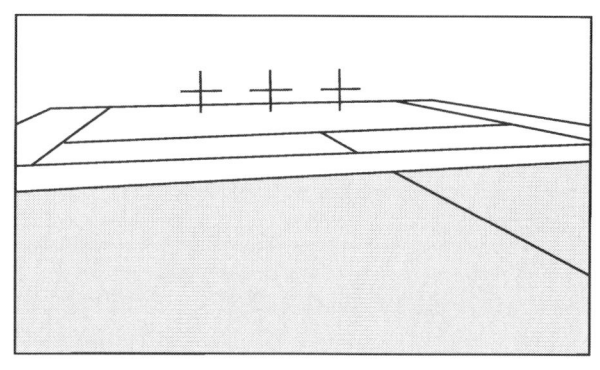

5b As you close into the net the volley targets get even closer together. The angle required to shoot the ball to left and right side of the court is less the closer you are to the net.

The High-Angle Volley

One very important shot selection when volleying is the high-angled volley. This is an essential shot to develop if you want to become successful at net play. This shot is hit on a tight angle; it lands about halfway up the court, near the service line. Let's talk about the target architecture for this shot.

High-Angle Volley from the Left and Right Sides of the Court

It is best to hit the high-angle volley when shooting from the side of the court. This shot is also most effective when shooting from a position close to the net. The target for this shot is very near the center tape. This shot will produce a lot of winners and is easy to make if you know where to aim. If you hit this shot too hard, it will sail wide of the court, so a little pace should be taken off this shot. The next time you watch a match, notice where high-angle volleys cross the net—very near the center tape. Use this target for your high-angle volleys, and go for this shot with confidence.

Figure 6 shows the aiming architecture for the high-angle volley from the right side of the court; Figure 7 shows the target for the high-angle volley from the left side of the court. These targets are very near the center tape. Use the tape as a visual reference for building your high-angle volley targets.

Forehand: High Angle Volley

high angle target

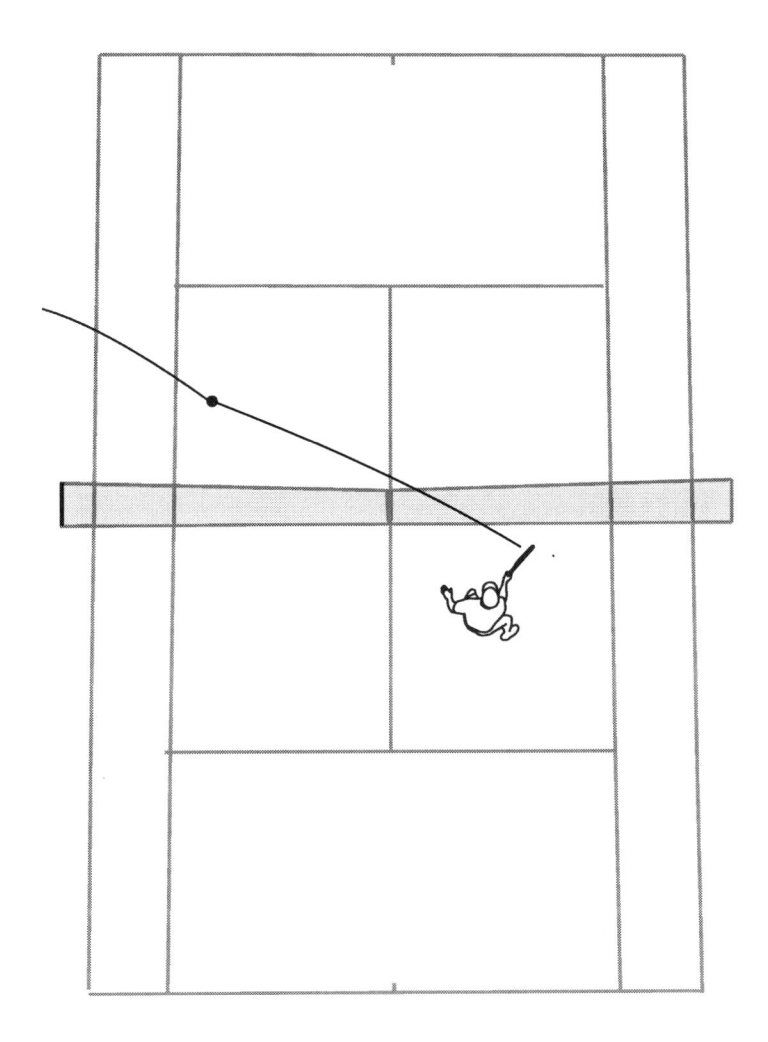

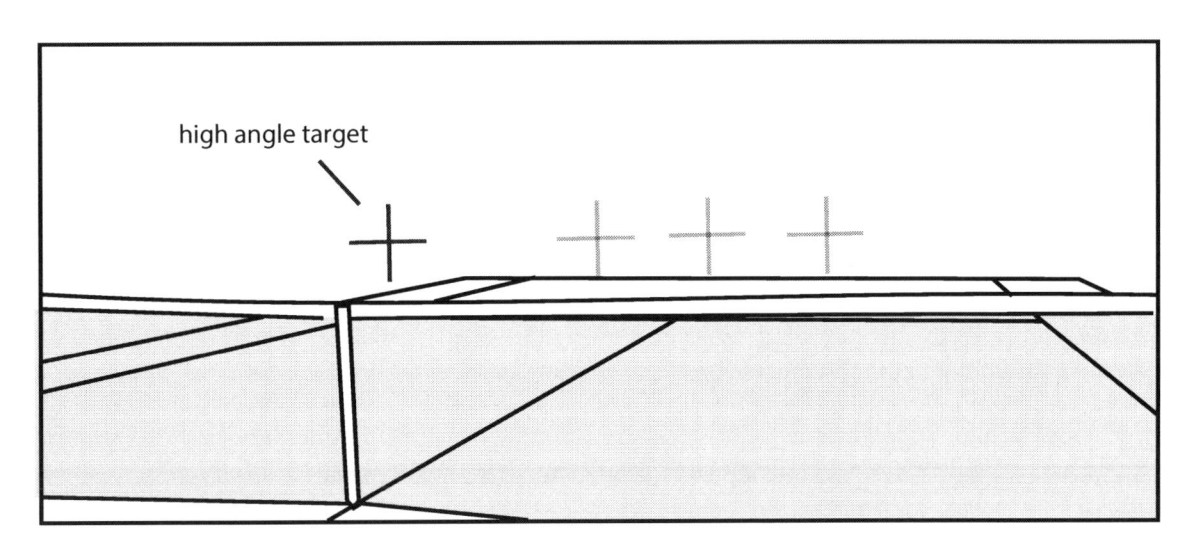

Fig 6. High angle volley from the right side of the court. Shooting near the center tape target creates an extreme angle. Pace must be taken of this shot to keep it in the court.

APPENDIX 1: VOLLEY TARGETS | 181

Backhand: High Angle Volley

high angle target

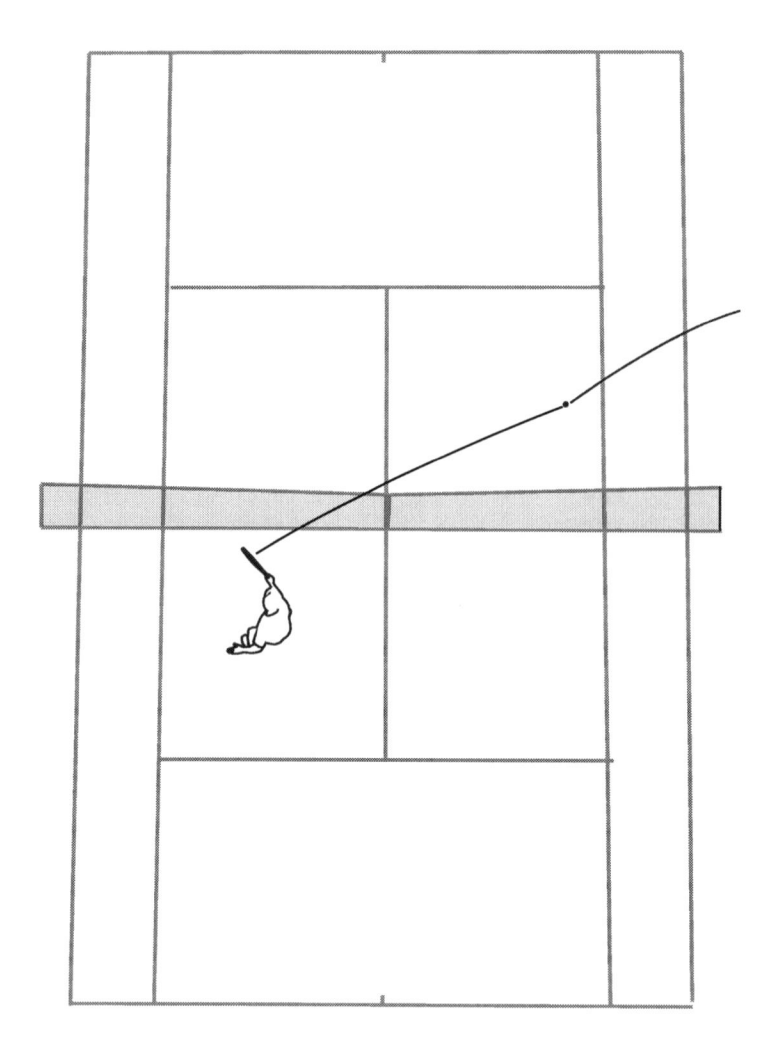

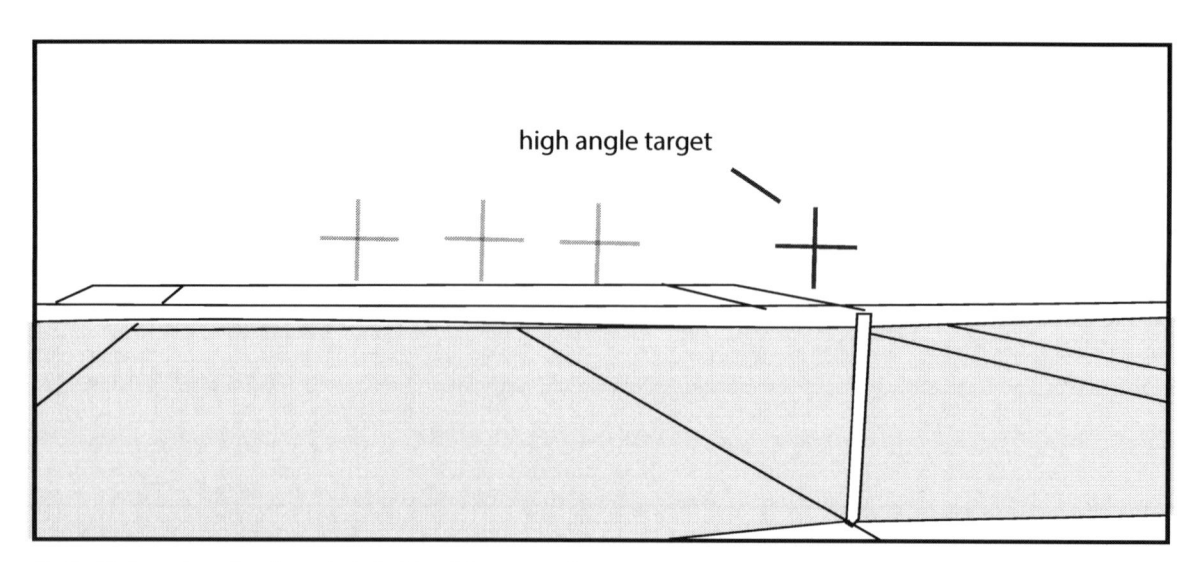

Fig 7. High angle volley from the left side of the court. Shooting near the center tape target creates an extreme angle. Pace must be taken of this shot to keep it in the court.

High-Angle Volley from the Middle of the Court

The sharply angled volley is a more difficult shot when you are shooting from the center of the court. The distance the shot travels is much less than when shooting from the side of the court. Because of this, you need to take more pace off the shot. This requires a good deal of finesse and practice. The target for the high-angle volley when shooting from the center of the court is a little wider than the normal volley targets (see Figure 8). Most players miss this shot because they choose too wide a target.

It is best to go for the high-angle volley when you are shooting from the side of the court. The target is simple and visually obvious. All you have to do is drive the ball right over the center tape, and good things will happen. You will bag a lot of winners by taking this shot.

The High Volley

This shot is subject to more nervous, cement-elbow errors than any other shot. Players frequently bungle volleys at high, slow-moving balls. What looks to be the easiest shot in the world is often sent over the baseline or hammered into the net. This easy sitter can be your most agonizing mistake.

The high angle volley target from the middle of the court are just outside the targets for the left and right side of the court. The target is also slightly lower. Most players shoot for targets too wide left and right. This creates too great an angle and lots of errors wide of the court.

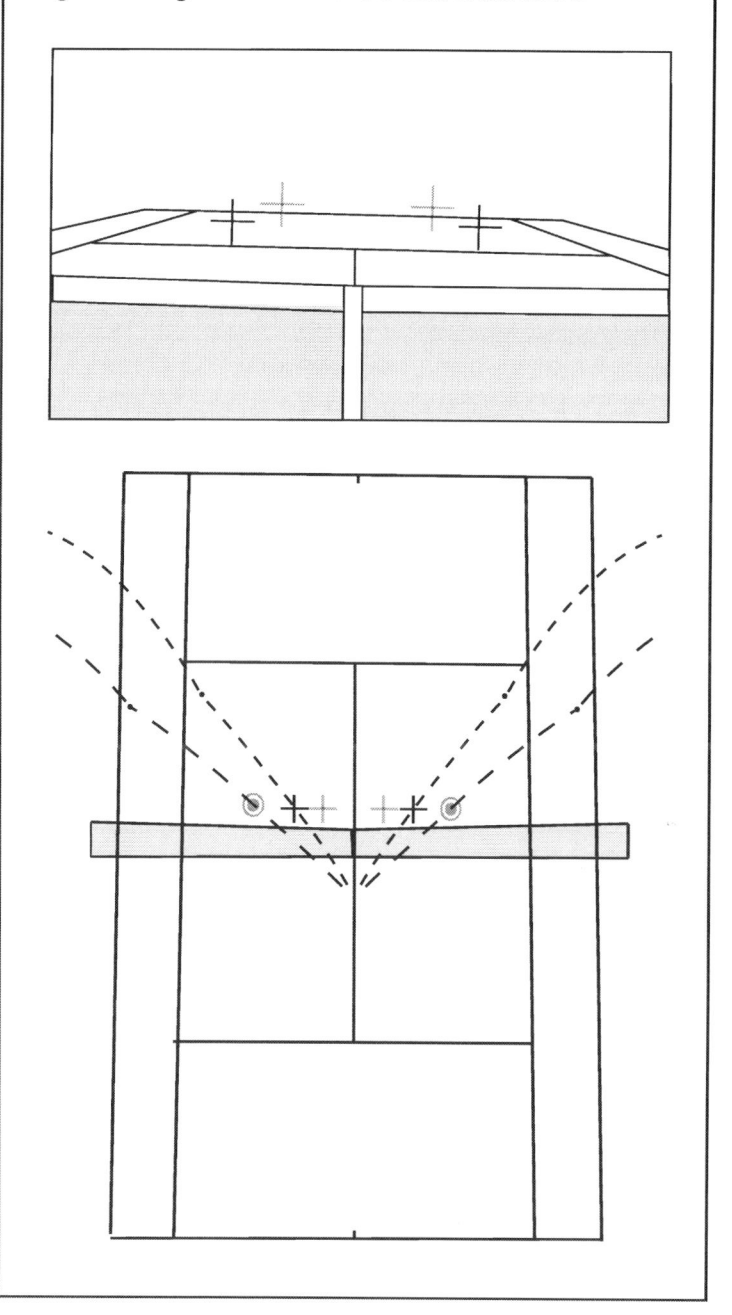

Fig 8 High angle volley targets from the middle of the court. See bird's for common errors shooting high angle volleys from the middle of the court. Most players shoot for targets too wide left and right. These "too wide" targets are depicted with circles. These locations creat too great an angle, producing lots of errors wide of the court.

There are at two reasons this "easy" shot is so often missed. First, this error occurs because most players go for too good a shot. That is, they try to hit the ball too close to the sidelines. This is essentially bad shot selection. Since you have learned that you never really aim close to the lines, you should have a lot more success on this shot from now on.

The second, and more important, reason that players miss this shot has to do with vision. When you receive the high volley, your field of view is dragged up as you watch the ball. As your eyes go up, you lose your view of the net and the court. As you lose your view of the court, it becomes difficult to hold a good visual target. This applies to all tennis players, even those who know nothing about targets or aiming. Tennis players with no clue use what they see of the court to make a shot, even though they are unaware that they are doing it. Because of this, they often misdirect the ball, and the error occurs.

To solve this problem, you need to do the following.

Choose a Correct Target Height

The most important thing on any high-volley shot is to choose a target height that will bring your shot down into the court and keep the ball out of the net. This target is higher than your normal volley target. If the ball you are hitting is so high that you lose sight of the net, use a target that is a couple of feet below the height of the ball you are striking. In this situation, you are basing your target on the height of the ball, since it is in your field of view. If the net is still in your peripheral vision, use a target midway between the top of the net and the height of the ball you are striking. These targets will ensure that you clear the net and drive the ball down into the court. Your goal for high, sitter volleys will be to smash the shot down at the service line really hard.

Shoot Very Close to the Middle of the Court

When you are playing the ball from the center of the court, you should shoot your forehand volley (again, assuming a right-handed player) to the left side of the court. This is the "pull shot" into your strength. The target for this shot will be right over or just to the left of the center tape. If your vision has been pulled up so high that you cannot see the net, you will *not* be able to use the net to construct your target. In this situation you use the position of the ball to mark the location of your aiming cross. Place your aiming cross a couple of feet to the left and a couple of feet lower than the position of the ball (see Figure 9).

With the net in your field of view, choose a target between the height of the ball and the top of the net. This will give good net clearance and drive the ball down into the court towards the service line.

The target is slightly to the left of the ball you are striking. This produces plenty of angle to produce a winner with lots of margin for error.

High forehand volley net out of view

The net has dropped out of your field of vew so the target height is constructed a couple feet below and to the left of the position of the ball.

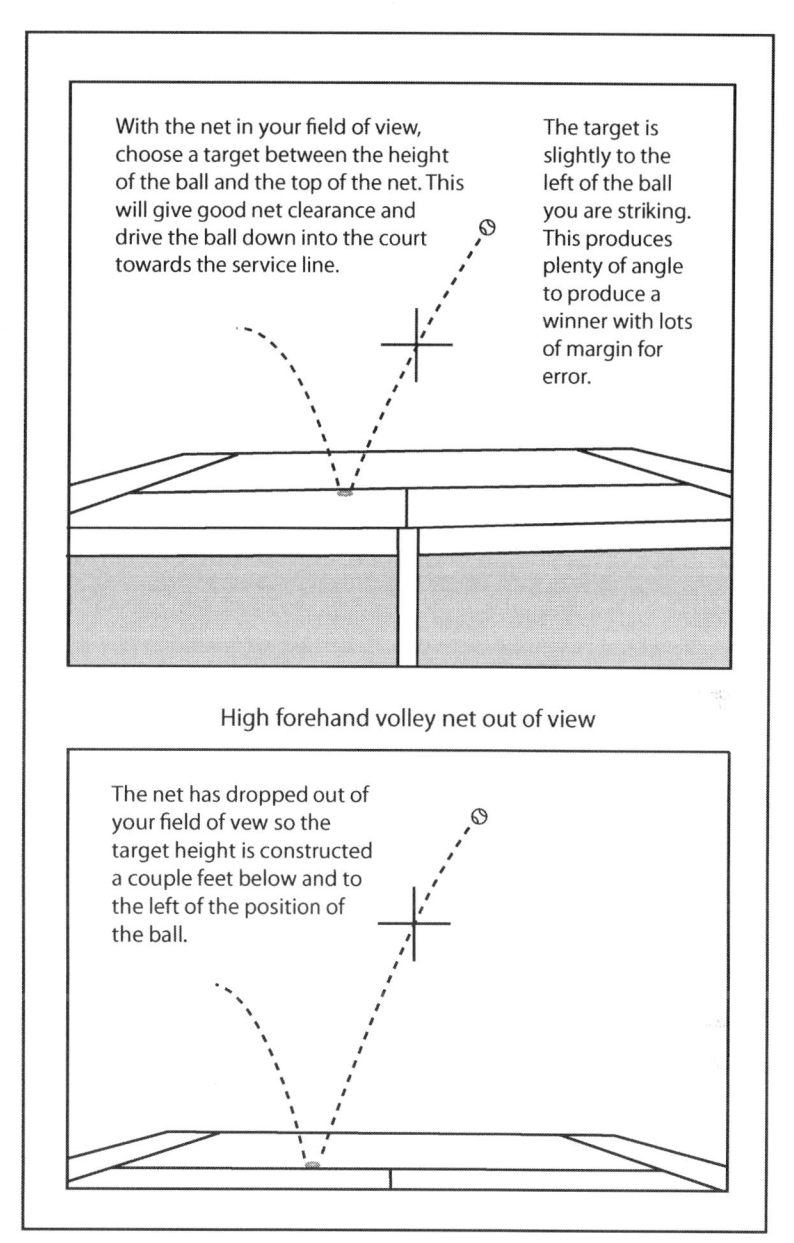

Fig 9. High forehand volley from the center of the court

APPENDIX 1: VOLLEY TARGETS | 185

Top panel — High volley net in view:

On this shot the net is in your field of view. The target height is between the net and the height of the ball.

A target right over the center tape produces enough of angle to make a winning shot with a huge margin of error.

High volley net out of view

Bottom panel — High volley net out of view:

The net has dropped out of your field of vew so the target height is constructed a couple feet below the height of the ball.

The target is slightly to the right of the ball you are striking. This produces plenty of angle to produce a winner with lots of margin for error.

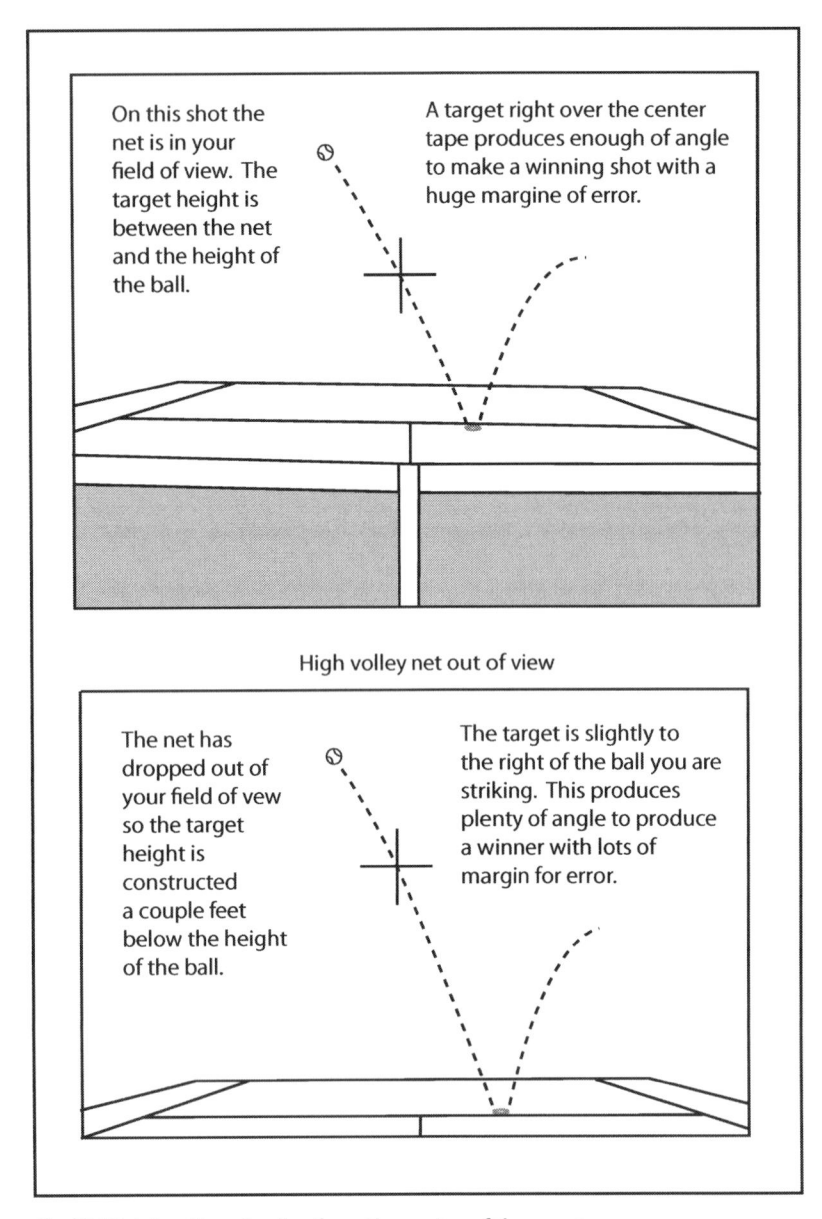

Fig 10 High backhand volley from the center of the court

If you are shooting a backhand high volley from the center of the court, you should choose a target that will shoot the ball to the right side of the court (right-handed player assumed). This target will be right over or just to the right of the center tape. If the net moves out of your vision, use the position of the ball to build this target. Mark your aiming cross a couple of feet to the right and a couple of feet lower than the position of the ball (see Figure 10). These are pull targets to your strength. These targets should shoot the ball near the service line on a decent angle, with lots of margin for error.

Shooting from the Side of the Court

When you are shooting the high volley from the side of the court, your goal should be to crush the ball right at the center T of the service court. A shot at the middle of the court will produce a good angle from this position. Targeting the middle of the court gives you the greatest margin of error you will ever have.

From the right side of the court, this target is between the position of the ball and the center tape. If you lose sight of the net as you play this high volley, you can use the position of the ball to mark your target. From the right side of the court, choose a target a couple of feet to the left and a couple of feet lower than the ball (see Figure 11).

The target between the center tape and the position of the ball produces a shot with plenty of angle. This shot is right at the center of the court. It has a huge margin of error.

On this shot the net is in your field of view. The target height is between the net and the height of the ball.

High forehand volley net out of view

The target is slightly to the left of the ball you are striking. This produces plenty of angle to produce a winner with lots of margin for error.

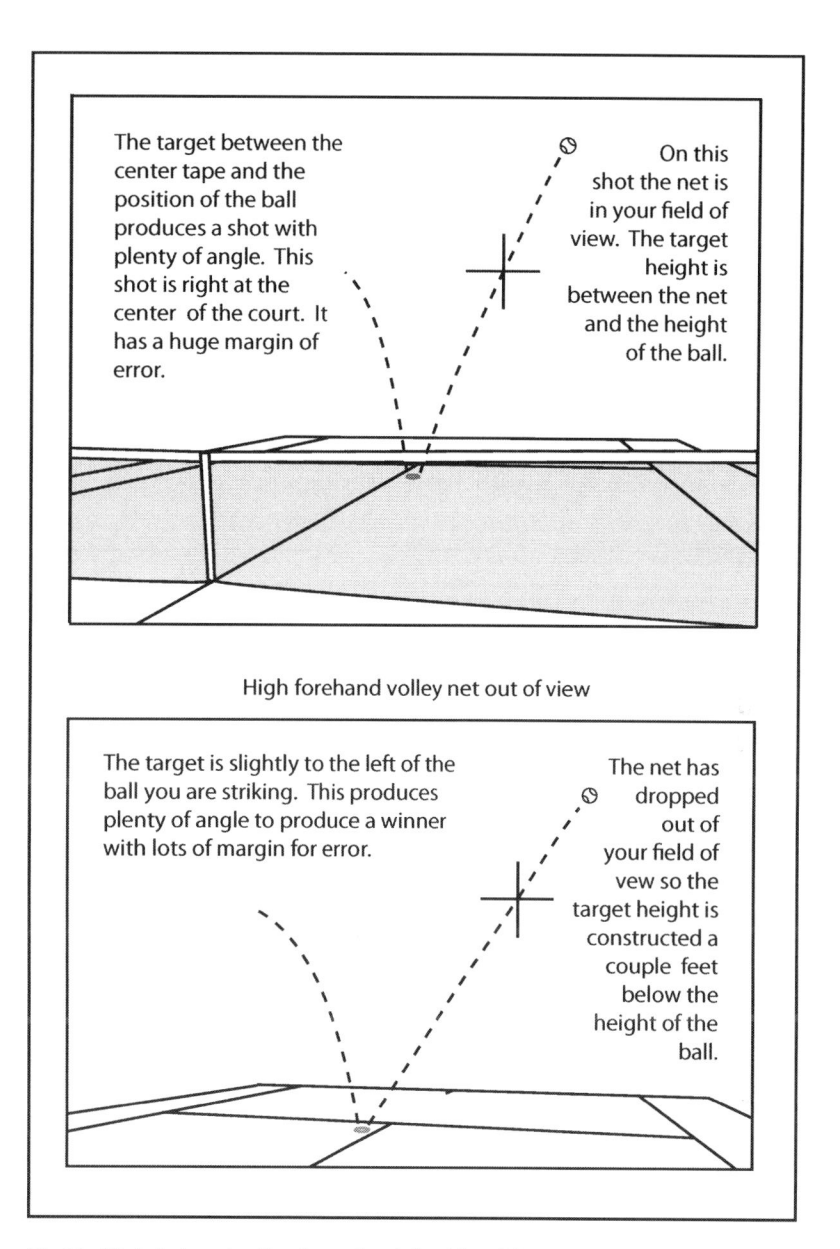

The net has dropped out of your field of vew so the target height is constructed a couple feet below the height of the ball.

Fig 11. High forhand volley from the right side of the court.

APPENDIX 1: VOLLEY TARGETS | 187

From the left side of the court, the target that will drive the ball to the center of the court will be to the *left* side of the center tape. It is between the position of the ball and the center tape. If you lose sight of the net, choose a target a couple of feet to the right and a couple of feet lower than the ball. This should drive the shot on a good angle right at the middle of the court (see Figure 12). Hit this ball *hard*. *Crush* the high volley. Even if your opponent returns it, it will be a weak shot. Then you can crush the high volley again. You will win this point in one or two shots. It is better to hit this ball hard right at your opponent and then set up a second easy ball than to miss shooting for a low-percentage shot.

So, to never (or almost never) miss another high-sitting volley, do this: Choose a target that will shoot the ball very near the center of the court. Shoot midway between the net and the height of the sitting ball if you can still see the net. If you lose the net in your peripheral vision, use a target below the ball you are striking. Choose a target over the net that will shoot the ball to the service line. And most importantly, *crush this ball! Go for it!*

On this shot the net is in your field of view. The target height is between the net and the height of the ball.

The target between the center tape and the position of the ball produces a shot with plenty of angle. This shot is right at the center of the court. This target has a huge margin of error.

High bachand volley net out of view

The net has dropped out of your field of vew so the target height is constructed a couple feet to the right and below the height of the ball.

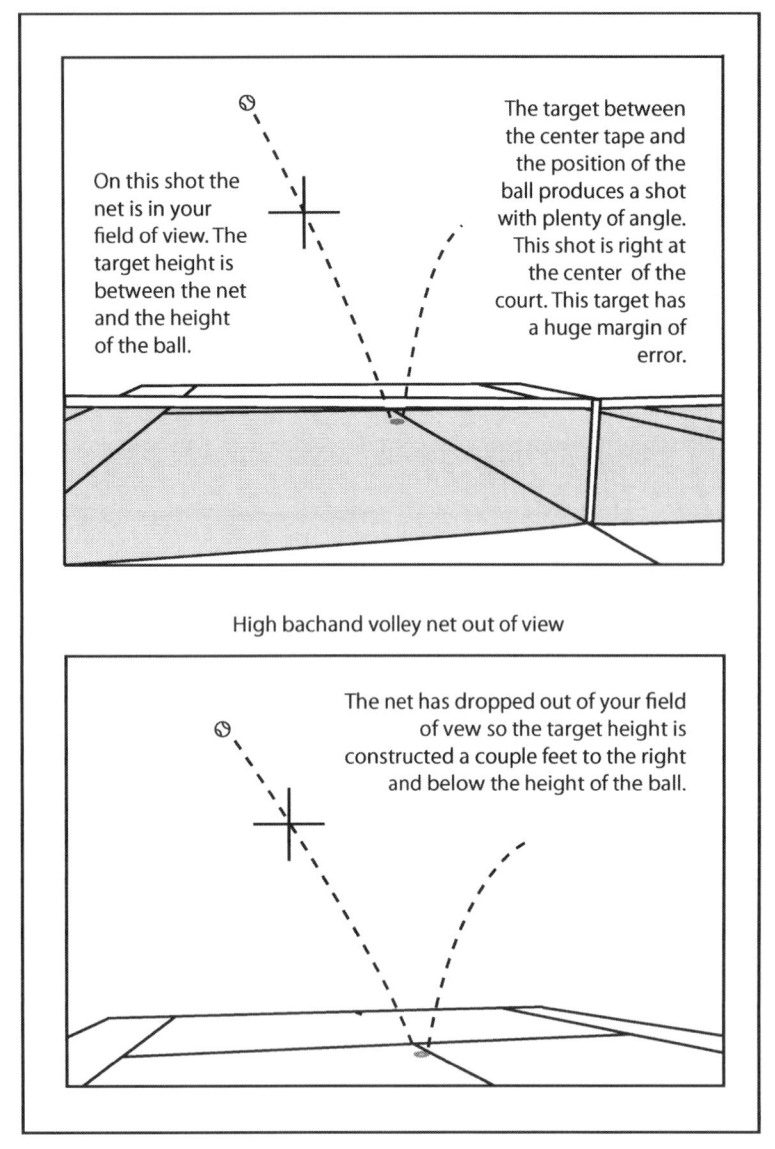

Fig 12. High backhand volley from the left side of the court.

Volley Summary

Most volley errors wide of the court occur because players do not understand the volley-aiming architecture. Even though they might not be choosing specific targets to aim for, the area of the court they want to hit becomes their visual cue. If a player is shooting for the corner of the court, that portion of the court becomes the target. This visual target, the corner, becomes the point over the net that the shot is driven to, and that point produces too great an angle. Figure 13 shows how an area of the court becomes that target. When the player uses that spot to direct the vector of the shot, it produces too severe an angle, and the shot goes wide. Using over-the-net targets based on a solid aiming architecture will drive the ball on an accurate flight path to your conservative-target goals. By using the center of the net as a visual fix for creating your targets, you control the vector of your shot. Knowing where the correct targets are will eliminate these gross errors wide of the court.

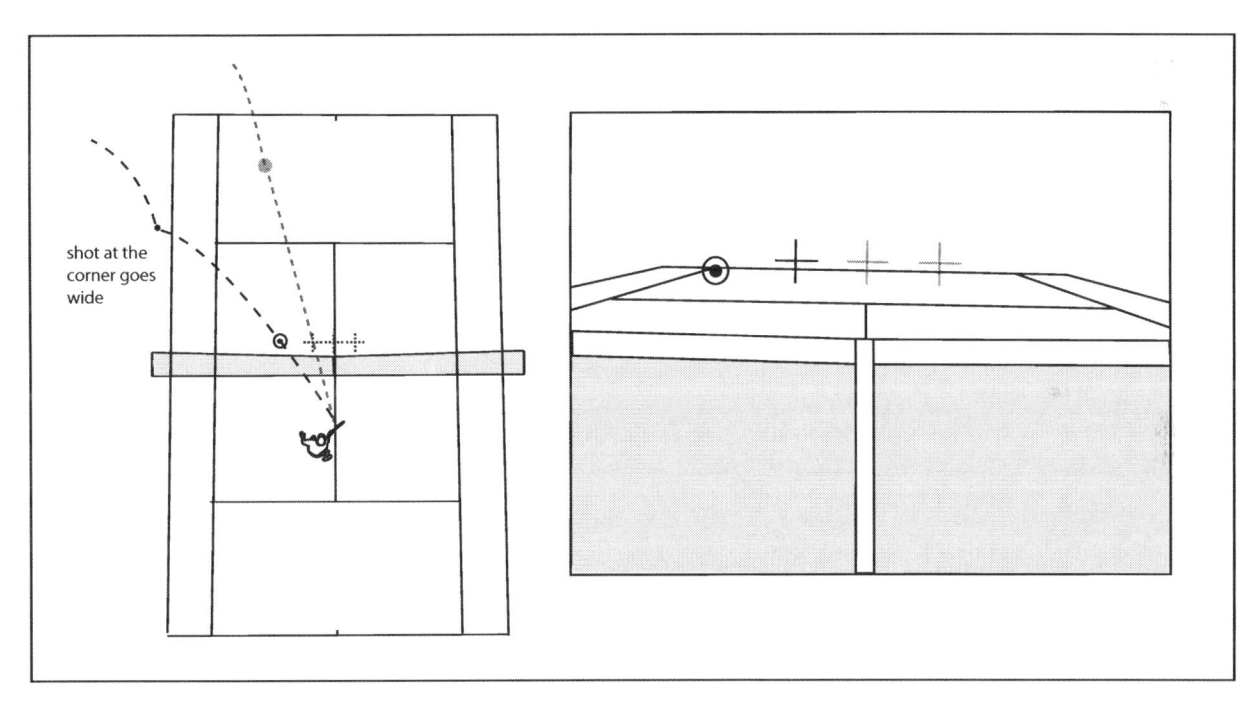

Fig 13. Here the player wants to shoot the ball to the corner of the court. The corner becomes the visual target that the shot is driven to. This produces too great an angle and the shot goes wide of the court.

As you shoot your volleys, the basic concept of aiming and adjusting your aim points based on your errors still applies. Strive to never make the same error twice. Make continuous corrections around your target with every shot. Demand of yourself that your accuracy improves with every ball you hit.

APPENDIX 2

Service Targets

The service targets are also based on targets over the net; where those targets will be for you will depend on a couple of things. One is whether you are left-handed or right-handed. All of these examples are for right-handed players; if you play left-handed, reverse the targets for each side of the court. The second issue is how advanced a player you are. Many lower-skilled tennis players hit their serves very flat. Their racket strikes the ball directly from behind and in a downward motion. This type of serve has very little topspin and in some cases is hit with backspin. More advanced players hit the serve with a lot of topspin, striking up at the ball. This produces a pronounced right-to-left and downward-curved service arc (for a right-handed player). This discussion will be for the advanced, topspin-type serve with the right-to-left curve. Appendix three includes a tutorial for less advanced players to learn how to transition to using a more advanced, topspin serve. The *ball-control* goals for your service are:
1. To be able to shoot the ball to the right corner of the service box.
2. To be able to shoot the ball to the left corner of the service box.
3. To be able to shoot the ball to the center of the service box. (That would be the jam shot, directly into the body of your opponent.)

Another important skill to learn is to be able to hit your second serve to your opponent's backhand (right-handed server and right-handed opponent assumed). Most players get "tight" and are unable to get the second serve to the backhand side. You will learn to fix that.

A Special Note about the Serve

The serve is unique in that it is the only static shot in tennis. If you have a consistent toss, you are striking a ball that is barely moving. You are hitting a ball that is stopped in space at about the same spot every time. Because of this, you don't have to take into consideration the energy (arc and vector) of the ball. You can be more refined in your accuracy. You must choose targets that will make your shot land closer to the lines.

To make this discussion understandable, we will make a couple of assumptions: one, that you are a right-handed server, and two, that your opponent is also right-handed. If you serve left-handed, the targets are reversed for each side of the court. If your opponent is left-handed, shooting to the backhand or forehand is reversed. Also, it is not as challenging for the right-handed server to get the second serve to the backhand side due to the right-to-left curve of the serve.

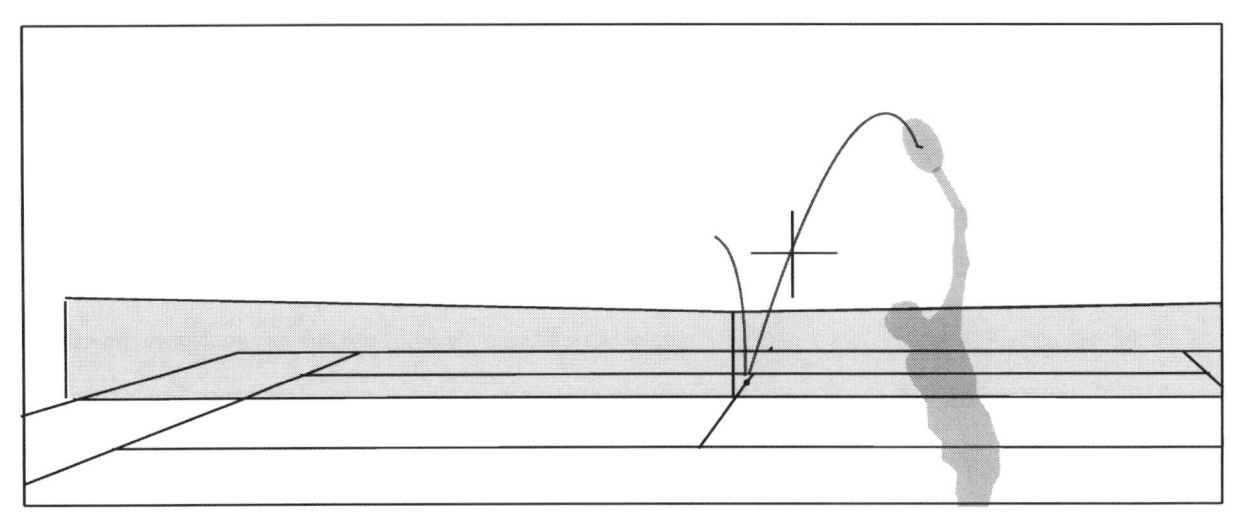

Fig 14 First serve target from forehand side of court to your opponents backhand.

Service Targets from the Forehand Side of the Court

To get the ball to go to the right corner of the service court (the backhand side of your opponent), use a target that is one to two feet to the right side of the tape and about two feet over the net (see Figure 14). If you look right through this target, you will see that you are directing the ball at the wrong service court. This target takes into consideration the right-to-left curve of the serve. The spin of your serve will curve the ball into the right corner of the service court, at your opponent's backhand. It is important to note that your service shot might not pass right through this target. What you are directing is the initial vector of the shot. The spin of the serve may move the ball to the left and lower than the initial target. This is true for all your service targets. What you are building here is an architecture of targets to get your serve to go where you want it to go. You will

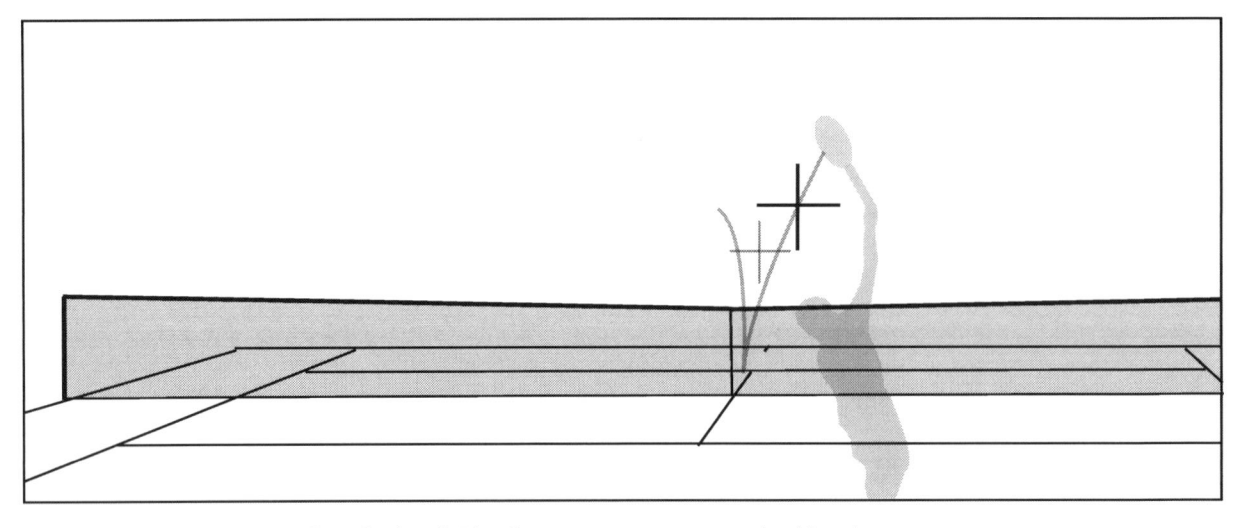

Fig 15 Second service target from forehand side of court at your opponents backhand. The target moves up and right for the second serve.

have to experiment and find where you need to target in order to be successful. Start with these targets. As you gain experience and get more data through errors and successes you will find the target location for your serve.

On your second serve, you need to choose a target even farther to the right of the tape, and slightly higher (see Figure 15). This is because the second serve is almost always hit with more spin, and it will curve more dramatically from right to left and down into the court. You might feel that you are shooting the ball way too high and too far to the right. Get over this fear, and go for this target. Once again, your shot may not go through this target. What you are controlling is the initial vector of your service shot. The spin of your second serve will move this ball down and to the left. Experiment and find where this second service target is for you. This target takes courage and a willingness to risk an error.

Why is it so hard to hit your second serve to your opponent's backhand side? One reason is that the second serve is usually hit with more spin; it therefore curves more from right to left and down. If you use the same target on your second serve that you did on your first serve, the ball will curve into your opponent's forehand—and maybe into the net. The second reason is that everyone gets tighter on his or her second serve. The bigger the point, the tighter most players get. As you get tighter, your arm action is restricted, and your

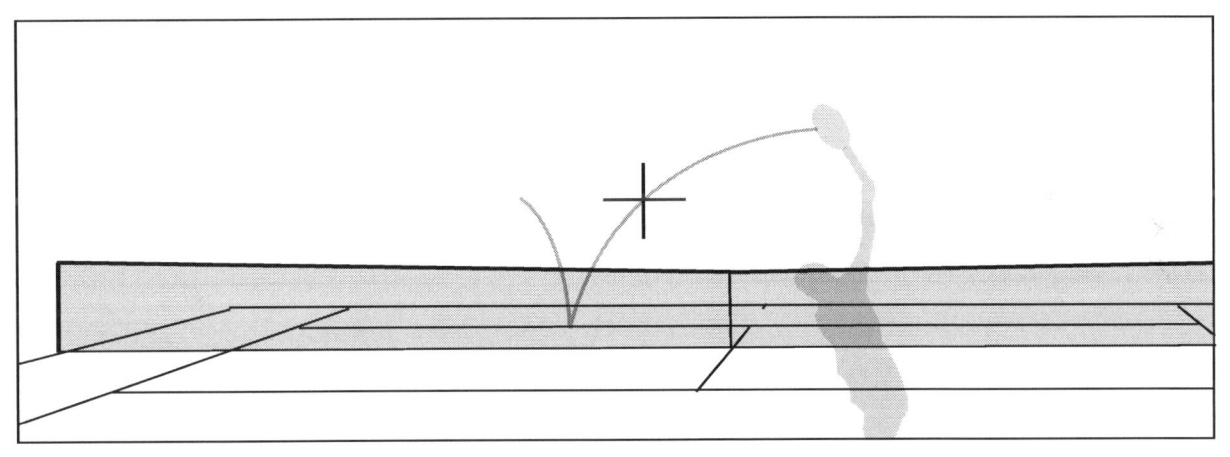

Fig 16 This target shoots the ball at your opponents body from the from the forehand side of the court.

service motion is pulled down and toward your body. This shoots the ball over to your opponent's forehand side. Sometimes it pulls the ball right into the net. That is why it is absolutely necessary to move your second-service target up and to the right. What you are controlling is the initial vector of your service shot. After the shot strikes out at the target, it will curve left and down into the court and may not go through the target. It takes courage to shoot for this target. You will have to miss a few second serves long and to the right of the service court as you build this part of your aiming architecture. But once you find the target that works for you, you will be able to smash your second serve with confidence and get it to your opponent's backhand side.

Use the aim-point adjustment techniques you learned earlier to refine your accuracy around these targets. Your serve is unique. You will need to experiment to find the right location for the targets. But these locations are a great starting point to finding your service targets to the backhand side of your opponent.

To get the ball to go right into your opponent's body, you should use a target directly over or just to the left of the tape, about two feet over the net (see Figure 16). The right-to-left curve of your serve will bend the ball right into your adversary's waistline. You are trying to shoot the ball so that it lands a few feet from the right corner of the service court. The ball will then curve into the body of your opponent. Just where this target will be depends on how much your serve moves from right to left; it also depends on where your opponent is standing to receive the serve. Use the aiming techniques to improve your accuracy around this target.

To swing the ball wide, out to your opponent's forehand, you should use a target near the middle of the service court, about one to two feet over the net (see Figure 17). This probably doesn't seem wide enough, but the most effective serve out to your opponent's forehand has less topspin and more sidespin. This

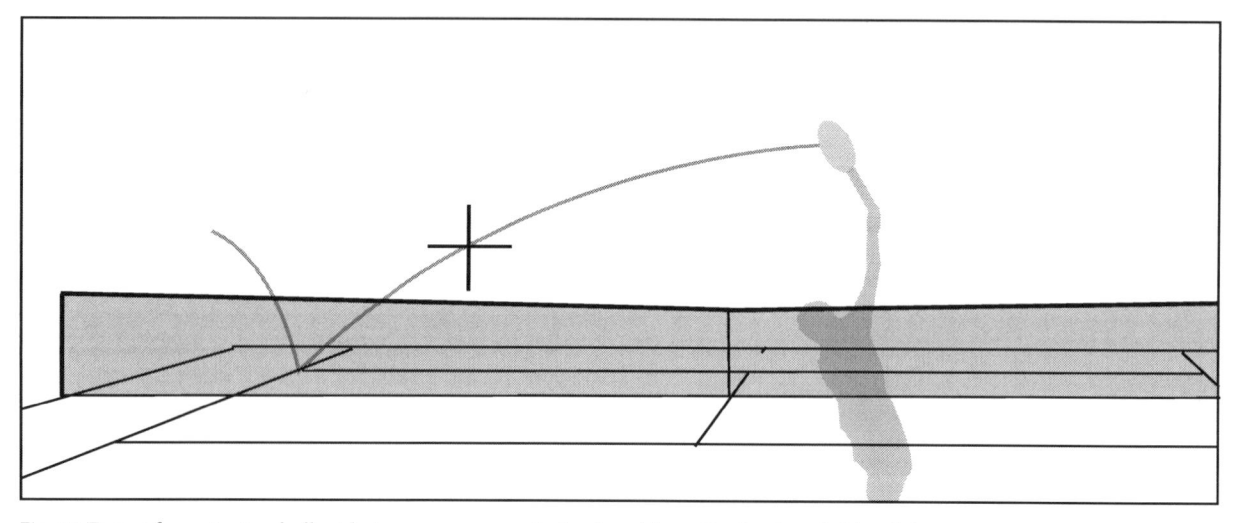

Fig 17 Target for swinging ball wide to your opponents forehand from the forehand side of the court.

sidespin, or "slice," causes the ball to make a big curve from the right to the left. If you aim for a target that is closer to the sideline, or right over the sideline, the ball will go wide. You want this serve to curve big-time. You want it to land in the corner of the service court, or even a couple of feet up from the back of the service court. It is essential to find where this target is for you. Once you have built this part of your aiming architecture, you can use this target to confidently "burn" an opponent who is moving over early to hit a forehand return.

Play with these targets. You will have to move them around to fit your serve. If you hit a big flat first serve, you will move the targets to the left for that serve. That's because the ball will curve less. If you don't put much sidespin on your serve wide to your opponent's forehand, you will need to move the target over to the left. Get a bucket of balls and find these targets!

Service Targets from the Backhand Side of the Court

To get the ball out to your opponent's backhand, you need to choose a target that is over the doubles alley, about three feet over the net. You are trying to shoot the ball so that it lands in the right corner of the service court. Because that corner of the service court is farther away, this target needs to be higher than you think (see Figure 18). Once again, your service arc may not pass through this target. You are controlling the initial vector of the shot. As your shot strikes out for the target, it will curve left and down into the court.

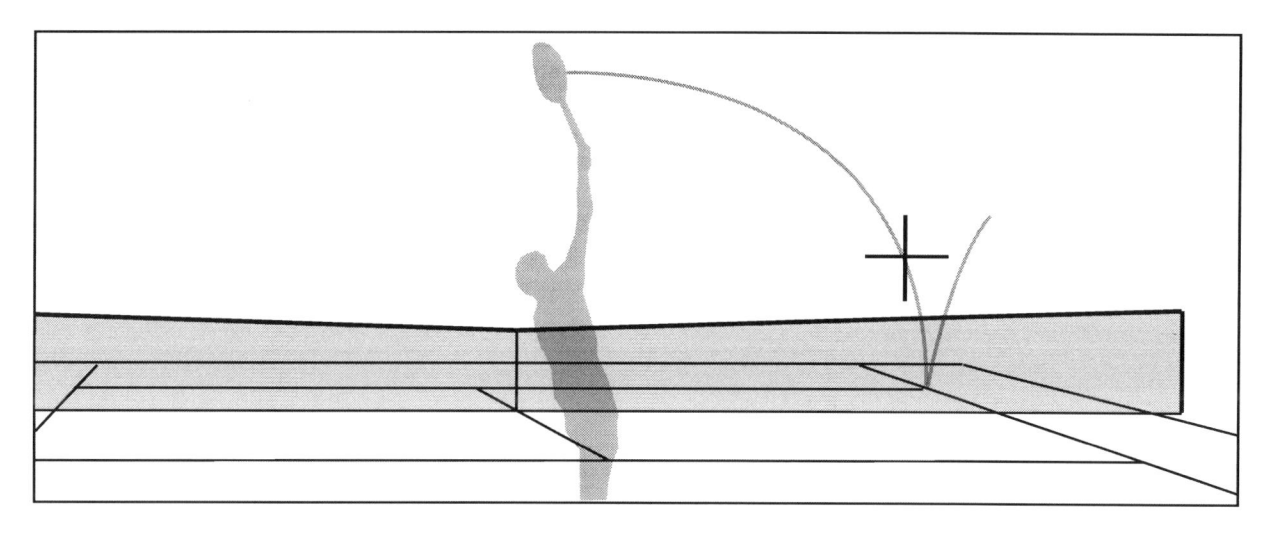

Fig 18 First serve target to opponents backhand from the backhand court.

For the *second* serve out to the backhand, you will need to move the target farther over to the right and even higher (see Figure 19). This target might look wrong. It might seem way too far over to the right and way too high. But remember, the second serve has more spin and will curve down and left more.

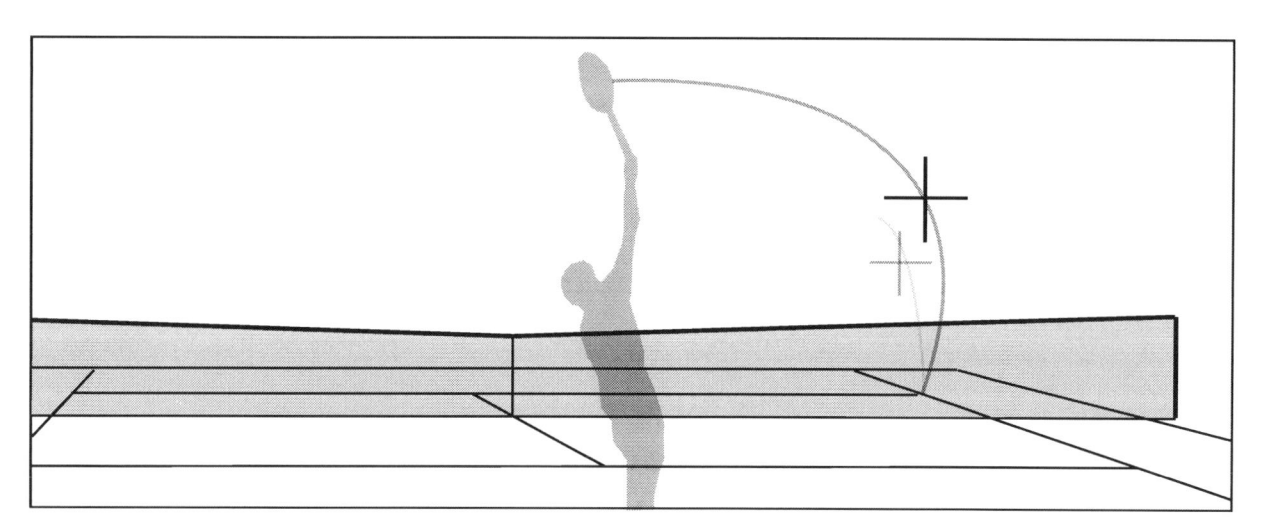

Fig 19 Second serve target to opponents backhand from the backhand court. Target moves up and right from the first service target.

You need to drive the initial vector of your second serve out to the target and let the spin do its work. The exact location of this target will depend on how much spin and curve your service shot makes. You need to play around with this target until you get the right location for your serve. Bear in mind, though, that this target will be much higher and wider than you think it should be.

To get the ball into your opponent's body, serving to the backhand court, use a target that is in line with the right corner of the service court, about three feet over the net. Once again, the right-to-left curve of your serve will take the ball into your opponent's body (see Figure 20). Remember, this target will be unique to your serve but very close to this spot. It will also depend on where your opponent is setting up to receive your serve. Play around until you find the right target for you.

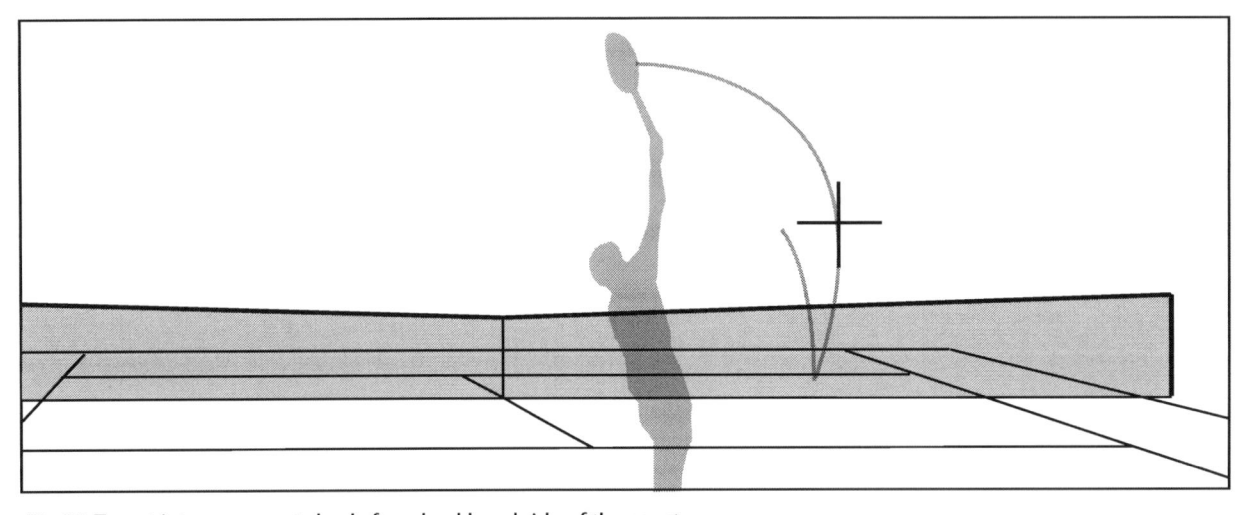

Fig 20 Target into opponents body from backhand side of the court.

To get the ball to go to the left corner of the service court, right at the T intersection of the court, use a target about two feet to the right of the net tape and about one or two feet over the net (see Figure 20). Unlike serving wide to your opponent's forehand from the forehand side of the court, you want this serve to bend a little less from right to left. This serve should be hit harder and flatter, with less sidespin. Like all the service targets, you need to find the target location that works best for your serve. Finding out where this target is is critical. You can use it to burn a player moving over early to make a forehand return.

These targets are for the average situation. If your opponent is "shading" well over toward her backhand, looking for a forehand return, things will change. The target that normally puts your serve onto her body may put the ball right into her "wheelhouse" on the forehand. But since you now have ball control and can put your serve where you want it, burn her by slicing the ball out to her forehand side. You can find exactly where this target is and hit it at will. Have courage. Shoot your second serve right ant the T. You can do it, and it's fun!

If you are playing doubles or are serving from extremely wide in the court, your targets will need to be shifted over to compensate for your position and the angle that your serve will travel to the court.

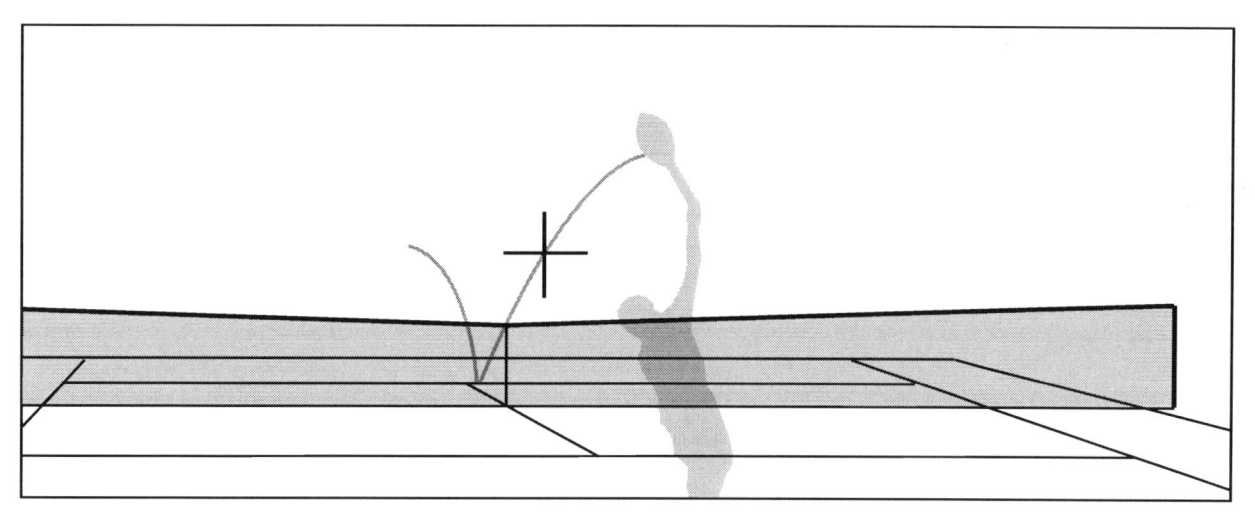

Fig 21 Target to opponents forhand from backhand side of the court.

The bottom line is that you need to find out where the targets are that will put your serve into the right corner, the left corner, and the middle of the service box. The targets described above are good starting points. Your serve will be unique, so you will have to define your own targets.

Play with these targets. Remember: you are controlling the initial vector of the service shot. Get a bucket of balls and practice your serve. Don't worry about your form and stroke. Go with what you've got. What you need to do is figure out *where* you have to *aim* your serve to get it to go *where* you want it to go!

Experiment: Treat Your First and Second Serve as Shot One and Two of an Aiming Sequence

The greatest thing about the serve is that you have two shots. Because of this, it is the perfect chance to use the aiming techniques. You can choose your target, take a shot, and analyze your error. Then you can make an aim-point adjustment and fire again. Unfortunately, most players exhibit a dramatic difference between their first and second serves. Because of this, there is a big difference between the first-service and the second-service targets.

I want you to experiment with a new mind-set on the serve. Treat the first and second serves much more equally. Take a little off your first serve and hit your second serve just as hard as your first. Make them shot one and shot two of an aiming sequence.

First, you should simulate this on the practice court. Take a bucket of balls out there and hit a bunch of first- and second-serve sequences. Pick out your target and go for it. On the second serve, make an aim-point adjustment and fire the serve again. Do not be concerned about double faulting. It is essential to get past this fear.

Now, experiment in a practice set. Accept the fact that you are going to double fault a few times. Do not worry about losing the set. Get the feel for hitting your second serve hard. Make the good aim-point corrections. Give it a try.

Unfortunately, the two-shot aiming sequence doesn't work all the time. Sometimes you might try to hit the ball wide to your opponent's forehand on the first serve and miss. On your second serve, you might want to hit the ball to your opponent's backhand. The "second-serve mind-set" discussed below will help your approach to this situation.

The Second-Serve Target

If you are *not* hitting your second serve as shot number two of an aiming sequence, you must always bias your target up and to the right (up and to the left for a left-hander). This is because the natural inclination in pressure situations is to tighten up. This will pull the ball down and to the left. Also, if you are imparting a little more spin to the ball, your shot will travel a shorter distance. If you do not bias the target up and right, the ball will land short in the service court. It will also curve into your opponent's waiting forehand.

Over time you will develop a good second-serve target for both sides of the court. With this biased target and a mind-set of going for the shot without concern for missing, you will develop a very potent and aggressive second serve.

The Second-Serve Mind-Set

When most players are hitting a second serve in a pressure situation, they choose to take a lot off the shot. They usually hit the ball with a bunch of spin. They tend to tighten up in a big way. This produces one of two things: a weak, slicing ball that slides over to their opponent's forehand, or worse, a cement-elbow, choking error into the net for a double fault. This attempt to "not miss" produces a weak shot, or even the opposite outcome: a double fault.

To forever eliminate this embarrassing result, you have to change your brain. You have to approach your second serve with courageous abandon. To develop an aggressive, hard-hit, and gutsy second serve, you have to embrace double faulting. What I mean is you have to say to yourself, "I don't care if I miss this second serve. I am going to go for it. I am going to choose my target, select my aim point, and hit out." You need to be of the mind that if you double fault, so what; it is just one point.

Once you have defined where your best second-service target is, you can have confidence in shooting your second serve hard and aggressively. Pick out your target, hold it in your mind's eye, and crush your second serve at that spot. You are thinking like a warrior here. You couldn't care less about double faulting. All you care about is smashing your second serve at your target. An error only means that on your next second serve, you will make an adjustment and will have a better aim point to shoot for.

You need to try this game plan. It is the best way to develop an aggressive and confident second serve.

APPENDIX 3

How to Transition from a Flat, Novice-Type Serve to a Topspin Serve

What I mean by a "novice-type serve" is a serve that is hit in a straight-ahead, pushing motion. The racket is taken straight back over the shoulder. The player is facing the court pretty much straight on and strikes the ball directly from behind. The racket usually comes from above the ball to below the ball. The racket is held in a forehand-type grip. There is no topspin on this serve. There is no sidespin on this serve. If there *is* any spin on the ball, it is usually backspin.

Everyone has seen this kind of serve. Every beginner starts serving this way. Some players never transition to a more advanced topspin serve. Some players hit their first serve in the more advanced topspin way and then transition to the push-type serve on their second serve. Changing from the push serve to the topspin serve can be frustrating, but it is very doable, especially since you now know about aiming techniques.

In order to change from a push serve to a topspin serve, you have to stand more perpendicular to the net, with your left shoulder pointing at the service court (assuming a right-handed player). You also need to turn your grip over to a more continental-style backhand grip (see Appendix 5). When you strike the ball, your arm moves in an upward, throwing motion. The forearm and wrist "pronate". This is a natural throwing motion. The racket strikes the ball in an upward direction, moving from the low-left side of the ball to the high-right side of the ball (right-handed player).

The change of grip is what makes this transition difficult. When an inexperienced player first tries this serve, the ball careens off to the left, extremely wide of the service court (right-handed player). This is because the player is not accustomed to the new throwing motion, and the forearm and wrist do not pronate enough. This causes the racket to strike the ball way over on the right side. That is what causes the dramatic error off to the left. The trick to solving this error is to follow the aim-point adjustment techniques to the letter. Let's say you are serving into the forehand court. You choose a target directly over the middle of the net. When you try your new grip and the new throwing motion, you might miss the target fifteen feet to the left. You might miss over the doubles alley and wide of the court. This is a normal error in this transition. What you need to do now is adjust your aim point the full distance of the error. This might even mean that you have to aim into the doubles alley on the right side of the court! As you make this dramatic aim-point correction, you will find yourself shifting your body so that your shoulder points more over to the right. This is also normal. Make the big correction and go for it. You will find that your shot will go very close to your target, right over the middle of the net. From the backhand side of the court, you may even need to aim into the tennis court to the right of the one you are playing in (see Figures 22 and 23).

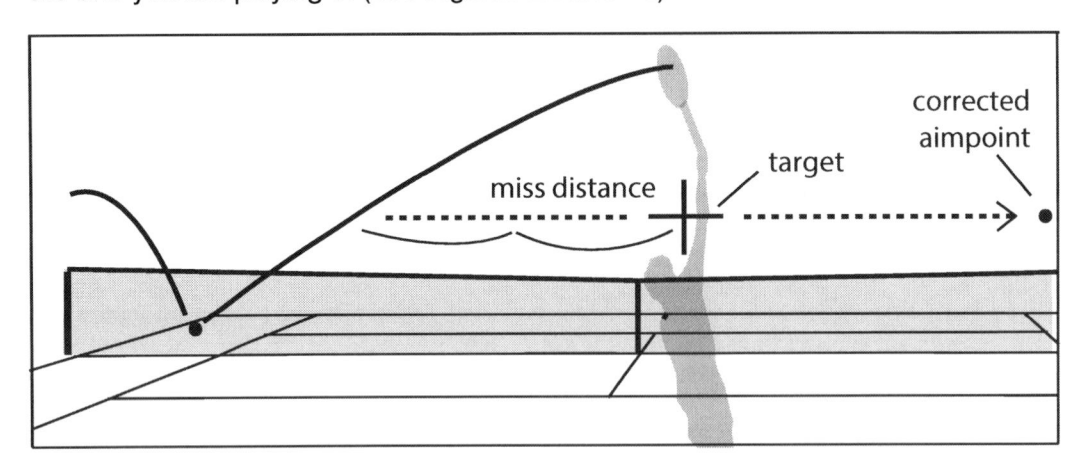

Fig 22 Aimpoint correction required when transitioning from push serve to topspin "throwing motion" serve from forehand side. Here the server attempts to thit the target, but misses many feet to the left. The new aimpoint is corrected the same distance as the error over to the right. This correction is huge and is difficult to "buy into". But, the big correction is a must in order to make the transition to a "throwing motion" serve.

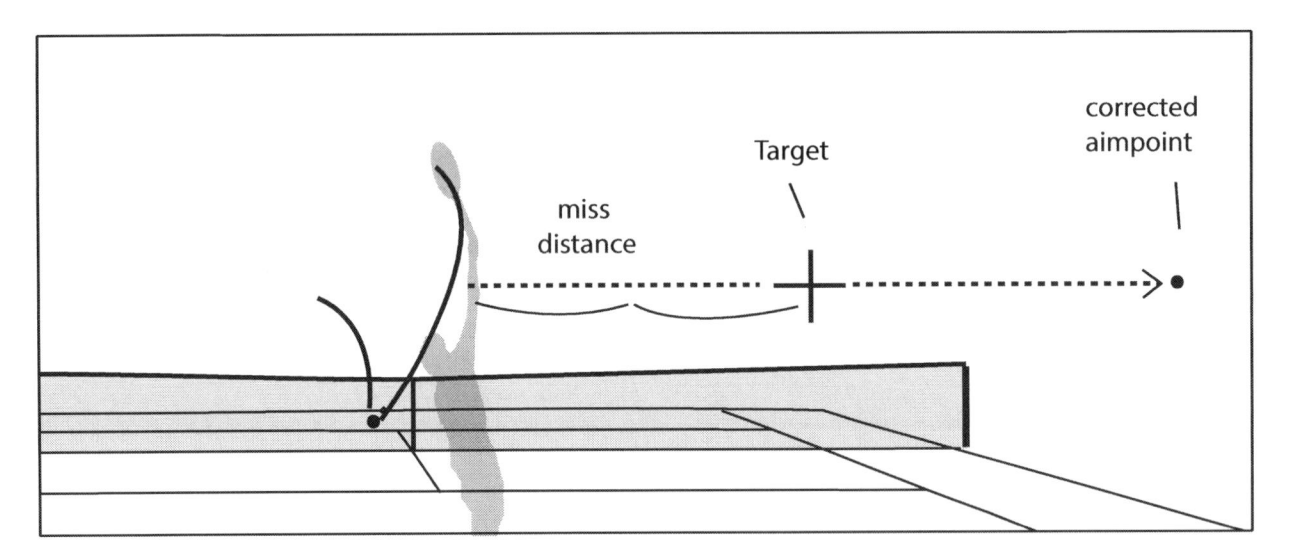

Fig 23 Aimpoint correction required when transitioning from push serve to topspin "throwing motion" serve from the backhand service court. Here the server attempts to thit the target, but misses many feet to the left. The new aimpoint is corrected the same distance as the error over to the right. This correction is huge and is difficult to "buy into". But, the big correction is a must in order to make the transition to a "throwing motion" serve.

You will need to practice this new serve for a while with a bucket of balls, by yourself, on the practice court. Trust what you have learned about targets and aim points. As you continue to develop this new, throwing-motion serve, your forearm and wrist will pronate more and more. You will develop a looser throwing motion up at the ball. As you do this, the ball will start to go closer and closer to your corrected aim point. As your shots get closer to your corrected aim point, continue with the aiming techniques. You will slide your correction back toward your intended target. Pretty soon you will be driving the ball directly at your target, with your aim point right over the aiming cross. This may take some time. You may have to use the big correction for a few weeks. Hang in there and believe in what you have learned. This is the perfect example of developing ball control.

APPENDIX 4

How to Crush Your Service Return

The secret to crushing service returns is all about how you play the service arc. First, let's review what happens when you play the arc. The energy of the ball—its speed, spin, and vector—create its arc. The arc is the signature of the oncoming shot's force. When the arc is played, the hitter conserves that energy by moving the racket around the shape of the arc with the foreword swing of the stroke. The energy of the arc is contained in the motion of the racket, and it is launched into the resulting shot. A tennis shot can be hit very hard with relatively little effort because the power of the oncoming arc is conserved and transmitted into that shot. The better the arc is played, the more powerful the shot. If the arc is not played correctly, the energy of the inbound shot will deflect off the movement of the racket. This produces a weaker shot. The energy of the oncoming arc is dissipated, and the shot is random in both direction and power.

Players with great service returns seem to hit their returns harder than the serve they are playing. Andre Agassi, for instance, was a great example of this. His returns were rockets. His service-return strokes were very short and effortless. His returns seemed to launch off his racket faster than the oncoming serve. The better word here is *rebound*. That is what happens when the service arc is correctly played. The ball rebounds off the racket with the power of the oncoming serve stored and launched into the return.

But we play the arc on every shot, right? So what is different about playing the arc on the service return? When a player plays the arc from a ground stroke, she uses the second half of the arc to guide her racket. We have named that part of the arc the "playable portion" of the arc. The playable portion of the arc starts at the highest point of the arc and ends when it hits the ground. That part of the arc is the guide for your racket when you hit a ground stroke (see Figure 24).

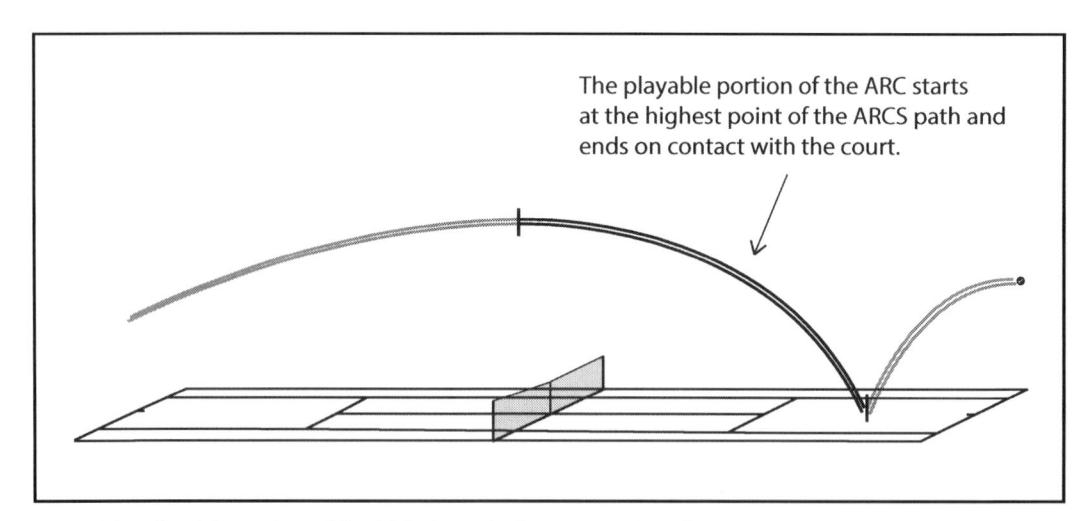

Fig 24 The playable portion of the ARC when playing a ground stroke

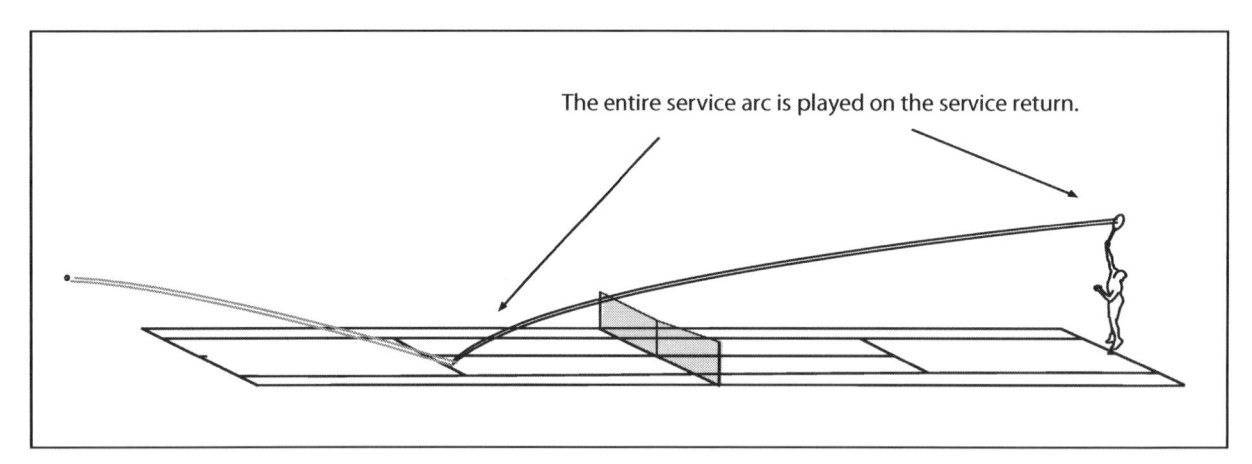

Fig 25 The playable portion of the service arc is the entire shape; from its point of origin, off the racket, to its contact point on the court.

The service arc is different. It comes at you from a higher point. It does not rise to clear the net and then fall into the court. There really isn't a peak, or highest point, on the service arc. It is launched out over the net and then curves down into the court. The highest point of the service arc is its origin, at the top of the toss. So, the secret to playing the service arc is to use its whole shape. The playable portion of the service arc starts from where it is struck and ends when it bounces on the court. The forward swing of your racket launches out along the entire arc of the serve, toward its point of origin (see Figure 25). When this is done correctly, all of the energy of the incoming serve is conserved and then launched into the return. Playing the service arc from its origin—from where it is struck—is the secret to crushing the service return. We'll now discuss how to hit the service return.

Preparation and Backswing

We assume a topspin, low-to-high-stroke service return in this discussion. How you flow with the service arc depends on how hard your opponent serves. If you are facing a hundred-mile-per-hour-plus serve, for example, there isn't much time to flow with the arc, but the flow principle still applies. To prepare for the service return, your racket must move instantly with the movement of the ball. You start your preparation for the return the moment you see which side the ball is going to: backhand or forehand. The most important move is the shoulder-and-torso turn. The movement of your racket is still the basic figure-eight motion, but it is shorter and more compact. The faster the serve you are playing, the shorter and more compact the backswing. Work to connect your shoulder-and-torso turn with the figure-eight movement of your backswing.

Forward Swing

The return is struck from low to high, playing the entire arc of the oncoming serve. The forward swing of your racket moves out and into the shape of the service arc. This is a more outward and upward movement along the entire shape of the oncoming service shot. The critical action that will supercharge your returns is to drive the forward swing of your racket up and out to the point of origin or the service arc, where it is struck off the service toss. Figure 26 shows a forehand return; Figure 27 shows a two-handed backhand return.

Service arc

Shape of the service arc

The sevice arc must be played out to its point of origin, where it is struck off the service toss. This captures and conserves the energy of the serve and transmits it into your return.

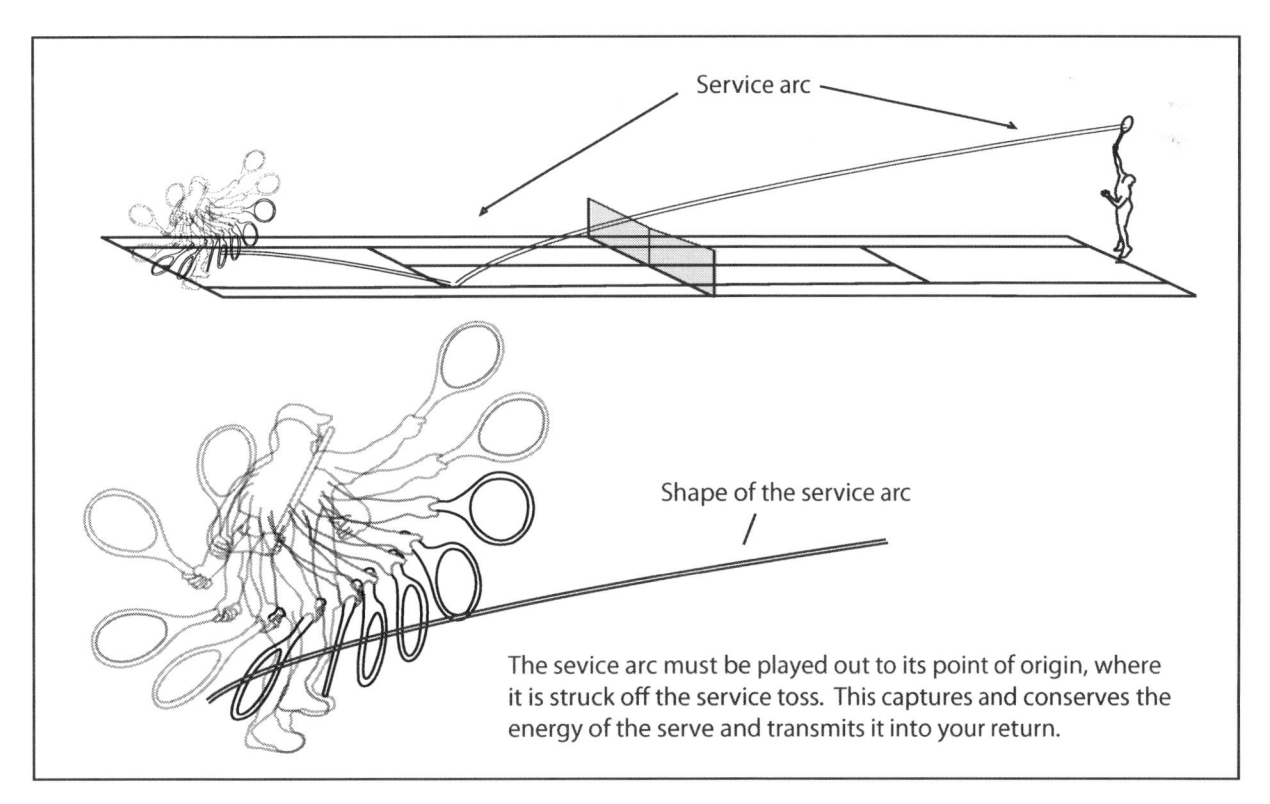

Fig 26 The entire service arc is played on the service return.

Service arc

Shape of the service arc

The sevice arc must be played out to its point of origin, where it is struck off the service toss. This captures and conserves the energy of the serve and transmits it into your return.

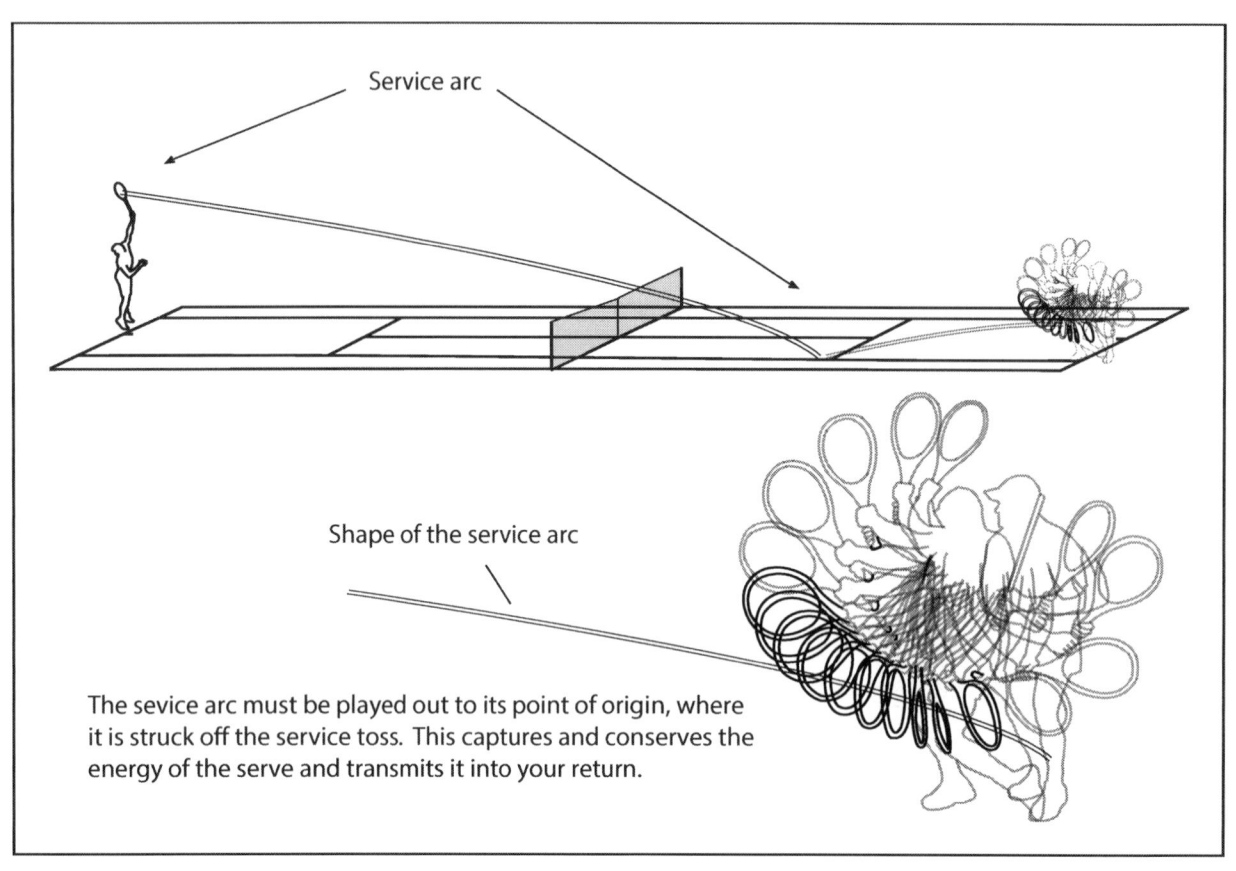

Fig 27 The entire service arc is played on the service return.

This power-service return should be played with a rolling topspin. If you try to flip your racket too much, you won't conserve the energy of the serve as well. This doesn't mean you can't hit big topspin service returns. But to hit a high-energy, big return, you need to moderate the amount of spin you are trying to impart. There is room to experiment here. Try a few returns with rolling topspin and a few with more flipped topspin: you will find more power and success with the rolling-topspin, flatter shot.

This return is an explosive shot. Your racket rides out along the service arc with venom and purpose. Your preparation and backswing differ slightly from the ground stroke. But you don't have to make this a conscious change. Focus on flowing instantly with the service arc. Your backswing should get more compact as the speed of the inbound serve increases. I recall people asking me, "You hit your return really hard, but you hardly have any backswing. How do you do that?" I did not have an answer at the time, and I still don't. It was something I just did. It will also be something that you will "just do" as you work to flow instantly with the serve and rip into the entire shape of the arc out to its point of origin.

When you first attempt this technique, you will feel like you are driving your shot too high and out of the court. But what you are doing is conserving the energy and power of the serve that your opponent hits to you. By playing up and into the entire service arc, its power and energy is conserved and transmitted to your service return. You control the direction of your return with targets and aiming.

Service-Return Targets

We will base our service-return targets off the vector of the oncoming serve. The three targets to choose from will be: exactly on the vector of the oncoming serve, slightly to the right of the vector of the oncoming serve, and slightly to the left of the vector of the oncoming serve. Strength and position logic remain the same. If you have time to cover more of the court with your strength, you have more target options. Deflection-factor logic is the same as described in the chapter on strength and position. Deflection factor does, in fact, dominate in choosing the high-percentage target on your service return.

Target height is also very important. As you start playing the service arc out to its point of origin, you might initially shoot a few balls too high out of the court. Use aiming logic to adjust for any errors. At first you may need to bring your target down closer to the top of the net to compensate for this. You still rip the entire shape of the service arc: the target adjustment down controls the vector of the return. Eventually, as your ball control improves on the return, you will find the target height that works for you.

The following discussions assume right-handed players.

Returning from the Forehand Court with a Serve to Forehand

The target that is directly on the vector of the serve is a very high-percentage target. Zero deflection factor ensures maximum energy conservation and power on your return. Most of the time this target is in strength. Even if it is slightly out of your strength, it is a high-percentage target, since you are crushing the shot on vector (see Figure 28).

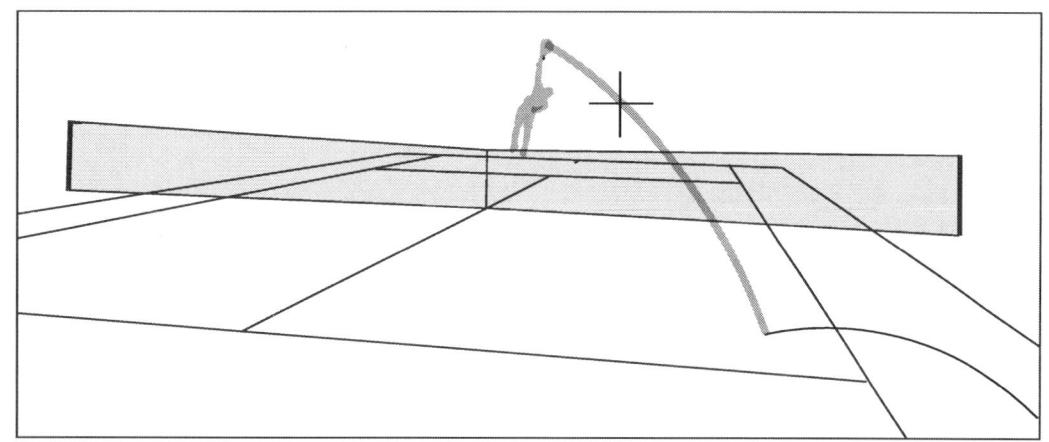

Fig 28 On vector service return target from the forehand. This target is very high percentage because it is on vector and in strength.

The highest-percentage target is to the left, increasing the angle farther into strength. The target is off vector, so there is some deflection factor. But this target is farther into strength, so it is a very high-percentage shot (see Figure 29).

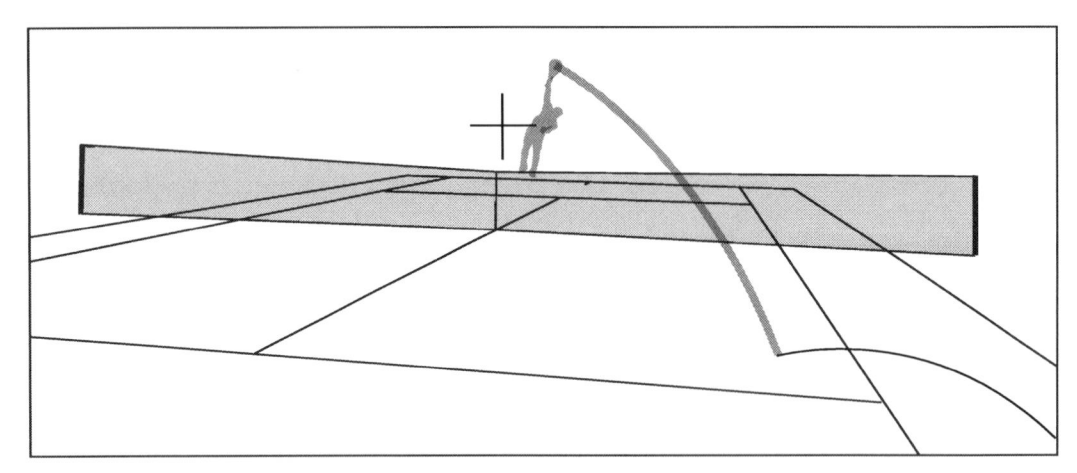

Fig 29. This target, further in strength, is the highest percetage target returning from the forehand side. It deep in strength and shoots for the longest part of the court. Deflection factor will be controled by strength.

The lowest-percentage target is to the right of the vector of the serve. It is off vector, so there is a deflection factor. Also, depending on your preparation, this target can be out of strength; at any rate, it will be on the edge of strength. Your ability to shoot for this target will depend on how much time you have to position your shoulders and torso to bring your strength to that side of the court. If you are returning a slow serve, and you are in position with your strength covering both sides of the court, this target can be high percentage. I still recommend being conservative here. The target should not be too close to the sideline, since the deflection factor and nearness to the edge of your strength will cause errors wide of the court (see Figure 30).

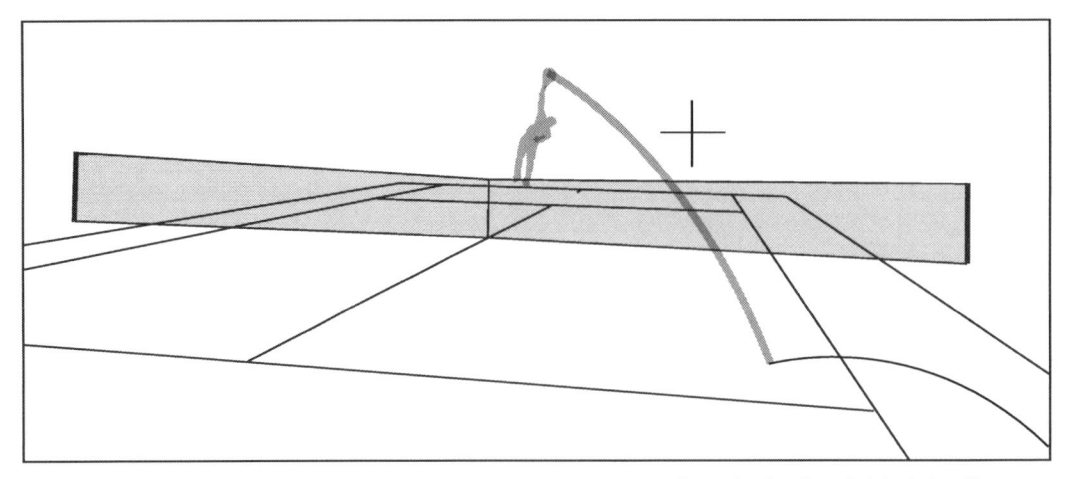

Fig 30. This target is the lowest percentage service target returning from the forehand side. It is off vector and usually out of strength. Good preparation is essential to get this target covered by your strength. If you prepare well you can take this risk.

Backhand Service Return from the Forehand Court

When returning a serve off your backhand from the forehand court, the pull target off vector into your strength is the highest-percentage target. There is a deflection factor, but this target is in strength, and deflection should be controlled (see Figure 31). The next-highest-percentage target is right on the vector of the serve. This

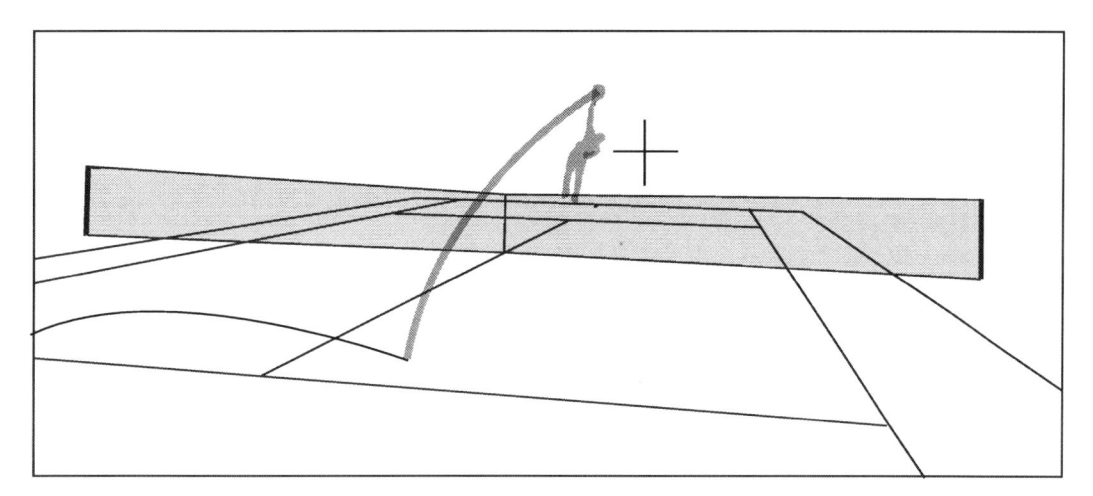

Fig 31 Strong side backhand service return target. This target is in strength and can be crushed. Deflection factor will be controlled by your strength.

best conserves the energy of the oncoming arc. This target might be slightly out of strength (or on the edge of your strength), but it is a high-percentage target, since you are driving right on the vector of the oncoming serve (see Figure 32).

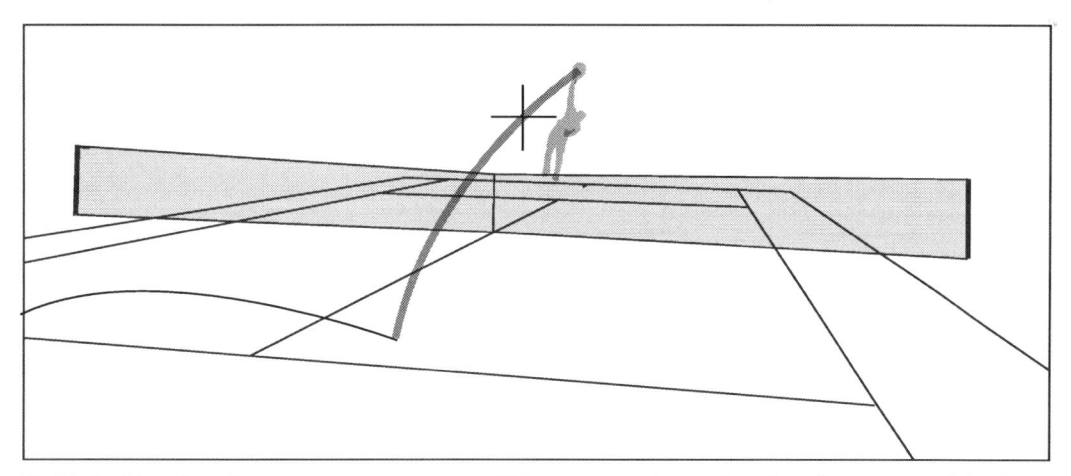

Fig 32 Backhand service return target on vector. This target may be on the edge of your strength but by shooting here you are conserving all the energy or the oncoming serve.

The lowest-percentage target is to the left of the vector of the serve. It will generally be out of strength. It is also off vector, so there will be a deflection factor. You are shooting at the longest part of the court, however, so this will increase your chances. If the serve is weak, and you can position your strength to cover both sides of the court, this can be a high-percentage target. Here, your torso turn and foot positioning need to be good so that your strength is covering the target well (see Figure 33).

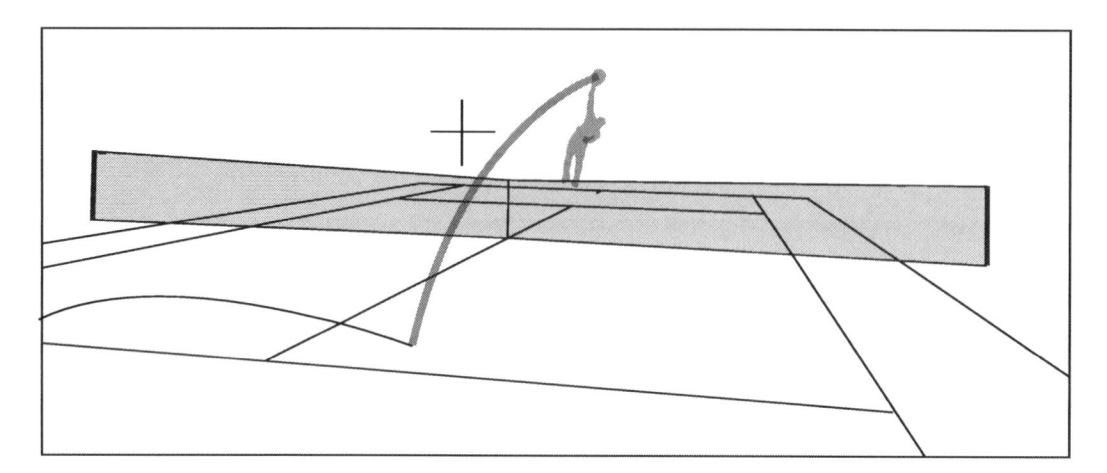

Fig 33 Off vector service return target usually out of strength. This target is the lowest percentage target to choose off the backhand return. It is usually out of strength unless you prepare very well for the shot. However, you are shooting into the longest part of the court giving you extra margin for error.

Forehand Service Return from the Backhand Court

The highest-percentage target returning from the backhand side of the court on your forehand is the target to the left side of the court, slightly to the left of the vector of the serve. This target is deep in strength. It is off the vector of the oncoming serve, but your strength should overcome deflection (see Figure 34).

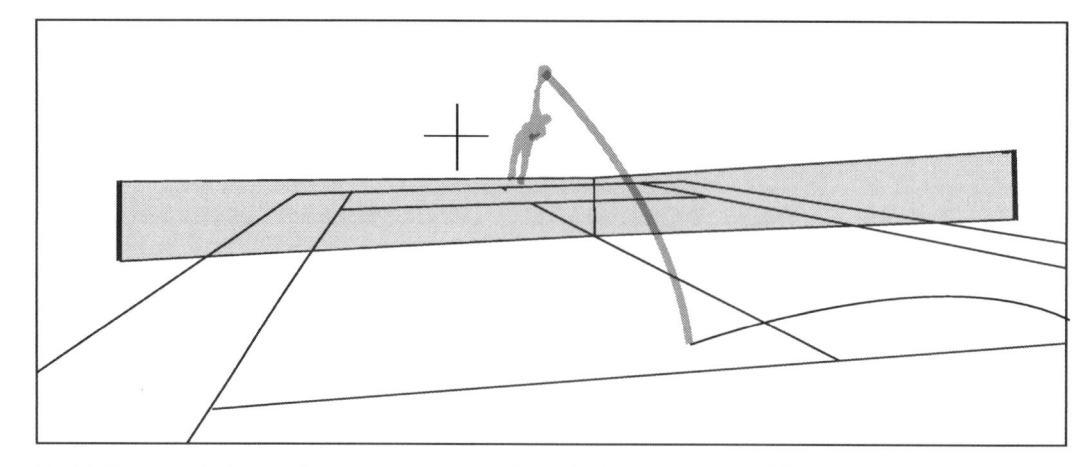

Fig 34 Strong side forehand service return target from the backhand court. This target is in strength and can be hit hard. Deflection should be overcome by your strength.

The other excellent target here is right on the vector of the oncoming serve. You can crush this shot even if the target is on the edge of your strength. You are conserving all of the serve's energy, with zero deflection factor. This on-vector target is a high-percentage shot, even if it is slightly out of your strength. You are also shooting over the lowest part of the net, and the court is long here (see Figure 35).

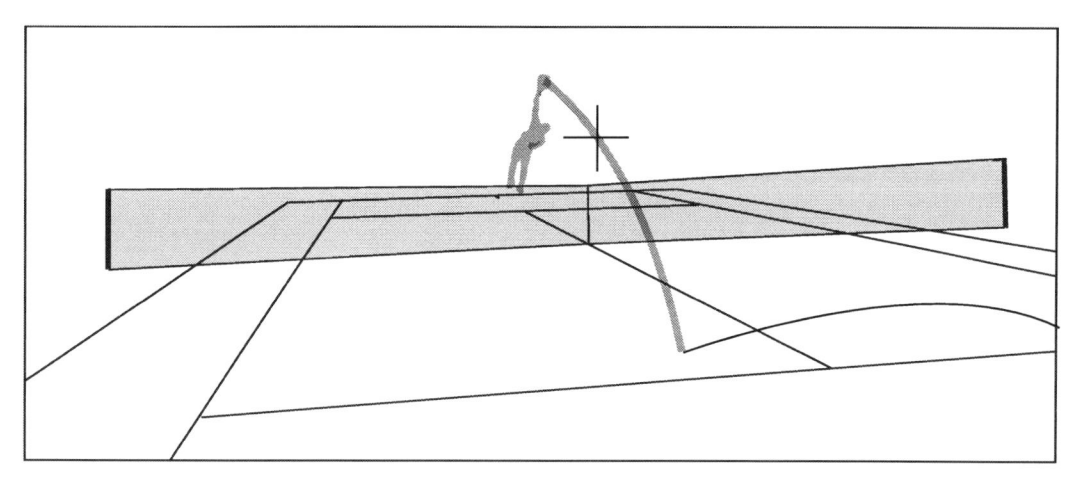

Fig 35 On vector forehand service return target. This is a great target even if it is on the edge of your strength. It conserves all the energy of the oncoming serve and shoots over the lowest part of the net.

The lowest-percentage target is to the right of the vector of the serve crosscourt. If you can get your torso turned and your strength covering this target, it is a "good risk" shot. You have a lot of court to miss when taking this shot. This inside-out return will surprise your opponent and can win you points (see Figure 36).

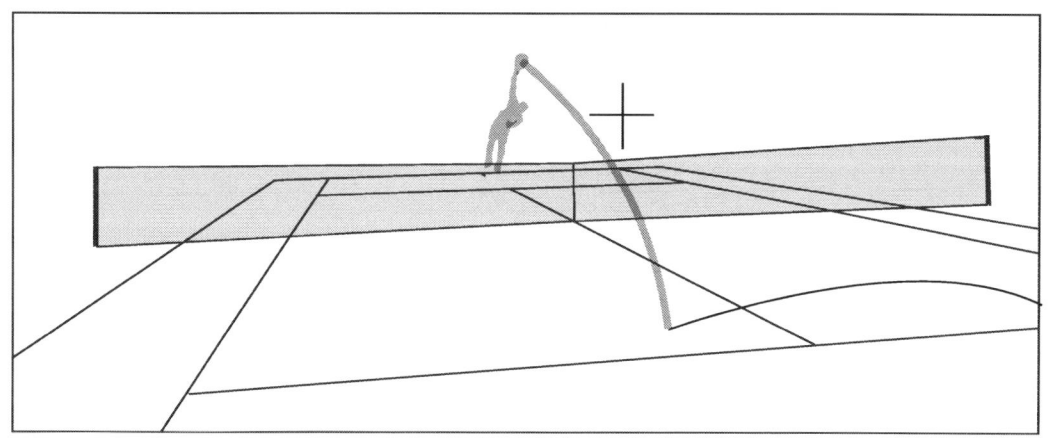

Fig 36 Forehand service return targe off vector cross court. This target is usually out of strength and is off vector. Because of this it is the lowest percentage return target from the forehand side. With good preparation however, you can shoot for this target with success.

Backhand Service Return from the Backhand Court

When hitting a backhand return from the backhand side of the court, the target directly on the vector of the serve is a very high-percentage target. The zero deflection factor ensures maximum energy conservation and power on your return. This target is usually in strength. You can strike this shot hard with very high success (see Figure 37).

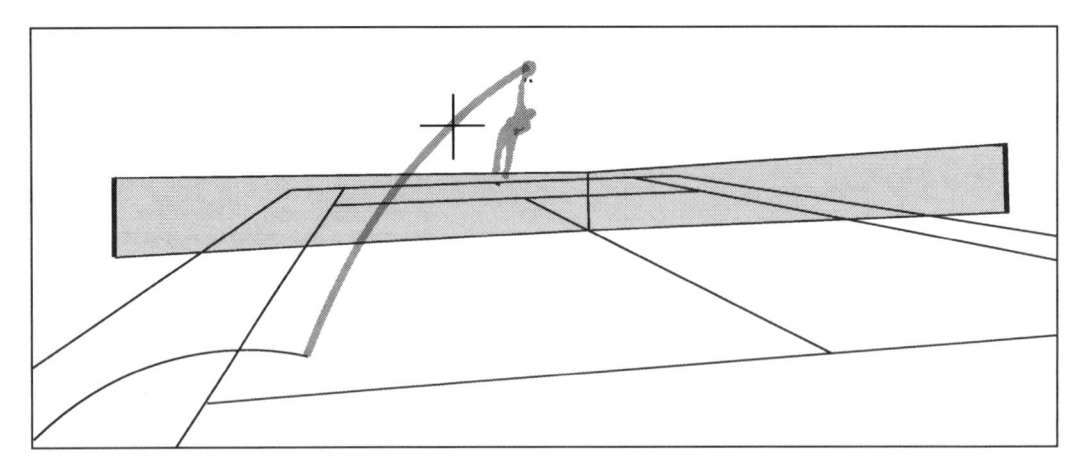

Fig 37 On vector target shooting a backhand return from the backhand court. This target is very high percentage as it is on vector and will conserve the energy of the oncoming serve 100%.

The other very high-percentage target off the backhand is to the right of the vector of the serve, farther into strength. This target shoots for the longest part of the court over the lowest part of the net. The deflection factor will be controlled by your strength. This return can be crushed (see Figure 38).

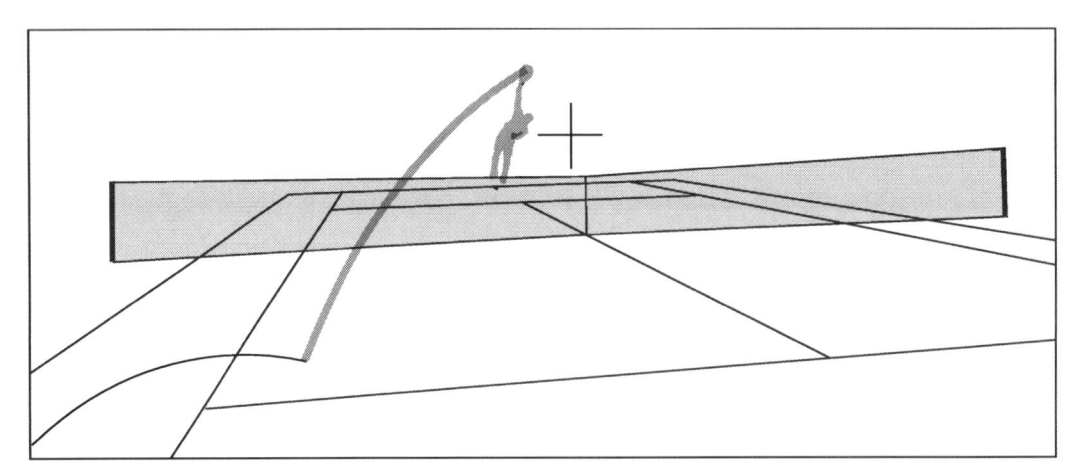

Fig 38 Cross court service return target off the backhand from the backhand court. This target is very high percentage as it is well in your strength and shoots for the longest part of the court. Your strength will overcome delflection here. Crush this return with confidence.

The lowest-percentage target is to the left of the vector of the serve. The deflection factor will be hard to control, as the target will probably be out of strength. You can successfully use this target if you have time to make a good torso turn to bring your strength over that part of the court. If you do go for this shot, choose a target that is not too far off the vector of the oncoming serve. If you are conservative, your errors will deflect into the court (see Figure 39).

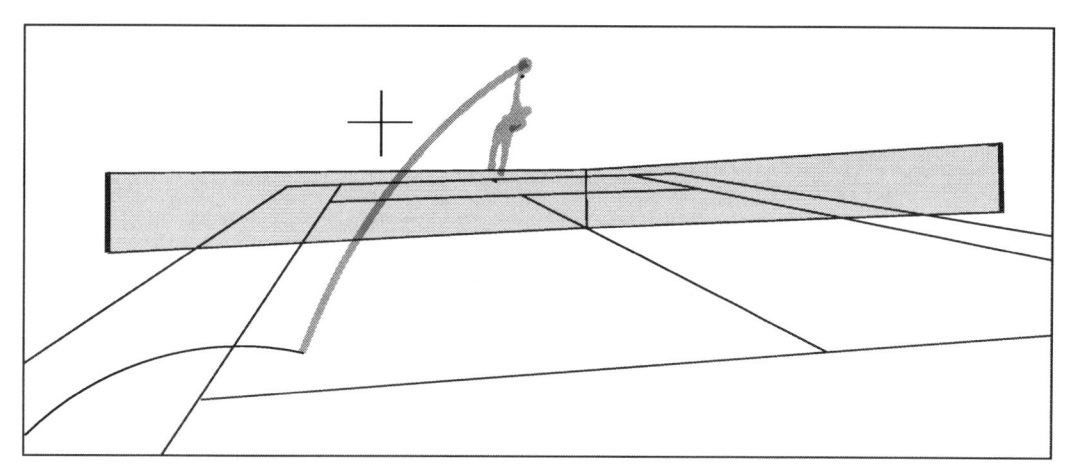

Fig 39 Lowest percentage retrun target off the backhand from the backhand court. This target is a high risk shot. It is usually out of strength and shoots for the shortest lenght of the court over the highest part of the net. You need to get in good position with your strength over that part of the court to have success on this shot.

The Most Important Thing

You have to play the total service arc. Your racket must drive along the arc up to its point of origin. This will conserve all of the energy of your opponent's serve and fire it back at her in spades. To do this, you must accept that you will make a few errors as you get a feel for playing the entire arc. Use the targets shown here as a starting point. Use the aiming techniques to find out where you must aim to get the ball into the court. Once you find those aim points, you can use them as the target for your return. Know that you may need to choose targets that are a little lower than usual until you "metabolize" this technique into your game. Please go for your shot. Choose the high-percentage service-return targets and crush your returns with confidence. Get started on changing this very important part of your game.

APPENDIX 5

Grips

The easiest way to get a closed racket face is to change the way you grip the racket. Let's review the conventional names and descriptions of tennis grips. These terms and descriptions are just for reference. The grips aren't absolute, and are not meant to constrain you from experimenting with how you hold your racket. As you move away from stroke control and other straitjacket approaches to the game, your grips will float around and you will find what fits you and your shot-making best.

Forehand Grips

Forehand grips come in three main varieties: western, continental and eastern.

Western

With the *western grip* the racket is held so that its face is closed. The western grip enables the player to strike the ball aggressively with a low-to-high movement that imparts lots of topspin. Since the racket face is closed by the western-style grip, the player doesn't need to turn his wrist to close up the racket face as he contacts the ball. He can use the flipping motion of his wrist and forearm to produce racket speed for power and spin using this grip. High-bouncing balls are much easier to play with the western-style grip. Novak Djokovic, Roger Federer, Rafael Nadal, Serena and Venus Williams, Maria Sharapova, and most other current great players use this grip on the forehand (see Figure 40).

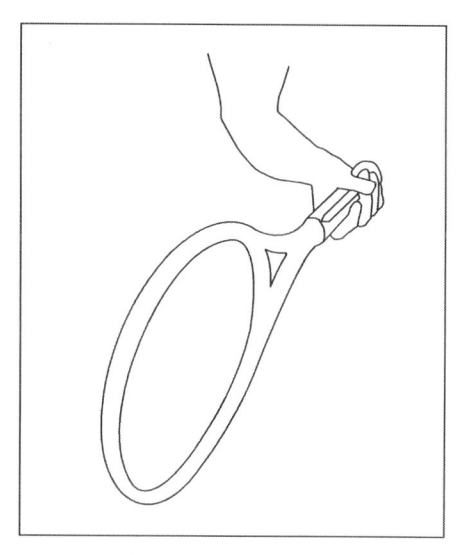

Fig 40 Forehand western grip

Continental

The *continental grip* was developed as a unitary grip for the forehand and the backhand. With the continental grip the racket is held so that the racket face is slightly open for both the forehand and backhand sides. Using the continental grip, topspin shots are often struck with an open racket face as the racket is flipped around the ball. The movement of the wrist must close (or nearly close) the racket face at just the right time to impart the spin. This is a difficult skill to acquire. The precise timing required for the wrist flip makes topspin shots with the continental grip inconsistent. The continental grip does work well for low-bouncing balls. Rod Laver used this grip. Except for the clay surface, most tennis courts during his time were faster and produced lower-bouncing balls, so the continental grip worked well for him. Most tennis courts today are slower and produce higher-bouncing balls. If you use this grip, topspin shots will be more difficult and more inconsistent. High-bouncing balls will be even more difficult to play with topspin. The continental-style grip is illustrated in Figure 41. The continental grip is the preferred grip for conventional backspin volleys off the forehand and backhand sides.

Eastern

The *eastern grip* lies between the western and continental grips. The racket face is closed, but not nearly as closed as with the western grip. Although rolling- and moderate-topspin shots are easily hit with the eastern grip, this grip is not ideal for hitting the ripping topspin shots that characterize the modern game. The eastern grip is illustrated in Figure 42.

I recommend that you experiment with a more western-style grip on the forehand side. Most great players today use this grip. The western grip's closed racket face makes hitting big topspin shots much easier. Take a look at how your favorite professional grips her racket and try that.

One-Handed Backhand Grips

Continental

The continental grip can also be used to play backhand shots. With the continental grip the striking face of the racket is slightly open. So, if you hit a topspin shot with the continental grip, your wrist and forearm must be turned as you strike the ball. This wrist turn closes (or nearly closes) the racket face as you strike the ball. Because of the need for exact timing, topspin-backhand shots with the continental grip tend to be inconsistent. The continental grip is good for hitting low-bouncing balls off the backhand. Hitting topspin backhands off high-bouncing balls is very challenging with this grip. The continental grip is an excellent grip for hitting backhand under spin shots. The racket face is open and already set up for the backspin play. The continental grip is the preferred grip for conventional backspin volleys. The racket face is slightly open and ready to impart backspin. Another benefit is that no grip change

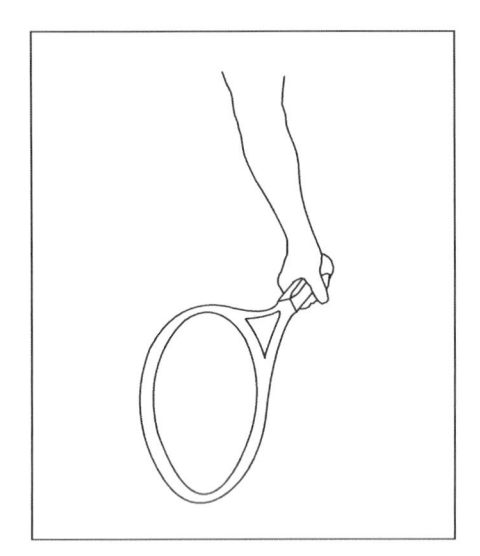

Fig 41 Forehand continental grip

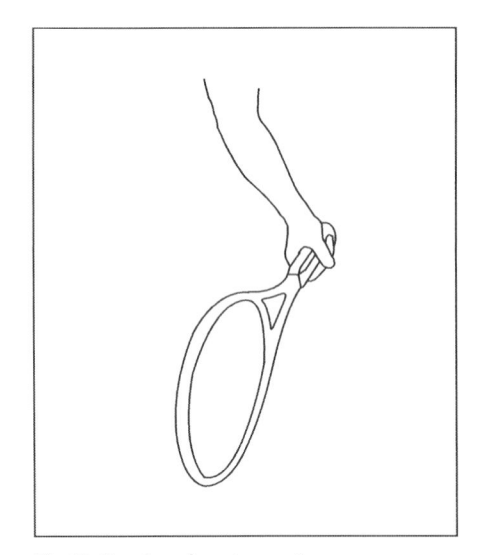

Fig 42 Forehand eastern grip

is required from the forehand to the backhand side when volleying with this grip (see Figure 43).

Eastern

With the eastern-style backhand grip, the striking face of the racket is closed. Backhand topspin shots using the eastern grip are more consistent and easier to hit than with the continental grip. The ball is struck from low to high, and no wrist turn is required to close the racket face. Your wrist and forearm can move freely and aggressively on topspin shots using this grip. The eastern grip is also good for playing high-bouncing balls. Backspin shots are also easy to play with the eastern grip. The wrist might need a little turning to open the racket face for the backspin, but backspin shots don't require a violent movement of the wrist and forearm to produce spin. You can hold a slight turning of the wrist and forearm throughout a backspin shot without making the shot inconsistent. The great one-handed backhand strikers of today all use the eastern grip. Federer is the best example. If you hit a one-handed backhand, this is the recommended grip (see Figure 44).

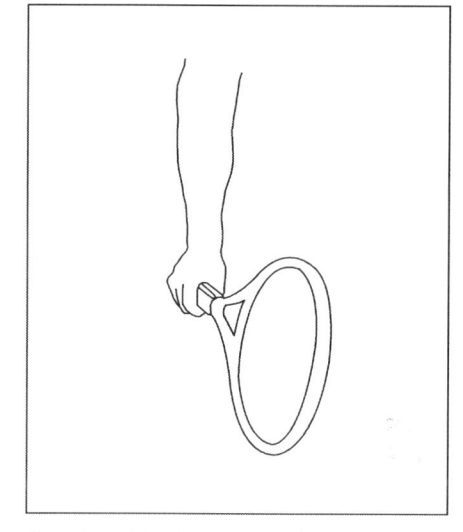

Fig 43 Backhand continental grip

Western

The western backhand grip holds the racket face more closed than the eastern grip. This grip is excellent for hitting topspin shots off high and medium height bouncing balls. Lower bouncing balls will be difficult to play with this grip. The western one-handed backhand grip is not optimized for hitting backspin shots. The wrist must be turned a great deal to open the racket face up for this play (see Figure 44).

Two-Handed Backhand Grips

Two-handed backhand grips should hold the racket face slightly closed. If you use the western-style grip for your forehand, then placing your left hand on top of your right produces this closed racket face. No grip change is required here. This is the recommended technique for two-handed

Eastern backhand grip.

Backhand Western grip. Racket face is far more closed than Eastern grip.

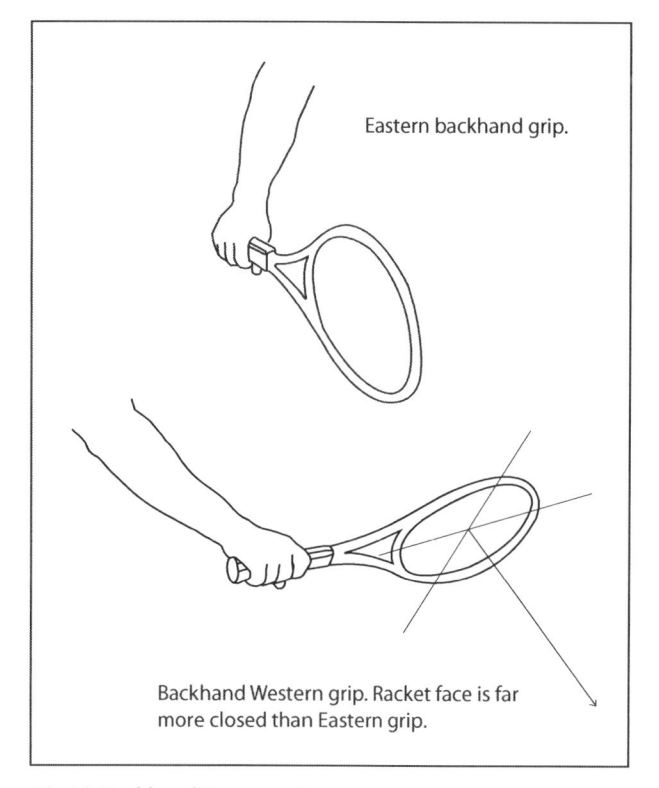

Fig 44 Backhand Eastern grip

APPENDIX 5: GRIPS | 217

backhand players. Regardless, if you hit two-handed on the backhand side, your grip should hold the racket face closed. The closed racket face will optimize topspin shots off the two-handed backhand (see Figure 45).

Take a look at professional players in action and observe their grips. Pick out someone to emulate, and go with that style. As you get better and better, your grip will actually float unconsciously to accommodate the plays you are making.

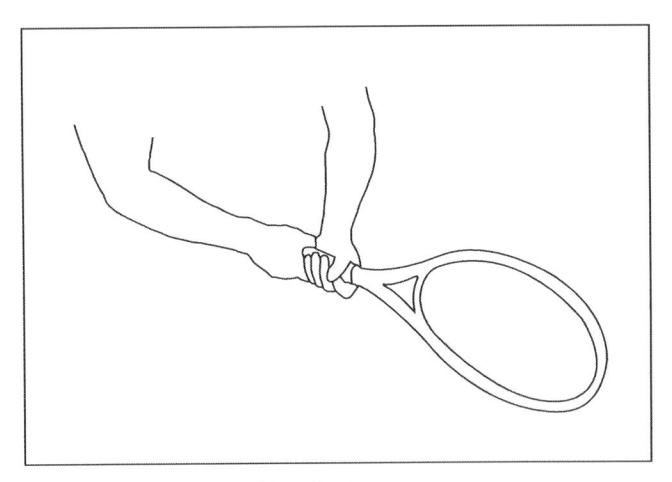

Fig 45 Two handed backhand grip

Printed in Great Britain
by Amazon